# DANTE AND DERRIDA

SUNY Series in Theology and Continental Thought

_____

Douglas L. Donkel, *editor*

# DANTE AND DERRIDA

*Face to Face*

FRANCIS J. AMBROSIO

STATE UNIVERSITY OF NEW YORK PRESS

Published by
STATE UNIVERSITY OF NEW YORK PRESS
Albany

© 2007 State University of New York

For information, address
State University of New York Press
194 Washington Avenue, Suite 305, Albany, NY 12210-2384

Production, Kelli W. LeRoux
Marketing, Michael Campochiaro

**Library of Congress Cataloging-in-Publication Data**

Ambrosio, Francis J.
    Dante and Derrida : face to face / Francis J. Ambrosio.
        p. cm. — (SUNY series in theology and continental thought)
    Includes bibliographical references and index.
    ISBN-13: 978-0-7914-7005-3 (hardcover : alk. paper)
    ISBN-13: 978-0-7914-7006-0 (pbk.: alk. paper)
        1. Dante Alighieri, 1265–1321—Influence. 2. Derrida, Jacques. I. Title. II. Series.
PQ4335.A43 2006
851'.1—dc22                                                                    2006014433

10   9   8   7   6   5   4   3   2   1

*For Deborah,*

"Vedea visi a carità suadi,

D'altrui lume fregati e di suo riso"

(*Par.*, xxxi, 49–50)

# Contents

# On the Pre-text *or* As a Pre-face

"How can another see into me, into my most secret self, without my being able to see in there myself? And without my being able to see him in me. And if my secret self, that which can be revealed only to the other, to the wholly other, to God if you wish, is the secret that I will never reflect on, that I will never know or experience or possess as my own, then what sense is there in saying that it is my secret, or in saying more generally that a secret belongs, that it is proper to or belongs to some one. It's perhaps there that we find the secret of secrecy. Namely, that it is not a matter of knowing and that it is there for no one. A secret doesn't belong, it can never be said to be at home or in its place. The question of the self: who am I not in the sense of who am I but rather who is this I that can say who? What is the I and what becomes of responsibility once the identity of the I trembles in secret." (*GD*, 92)

Truly, I do not know why I must write this book, so I must begin by asking for your forgiveness for having done so without knowing why and therefore, necessarily, without knowing how. Having said this, I have in effect said in a different way all that I believe the book truly has to say. So if you read further, it is your responsibility and it will be for the sake of that difference, to decide whether or not you believe it truly makes a difference and, more precisely, how.

For myself, I believe that the difference the book makes is this: it traces and remarks in the texts of Dante and Derrida two episodes in the history of forgiveness. These episodes appear as the signs of an "autobiographical" element that figures decisively in these texts, specifically in the confessional voices in which they are written. As confessional autobiographies the texts of Dante and Derrida that this book considers are religious in character. In these texts "religion" signifies a passionate concern for constant conversion to personal responsibility instigated by the need for forgiveness. The religious experience of the need for forgiveness is the context for all questions of personal identity and responsibility. But this experience is problematic in the strongest sense: it locates both the necessity and the impossibility of love in the face of the "Other," that is, in the face of death. The experience of the necessity and impossibility of love in the face of the Other/death marks the texts of both

Dante and Derrida as religious scriptures. These texts reveal the truth of for-giveness without yielding knowledge of it by soliciting faith and encouraging hope to do that truth in love. The religious "way" of life, marked by faith, hope, and love in the face of the Other/death inscribes the texts of Dante and Der-rida within the history of scripture and the scripture of history as revelations without knowledge of the truth of forgiveness done in love.

"  . . . *TANTO PADRONE, ET PADRE*"

Shortly after arriving in Fiesole for the spring semester at Villa Le Balze, Georgetown University's Study Center outside Florence, I learned of an exhi-bition in progress at the Casa Buonarotti that was shortly to conclude. With my wife, Deborah, I visited the exhibition, entitled "Daniele da Volterra, amico di Michelangelo," on the day it was to close, January 12, 2004. To my surprise and delight, the exhibition included the original drawing by Daniele Ricci-arelle designated, *Studio di figura femminile piagente per la Deposizione Orsini*, from the collection of the Musée du Louvre. Jacques Derrida had chosen this drawing, referred to as *Woman Weeping at the Foot of the Cross*, as the final work displayed in the exhibition *Memoirs of the Blind*, which he had been asked to curate at the Louvre as the first in a new series of exhibitions entitled *Parti Pris*, "Taking Sides." This exhibition was held from October 26, 1990 until January 21, 1991.

In viewing the exhibition in Florence, I learned the reason for its title. Daniele da Volterra had indeed been an intimate friend of Michelangelo, so much so that when Michelangelo fell gravely ill with a fever that would prove to be fatal, he sent word to Daniele on February 14, 1564, for him to come immediately and stay at the dying man's house. On seeing him, Michelan-gelo begged him, "O Daniele, I am done for; I beseech you, do not abandon me." Michelangelo had him write a letter to his nephew, Leonardo Buonar-otti, in Florence, informing him that death was upon him and that he must come immediately. Despite his best attempts, Leonardo arrived three days after Michelangelo's death on February 18. In a letter to Giorgio Vasari, dated March 17, 1564, in which he gives an exact inventory of all the works by Michelangelo's hand that were in the house in Rome where the master had been living for many years and where he died, Daniele reveals the intensity of his feeling toward his friend and the way in which he viewed their relation-ship. He says that of course he feels all the grief that the death of "so great a patron, and a father" behooves him to suffer.

Most startling to me, however, was learning that this filial piety that Dan-iele expresses was acted out in a gesture of mourning and memory that brought home to me with an unnerving immediacy certain issues that had been run-ning through this study of Dante and Derrida. I had come to Florence, in part at least, to complete this work. Even before he wrote to Vasari, Daniele had already been commissioned by the nephew of Michelangelo, Leonardo, to cast in bronze two portrait heads of his uncle, probably modeled from the death mask and bearing the image of the death of the father in the eye of the son. In these sculptures and in the drawing of the face of "an apostle, with the features of Michelangelo," for his della Rovere Assumption, Daniele gives to history the face that has been and will always be that of Michelangelo, the face that is the signature on the text of humanity that has quite possibly enkindled more love than any other come from a single hand.

This work of filial piety moved me as it did because, in addition to being a graphic evocation of that to which Derrida refers in *Memoirs of the Blind* as the "ruins of memory," it also clarified for me what I had been trying to formulate in the text on which I was working as "face-writing," what I understood to be the "referent," if that term can be used here, of Derrida's notion of "archi-writing." In an instant, I had found gathered in the Casa Buonarotti, a familiar place, the traces of Derrida writing of Daniele, who was writing about Michelangelo and who had written the finality of Michelangelo's face in his portrait bust. Daniele had received the finality of that face as the gift of his "father's" death, a text which, if memory serves, had been written there in the face of Michelangelo by Dante, the author of the poem most of which Michelangelo knew by memory, that is, by heart. Vasari says that the *Commedia* was Michelangelo's favorite reading. One can easily imagine that it was the text of living memory from which Michelangelo read the images to which he gave flesh in so many of his greatest works, especially in their bodies, hands, and faces. In that instant, I found what I had been hoping for, what I had believed from the beginning was both necessary and possible: there in Daniele da Volterra's face of Michelangelo, I found Dante and Derrida, standing face to face.

# Acknowledgments

Much of the research and the first stages of writing for this book were supported by a sabbatical grant from Georgetown University. I undertook an initial exploration of the present subject matter in an essay entitled, "Dante and Derrida: The Promise of Writing and the Piety of Broken Promises," which appeared in *Styles of Piety*, eds. S. Clark Buckner and Matthew Statler (New York: Fordham University Press, 2006).

This project as a whole would not have been possible without the insight and scholarship of John D. Caputo's exceptional study *The Prayers and Tears of Jacques Derrida: Religion without Religion.*

I am grateful to all of my students at Georgetown who have over the years participated in my "Dante and the Christian Imagination," and especially to Jessica A. McKinney and James F. Zumberge, who worked diligently and skillfully on preparing the manuscript.

Finally, I owe a debt of gratitude that exceeds all resource to my family. From them I first learned to see the White Rose.

# List of Abbreviations

The following abbreviations are used in the body of the text:

*Circum.*   Cirumfession: *Fifty-nine Periods and Periphrases*. In Geoffrey Bennington and Jacques Derrida, *Jacques Derrida*. Chicago: University of Chicago Press, 1993.

*GD*   *The Gift of Death*. Trans. David Wills. Chicago: University of Chicago Press, 1995.

*Inf.*   *Inferno*. Trans. John S. Singleton. Princeton: Princeton University Press, 1970.

*MB*   *Memoirs of the Blind*. The Self-Portrait and Other Ruins. Trans. Pascal-Anne Brault and Michael Naas. Chicago: University of Chicago Press, 1993.

*Par.*   *Paradiso*. Trans. John S. Singleton. Princeton: Princeton University Press, 1975.

*PTJD*   *The Prayers and Tears of Jacques Derrida: Religion without Religion*. John D. Caputo. Bloomington: Indiana University Press, 1997.

*Purg.*   *Purgatorio*. Trans. John S. Singleton. Princeton: Princeton University Press, 1973.

TF   "To Forgive: The Unforgivable and the Imprescriptible." In John D. Caputo, Mark Dooley, and Michael J. Scanlon, *Questioning God*. Bloomington: Indiana University Press, 2001.

# Introduction

How does it happen that, as persons, we are given to writing?

As it turns out, this question seems to be one way of identifying the human concern generally referred to as "religion," at least in the sense that we speak of "religions of the Book," religions that trace their history back to Abraham, "the father of faith."[1] Still the faith of Abraham is only a beginning, only one possible beginning, in a long history of religious scripture, of history as the memory of religion in writing and as writing, of writing as the trace of what passes, passes over and passes on, the memory of life and death written in and as the memory of persons. Perhaps we are given to religion as writing because we ourselves, our lives and deaths, are written in flesh and blood, like paper and ink. For our memory too is bodily.

In the memory of Abraham we find written traces of how it happens that, as persons we are given to writing. These traces appear in traditional religious texts as events in the lives and deaths of persons, like Abraham: questions of naming—call, promise, and conversion; of sexuality and family—pair-bonding and breaking, the birth of triangles, the one, the other, and all the others; of hospitality—the stranger, the gift; of conflict—sin, sacrifice, and atonement. These are all questions of the way it happens that as persons we are fundamentally and universally given to writing. They are questions of religion, that is, of faith in writing and the writing of faith in response to questions of life and death. They are, in other words, questions of "revelation," of putting faith in writing, of putting faith in traces, in marks of difference that make no difference except in passing. These marks have no purpose or meaning except to pass over and pass on what is impossible, what is written in the body as hunger and thirst and libido, all that it is impossible to satisfy, end, or finalize. It is impossible to know, to tell or to hear the secret that is encrypted in our bodies. Religion might then be faith in the impossibility that is first written in human existence, so that we are given to put faith in writing, in marks that trace in the memory of persons, a passionate history of suffering the impossible in the hope of beginning to do again what, finally, cannot be done. The only hope of faith might be that of always beginning again without end, the hope of the passion that always says, "Here I am! Ready! Yes, let it be; yes, let it come! Again and again and always again." Love forgiven?

1

What would happen if the history of religion, the history of Abraham and Jesus, the history of faith and of forgiveness, the history of promises made and promises broken, of secrets revealed and kept, were put into question and written differently, transcribed into different contexts according to different styles of writing? Is it possible to write the same history of faith, hope, love, and forgiveness differently? More specifically, as a beginning, what might happen if we were given to writing such a history beginning again at the beginning, before the history of religion comes to be written as the history of sin and sacrifice? Is it possible to rewrite history and religion in this way? One never knows; one must believe. "We must always start over," Derrida says (*GD*, p. 80).[2]

The ultimate goal of this study is to interpret the relation between Dante and Derrida within the history of religious scripture in the light of the fundamental and universal questions that pervade their texts, but the horizons of which necessarily exceed the scope of either, indeed any single writer. These are questions of what it means to be a person or to have an identity as a person (Who am I? Who are you? Who are we?), the question of what it means to be ultimately and absolutely responsible for one's own identity to other persons, and, therefore, to be free; and what it means as a person to be mortal, to be destined for and by death. I will argue that these are universal questions that define the character of personal existence as fundamentally religious, prior to and independent of any relation to a "religion" or to the existence of a divine "Being." I will show that Dante and Derrida are both religious writers in the most radical and effective sense of the term: they share a religious identity as writers that arises from the human experiences of faith, hope, and love in response to the divine mystery of absolute responsibility and freedom. In the end, I will contend, for both Dante and Derrida the religious experience of absolute responsibility and freedom resolves itself only in the aporetic dynamics of forgiveness, the Secret that these two reveal without being able to share.

Dante's *Commedia* is first of all a poem of Christian faith in the resurrection of Jesus. That faith affirms resurrection as a real historical event, though not necessarily an empirical one. In this event, the death of Jesus is traditionally, though problematically, understood as a "sacrifice" of innocent suffering offered in expiation of sin. The death of Jesus occasions in response a second act of divine creation, a new genesis, a different way of giving the gift of life that transforms and finalizes the identity chosen by Jesus in his death on the cross. This identity takes the form of the freedom effected by forgiveness. Through this transformation, Jesus' identity becomes centered in forgiveness as the flesh and blood substance of his relationship to all who, through baptism, accept the offered gift of his death and take it on themselves in faith, hope, and love as the meaning of their own death. This exchange of a "gift of death" among Jesus and those who identify themselves with his resurrection finalizes the meaning of love effected through forgiveness as the identity of human freedom. The resurrection is the revelation of that identity as the historical realization of the promise made in secret to Abraham, the promise of the impossible, the promise of God among us, the kingdom of God on earth—the promise written in secret in the flesh of Abraham that faith will always go on beginning again. The history that begins with Abraham reveals that the writing of faith, faith in writing, is from the beginning a promising business, a history and a religion of responsibility.

As a poem, the significance of the *Commedia* is singular. Many claim for it the status of the greatest poem of Western literature. Particularly among poets, including, perhaps even especially, among contemporary poets of widely diverse religious persuasions and nonpersuasion, Dante is revered as both towering visionary and master craftsman. Without interruption, generation on generation of readers have found within the *terza rima* verses of the poem a mirror, by turns hauntingly spectral yet compellingly familiar, in which they "come to themselves again." Historically, the *Commedia* stands at the frontier between the old and new worlds of Western culture. Deeply rooted in Greco-Roman classical antiquity and the Judaeo-Christian religious cultural tradition, the poem stands, with the *Summae* of Thomas Aquinas, as the capstone of the spectacular intellectual synthesis of the High Middle Ages. At this point in history, Europe pauses to take in the vision of the heights to which it had climbed and to survey, with a thrill of anticipation, the new horizons that lay open before it. The *Commedia* culminates in a moment of vision that pierces to the very heart of the Renaissance, and reaches beyond to catch us in our "postmodern" situation today in its prophetic gaze.

All this seems undeniable; it is hardly controversial, and so hardly challenging. So wherein does the singular vitality and power of the *Commedia* lie? If we answer, "in its beauty as a poem," we commit ourselves not just to the formidable task of explaining how beauty happens as poetry, but to the all-but-impossible venture of representing in another way what the poem already is in the singularity of its own identity. Nevertheless, neither prudence nor scientific circumspection obviate the situation of total responsibility in which every reader of the *Commedia* finds herself (again), standing addressed by Dante's words at the opening of the *Paradiso*:

> O you that are in your little bark, eager to hear, following behind my ship that singing makes her way, turn back to see again your shores. Do not commit yourselves to the open sea, for perchance, if you lost me, you would remain astray. The water which I take was never coursed before. Minerva breathes and Apollo guides me, and nine Muses point out to me the Bears.
>
> You other few who lifted up your necks betimes for bread of Angels, on which men here subsist but never become sated of it, you may indeed commit your vessel to the deep brine, holding to my furrow ahead of the water that turns smooth again. (*Par.*, ii, 1–15)

Just as it required faith of Dante to follow Virgil, faith, as the absolute condition of companionship, is required of the reader to follow Dante, not just

in the passage into the "deiform realm" of Paradise, but from the beginning of
the journey to its climax, because the journey is one movement, the movement
of life into the gift of death, by which it is transformed into new life. Therefore, to read the poem responsibly requires religious faith, though not necessarily in the form of commitment to a religion. Those who seek beauty only
as aesthetic recreation cannot follow Dante's way because, from the beginning,
the poem requires the responsibility of faith, the faith that lifts its neck to
feed on the "bread of angels," the Paschal meal that feeds on the word made
flesh and offers a second Eucharist in return for that food, a transformed gift,
the flesh made word again. The poem's beauty gathers itself in its articulation
of a true-to-life-in-death image of the resurrection: *the poem is the resurrected
body of Dante revealed to the reader as a sacrament of faith, hope, and love.* In its
words, it incarnates the Spirit of resurrection, the Spirit promised by Jesus to
his friends before and again after his death, as the gift of his death, as the final
gift, the gift of finality, of a forgiveness that ends in death and by so ending
in the flesh gives the gift of "spirit," the articulated breath of life. The word
goes on becoming flesh again and always without end. The poem's beauty and
power resides in its finality, its integrity, as an image of resurrection. The Spirit
of resurrection animates and enkindles its language, making it a tongue of fire
that burns in the ear and the eye and the heart of the imagination, as the bread
of its words and the wine of its sound are tasted by those whose faith compels
them to "lift their necks" in the gesture of freedom, to feed on it. The Spirit of
resurrection becomes incarnate in the language of the poem, revealing itself in
and as beauty and power, truly human, truly divine.

The guiding concern—less rigid and more flexible than a contention—of
the study that follows is to ask whether the style of writing with which Jacques
Derrida has identified himself, generally labeled "Deconstruction," might
prove to be singularly effective in aiding contemporary readers to understand
the power and beauty of Dante's writing, and most particularly, to understand
how today that power and beauty might be read as expressing a revelation of
the Spirit of resurrection differently. As a concern and a question, what follows
in this study is instigated by and deeply indebted to the work of John Caputo,
particularly in *The Prayers and Tears of Jacques Derrida*,[3] who has both recognized and convincingly articulated the fundamentally religious concern and
character of Derrida's work. In this important and influential study, Caputo
has argued convincingly that in Derrida's more recent writings we discover to
our surprise that Derrida has "gotten religion," or more accurately, that it has
gotten him; in fact, it already had him in the beginning. In *Circumfession*, Derrida reveals that the "cut" that Deconstruction traces in writing copies the style
of the cut of circumcision made by the mohel in Derrida's infant flesh. He
finds that both styles of cutting mark the text they inscribe with an unavoid-
able ambivalence: the "double bind" of a promise destined always to be broken,
a covenant that requires keeping. Caputo reads *Circumfession* as a "confessional
testament," in the spirit and style of St. Augustine's *Confessions.* Each traces a

conversion in writing, remarking in memory both a history of broken promises and a covenant kept in secret by the power of the question that Augustine and Derrida share: What do I love when I love my God? One objective of the study undertaken in *Dante and Derrida* is to add another evidential link to the chain that binds both Augustine and Derrida back to Abraham and Socrates, binds them back as men of "religion" to the father, that is, Abraham the father of faith and Socrates the father of questioning. It binds them as well as to their wives, Sarah and Xanthippe, of whom little is written, except that they laughed and cried inappropriately, at least according to their men. That evidential link is Dante Alighieri.

The evidence for both the claim of a singularly close relationship and the claim for the signal importance of that relationship is to be drawn principally from works by each writer that can be justifiably labeled "autobiographical," if not in the strictest, then at least in some relevant sense of the word. Dante's *Vita nuova* and *Commedia* must in the end be read as autobiographical, regardless of whatever appropriate qualifications might need to be made to this understanding. The place of Derrida's excursus into autobiography across the much broader range of his philosophical writings might at first seem more problematic and less central in comparison, but this appearance belies a decisive reality. The situation of *Circumfession* as, literally, the subtext of Geoffrey Bennington's *Derridabase,* is rooted in a double confrontation, the effect of which is to bring Derrida face-to-face with himself "where he lives," at home, in his writing. Bennington's thematic portrait of Derrida's work is, on its own terms, an altogether admirable work of explication and commentary. In fact, it could with good reason be viewed as a Derrida's "authorized" intellectual biography. But precisely as such, both Bennington and Derrida recognize it for what it is: a formal, theoretical, and, therefore, basically metaphysical understanding, the ultimate *telos* of which is comprehensive understanding, drawn inertially toward total systematization. Derrida recognizes that the only hope for escape open to rescue the singularity of his writing would be to surprise Bennington's system with an unforeseen variable that could not have been anticipated and preprogrammed. *Circumfession* becomes "Derrida's wager," to come up with something altogether new, unexpected, and surprising, that will, at least for now, halt the inexorable, glacial advance of the system toward "monumentality," toward the transmogrification of Derrida's corpus, his body in writing, into a corpse for which Bennington's commentary would serve as grave, tombstone, and epitaph. The surprise Derrida pulls is to display his circumcision in writing, or rather as his writing, to trace the figure of the cut of circumcision that he bears as a kind of bizarre shibboleth. It is impossible to say whether circumcision is the shibboleth of writing or writing of circumcision.

But the real surprise factor in this display, which makes it a genuinely shocking, singular event rather than just a clever tactical trick, is that Derrida's purpose in bearing his circumcision is not primarily to make good on his wager with Bennington, but to cover another bet, this one on a race with death, a headlong pursuit of and by death that he must contest with his mother, Georgette, who is terminally ill and whose death is feared to be imminent. The stakes here are much higher than in the first wager; he fears his mother will die believing her son has abandoned his faith, the faith of their people, that he has become an atheist. To make matters worse, the stakes have been doubled by the onset of a disease from which Derrida himself suffered during his mother's period of crisis. So the deathwatch has been doubled and redoubled: the death of the mother to her son, of the son to the mother, and of the alliance between them.

It is this configuration of the second wager that invokes the spirit of St. Augustine to come to Derrida's aid, just as Beatrice invokes the spirit of Virgil to come to Dante's aid. It is this configuration that gives *Circumfession's* truth claim its proper form—confession. "Every autobiography is a confession," Derrida states; but a confession of what? To whom? Why? To what avail? These questions will pursue our understanding of *Circumfession* as a sort of spectral presence haunting and hounding our tracks throughout.

Caputo's line of interpretation contends not simply that Derrida's scriptural testament is written in a different style than the canonical scriptures of Abrahamic faith, a "religion without religion," but also that this specific difference reveals something significant about all "revelation," the style of religion that is given to writing. In the hope of confirming and advancing this line of interpretation, this study's heuristic hypothesis is precisely that *Derrida can act as a sort of Virgil to contemporary readers of the Commedia,* since Dante too writes his scriptural testament differently than his tradition would expect. Both write confessions of the love of a woman.

Dante takes two classic works as exemplars for his *Commedia*: one, of course, is Virgil's *Aeneid;* the other, Augustine's *Confessions.* The *Confessions* establishes the pattern of religious autobiography as the attempt to take responsibility for one's own personal identity. Augustine traces the story of undergoing a conversion from sin through repentance to forgiveness that begins a new life of discipleship. The confession of a conversion in writing is for Dante, as for Augustine in *Confessions* and Derrida in *Circumfession,* a confession of the double bind of religion, of sin as broken promises and forgiveness as covenant kept, with a difference. Specifically, I want to suggest that Derrida's style of piety allows Dante's poem to resonate differently in the ears of contemporary readers for whom the late medieval synthesis of faith and reason can no longer ring altogether true. In effect, I wish to say that Derrida's style of writing and reading opens up a specific and concrete possibility of a resurrection for the *Commedia* in our historical and cultural situation, a possibility that is both strictly necessary to the poem's identity, yet altogether contingent on the occurrence of occasions that create the determinate conditions for the singular event of such a resurrection to take place. One objective, therefore, of the present study is to display the evidence for the claim that Derrida's writing presents such an occasion and to frame a context in which the significance of this claim can be appropriately estimated and its implications tested.

The progressive development of "Deconstruction" by Derrida as a style of writing can be read, like Dante's *Commedia*, as a "scriptural revelation," a testimony in writing to a "new truth" about the human relationship to the divine and about history. It leads, indeed, to a new understanding of the way the meanings of truth, of religion, and of history mutually determine one another. It goes without saying that, at least in relation to Derrida, this statement cannot be taken as making metaphysical claims about truth, God, or human existence. It does not go without saying, however, that the same is true with regard to the *Commedia*, seen as a "scriptural revelation." Nonetheless, that is one implication of what I am suggesting here and will develop in what follows. The possibility of reading both the *Commedia* and certain of Derrida's texts as "scriptural revelations" constitutes the common ground on which the trajectory of these texts can meet and cross one another, establishing a relationship of singular importance. This suggestion of a significant relationship between Derrida and Dante is not simply to the effect that there is a similarity between them, or that they exhibit a number of noteworthy but, ultimately, isolated points of similarity. Rather, the point is that the relationship between them as a whole, composed of both striking similarities and irreducible differences, reveals something about "revelation" itself and therefore about the relationship between the divine and the human. It reveals something about the occurrence of revelation in writing and therefore as history, as well as about the traditional structures of the human religious imagination and human philosophical and scientific understandings of truth in which the notion of scriptural revelation is embedded.

The relationship between Dante and Derrida testifies to the ongoing, historical human experience of the transformation of life through death, what Dante calls "Resurrection" and Derrida calls "the Gift of Death." Another traditional religious theme, *conversion,* hints at the nature of this transformative gift. The relationship between Dante's styles of writing and of piety and Derrida's styles reveals the way in which the inscription of human experience in writing always involves conversion, and as such, is fundamentally religious and spiritual. A styled writing always bespeaks faith, hope, and love because all conversion necessarily becomes involved in questions of a "gift of life," and therefore of a "gift of death." Writing is religious and spiritual because it necessarily solicits human concern with the finality of freedom and the unconditional responsibility born by every person for the question of identity, "Who am I?" in both my living *and* my dying, precisely in so far as either life or death can be *my own*. The writings of Jacques Derrida, seen through the lenses of certain of his works, most particularly *Circumfession* and the closely related texts, *The Gift of Death, Memoirs of the Blind,* and the lecture "To Forgive," show him, as Caputo suggests, to be unmistakably and primarily a religious writer, as is Dante. Finally, it is Derrida's way of writing that brings him into close companionship with Dante, sharing a pilgrim's journey of conversion in writing, whereby both similarities and differences constitute the strength and intimacy of the bond between them.

The relationship of Dante and Derrida is, however, more specific than simply sharing the genre of confessional autobiography. It extends to and is centered on the style of writing by which the work of confessing a conversion in writing inscribes itself. The proposed study attempts to show through a close reading of certain texts of both writers that they share strong and sustained stylistic patterns of inscription that mark their respective ways of writing. The "scriptural testaments" of conversion by which they both seek to take responsibility for the question, "What do I love when I love *my* God?" which is at the same time the question, "Who am I?" testify to this bond. Central to this attempt, however, indeed very close to its heart, is the conviction that the "shared patterns of inscription" traced and remarked in these texts are the marks of a revelation about style. They refer not only to the styles of Dante or Derrida as authors, but to the style of religion itself, the way in which religion happens in writing as scripture, and about the style of responsibility, the way in which responsibility happens in writing as *conversion:* a revelation of word turning into flesh and flesh turning into word again in writing, as writing, instigated by a recognition of the absolute need for forgiveness. Central, then, to this consideration of the relationship of Dante and Derrida is a concern for the ways at least four specific stylistic patterns of conversion have been inscribed historically in the figures of religion, responsibility, and writing that mark the legacy of those who in some way trace their descent down from Abraham and Socrates. These four stylistic patterns of constant conversion are: (1) a recognition of the need for forgiveness in personal existence, an "absolute" forgiveness for all beginnings, not just that beginning in which sin originates; (2) religion as the history of responsibility arising out of this recognition, and also as the revelation of the freedom that forgiveness promises as its singular gift; (3) faith, hope, and love as the style of living distinctive of religion; and (4) what Dante would call "Resurrection" and Derrida, "the Gift of Death" as the joy of a love that always begins again, fulfilling the promise of absolute forgiveness of all beginnings.

The present study certainly cannot aspire to offer a comprehensive interpretation of the work of either Dante or Derrida. It confines itself to one line of development in certain major texts of each writer that could in some significant sense be regarded as autobiographical, though in neither case in a simple or straightforward sense. For Dante these texts are the *Vita nuova* and the *Commedia;* for Derrida, they are *Circumfession, The Gift of Death, Memoirs of the Blind,* and the lecture, "To Forgive." In the case of Derrida, this grouping of texts, closely related both thematically and chronologically, represents a relatively narrow cross-section of his work. Nevertheless, as Derrida has himself said and Caputo has shown more generally, they locate a decisive moment that is revelatory of both an unrecognized continuity in his writing, his "religion without religion," and a heightened immediacy of concern with the direction that his writing has taken. In the case of Dante, these two works demarcate the entire scope of his life in writing and have generated an entire universe of commentary and discussion. In the context of this study, however, it is the dynamic of religious conversion carried out in writing that focuses consideration of the two texts. Let us attempt to clarify in a preliminary way the implications of this line of interpretation for the present study, especially as regards its ultimate goal.

First, the relationship we are considering resides among these texts, not between their authors. Nothing is being said of the historical individuals Dante Alighieri and Jacques Derrida, their intentions, motives, convictions or identities, except insofar as these enter into the transformative expression that is their writing. Put another way, nothing is said of these persons except insofar as their identities are incarnated in their writing. Second, insofar as Dante can be taken as exemplary, though certainly not typical, of the Christian religious imagination, and in the same way, Derrida of the Jewish religious imagination, the relationship between them challenges our understanding of the relation between Christianity and Judaism, both as styles of religious imagination and as revealing the religious dimension as a constitutive element of all human personal identity. Neither Dante nor Derrida, however, is in a position to initiate or to respond directly to this challenge. It stands as an urgent concern only for a point of view that is different from either of theirs, and which, while attentive to their texts, simultaneously recognizes in them a movement beyond themselves, an openness to being understood otherwise, what Derrida would call a tendency to auto-deconstruction, or what Dante might identify as the sure hope of resurrection. This is the necessary yet impossible transformation of life through death. In some sense, it must be acknowledged that our attention to these two writers, however great the one and provocative the other, is finally motivated by a human concern in which all persons have equal share, and that this tension is experienced as a question of personal identity (Who am I? Who are you? Who are we?).

Two more specific implications follow from casting Dante and Derrida in this role. First, we must ask: Why Dante and Derrida? Why these two writers, these sets of texts? Why not Dante and Joyce, or Milton and Derrida? Why not, indeed, any two "significant" writers? Beyond the exercise of comparison and contrast, what is the heuristic value of evoking a relationship rather than focusing on the religious imagination of one or the other, or even each separately?[4] A second question follows as a practical consequence of the first: How could any study of the relation of two such writers from whatever perspective be responsibly undertaken given the vast scope, the stylistic differences, and the wild diversity of the universes of cultural reference that separate them. How is the reader not already securely, if not expertly, familiar with these texts and their contexts, to understand and judge whatever might emerge from such a study. The answers to these two questions are interrelated and can usefully be addressed here, at least in an anticipatory way.

First, as has been said, the relationship between Dante and Derrida exhibited in these texts is centered on the religious experience of "conversion," not as some broad, archetypal religious category, or even as in the paradigmatic case of St. Augustine, as the explicit subject matter of confessional autobiography, but most specifically as a conversion in writing and in relation to writing. It is a conversion that occurs in the act of writing about a change in one's relationship to and understanding of writing. This is the case, as I believe these texts will show, because both Dante and Derrida, each in his own way unmistakably understands religion in terms of writing and writing in terms of religion, for writing as religion reveals the relationship in human existence between life and death in the transformative light of occurring without beginning or end. This is so neither because the relationship is either eternal or immortal in a metaphysical sense, nor because it is chaotic and absurd, but because it occurs historically as a movement of always beginning again anew. For both Dante and Derrida the history of all human existence is a Book of Genesis, a history that begins without explanation or apology and never delivers a finale, but constantly converts each ending into a new beginning.

For both Dante and Derrida the necessary choice to identify oneself decisively with this movement of history, or to refuse to do so, to finally say "Yes!" or "No!" to this particular configuration of life and death, makes human existence the historically incarnate, testamentary scripture of trust and betrayal, hope and despair, love and hate into which all personal existence, human and divine, is absolutely inscribed. The inscription in flesh and blood of the history of life and death, "Yes!" and "No!," love and hate, hope and despair, trust and betrayal: this is the religion of the Book that Dante and Derrida openly and unmistakably share in a companionship that is made all the more compelling by the irreconcilable differences between them. One is a theist, the other an atheist; one is a Christian, the other acknowledges being indelibly marked by Judaism; one is a poet, the other a philosopher. But through these differences, not despite them, both understand the history of personal existence, the religion of life and death, and the writing of "Yes!" and "No!" to be a matter of a certain style. For both Derrida and Dante that style is signified by the word "forgiveness."

To term forgiveness a "style" seems peculiar at best. In at least one sense, however, this usage attempts to be quite precise: forgiveness refers to a way of going on, a way of beginning anew, of beginning without explanation, condition, or apology for the absence of a cause or a sufficient reason, without apology for the absence of any absolute or necessary first beginning or final end. Forgiveness characterizes the style that marks the history of personal existence insofar as that existence is identified primarily in terms of the freedom and responsibility that mark a way of life that is directed along the path which faith, hope, and love open up. Faith, hope, and love articulate the way forgiveness takes place historically, the path along which it journeys; forgiveness is the way all things go on.

Therefore, before all else, this is a book about forgiveness. Earlier, in the Pre-face/Pre-text, I stated that I take the texts of Dante and Derrida under consideration here to constitute two exemplary episodes in the history of forgiveness. It is only from this perspective that the justification for this study can be understood. The relationship of Dante and Derrida has been chosen as its subject matter because of the way in which their texts offer inspired scriptural testaments, a kind of "divine" revelation regarding what is most fundamental and universal in the existence of all persons. Like all divine revelation, however, this truth takes the form of an aporia, the aporia of forgiveness, in which the hidden Secret, the divine mystery, of the person is revealed without being disclosed, passed on without being shared.

Having identified in a preliminary way a justification for juxtaposing certain texts of Dante and Derrida ultimately on the strength of their shared commitment to forgiveness as the fundamental and universal concern of the religious dimension of personal existence, we are now in a better position to turn to the second difficulty that faces such a study: How could any study of the relation of these two writers, from whatever perspective, be responsibly undertaken given the vast scope, the stylistic differences, and the wild diversity of the universes of cultural reference that separate them? How is the reader not already securely, if not expertly, familiar with these texts and their contexts to understand and judge whatever might emerge from such a study?

Certainly, these are two separate questions, but in fact they converge on the issue of difference, which can be said without fear of contradiction to be close to the hearts of both Dante and Derrida. Are not these two writers simply too different to be responsibly compared? And as one immediate aspect of that difficulty, how practically is such a study to begin without genuine familiarity on the part of the reader with the style of writing with which each is identified—presuming that the audience who have read the texts of both these writers are "fit but few." This issue is particularly relevant since the claim being advanced here is precisely that it is in the *style* of each writer that the relationship resides and through which its revelation occurs. But the issue of difference *is* the question of beginning; to begin is to differ, as well as to defer. To begin is to be separated, cut off both from all that has already begun as well as from all endings. Existence, history, religion, responsibility, and writing: all are without beginning and without end for Dante and Derrida. Beginnings always take place *nel mezzo*, in the middle, the words with which Dante begins his poem. In the middle, at the center, at the turning point, the decisive instance, the point of crisis in the moment of judgment—this is the difficult place of all beginnings. Dante's beginning is in a Dark Wood, *esta selva selvaggia e aspra e forte*, "this savage forest, dense and difficult," what Derrida refers to as "Khora." We must begin in the only way that one can, by entering into the middle of what is already underway in these two different styles of writing, in their texts and in this one, entering on the common path, the *via diritta*, which Dante says does not stray, even though he had lost sight of it. What is the common path that begins in the middle of our shared human journey of life (and death), *nostra vita*, our life, and therefore forms the crux, the crucial center of the relationship between Dante's texts and Derrida's, at the center of the concern that guides the present study? As previously stated, it is the question of forgiveness. But now it must be said explicitly that the question of forgiveness secretly shelters within itself *both* the question of difference *and* the question of beginning. Existence separates, Kierkegaard said. Forgiveness is the style in which all existence occurs, the way in which all difference and singularity take place in existence, without reason or cause, "out of nothing" the Book of Beginnings says, as a gift of love and freedom. Forgiveness is the style of the stroke that cuts out and cuts off every beginning and ending, each life and death, and all writing, all history and religion, all responsibility. Forgiveness is at the center, in the middle, of all things. It is the beginning and the end.

So the present study seeks the forgiveness of which it speaks, forgiveness of the difficulty of beginning to be familiar with the style of writing that Dante and Derrida share: religious, autobiographical, confessional writing of conversion. It seeks forgiveness for the necessity to allow what is the same to remain scattered and intertwined with what is different, for the sake of Dante's and Derrida's identities, but ultimately for the sake of our own identities as well, what each calls "mine," which can be separated no more or less than the identities of these two. The difficulty must be faced practically and straightforwardly, offering what minimal help can be afforded by way of a close reading of their texts, demonstrating and explaining to the extent possible what is distinctive and peculiar to each. Ultimately, however, we must begin and remain *nel mezzo,* in the middle, between two confessional testaments, forced to substitute style for substance, in the faith that the style of these conversion stories, the stories of word become flesh become word again, is offered here as food, the "bread of angels," to sustain the journey of our own conversions. We begin then, necessarily, in the faith that close attention to the style of writing in these texts can reveal the profile of the relationship between Dante and Derrida, reveal it in its human truth and urgency, in the same way that the features of two faces can reveal in their singularity the shared blood of the familiar.

On the other hand, we must not become disoriented if we find a sort of aporia developing around this way of beginning. As we entertain the possibility of recognizing in Derrida the figure of (our) Virgil, then we must inevitably go on to recognize another figure behind his. It is the figure of "another" Dante: not the pilgrim to whose rescue Virgil comes, but rather Dante the poet, the one who imagines the possibility of both rescue and rescuer, the Dante whose signature as author of the poem we are wagering here awaits and requires Derrida's countersignature to liquidate the reserves of the inheritance, to dispense them, let them flow, to find a grace period for the poem, a *kairos* (a bank holiday) in the place of a Khora—to speak in Derridean for a moment. In plainer terms, the aporetic point here is that if we need Derrida's guidance to read Dante better in our own time, perhaps we also need Dante in order to be able to recognize Derrida as our Virgil. Even more pointedly, we can use the account of conversion that Dante the poet has written into/as the journey of the pilgrim in the *Commedia*, in order to read differently the figures of conversion inscribed in the style of Derrida in *Circumfession*. Derrida to deconstruct Dante; Dante to deconstruct Derrida. . . . Too neat? Perhaps; it remains a question.

The study begins by tracing the parallel of *Circumfession* and Dante's journey in the *Commedia*; considers the *Gift of Death* as a testimony to Derrida's experience of conversion as the genetic code of Western history and religion in relation to Dante's account of conversion in the *Inferno;* turns to the aporia of forgiveness in Derrida's "To Forgive," in relation to Dante's portrayal of forgiveness in the *Purgatorio*; and finally, turns to consider *Memoirs of the Blind* as tracing a certain figure of human existence that reveals a faith, a hope, and a certain love that seem to lead back, across the cut of difference, to the experience of the Joy of Resurrection to which Dante testifies in the final vision of the *Paradiso*.

## CHAPTER ONE

# *Vita Nuova:* The Promise of Writing

In man, life sets itself the challenge of producing an animal capable of making promises.

—Nietzsche, *Genealogy of Morals*

Chapter 1 undertakes an interpretation of Dante's *Vita nuova* occasioned by the difference that appears in that text when it is read alongside the first essay of Derrida's *The Gift of Death*. Derrida's essay concerns itself with the history of Europe as the history of European religion and European responsibility, which Derrida reads together as a history of secrecy, the history of keeping secrets. Death is the seal of secrecy, the cut made by the impossibility of keeping the promise of life. Read from this perspective, the *Vita nuova* emerges as both a work of religious autobiography, a confession, and as the chronicle of a signal episode in the history of the invention of writing, the emergence of *il dolce stil nuovo*. In both regards, the *Vita nuova* is the account of a conversion, the record of a new identity that Dante takes on by taking responsibility for a secret covenant of promises: the secret of a "Divine" word given as a promise of love, revealed and made flesh in the person of Beatrice, and Dante's secret promise of a human word to be given in writing to memorialize the death of love. This reading of the *Vita nuova* in turn prompts an initial reading of Derrida's *Circumfession* according to the difference that appears in that text when it is read alongside Dante's *Vita nuova*. *Circumfession* is the history of Derrida's conversion in writing, a history of his religion without religion. There he attempts to take responsibility for his deconstructive style of writing as a way of keeping the secret promise of life that had been cut in his flesh at the beginning of his life in the face of the death of his mother.

## THE SECRET OF BEGINNING: A PARABLE

The promise of writing reveals a secret calling. This means that writing is a promising business: it is set to work by the need, the necessity, to make and keep promises. This necessity is absolute; without promise, nothing happens, neither world nor history. According to Genesis, the Book of Beginning, the history of the world, the universe, unfolds as the making of a promise: Let there be light! Let there be the revelation of something new, a beginning full of promise. Let a new dawn break, and break again and again. The world begins with promise, with the promise of light, revealing together the possibility of a world and of history. Light is the illuminating possibility of world history. Light calls into evidence the possibility of making promises and of keeping promises; that is, light is the calling into existence of persons, the being that is capable of promise making and promise keeping. Light is the calling of, the calling to, freedom. Light illuminates the possibility of the world as the place in which the history of freedom occurs.

The identity of the "person" here includes the possibility and the necessity of both divine and human persons, and also of their correlativity, that is, of their mutual codetermination of every aspect and perspective of the time, space, and history of their relationships as persons. "Divine" signifies the anteriority of promising as the revelation of a call for beginning, the origin of which is not and cannot be revealed but must remain secret, be kept as a secret, as the necessary absolute condition of genesis, of every beginning. Without the keeping of the secret, the very idea of beginning would be meaningless; meaning would never begin to happen as the world and history of persons.

Without keeping its secret, any idea of beginning is meaningless—empty, void, nothing, without possibility, unthinkable, absurd. The secret is in its own keeping, this keeping for itself of this empty nothing, this meaningless absurd, this impossible. The secret anterior to genesis, with which genesis begins, the Secret which is divine because it is absolutely necessary, is an empty secret. It conceals nothing; at least, nothing meaningful, not even the possibility of meaning, for that too is revealed and begins with the word that calls into the void with the promise of light, the promise of meaning that articulates the space and time of the world and history. Genesis: the story of the theory of relativity; the story of light, space, and time as correlative; of human and divine persons, also as correlative. All necessarily emerge together as promising meaning and keeping the secret of promising, which is an empty secret making empty promises that must be kept.

How to keep an empty secret, empty promises? This is the question posed by the calling into existence of the human person, God's co-conspirator in keeping the empty promise of an empty secret. Humans, too, are persons; like divine persons, they too are capable of making (empty) promises and keeping (empty) secrets. Woman/man made in the image and likeness of God; male and female, another correlation, another conspiracy; another uncertainty principle, history's first recorded triangle, the first trick of three, the best way to keep the empty promise of an empty secret—dissemination, sowing the seed of difference, which sprouts into weeds among the flowers, planting the seeds of dissimulation, of deception and discord, calling attention away from the secret hidden at the center of the garden, the tree of life that articulates space and time, situating all involved in a scene of uncertainty where the possibility of the correlation, the site of relation and meaning, is kept hidden, guarded by the trial of prohibition, by calling attention to another site, the site of temptation occasioned by the fruit of secrecy, the knowledge of good and evil, the first fruit of cultivation and of culture, the harvest that fulfills the empty promise of the empty secret: sin, the final seal, which assures that the empty promise of the empty secret will both be kept, empty. Eating—the occasion of sin, the strategy shared by divine and human co-conspirators, designed to give the history of the world the semblance of meaning through substitution, so as not to give away its secret at the beginning.

It is a rather charming story; really quite a comedy, and quite effective: it opens up the possibility of multiple complications, some rather terrifying, altogether effective at sowing further seeds of discord, further distracting from the emptiness of the promise and the secret it keeps. But in the end, all shall be well; all manner of thing shall be well, for the story promises a happy ending. It is necessarily written that way, full of promise and light from the beginning because writing is a promising business, a secret calling to be kept secret in writing, the articulation, according to a certain theory of relativity and principle of uncertainty, of a real possibility, in the end, for meaning to be inscribed in space and time, in the world's history, as a story with a happy ending, a Comedy. The structure of promising, in other words, is faith, hope, and love, the virtues of every religion.

## THE PROMISE OF A NEW LIFE

### Poetry

And it was at that age . . . Poetry arrived in search of me.
I don't know, I don't know where it came from, from winter or a river.
I don't know how or when, no they were not voices,
they were not words, nor silence, but from a street I
was summoned, from the branches of night, abruptly,
from the others, among violent fires or returning alone,
there I was without a face and it touched me.

I did not know what to say, my mouth had no way
with names, my eyes were blind, and something
started in my soul, fever or forgotten wings, and I
made my own way, deciphering
that fire, and I wrote the first faint line, without
substance, pure nonsense, pure wisdom
of someone who knows nothing, and suddenly I saw
the heavens unfastened and open, plants, palpitating

plantations, shadow perforate, riddled
with arrows, fire and flowers, the winding night, the universe.

And I, infinitesimal being, drunk with the great starry
void, likeness, image of mystery, felt myself a pure
part of the abyss, I wheeled with the stars, my heart
broke loose on the wind.

Pablo Neruda[1]

"In the book of my memory, after the first pages, which are almost blank,
there is a chapter headed *Incipit vita nova* [here begins a new life]."

(Dante Alighieri, *Vita nuova*, i) [2]

The book of New Life. A new Book of Beginning. Genesis—a book of new beginning(s), of (always) beginning anew. A revelation in writing; a scriptural revelation of a new genesis, a new triangle, a new trick-of-three. A new promise of new writing, in a new style (*il dolce stil nuovo*), a new way of keeping secret. Dante's *Vita nuova* is a strange work: strange, because it is (almost) altogether new, because it is so promising. It is stranger still because it probably promises too much in writing—in the face of death, it promises a new life, a new beginning. It promises a gift of writing in the face of death, promises in writing the Gift of Death. The promise of writing is the Gift of Death.[3] *Vita nuova* promises to give a new name to the face of the Gift of Death. The Book of Beginning, written in a new way, tracing the beginning of a conversion. The conversion story of the *Vita nuova* tells of conversion deferred, a conversion that ends by promising yet another conversion (for it promises in writing another writing that will require another new beginning). The *Vita nuova* concludes with the lines:

> After this sonnet, there appeared to me a marvelous vision in which I saw things which made me decide to write no more of this blessed one until I could do so more worthily. And to this end I apply myself as much as I can, as she indeed knows. Thus, if it shall please Him by whom all things live that my life continue for a few years, I hope to compose concerning her what has never been written in rhyme of any woman. And then may it please Him who is the Lord of courtesy that my soul may go to see the glory of my lady, that is, of the blessed Beatrice, who now in glory beholds the face of Him *qui est per omnia saecula benedictus* (who is eternally blessed). *(Vita nuova, xlii)*[4]

Contained here is the promise of a new, "more worthy" writing, the beginning of which would in fact be postponed for more than a decade, despite the reference to being spared "for a few years." What is the significance of this promise, what secret does it keep that prevents it from being kept for so long? What conversion does it articulate and what conversion does it anticipate, so long in arriving? And, perhaps most important, what should we make of the prodigious prodigality of this promise? Something absolutely new? Never written before? Of a woman? Impossible!

The promise is predicated on a long series of visions that culminate in the decisive one mentioned but not described in the above citation. This final vision is anticipated not long before by a lesser one, more an "impression" than a vision, though still vivid, which prefigures the manner and matter of the one yet to come:

> I seemed to see Beatrice in glory, clothed in the crimson garments in which she first appeared before my eyes, and she seemed as young as when I first saw her. Then I began to think about her and as I recalled her through the sequence of time past my heart began to repent sorrowfully of the desire by which it had so basely allowed itself to be possessed for some days against the constancy of reason; and when this evil desire had been expelled all my thoughts returned once more to their most gracious Beatrice. And I say that from then onwards I began to think of her so much with the whole of my remorseful heart that frequently my sighs made this evident, expressing as they issued what my heart was saying, that is, the name of this most gracious soul and how she had departed from us. (*Vita nuova*, xxxix)

Dante-the-lover prepares the final vision by circling back to the original vision that already contained the seed of the final one. By following in living memory the sequence of time past, he returns to himself again as he had been and as he now begins to be again, to his thoughts of Beatrice as she had been in his eyes in the beginning. And now his tears begin to wash clean again the vision of her that had until this episode been dimmed and obscured for a while by his succumbing to the temptation to seek consolation for his loss of her to death in the pity of the "lady of the window."[5] Enkindled by his sighs, inarticulately expressing what his heart would say, the name of Beatrice, his eyes become "desirous only of shedding tears" of repentance, expressions of a rethinking, a change of mind, of a conversion. Thus bathed and cleansed, thus baptized, his eyes die by going down into the waters over which the sighs of God had first breathed, in the beginning, the first "inspiration." From these waters, his eyes emerge to the final vision and the promise it expresses: the promise of new writing, of new tears, to be inscribed in a new style in a new book of his memory.

This final vision contains within itself and reveals its beginning in a new light. Here the structure of the *Vita nuova* becomes apparent. The Dante who writes the work or, more accurately, compiles it, probably in 1292–1293, writes in an attempt to read himself, rereading his poems written at various times probably over the preceding ten years, and trying to "come to himself again," by rereading and rewriting in narrative commentary what he finds written in the book of his memory.[6] Through this triple inscription, Dante the writer recounts the story of Dante the lover, whose new life begins with his "first vision" of Beatrice "when they were both about nine" (*Vita nuova*, ii). They were two children at a feast hosted by her father, two children who could not yet see that their names had already been written down together by another in the book of history, divinely prescribed for each other: a new Adam and Eve at a new garden party. From the start, this book is written binocularly to achieve maximal depth of field: one eye angles the story from the perspective of the young lover, the initiate who is being inducted into love's secret ways; the other eye sees from the perspective of the adept, the seer who has already participated in the ecstasy of the mystery. This double vision, however, is itself redoubled: it is a rewriting of what had already been written twice and written differently—first in the book of memory, then in the poems. Now these writings are reinscribed into the prose commentary that constitutes the confessional voice in the work, the poet's voice confessing that he was all along being called. He confesses that he had received a vocation to be the poet of Beatrice. He is trying to confess to being called by Beatrice to see himself in a new light. It is Beatrice who calls, Beatrice who was his beloved Lady; Beatrice who was the inspiration of his poetry; Beatrice who was the "desired of God" and of the Heavenly City; Beatrice who is the threefold arrival of the Gift of Death, the trinitarian revelation of the secret of beginning, the promise of a new life.[7] It would seem, however, that although the writer saw differently than the lover, neither suspected the unpromising and highly improper role of yet another, a third Dante, absent yet present in the writing, on whom still further visions would be visited and of whom another conversion would be required in order to make good his promise to keep the secret of the Gift of Death in a new writing, and thus to remain faithful to his Lady.

But that is another story, yet to be told. The story of this promise still needs to be traced back to its promising beginning of a new life and a new style of writing, the revelation of a new way of keeping a secret. The First Vision, recounted in *Vita nuova* ii, is the seminal one of the lover's first sight of Beatrice, whom the writer already identifies as the woman whom "my mind [now] beholds in glory," though that beholding has yet to germinate into the form of vision that it will take in the writing of the *Paradiso,* with Beatrice taking her proper place in the White Rose of the Empyrean. Dressed "in a very noble color, a decorous and delicate crimson," he recognizes her as a divine revelation. He knows this by the style of writing by which she is inscribed into the book of his memory. "The moment I saw her, I say in all truth that the vital spirit, which dwells in the inmost depth of the heart, began to tremble so violently that I felt the vibration alarmingly in my pulses." This revelation is traced by its pulse strokes in his heart and blood, "even in the weakest of them." He undergoes tremendous trembling of blood-writing, articulated without words in the fleshy tablet of the heart with the violence, the violation, the transgressive, incising bite that is characteristic of the divine style of wording itself: it always marks itself in the flesh first, cutting open a bloody trace with which it binds and ties its victim (Beatrice wears a girdle over the crimson, "trimmed in a matter suited to her tender age," the victim bound for sacrifice; another Iphigenia, another Isaac).[8] His trembling heart utters the words that are wrung out of it by the master power that keeps the secret of the divine, the secret of the beginning, enclosed within itself as it expresses itself in the flesh of another. *Ecce deus fortiori me, qui veniens dominabitur mihi.* "Behold a god of greater power than mine, who comes to lord it over me." This is how the secret writes itself in the flesh: the Lord, the dominator, exercises its dominion by "taking place," happening as the subjugation of the fleshy tablet, there to disseminate itself by conjugating, verbalizing itself in the pulse-strokes of blood-writing.

The conquest quickly spreads to a new front: "At this point, the spirit of the senses which dwells on high in the place to which all our sense perceptions are carried, was filled with amazement and, speaking especially to the spirit of vision said, 'Now your joy has been revealed.'" The power transgresses further along the path that life follows to the eyes that sustain a second blow—the envisioning of revelation. This further transgression, transferring the blow of power, inspires a new register, reaches a new registry, and transcribes itself into yet another style of writing: "Whereupon the natural spirit which dwells where our nourishment is digested, began to weep and, weeping, said, 'Woe to me! For I shall often be impeded from now on.'" This must have been something like the way YHWH's Spirit breathed life into the inert clay of Adam, violating the dumb dirt with blow after blow, inspiring it with senses and articulating it with various strokes, inscribing it with different styles of writing. But with a difference: here in Dante's vision the woman comes first and the man is induced through her, as seems more natural, or at least more familiar. Furthermore, this water-writing in tears is an unresponsive, irresponsible substitute for inspiration of the Spirit that first breathed over the waters and inscribed in them the secret promise of life. This substitute water-writing in tears blurs the vision and registers itself as the dismay of digestion, that dyspepsia that inhibits eating, the presence of the other that discomforts the void within the place of the secret where the fruit is buried after it is eaten, substituting flesh for the hunger for the word that must be kept secret, substituting a watery ink that vanishes for the lasting stain of blood. Eating flesh—flesh of fruit, flesh of animal, flesh of men—all flesh-eating is a sorry substitution, an empty promise of the empty secret which is the only food that truly sustains life—the secret revelation encrypted in the vision of the sole source of the soul's vital joy. Only the eating of flesh made word again will turn the water of tears into the wine-blood of joy, turn the salt of tears into the bread-flesh of life. Eucharist—the conversion of eating from animal nourishment into feasting as celebration, the change in the signification of eating that Dante will have to inscribe in the promised writing, is already inscribed, prefigured, in the biopsychology of this passage.

The text of *Vita nuova,* ii continues, "From then on indeed Love ruled over my soul, which was thus wedded to him early in life, and he began to acquire such assurance and mastery over me, owing to the power which my imagination gave him, that I was obliged to fulfill all his wishes perfectly."

Inscribing itself in the fleshy tablet of the body, the divine power consummates its nuptials with the soul, its voice inspiring the cords of imagination to resonate and amplify its significance, and impregnates it with the seeds of new visions yet to come. Dante's imagination grows big with the promise of new life written in the virgin blood of that wedding night. Domination, mastery to the point of servitude, even enslavement: the pattern of divine power written into human flesh, that kenotic emptying out that St. Paul transcribes, the secret that is constantly kept by reinscription into human flesh. The transgressive and violent impropriety of this pattern had long ago been given a proper name: Incarnation.[9]

Dante the poet recognizes that in one sense, the lover's revelation is an old story, recorded countless times in old testaments: "I often went in search of her, and I saw that in all her ways she was so praiseworthy and noble that indeed the words of the poet Homer might have been said of her, 'she did not seem the daughter of a mortal man, but of a god.'" Yet the poet recognizes too the note of an irony that registers its trace here, planting a seed that will germinate only much later, "Though her image, which was always present in my mind, incited Love to dominate me, its influence was so noble that it never allowed Love to guide me without the faithful council of reason, in everything in which such counsel was useful to hear." The dominion of Love here, however triumphant, is circumscribed by the prescription of another style of inscription, another as yet ungerminated seed of conversion that will produce in imagination other figures of mastery and direction that come to life in the *Commedia*. The voice of reason, which prescribes another rule to which the Love of the "praiseworthy and noble" pays heed, is yet to be figured forth, and the style of its writing yet to be traced out in imagination in this episode of Dante's conversion story.

*Vita nuova* traces the secret of beginning ambiguously inscribed in the promise of Dante's writing and in Dante's promise of writing. It is the Book of Genesis in the scriptural testaments of Dante the poet, the Book of the Dead in the confessional testimony of Dante the lover, the Book of Revelation in which the Secret calling, the vocation to conversion and new life, is inscribed into the heart, viscera, eyes, and mind of Dante, the child of the Promise of Writing. But the promise of writing is always and only fulfilled through the Gift of Death, which pays the price for the an-economy[10], the prodigious prodigality and hyperbolic excess of the promise of a genuinely new beginning, of a true singularity and singular truth. A promise is always an act of impropriety and importunity; whatever it promises, it draws on credit, offering present property as collateral for future gift. But the asymmetry between its structural elements, property and gift, present and future, reveals the impossibility of promising, the unpromising possibility contained within the structure of promising itself: its necessary, secret emptiness. The promise is a substitution, a subterfuge that tries to draw attention away from the impropriety of the future, which we do not yet have, and the expropriation of the past, which we no longer have. It plants a seed that germinates into the fruit of promise, which is "attractive to the eye and good to eat," because it promises present knowledge. Knowledge seems to offer the promise of enabling the one who eats to ingest the past and future whole, transforming the one into the other, digesting the otherness of the Other and transmogrifying it into one's present property—"Ye shall be as gods." (Much as Ouranos, Kronos, and Zeus all had to do, that is, ingest everything, including their own offspring, in the ultimately futile attempt to stabilize their fateful dominion.)

If the vision of *Vita nuova,* ii is the vision of creation and the revelation of its promise of new life, *Vita nuova,* iii is the revelation of the ambiguity of that promise born of its emptiness, of the seductive, tempting power of the secret of promising as the beginning of a hopeless economy of debt and deception. It reveals the history of an eating that neither nourishes nor satisfies, yet which reveals a new possibility for the story, tracing a new chapter in the water-writing, a trail of tears and sweat, a new transcription in blood-writing, as blood sacrifice and bloodbath. The seed of this new writing is planted in the second vision of *Vita nuova.* That seed will not germinate, however, or flower or bear the fruit of difference, a different way of eating and writing, until long years of gestation have passed. Then the alchemy of the soul, like the pregnancy of the womb, brings forth something singular and new: the an-economy of conversion—changing the blood, sweat, and tears by which must be earned the daily bread, that which substitutes as food but does not satisfy, into the bread of life by which the promise is converted and kept through the revelation of the Gift of Death, through the experience of forgiveness as a new way of keeping promises and secrets in writing. Forgiveness means always beginning anew: the deferred conversion of the poet of the *Vita nuova* becomes the pilgrim's journey of conversion reimagined in the *Commedia.*

The vision of *Vita nuova,* iii is terrible: it is a further revelation of the Secret calling for the promise of writing, the promise written in the blood, the blood of sacrifice. It is a vision of "heart-eating," of the violence that tries to redeem the debt of substitution through the economy of sacrifice, succumbing to the temptation to consume and devour the promise of writing and digest it as present property expressed in writing. Situated as occurring "exactly nine years" after the first vision, the second is recorded in the same divine space, the doubled square of time-space that bespeaks the reciprocity of the relationship that locates the religious dimension of human existence. The vision occurs improperly, that is, as a dream, the unconscious articulation of a desire that is temporally (temporarily) dissociated from the voice of reason, at liberty to express itself without regard to the responsibility to discipline itself according to the word made flesh appearing as the restraining presence of the other—Beatrice as she appeared in the flesh: nine years prior in the first vision, and again in the flesh on the day preceding this dream. Yet it is her flesh made word that supplies the occasion for the dream, itself a continuation of a revelry that becomes the substitute feast for her living word:

When exactly nine years had passed since this gracious being appeared to me, as I have described, it happened that on the last day of this intervening period, this marvel appeared before me again, dressed in pure white walking between two other women of distinguished bearing, both older than herself. As they walked down the street she turned her eyes toward me *where I stood in fearing and trembling,* and with her ineffable courtesy, which is now rewarded in eternal life, she greeted me. *As this was the first time she had ever spoken to me, I was filled with such joy that, my senses reeling, I had withdrawn from the sight of others. So I returned to the loneliness of my room and began to think about this gracious person.* (*Vita nuova,* iii; emphasis added)

The location of the episode in the square of divine time-space (nine equals three times three, the Trinitarian figure "squared," rectified with its human image) is redoubled by the location of Beatrice herself appearing as the central member of the trinity of women, securing her figural identity as the revelatory word, her *"salute,"*[11] the "greeting" which is recognized as expressive of her role as the embodied promise of his salvation, the annunciation of his new life communicated in the script of her eyes that behold him in "fear and trembling," prefiguring the act of fevered imagination in which the dream will rescript her promising greeting in the idiom of sacrifice. Before his eyes, the dream-vision will encrypt her actual appearance in the flesh inscribing it in the image of sacrifice as a substitute for the Gift of Death. The purity of the white in which she is dressed is the color appropriate to the innocence of the victim to be offered in sacrifice. But something goes wrong. In a parodic echo of the visionary biopsychology of *Vita nuova* ii discussed earlier, Dante withdraws from the sight of others into the privacy of his own room, and attempts to secret himself away into the reverie (senses reeling) of an enclosed space, a secret garden of earthly delights, the seductively tempting delight of thinking his own thoughts as a substitute for her lost presence in the flesh-made-word of her greeting. He sleepily begins to lose himself in the project of transforming his private property ("the loneliness of my room") into sacred precincts to set the scene for a liturgical ritual of his own devising. The stage is set for the fateful drama about to unfold: the encryption of the Secret calling in the promise of writing, the substitution of another secret, the secret Dante dreams up in the crypt of his own private property, the encrypted substitution imaginatively kept secret by role reversal: male for female, tempted for tempter, victim for priest/executioner. The duplicity of this encrypted substitution is signaled and signified by the "redress" that Beatrice undergoes in the dream for transgressing the boundary confines of Dante the unconscious lover's private garden-party world of exclusion of the other ("the loneliness of my room") with the violence of her address (*salute*). Now Beatrice is dressed again in the crimson-blood red of the passion of her first appearance before the word of her greeting had transgressed the silence, piercing the virginal hymen of his hearing, which had not yet been ravished as had his seeing and tasting/

smelling (eating) within the first vision. This rapture/ravishment stains her white garment blood red and ignites the bonfire of desire for the sacrificial holocaust his secret substitution of his dream image for the reality of her flesh made word would call for:

> As I thought of her I fell asleep and a marvelous vision appeared to me. In my room I seemed to see a cloud the color of fire and in the cloud a lordly figure frightening to behold, yet in himself, it seemed to me, he was filled with a marvelous Joy. He said many things of which I understood only a few, among them were the words: *Ego dominus tuus* (I am your Master). In his arms I seemed to see a naked figure, sleeping, wrapped lightly in a crimson cloth. Gazing intently I saw it was she who had bestowed her greeting on me that day. In one hand the standing figure held a fiery object, and he seemed to say, *Vide cor tuum* (Behold your heart). After a little while I thought he awakened her who slept and prevailed on her to eat the glowing object in his hand. Reluctantly and hesitantly she did so. A few moments later his happiness turned to bitter grief, and, weeping, he gathered the figure in his arms and together they seemed to ascend into the heavens. I felt such anguish at their departure that my light sleep was broken, and I awoke. (*Vita nuova,* iii)

It will not prove too much to say that the dream vision recounted here sets in motion Dante's "salvation history," that is, both the history of his "original sin" and the long history of his conversion, repentance, forgiveness, and resurrection that is inscribed in the *Vita nuova* and *Commedia,* the "Old and New" confessional testaments that comprise his "scriptural revelation." In this passage Dante and Beatrice figure Adam and Eve, though their identities are partially encrypted in the reversal of gender roles noted above. The full anticipatory significance of this claim, especially with regard to the *Commedia,* must await further explication, but this much can be asserted here with substantial textual reliability: when Dante "came to (find) himself again," astray in the Dark Wood in the opening lines of the *Commedia,* "the straightway having disappeared," at some moment of oblivion when he was "so full of sleep" that he failed to recognize the substitution of a "false" for and a "true" way of envisioning both Beatrice and himself, this is the moment which the Pilgrim unwittingly, and the poet in the full consciousness of the final vision, is recalling, reconstituting, reliving, submitting for conversion. This is the moment of "original sin" in writing, in the writing on his heart, in his senses, in his memory, in his imagination, in his blood, in his poetry and his self-interpretation, of which Beatrice will convict him in their encounter in *Purgatorio,* xxx–xxxi, for which he will shed tears of repentance and receive forgiveness, thereby allowing the promise of writing, its secret calling, to be resurrected in the "new life" which the conversion recounted in *Vita nuova* only dimly prefigures.

The vision described here concerns the ironic history of eating; it recapitulates salvation history as the mirror play of the origin and growth of sin, while at the same time and through the same events revealing the dissemination and germination of the growth of forgiveness and redemption. Together these perspectives form one account of the history of the (empty) Secret of Beginning, the story of the Impossible which calls for and promises, in writing, the Gift of Death. This ironic history of eating turns on the necessary ambiguity of its structure as substitution: to eat means to substitute the death of the Other for the empty promise of life. Eating is both necessary and impossible. The flesh of the Other can be consumed and digested to be transformed into the proper property of one's own flesh, but the death of the Other cannot be appropriated, so that, in attempting to feed on it, the empty stomach of life becomes engorged and must expel the other/death (the work of mourning) in order to become free again, open, empty, for the proper impropriety of its own death, for the giving of death as a Gift, for-giving its own death rather than feeding on the substituted death of the Other. Life is fed only by faith, hope, and love consumed as the word made flesh of the Other, given as the Gift of Death.

This ironic history of eating as substitution, ambiguously signifying both transgression and forgiveness, is also the history of gender and sexuality, equally ambiguous in their significance. Sexuality and gender, both biologically and psychologically configured, are movements of substitution. Reproductively, the life of the child substitutes for the life of the parents, which is sacrificed for the life of the child; erotically, lovers feed on the flesh of the other immolated by the fire of passion for the (substitute) death of the other in his or her orgasmic climax, while paying the price, making the sacrifice of one's own (substitute) orgasm-death (Sartre's sexuality as sado-masochism). Eating and sexuality: both exhibit the ambiguity of their sacrificial structure. Sacrifice here is but an element of the structural dynamics of the original sin of substitution. All eating, all intercourse—always sinful and in need of forgiveness (St. Augustine was right at least to this extent: sexuality (as eating) is the "original sin"; but apparently he did not also recognize it also as the original scene of forgiveness).

In the dream, Beatrice is required by the god Amor to eat Dante's burning heart, which she does reluctantly and hesitatingly. While both the sexual and the eucharistic connotations in the image are clear, it is precisely the structure of sacrificial substitution that calls for attention here. Dante's unconscious (sleeping) imagination scripts itself in the role of male sacrificial victim whose heart, on which Love has already inscribed its secret, is consumed both by the fiery passion which is the aura of love's divine necessity and by Beatrice's feeding on his orgasmic death. But it is Beatrice who wears the blood sash/slash of the love wound, she who bears the blood-mark on the sacrificial victim, "reluctantly and hesitantly." It is a scene of rape: her mouth is raped by dominating Love that forces the phallus of its words of dominating power, inscribed on Dante's heart, into her mouth and down her throat, gorging the emptiness of her stomach/open wound with the food of substitution: his death for hers; the forced violence of an uninvited intercourse, an inhospitable last supper. The violence of this transgression is revealed immediately as the guilty conscience of Amor, whose complicity as instigator and intermediary, indeed as pimp, is unmistakable when his joy quickly turns to "bitter grief" as "weeping, he gathered the figure [of Beatrice] in his arms and together they seem to ascend into the heavens." The image is one of postcoital embrace, which ironically is interpreted by Dante the writer as a heavenly ascent, instead of the descent into the oblivion of sleep, the death of desire following its satiating climax, which postpones the necessary work of mourning. The standard interpretation in the literature of the *Vita nuova* of this onset of grief and anguish is that it foreshadows the multiple deaths of Beatrice to Dante, which the text will recount: first, her marriage to another, then her physical death, and finally her death as his Muse of poetic inspiration in the long years that follow the promise with which the *Vita nuova* concludes, "to write of her what never has been written in rhyme of woman before." This is, in itself, certainly valid; but as the *Commedia* will eventually make clear, the grief and anguish that the dream displays are also an unconscious registry of Dante's guilty conscience for his authorship of this masque in which he encrypts his own identity as Eve, Beatrice's as Adam, and Amor's as the beguiling serpent. They are envisioned as a trinity of substitution, the substitute Trinity that distracts in guilty sleep from the conscious awareness of the original Trinity in which the secret promise of life is kept. This loss of consciousness of the empty secret, engorged by feeding on the death of the Other, incurs the guilty debt, the bad conscience of substitution and will require the work of mourning expressed in the promise of writing to convert the loss of joy and its substitution by grief and anguish into the figure of resurrection. The transformation of death into gift, one's own death taken on oneself freely in full consciousness, given as food by the Other, in the an-economy of forgiveness.

There is another mechanism of substitution at work in the writing of the dream vision. In the first major movement of *Vita nuova* (i–xviii) Dante the writer portrays Love as an independent entity, separately embodied and endowed not just with agency, but with dominant power and initiative, and this is undoubtedly accurate to the experience recorded in the book of his memory. Gradually, however, beginning in the second and culminating in the third movements of the *Vita nuova*, Dante comes to recognize the figure of Amor as the projection of his own need, his enthrallment to the passion of his own desire, and indeed of his own will to power. In other words, as the *Vita nuova* progresses, Dante the writer begins to suspect unwillingly and hesitantly that Amor is an idol, a false identity. Amor becomes the shadow in his imagination of the authentic power of the Other that has transgressed the boundaries of his heart, his senses, and his mind, a transgression which, impossibly, demands avenging. In much the same way, Cain avenges himself on Abel by murdering him on account of Cain's guilty conscience over the debt he incurs through his substitution of blemished meat for the best grain food offered by Abel—the image being itself a parable of degrees of self-deception and oblivion pertaining to the sacrificial structure of substitution as it relates to both eating and sexuality—since the brothers would, of necessity, have been at least potential sexual rivals for their sisters.[12] And as the figure of incest is necessarily involved in the story of Genesis, so must it be in the reading of *Vita nuova* as Dante's Book of Genesis. Amor, functioning as the avenging angel of Dante's unconscious imagination in rescripting the story of his own violation and sacrificial wounding (the extraction of his heart) by that same Amor, rapes and wounds Beatrice.

But Amor, in its initiative and mastery over Dante, must be read as more than the externalization of Dante's own libidinal, instinctive desires. Amor is also the instinct and impulse to writing. It is the impulse that leaves him in grief and anguish and that, when he returns to consciousness, shocked by that horrifically bad dream, prompts Dante to turn to writing as a means of working out that grief and anguish over the double violation that produces the violence of the dream. He writes a sonnet, further encrypting in it the text of substitution already encoded by his imagination in the dream. Again attributing the power and initiative to Amor, Dante decides to disseminate the cryptic message in writing, inviting interpretation, and thereby diffusing responsibility for the original scripting, giving it out over the substitute signature of Amor:

> To every captive soul and gentle lover
> Into whose sight this present rhyme may chance,
> That, writing back, each may expound its sense,
> Greetings in love, who is their Lord, I offer. (*Vita nuova,* iii)

A further substitution, a deeper encryption: dissemination in writing, initiating an economy of circulation among a "captive" audience further ensuring that the secret calling of the promise of writing will be kept secret. And indeed, it is. "This sonnet drew replies from many, who all had different opinions as to its meaning. Among those who replied was someone whom I call my closest friend [Calvalcante]; he wrote a sonnet beginning: *"In my opinion you beheld all virtue"* (*Vita nuova,* iii). Now the tomb of the guilty, encrypted substitution is sealed; there is no going back, only forward, through writing.

This pattern of substitution continues and intensifies throughout the remainder of the first movement of *Vita nuova* (v–xviii). Driven by the impulse to encryption and masking as a way of keeping its guilty secret, the writing of the poetry and its interpretation devises another substitution, that of screening Dante's enthrallment to the love of Beatrice behind the simulation of romantic devotion to first one, then another lady, so as to deflect public attention away from its actual but secret object. Dante adopts dissimulation as the occasion and style of writing both the poems and their later interpretation. This seals the contract in writing between Dante and Amor. It also clarifies the identity of both figures in this first melodramatic episode of the secret calling to enter into the larger drama of conversion contained in the promise of writing. Dante the love-slave and the lordly Amor are the dissociated elements of a concretely existing personal freedom, the historical *person* Dante, to whom the vocation to writing and the call to conversion are addressed as the truth of the revelation he experiences in the *person* of Beatrice. In this larger configuration both the Incarnational and the Trinitarian structures that are central to and pervasive in Dante's poetic work become apparent: *the word is made flesh and the flesh is made word again.* As an historical person, Beatrice incarnates for Dante the revelation of Divine Love (dimly figured in the *Vita nuova* as Amor). This trinity of personal freedoms configure the historical time-space of incarnation, that is, the Divine Word revealed in the flesh and, through the Gift of Death, that flesh resurrected into spirit, the tongue of fire that inspires and articulates the conversion of the Divine Word into the human Word: a new life, a converted pattern of substitution, a redeemed pattern of eating. Resurrection reveals Love as the impossible truth of life, the Gift of Death, the secret that is always empty because history only begins as the pouring-itself-out of Love in forgiveness. Divine Love articulates itself as the resurrection of life through the Gift of Death, given as forgiveness. Resurrection configures itself historically in the trinitarian and incarnational patterns of human personal identity. Freedom names this patterning of personal existence as the experience of absolute or total responsibility for transcribing and encrypting the revelation of the divine Word of Love into the flesh and blood of human personal identity. Resurrection is written in the flesh of human personal identity through the experience of conversion to the freedom that transcribes the divine Word of Love into Spirit, articulated by the human Word. Spirit is the resurrection of the flesh as word, the word through which the Gift of Death is forgiven. Spirit keeps the secret of life by encrypting it in the human Word. Freedom names the total responsibility for human identity that gives itself the Gift of Death as the Spirit of Resurrection.

The dynamic of this freedom as conversion to total responsibility for personal identity is already prefigured, though dimly and in dissociation, in the historical situation of Dante's writing of the *Vita nuova* with its story of Amor, Beatrice and the writer himself. In it, Amor certainly figures the god of love, but also the god of writing: he is flesh-writing, blood-writing, water-writing. Amor figures the divinity of writing, divine writing incised and inscribed into human experience. Amor is the love of writing and the writing of love into human history as a new revelation, a new beginning. Dante has his heart in writing because love has been written into his heart; through the love of writing, his heart is open to becoming the location to which this revelation can be historically traced. But Amor is only a figure of Divine Love in the history of writing and is therefore an idol, a local pagan deity, historically situated by the event of its revelation as a figure. Amor is a substitute for the Divine Word of Love, and its revelation inaugurates an historical epoch, rather than initiating history itself, a figure of genesis that keeps the Secret of Beginning by sharing it without possessing its truth.

It is a commonplace that Dante is the first great vernacular poet of postantiquity Europe, the originator of *il dolce stil nuovo,* a precursor of Renaissance humanism and of the modern conception of self. He is also acknowledged as the legitimator of individual experience as the substance of epic poetry, paving the way for both modern drama and the novel. Dante's heart, senses, and mind, all inscribed with love for Beatrice, are the location for a new revelation in writing, a new style of writing that, marked by the love of writing and the writing of love as the trace-marks of a new possibility for human personal identity. Amor is the local deity of this new historical situation of writing.

In chapter xxv of *Vita nuova,* Dante briefly sketches out the boundaries of the historical situation of writing in which he found himself and through which he would later "refind" himself (*Inf.,* i, 2). At the same time, from the developed perspective of the second movement of the *Vita nuova,* he acknowledges, at least to a certain extent, that Amor, the god of love/writing, is not an independent entity, but inheres in his experience of love/writing and is the familiar spirit of its historical practice:

> At this point someone whose objections are worthy of the fullest attention might be mystified by the way I speak of love as though it were thing in itself, and not only a substance endowed with understanding but also a physical substance, which is demonstrably false; for love is not in itself a substance at all, but an accident in a substance. . . . To clarify this matter, in a manner that is useful to the present purpose, it should first be understood that in ancient times the theme of love was not taken as a subject for verses in the vernacular, but there were authors who wrote on love, namely, certain poets who composed in Latin; this means that among us . . . those who wrote of love were not vernacular but learned poets. It is not very many years ago since the first vernacular poets appeared. . . . That it is not long ago that this happened can be shown to be the case if we study the literature of the *langue d'oc* and of the *lingua del si,* for there is nothing written in these languages earlier than 150 years ago. . . . The first to write as a vernacular poet was moved to do so because he wished to make his verses intelligible to a lady who found it difficult to understand Latin. This is an argument against those who compose in rhyme on themes other than love, *because this manner of composition was invented from the beginning for the purpose of writing of love.* (*Vita nuova,* xxv; emphasis added)

This is a strangely didactic, almost pedantic excursus, breaking both the poetic and narrative flow of the work. It offers, however, a clarification of Dante's self-understanding, his sense of his own historical situation and that of his writing, which obviously he took to be crucial to interpreting the work: the divinity of Amor inheres in and is inseparable from *the style of writing poetic rhymes in the vernacular for the purpose of communicating one's experience of love and of taking personal responsibility for it.* The sense of personal responsibility for explaining the meaning of that which one writes and establishing its claim to authority on that basis, emerges forcefully in Dante's conclusion to the excursus:

> And lest any uneducated person should assume too much, I will add that the Latin poets did not write in this manner without good reason, nor should those who compose in rhyme, if they cannot justify what they say; for it would be a disgrace if someone composing in rhyme introduced a figure of speech or rhetorical ornament, and then on being asked could not divest his words of such covering so as to reveal a true meaning. My most intimate friend [Cavalcante] and I know quite a number who compose rhymes in this stupid manner. (*Vita nuova*, xxv)

As has been well documented, the tradition of vernacular rhymes, "no older than 150 years," to which Dante refers under the appellation of the *langue d'oc* and the *lingua del si,* is the style of composition practiced by the Provençal troubadours beginning in the 12th century and shortly communicated to Italy and other regions. The subject matter of these rhymes was of course love, but it was a very specific dispensation of love, inscribed in the rubrics of the literature of the Courtly Love tradition. Both the style of love and the style of poetry that we might say was, broadly paraphrasing the spirit of Dante's magisterial pronouncement, hypostatically united with it, blossomed from the culture and code of chivalry that took as its canonical scripture the Arthurian legends. The Courtly Love tradition and the style of poetry that disseminated it have been identified as epoch-making in the cultural evolution of Europe and the West because together they constitute the revelation of a new possibility for imagining the meaning of human existence: the emergence of the conception of personal identity in function of the freedom of responsibility in relationship to other such responsible freedoms. As Dante says, the structure of this conception of personal identity and its transcendent, or divine, element of freedom as total responsibility to the Other, existed only by its accidental inherence in the written "substance" of the Romantic literature of that time. A closely related conception of personal identity had no doubt been inscribed into the Christian doctrines of Resurrection, Incarnation, and Trinity. The effective significance of these doctrines, however, had become progressively more dysfunctional, distorted in their effective significance as they were by having been encrypted into the larger cultural idiom and discourse of Catholic Europe under the influence of Byzantine liturgical, spiritual, and artistic styles of expression. The Byzantine style expressed a religious sensibility that placed greater emphasis on the mystical, transcendent, and otherworldly elements of divinity, and proportionately less on the explicitly incarnational and experiential.

Drawing ultimately if indirectly on the Platonic doctrine of the *ascesis* of the soul (*Symposium* and *Phaedrus*), the educatory disciplining of the soul's desire (Eros) for Beauty in order to rise through the ascending orders of being to mystical union with the One source of every beautiful image, the Courtly

Love tradition manifests the ambiguity that is central to that (neo-)Platonic doctrine: the ascent of Eros, as an educational discipline, is empowered by a drive that simultaneously affirms and negates the images of beauty on which it feeds. Eros affirms the image in so far as the image awakens in the soul the memory of the vision of Beauty that it once enjoyed, but from which it has fallen, thus resurrecting in the soul the spiritual vision that had sunken into oblivion beneath the weight of material embodiment. At the same time, however, it negates the image in the dynamism of transcendence, which, tasting the poison in that on which it feeds, scenting death in the finitude of Beauty's limited capacity to infuse the dross of matter with its immaterial radiance, soon grows restless with the urge to surpass its satisfaction by seeking higher and more transparent images of Beauty. One of the most significant, indeed perhaps the critical, manifestation of this primal ambiguity of the experience of love, which originates in the Secret that love keeps in giving all its gifts—that, radiant with promise though they be, that promise necessarily remains empty—is the ambiguity of sexual gender identity. Whether in the sexual ethos of Plato's Greece or the altogether differently stylized courtly mores of feudal chivalry, the "flight from woman," as Jung terms this dynamism, is apparent. Revelation and dissociation, inspiration and temptation, the scripting of the role of woman as Other historically situates the Courtly Love tradition and Dante's *Vita nuova* in a moment that is both timeless in the sense of being utterly original, and timely in the sense of announcing an epochal change in the history of the Other, specifically the sexually gendered other, in the evolution of both a concept and characterization of human personal identity. The argument can and has been made that in the Courtly Love tradition the idea that human identity is realized for the first time, not through participation in any social group or institutional structure, but rather through the bonds of personal responsibility within an interpersonal relationship, and that among the types of such relationship, romantic love enjoys a unique revelatory privilege.[13]

For Dante, however, the full authority for this revelatory privilege does not rest solely with the credibility of the literature of Courtly Love. Rather, for him it receives its full incarnational figure, and with that its full sovereignty over his imagination, through its embodiment in the life and spirituality of St. Francis of Assisi. Indeed, it will become apparent that as influential in Dante's personal and poetic formation as St. Augustine unmistakably was, St. Francis is at least as powerful a force of imagination, and in certain crucial respects, ultimately more compelling for Dante. St. Francis's "*Vita nuova*," his conversion story, revolves around the trinity of the courteous son of a cloth merchant, inflamed with youthful dreams of knightly glory, the God of love who speaks to Francis in the image of the crucified one in the ruined chapel of San Damiano, and the image of the beloved woman to whom Francis is espoused in mystical marriage, Lady Poverty.[14]

In Canto xi of *Paradiso,* Dante recounts his own version of the form that the bliss of this nuptial union takes in the life of St. Francis in a passage that is crucial for understanding the conversion of Dante's imagination, and particularly his conversion to a new, yet old image of Beatrice as the incarnation of Divine Love in the last movement of the *Commedia*. From the perspective of that advanced stage of his journey, it is possible to recognize the full ambiguity, in the form of dissociation, at work in Dante's image of Beatrice as revelation. From the beginning, her image expresses the risk of life, both its joy and sorrow, both its promise and its portent of death, both salvation and bereavement, inspiration and accusation. As has been shown, the first movement of *Vita nuova*, portrays the ambivalent dominion of the lover by the Lord of love, Amor, through the constrained instrumentality of the beloved. The poet/commentator is first captivated by love and then conscripted into the slave-labor of devising patterns of substitution in writing that distract him from the work of mourning, which is the proper, albeit impossible, vocation to which love is dedicated. In *Vita nuova*, xvii, Dante announces a renunciation of the dirge-work of recounting the pains of his love-wound and the taking up of a "new theme, one more lofty than the last."

Dante announces this new theme in *Vita nuova*, xviii on the occasion of a dialogue between the poet and "certain ladies" who "knew my heart well," because "through my appearance many people had learned the secret of my heart." In this exchange, Dante is brought to the realization of the incompleteness, and therefore, the unworthiness of his prior theme, the suffering of love, due to the pattern of substitution and concealment at work in his writing until then.

> "Ladies, the aim of my love was once the greeting of one of whom perhaps you are aware, and in that resided all my blessedness and joy, for it was the aim and end of all my desires; but ever since she saw fit to deny me her greeting, my lord Love, in his mercy, has placed all my hope of that same joy in something which cannot fail me." (*Vita nuova*, xviii)

Importuned to reveal this new, more reliable source of joy, he responds, "in those words that praise my lady." His interlocutors press him on the point, charging that his prior writing must have had another, more self-serving motivation. There then occurs a conversion in writing: "Then I, thinking of these words that shamed me, departed from these ladies saying to myself, "Since there is so much bliss in those words that praise my lady, why have I ever spoken otherwise." He goes on to recount that for some time thereafter he feared that he had now undertaken "a theme too lofty for myself, so that I dare not begin writing," and remained frozen between "the desire to write and the fear of beginning" (*Vita nuova*, xviii).[15]

The poem that emerges from this experience of conversion, the canzone, "*Donne, che avete intelletto d'Amore*" (Ladies, refined and sensitive in Love), is generally identified by scholars as the official inauguration of "*il dolce stilo nuovo*," the "sweet new style" of poetry that not only sets a new course for European literature and wins for Dante the imitative admiration of Boccaccio,

Petrarca and of poets down to the present, but equally significantly discloses the specifically religious trajectory of the journey of personal transformation on which he is embarked. The turn to praise, the proper style of worship, is a turn toward transcendence. It is gesture of fidelity in keeping the Secret in the promise of writing, a turning, still partial and incomplete, away from a lesser image of Beauty to a higher one, from a lower, cruder pattern of substitution to a less opaque, more translucent one. The substitution of Dante's own words of praise for Beatrice in place of his reliance on the word of her greeting, her *"salute,"* marks a new form of responsibility emerging out of his experience of repentance, of thinking again about the promise of writing, of turning to a more promising style of writing, of putting on a changed mind (*metanoia*), which allows for both a new style of love and a new style of writing. This transformation takes the form of substituting a higher desire and a higher "reason" as the motive force for his love/writing than the more cramped and confined desire and reason that required her word to move his word. The canzone explains:

> To the all-knowing mind an angel prays:
> "Lord, in the world a miracle proceeds
> In act and visible, from a soul's deeds,
> Whose splendor reaches to this very height."
> One imperfection only Heaven has:
> The lack of her; so now for her it pleads,
> And every saint with clamour intercedes.
> Only compassion is our advocate.
> God understands to whom their prayers relate
> And answers them: "My loved ones, bear in peace
> That she, your hope, remain until I please
> Where one knows he must lose her, soon or late,
> And who will say in Hell: "Souls unconfessed!
> I have seen the hope of Heaven's blessed."
>
> My lady is desired in highest Heaven;
> Now of her excellence I'd have you hear. (*Vita nuova,* xix) [16]

"My lady is desired in highest heaven." The new pattern of substitution inscribed here is "more worthy" only to the extent that it is more transparent: according to him, his words are moved into writing not by his desire for her word, *but by heaven's desire for her.* Nevertheless, his explanation of his motivation still hides the empty secret of his own desire, veiled in the ambiguity of whatever is "owned," behind a substitute, an idol. Beatrice is portrayed as a "living miracle" on earth whose light reaches "as far as here." In this way, she reveals the pattern of incarnation anew: Beatrice as the figure of Jesus, who makes the power of Divine Love palpably present on earth, reversing the vector of cosmic time-space by shifting its directionality *from earth to heaven.*

Already here, long before its composition, Dante anticipates not simply the structure, but more significantly, the poetic tonality of the penultimate vision of the *Paradiso,* the revelation of the White Rose. In that moment, St. Bernard will transcribe the supplication of the "angel" in this canzone. Praying on behalf of Dante, that on account of Beatrice's presence among the blessed, Dante be vouchsafed the final vision that fulfills the promise of her *"salute"* heard by him on earth. The canzone continues:

> If any man she find who worthy be
> To look at her, her virtue then he knows,
> For, greeting him, salvation she bestows,
> In meekness melting every grudge away.

In other words, the salvation that she has the power to bestow is experienced through the humiliation of forgiveness. Here "humiliation" means the truth of human self-knowledge, as Adam, fashioned from clay, might ask, "How can flesh drawn from clay achieve such beauty and such purity?" The canzone reinforces the Incarnational pattern further by uniting vision to word in the creative and redemptive expression of the power of Divine Love, "This too has God Almighty graced her with: Whoever speaks with her shall speak with Him."

The third movement of *Vita nuova* announces another turning, the conversion of praise into a new hope for life, hope for a new life, life in its extreme, life resurrected as the hope of writing in the face of death. First, in the sonnets commemorating the death of Beatrice's magnanimous father, Folco Portinari, then in the prefigurement of the death of Beatrice in Dante's own serious illness (*"Donna pietosa e di novella etate,"* A very young and sympathetic lady), and then finally in his treatment of the death of Beatrice herself, Dante is moved to a new space and time, a new wilderness location, a place of fasting where freedom receives a vocation, the Secret calling to a responsibility that is total in its demand to repent, to change one's mind regarding life as a whole, in and through the encounter with death. In this place the long years of solitary exile begin, whose outward analog will not take shape in Dante's life for ten years yet, but the seeds of which are sown in his heart, his mind, and his writing here and now. In this desert place of trial and temptation, the inexorable ambiguity of the Secret of new life, given as the Gift of Death, breaks out again after the interlude of praise on which his desire fed for awhile, and a new fasting accentuates the alternating rhythms of hope and flight: the former expressed as the hope of Beatrice's continued presence to him as the object of praise, now having assumed her place in the heaven "where she is desired"; the latter expressed in a regression and reversion to the first pattern of substitution, but which now insinuates the substitute, the lady of the window replacing the screen lady, into a far more intimate place in Dante's writing than before, in response to a far more powerful and visceral desire to feed and eat, to ingest and inscribe the substitute into the flesh of his writing. These two conflicting impulses finally tear Dante's heart asunder and cause his writing of Beatrice to bury itself in the sleep of earthly death and be sealed in its tomb with the promise to "write no more of her until I can do so more worthily," a promise which would sleep in death and awake in the fear and trembling of the Dark Wood many years later in the hope of finding itself again in the Gift of Death, the Spirit of Resurrection, in writing.

One example of each of the dynamics of recurrent ambiguity at work in this period of Dante's conversion must suffice to sketch the pattern recurring throughout. Remarkably, Beatrice's death is not dealt with in poetry in the *Vita nuova*, at least not as Dante's first response. In what must be read as a highly artificial, even secretive explanation for this abstinence from poetry, Dante substitutes in *Vita nuova,* xxviii and xxx a double epitaph in which he inscribes Beatrice into the figure of three, the form of the Trinity, the trace of relationship and meaning that is the *arche*—the beginning, the first principle, as well as the *archon,* the dominating power—of writing itself. He gives three reasons, excuses really, for not writing the figure of her death in poetry, and then offers a highly stylized derivation of the number three, not simply as the marker of the space and time of both her birth and death, but as the very essence of her being, as the divine radical of her identity:

> But, thinking more deeply and guided by infallible truth, *I say that she herself was this number nine;* I mean this as an analogy, as I will explain. The number three is the root of nine, because, independent of any other number, multiplied by itself alone, it makes nine, as we see quite plainly when we say three threes are nine; therefore if three is the sole factor of nine, and the sole factor of miracles is three, that is, Father, Son, and Holy Ghost, who are three and one, then this lady was accompanied by the number nine to convey that she was a nine, that is, a miracle, of which the root, that is of the miracle is nothing other than the miraculous Trinity itself. Perhaps a more subtle mind could find a still more subtle reason for it; *but this is the one which I perceive and which pleases me the most.* (*Vita nuova,* xxix; emphasis added)

Did lover ever erect to beloved a more imposing monument to enclose her dead flesh than this Taj Mahal of allegorical interpretation? "She is a nine, or a miracle," the revelation in the dimensions of time and space of the power of divine love to keep the Secret of beginning, of new life, by encrypting in the flesh the secret formula of every meaning, of every act of imagination, of every image and representation, of all writing. That "she is a nine," says analogously that, as *imago Dei,* as the image of the trinity at the root of all relation, she disseminates in her flesh the radical of Love, and, cross-fertilized by the pattern of Incarnation, does so most fruitfully when the seed of her flesh is buried in the ground and sealed in the tomb of memory with the writing of truth as its epitaph.

But Dante, as did those witnesses turned scribes who preceded him, quickly discovers that her tomb is empty. After a brief period of apparition, the faith of resurrection must begin its ages-long fast of vigil-keeping, keeping alive the secret of the empty tomb, the Gift of Death, by writing it in tears and words:

> Tears of compassion for my grieving heart
> Such torment have inflicted on my eyes
> That, having wept their fill, they can no more.
> Thus, if I still would ease this aching smart,
> Which step by step brings closer my demise,
> Words must bring their aid, as weeping did before. . . .
>
> . . . Beatrice has gone to Paradise on high,
> Among the angels in the realm of peace,
> And you, ladies, she has left comfortless. . . .
> For light, ascending from her lowliness,
> So pierced the heavens with its radiance,
> That God was moved to wonder at the same;
> And a sweet longing came
> To summon to Him such benevolence;
> And from on high He called her by her name,
> Because our grievous life He saw to be
> Unfit for such a noble thing as she.
>
> From the fair person which on earth was hers
> Her noble soul departed, full of grace,
> To dwell in glory as befits her state.
> Whoever speaks of her and sheds no tears,
> His heart is stone, so evil and so base,
> No living spirit there can penetrate. (*Vita nuova,* xxxi)

There is more inscribed in this epitaph than the sorrows of the love wound, even when it has begun to fester and putrefy with deadly gangrene. Here, muted but resounding with eternally echoing rage of the ravenous, ever-growing hunger that cannot be fed, we see reenacted the scene of violation from the second vision, the divine rape of Beatrice's mouth by Amor with the borrowed stylus of Dante's heart. Here is the reenactment of every tale of Olympian predation, the necessary sacrificial price of the birth of heroes; here is the image of betrayal that later the pilgrim/poet will find inscribed in nether Hell, as the closest image the human imagination can evoke of the unimaginable treachery of Satan, the words with which Ugolino begins to tell the story that purports to account for his eternal gnawing on the nape of Ruggieri: "if you do not weep at this when do you weep? My heart was turned to stone."[17]

Is it too much to see in this betrayal of Dante by God in the death of Beatrice, the seed of his betrayal of her in the seeding/ceding of her place in writing to the Window Lady, one of the many betrayals with which Beatrice will charge him in *Purgatorio,* xxx–xxxi? Rather than seeing too much, it would be to recognize too little not to see this as the reciprocal, squared counter image of the miracle of nine that accompanied his first sight of Beatrice and to see the two together as one, to see a new trinity of ambiguity sealed with the Gift of Death and secretly kept encrypted in the promise of writing—the promise of a resurrection in writing.

## TRANSCRIBING THE PROMISE OF A NEW LIFE

At this point, it becomes appropriate to recognize openly that the voice of Derrida has all along been inscribed in the preceding reading of the *Vita nuova*. The tonality of Derrida's voice is most noticeable in the three themes that have in large measure guided that reading: the (empty) Secret of (all) beginning; the promise of writing, and the Gift of Death. Each of these themes is recurrent in Derrida's work, especially from the late 1980s until his death, but for the purposes of this study, it is their interweaving into the fabric of the texts of *Circumfession* and *The Gift of Death* that is the focus of immediate concern. In the first of the four essays which comprise *The Gift of Death*, "Secrets of European Responsibility," Derrida links together the concepts of secrecy, responsibility, and religion:

> In one of his *Heretical Essays on the Philosophy of History* Jan Patočka relates secrecy, or more precisely the mystery of the sacred, to responsibility. He opposes one to the other; or rather underscores their heterogeneity. Somewhat in the matter of Levinas he warns against an experience of the sacred as an enthusiasm or fervor for fusion, cautioning in particular against a form of demonic rapture that has as its effect and often as its first intention, the removal of responsibility, the loss of the sense for consciousness of responsibility. At the same time Patočka wants to distinguish religion from the demonic form of sacralization. What is religion? Religion presumes access to the responsibility of a free self. It thus implies breaking with this type of secrecy (for it is not of course the only one), that associated with sacred mystery and with what Patočka regularly calls the demonic. A distinction is to be made between the demonic on the one hand (that which confuses the limits among the animal, the human, and divine, and which retains an affinity with mystery, the initiatory, the esoteric, the secret or the sacred) and responsibility to the other. This therefore amounts to a thesis on the origin and essence of the religious. (*GD*, 1–2)

Derrida sees the interrelation of secrecy, responsibility, and religion primarily as a question of genealogy and therefore as necessarily an historical question:

> According to Patočka one can speak of religion only after the demonic secret, and the orgiastic sacred, have been surpassed. The subject of responsibility will be the subject that has managed to make orgiastic or demonic

mystery subject to itself; and has done that in order to freely subject itself to the wholly and infinite other that sees without being seen. Religion is responsibility or it is nothing at all. (*GD,* 2)

Furthermore, this history is inseparable from the history of sexuality:

> Since the concept of the *daimon* crosses the boundaries separating the human, the animal, and divine, one will not be surprised to see Patočka recognizing in it a dimension that is essentially that of sexual desire. In what respect does this demonic mystery of desire involve us in a history of responsibility, more precisely in history as responsibility? (*GD,* 3)

Thus, insofar as the *Vita nuova* is caught up in the issues of secrecy, religion, and the responsibility of promising, and all of these as the condition of beginning a "new life," we recognize the historical necessity of the freedom of the one, Dante, who tells us of this new beginning:

> "The problem of history . . . must remain a problem." The moment the problem were to be resolved that same totalizing closure would determine the end of history: it would bring in the verdict of nonhistoricity itself. History can be neither a decidable object nor a totality capable of being mastered, precisely because it is tied to *responsibility,* to *faith,* and to the *gift.* To *responsibility* in the experience of absolute decisions made outside of knowledge or given norms, made therefore through the very ordeal of the undecidable; to religious *faith* through a form of involvement with the other that is a venture into absolute risk, beyond knowledge and certainty; to the *gift* and to the gift of death that puts me into relation with the transcendence of the other, with God as selfless goodness, and that gives me what it gives through a new experience of death. Responsibility and faith go together, however paradoxical that might seem to some, and both should, in the same movement, exceed mastery and knowledge. The gift of death would be this marriage of responsibility and faith. History depends on such an excessive beginning. (*GD,* 5–6)

The *Vita nuova* is situated historically by the intersection of Dante's love for Beatrice with the three-stage evolutionary dynamic of human desire in response to the power of mystery which Patočka identifies: the orgasmic and orgiastic fervor for fusion of sexuality (demonic), the romantic/chivalric dedication of self in the form of the discipline of responsibility in writing as a poet (Platonic), and religious spirituality achieved in recognizing Beatrice as the secret radical that originates the history of salvation (Christian). The demonic or orgiastic form of mystery functions in Derrida's exegesis of Patočka as a kind of psychic principle of entropy, the instinct of consciousness toward fusion, oneness and dissolution of the polar tension between the emptiness of consciousness as a field of appearance, on the one hand, and its complete overdetermination, on the other hand, by its awareness of its "Other," all that it itself is not. This impulse toward the dissolution of the tension that surges up and continually irrupts toward self-consciousness at the same time as it plunges to immerse and lose itself in its environment, seeking release and discharge of tension in orgiastic fusion, giving free rein to orgasmic desire. Poetry especially has retained the memory of the instinctive life-drive toward entropic death in its long testimonial record of the proximity of orgasmic climax to the sleep of death. In the *Vita nuova,* the first appearance of Beatrice to Dante at the age of nine reveals to him the joy of life in the apparition of the Other as Beauty, but immediately there follows in the text the "squaring" of this apparition after another nine years have passed and its radicalization in the form of the orgiastic vision of divinely enforced violation and consumption, the sacrificial ritual of "heart-eating."

This image derives its terrific power, a power that resonates throughout the rest of the *Vita nuova* and down through the whole of the *Commedia,* in part from its primitive, essentially entropic impulse, expressed figuratively in the dream as Dante's unconscious desire to be consumed and digested, to lose his heart, to spill his blood, to disseminate his consciousness, to pour himself out into and lose himself in Beatrice. The poem that emerges from the dream, its dissemination to Dante's fellow devotees of love/writing, and the patterns of dissimulation and substitution that follow on it in the first movement of the *Vita nuova,* all constitute a liturgy of initiation into the mystery cult by which the guilty secret of the demonic is kept silent and unconscious by Dante, irresponsibly kept hidden, most of all from himself. So begins the history of Dante's mystification; so begins also the history of his salvation, of his conversion to another way of keeping the (empty) Secret of beginning—in writing.

As already noted, the device of the "screen lady," which leads, almost comically, to Beatrice's withholding from Dante of her *salute,* her greeting but also her saving grace, repeats in an external form the pattern of substitution inscribed in the dream vision. In the *Vita nuova* this device progressively reveals the inadequacy of the demonic, orgiastic experience of mystery as the source of inspiration for writing. In the ritual of this particular liturgical writing, Dante's poetic word moves only at the impulse of her word, it possesses no power of self-movement. It has no soul of its own because the impulse to converse with oneself is absent here. But as Derrida points out, this impulse is also a movement toward conversion, precisely the conversion into having a soul which, according to Patočka, is the form which the conversion to Platonic self-discipline takes. In this form, consciousness becomes for the first time conscious of itself *in secret,*[18] that is, as cut off from its Other, as separated from it by its movement of discipline, of reining itself in, of reigning over itself, holding itself back and keeping its distance from the Other, so as to open up for itself a space, a contemplative distance, across which it experiences "awe and reverence" at the site of the Beauty from which it keeps its distance and so keeps sacred.[19] In fact, it can be said that the vision of the Good toward which the soul aspires is precisely this perspective on the Beautiful which is enjoyed from the distance of the soul's self-withholding. Here one catches the precise sense of Patočka's use of the term "incorporation" to describe the relation of surpassing-while-retaining in which the mystery of the Platonic soul stands in relation to demonic mystery and which constitutes the soul's "immortality." By withholding itself, by holding itself within itself, the Platonic soul masters itself through the discipline of separating itself from the body, which is the medium of fusion, and so also of death and loss of itself. By *in-corporating* itself, by keeping to itself within the body, by not pouring itself out in the impulse to transgress the limits of the body, by practicing death in the form of sacrificing the demonic purge to disseminate itself in and through a body, the soul masters itself in the form of self-possession. By keeping to itself, separate and in secret, the soul passes beyond the body and the mystery of orgiastic fusion and into transcendence in the form of responsibility. The soul, thus disciplined and self-mastered, is able to move itself, to circulate within an economy of its own, to encircle and contain the bodily economy of unrestrained expenditure. Thus self-moved, it is able to converse with itself, to speak in response to its own word, that is, to have a conscience, an understanding of itself which is able to answer for itself responsibly. It becomes capable both of being with the Other and of being with itself. This transcendence through self-discipline into responsibility and conscience is freedom, the freedom of self-identity. Self-identical, it is immortal because it has come to itself, found self again through the practice of death until, having mastered death, the soul experiences itself as a gift of death, that is, the soul finds itself given to itself in death.

In the writing of *Vita nuova,* we find a figure that repeats the configuration of this discipline of practicing death, this self-possession of the soul in the responsibility of conscience and in the freedom of immortality through incorporation of the demonic mystery, which separates the soul from the body and enables it to keep itself in secret by keeping to the limits of the body. The conversion that marks the transition from the first to the second movement of that text is, as has been seen, inscribed and documented especially in the canzone, *"Donne che avete intelletto d'Amore."* The figure of immortality resides in the praise of Beatrice's beauty, which is "desired in heaven." Dante recognizes—but, as will emerge, only partially recognizes in the form of dissociated consciousness—that, until then, his writing of Beatrice has been unworthy. Its unworthiness resides in the fact that it has no soul of its own; its words have depended for their movement on her soul, expressed as the movement of her words, whether given as gift, anticipated or withheld. In fact, his conversion toward immortality and self-possession is triggered precisely by *her withholding of her words of greeting.* Thus, the conversion to self-discipline and the incorporation of the demonic impulse that the poem "Donne che avete" articulates remains ambiguous. It is in fact a conversion expressed in the writing of praise that recognizes the immortality of the beauty of her soul. Further, it includes a renunciation of the figure of the demonic in the form of the idol Amor, identifying it not as a genuine substance, but only as an accident or quality that inheres in a substance, and hence as not fully divine but only "daimonic," or as Plato says in *Symposium,* "half-way between the mortal and the immortal." Praise, the articulated recognition of the Good across the distance of contemplative self-mastery, is Dante's way of taking responsibility for the recognition of the soul's immortality, and also his way of exercising the self-possession of having a conscience regarding the style of his writing. Both of these recognitions, however, are expressed in and as the dissociation of his own soul from itself, and its screening of itself behind the simulacrum of Beatrice's nobility and the apparent gracious condescension of God, who allows her presence on earth, "for a time," because of Dante's abject dependence on her. This "presence for a time" is precisely a "presence," the simulacrum of the authentic Gift of Death, the donation of a closed economy in which debts must eventually finally be paid in full.

In the end, the praise of the mortality of Beatrice's beauty in these poems is merely a "down payment" or first installment on the debt of the guilty secret of the orgiastic mystery, which is not eliminated, but only incorporated into the soul's conscience and kept there within limits "for time," awaiting final discharge of its guilt and debt. Thus the praise of the Beatrice who is still "present" to him in glory is only a promissory note on the obligation to the eventual necessity of her absence, which is required if she is to become for him the Gift of Death. Inevitably, this note is called soon enough. Shortly thereafter in the *Vita nuova,* when the trinity of deaths described in xxii–xxx, the death of Beatrice's father, Dante's fevered dream of Beatrice's and his own deaths, and finally, Beatrice's actual death, forces Dante to confront consciously the absence necessarily implicated in the "present." What is apparent here is the significance that Derrida attributes in "Secrets of European Responsibility" to the recognition that both responsibility and religion are historical, that is, that they have histories, and that as such, they remain and must remain open.

One specific consequence of this recognition is the realization that the notion of the immortality of the soul as an historical accomplishment of responsibility and freedom still lacks the character of personal identity. The conversion into the self-possession of the soul is accomplished in its vision of the Good through the achievement of the contemplative discipline of self-withholding, keeping its distance from the Beautiful. As a result of this double contemplative separation, from the body and from the Good, by the incorporation of orgiastic fusion into the dissociation of contemplative vision, there is a price to be paid. The price for keeping the guilty secret of orgiastic mystery through responsibility is the sacrifice of the person, the historical self, the existing individual. The stoicism of Platonic self-discipline is the practice of death in exchange for the "present" of immortality, where immortality is no gift, because it comes at the price of the integrity of the person through the dissociation of the immortal soul from the material body. The absence of the person in exchange for the presence of the soul to itself is the law of an economy of sacrifice in which the body must be discarded and written off as the incriminating evidence of the soul's guilty substitution of incorporation of the orgiastic mystery within itself, keeping it for the soul itself in secret, separate from the body, where the soul can possess it by itself forever. The universe of Platonic immortality is in the end an impersonal one, for its condition of possibility is the isolation of the soul through its separation from the historical world of personal identity. The immortal soul is alone in beholding the Good, just as Aristotle's Prime Mover is alone in self-contemplation, because in both cases, it beholds without being beheld. Immortality is a move to separation from the Other, a sacrifice of responsibility to the Other in order to achieve responsibility for oneself.

This economy of sacrifice is mirrored in the secret rage identified earlier as encrypted in the canzone, *"Li occhi dolenti,"* in *Vita nuova,* xxxi, and as such is the trace in Dante's writing of that work of an incomplete conversion, the partiality of which is evidenced by his regression to the orgiastic in the substitution of the present "window lady" for the now absent Beatrice, who has been taken "to God," taken by God as divine paramour in the realm of immortality. Dante remains "below," bereft of the salvific joy of life, separated from Beatrice's immortality by the loss of her presence, separated from his own immortality because he is separated from his own soul. He has deposited the responsibility which is his soul in Beatrice's soul. He has attempted, impossibly, to deposit responsibility for his own death in her death. When her soul is separated from her body, his body is separated from its soul and therefore separated from the realm of immortality. Dante is alone not by some moral failing, or if so, by a moral failing that is a symptom of a failure of imagination, a secret guilt, a failure at secret-keeping, which will not be put right until the final vision of the *Commedia.* It must be noted now, to be recognized later, that this final vision cannot occur until after he has been reunited to Beatrice through forgiveness *and* separated from her again. Both these movements, reunion and separation, rehearse the first movements Derrida identifies as the history of religion as responsibility, demonic union, and moral separation, as the necessary movements toward conversion to the specifically Christian mystery, the *mysterium tremendum.*

Derrida also notes, however, that the *mysterium tremendum* is related to the demonic and the Platonic experience of mystery as a *repression* of the one (demonic) which now the other (Platonic) has incorporated within itself. It is this configuration of incorporation and repression that Derrida claims constitutes the distinction between secrecy or the "Secret" as he uses the term, and Patočka's use of mystery. The history of the Secret is the historical development of responsibility and freedom precisely as the historical constitution of personal identity through the conversion from the demonic and orgiastic, through sacrificial incorporation into Platonic self-discipline, and the repression of the memory of that incorporation through conversion to faith in the Christian mystery. But this latter conversion, both Patočka and Derrida suggest, has yet to be fully worked out, and the history of Europe, or we might say by extension, the entire West, has yet to take full responsibility for keeping its secret(s) in full consciousness.

The writing of the last movement of the *Vita nuova* prefigures the historical situation of Western religion and responsibility in relation to the Christian repression of earlier forms of mystery and secrecy that have continued to prevail up to the present time. To be more precise, this is the conversion promised by Dante in writing at the conclusion of the *Vita nuova,* a promise kept in the writing of the *Commedia* that prefigures the historical development in which the West remains involved today. This accounts for the remarkable timeliness of the 700-year-old-poem, a timeliness that is one of the basic assumptions of the present study. As a result, at the present stage of this inquiry, the task is to identify Dante's religious and moral situation in writing at the conclusion of the *Vita nuova,* on the grounds that it literally contains the promise that is to be fulfilled in the writing of the *Commedia*. Furthermore, that process of identification follows the trace of Derrida's use of the specifically Christian form of secrecy and secret-keeping, which involves the repression of Platonic secrecy (incorporation of the demonic) by the *mysterium tremendum.* The Kierkegaardian formulation of the Christian mystery has a particular relevance for Derrida's analysis, which turns on the "fearing and trembling" inspired by the faith of Abraham revealed in his willingness to sacrifice Isaac, which in turn anticipates the faith of the Christian believer who places faith in the Father of Jesus, who like Abraham stands ready to sacrifice his son to keep the secret of the covenant made with his people, the covenant that promises them a singular place in history. The repression that Christian faith accomplishes then is the repression of the memory of multiple gestures of sacrificial violence, that is, of a readiness to enforce substitution as a means of keeping an empty secret, the secret of an impossible promise: Abraham's, Socrates's, God the Father's, and also that of the Christian believer who places faith in and therefore takes responsibility for the death of Jesus as innocent victim. By way of anticipation, it can be said that what is here referred to as the Spirit of Resurrection points to the historical dynamic of the lifting of the repression of the Secret that lies buried in those memories.

To summarize, at the end of the *Vita nuova* Dante has fallen into a state of repressed consciousness of his own identity, expressed in his attempt to take responsibility for his love-writing, inspired by the revelation of Beatrice as the joy of his life, by promising a singular writing in her name. This state of repression, however, and the promise that proceeds from it, are ambiguous: both proceed through patterns of authentic, if partial, conversion as well as patterns of guilty substitution. At Beatrice's death, Dante finds himself at the extreme limit of the unconscious dissociation of his identity with which he is able to cope. As a result he does not know how to go on in writing; he is unable to find his way in writing responsibly, that is, in response to the vocation with which he has become identified. Caught in an unresolved tension between orgiastic desire for union with Beatrice and stoic self-discipline to the work of serving her by inscribing her in verse, he experiences himself drawn inevitably into the Christian *mysterium tremendum*. But, cut off as he now is from his soul that he has deposited in Beatrice's body, he fails, at least initially, to find in that experience of mystery anything other than the encrypted memory of an economy of sacrifice that has yet to come into full consciousness in the light of revelation, for example, specifically the revelation of the Spirit of Resurrection, or as Derrida might say, the Gift of Death. Venturing a risk at once prodigal in its extravagance and marvelous as a movement of faith, hope, and love, Dante sacrifices himself in the promise to write of Beatrice what never has been written in verse of woman before. This promise, encrypted in the conclusion of the writing of the *Vita nuova*, seals Dante in the tomb where he sleeps and dreams his way through more than the next decade of his life, until he wakes to find himself again in and through the Dark Wood (*mi ritrovai per una selva oscura*).

Up to this point we have been reading the *Vita nuova* from a certain Derridean perspective, with a slant toward the concerns and the styles—both religious and literary—of our own time and place. In one sense, this is as it should be, in part because it could not be otherwise. There is obviously, however, a risk and a danger involved in such a slanted, tendentious reading: the risk of going astray, of dreaming up meanings and significance for the text of the *Vita nuova* that are not proper to it, not really its own, whatever it might mean to speak of the text as a substance that might have proper or improper properties. Be that as it may, there does seem to be a need for exercising care and discipline in an interpretive encounter with the text, because the risk and danger seem real. Whether we can articulate that risk and explain it responsibly or not, we remain responsible for it.

The question of responsibility in this case might be put in this way: In what are we putting our faith when taking the risk of reading Dante through Derrida's deconstructive lenses? And further, what might we hope to accomplish by so reading? Regarding the act of faith being made here, it concerns a certain trust in Derrida, specifically, in the genuinity and authority of the religious impulse at work in his writing, and most particularly those writings being considered here, which, as has been suggested, seemed to document a conversion in writing. As far as hope goes, it would seem necessarily to be a specific instance of the hope that corresponds to the promise of writing itself: the hope of responsibility, the hope that the Other will address us, will come ("Yes!" "Come!") to us, and that we will wake, rise up and respond and that there might yet come an hypereconomic exchange of responsibility. Even further, it would seem to be the hope that we might be able to keep that economy open, keep it from closing in on itself, keep it from spiraling in on itself, keep it from going into a death spiral, at least somewhere for awhile. Specifically with regard to reading Dante's text in response to Derrida's, this hope would articulate itself in being able responsibly to sustain the desire to join the voice of an "early modern" religious vision in writing to that of a voice that is, as we ourselves are, on the verge of becoming "postmodern"—whatever that might mean. This hope is a specifically historical one; indeed, it is an expression of hope in history itself, in the "problem of history," a hope that history will keep coming, keep going, that it will not die, nor us with it.

If we take—on faith—the text of *The Gift of Death* to document and give testimony of a conversion in writing, we must take responsibility for acknowledging that it does not express itself "autobiographically" in any recognizable way, not even in the indirect and ironic sense that Dante's *Commedia* might plausibly be read autobiographically. But Derrida's *Circumfession* does express itself as autobiography, as has been indicated. In it we encounter an account of a personal conversion that at least arguably points toward a properly religious concern and question (What do I love when I love my God?), however improper the style of piety with which that concern and question are pursued. In fact, it is the very impropriety of Derrida's style of piety that enlivens the hope that it can keep alive the history of Western religious traditions with which it concerns itself, especially Judaism and Christianity.

So the hope that joins *Circumfession* to the *Vita nuova* is hope in the promise of writing: it is hope in the promise of writing with which the *Vita nuova* concludes and with which the *Commedia* begins ("I will tell the good I found there"). It is likewise the promise of writing that is the hope that first moves Derrida to respond and take responsibility in the writing of *Circumfession* for the race with death, not just his mother's death, or even his own, but the threatened death of the *alliance* between them.

*Circumfession* begins with blood, with images of writing as the opening of a vein, allowing blood to flow, being drawn with a syringe which, like a pen, draws outward what circulates closed within and expresses it, almost like mother's milk, into a receptacle, perhaps to use for analysis and diagnosis, perhaps to be transfused. Above the flow of blood in writing, stands a god, "Geoff," the godlike figure, an idol really, an image of a god graven in writing that will test and analyze the blood and put it back into circulation in another closed system, his "Derrida-base," a transubstantiation that happens in writing. Unlike Dante at the beginning of the *Vita nuova,* Derrida hopes to escape having his heart cut out, losing the source of the impulse that moves the circulation of his blood; he hopes to avoid having it fed to his mother, which she would be forced to swallow as the transubstantiated body and blood of her son in the form of the Derrida base which, Derrida says, seeks to transcribe the flow without the source of its impulse, into writing that has been less and less well-understood for twenty years now, so that "I rightly pass for an atheist." This is what his mother cannot swallow, so Derrida opens a vein, recalls another flow of blood that he hopes his mother will recognize, creates a shibboleth that he trusts will be familiar to her tongue and that she will recognize him by it. By inscribing the cut of his circumcision in writing, Derrida hopes to confess, to give testimony to the trace of the ring, the circle of an *alliance* that has not been broken. He hopes to give testimony that it is still alive in the flow and circulation that his own syringe/pen subscribes beneath the text of Bennington. Above, the writing seems to move inevitably toward the death spiral of a closed economy, a sacrifice to a false god. Below, Derrida hopes the writing of *Circumfession* can be his testament of hope in the promise of writing, the writing of his own *Circumfession,* written in his flesh and written as testimony in the word of his text, a promise made in the hope of life in the face of death, his lady mother's death, his own death, the death of his writing in the corpse of his corpus. He hopes to confess his circumcision, the indelible mark in his flesh of the promise of life, not his own promise, but one that has a claim on him nonetheless, because it is the promise made for him by another, the promise of him to Another.

It is the mark of an impossible promise, and excessive and prodigal covenant that must be kept precisely because of its impossibility, which exceeds and overpowers every possible claim. "Do you see the stars? I will make of you a great nation, more numerous than these" (Gen. 22:17). A prodigal promise: not just economic optimism—many from one—but many from none: impossible! Derrida is the problem child of an impossible promise, and now his only hope of escape is the hope of keeping his promise, the promise written into his flesh, by transcribing it in writing in the face of death. As a child of father Abraham, he has to make his apologies (Greek for the Latin-Hebrew con/circum/fession) in writing for who he is and who he is not to mother Sarah/Georgette before he or she dies. He is the prodigal son, the child prodigy of the promise; like all of his nation, he cannot be at home in the hope of a Promised Land that is still to come, not here, not yet. The promise of writing in the face of death is born of the gift of hope and is therefore impossibly excessive, like all gifts: they promise what is not "present."

Still it would be difficult to see in this promise of writing the hope of a conversion that can pass for religious were it not for the appearance of a compatriot, a brother-writer, a brother-son, more experienced in such confessional writing than the one who finds himself astray—a Virgil, so to speak, evoked in the name and over the signature of St. Augustine. Derrida recognizes himself in Augustine, and his own situation—in writing—in that of Augustine's. The text of this recognition needs to be read in its entirety because it resists paraphrase, while at the same time offering authoritative testimony to the point that is crucial here:

> If I let myself be loved by the lucky vein of this word, this is not for the *alea* or the mine it's enough to exploit by hacking out writing on the machine, nor for the blood, but for everything that all along this word vein lets or makes come the chance of events on which no program, no logical or textual machine will ever close, since always in truth has operated only by not overcoming the flow of raw happenings, not even the theologic program elaborated by Geoff who remains very close to God, for he knows everything

about the "logic" of what I might have written in the past but also of what I might think or write in the future, on any subject at all, so that he can rightly do without quoting any singular sentences that may have come to me and which that "logic" or "alogic" would suffice to account for, transcendental production of me, so that I should have nothing left to say that might surprise him still and bring something about for him, who you would be tempted to compare to Augustine's God when he asks whether there is any sense in confessing anything to Him when he knows everything in advance, which did not stop my compatriot from going beyond this *Cur confitemur Deo scienti*, not toward a verity, a severity of avowal which never amounts merely to speaking the truth, to making anything known or to presenting oneself naked in one's truth, as though Augustine still wanted, by force of love, to bring it about that in *arriving* at God, something should happen to God, and someone happen to him who would transform the science of God into a learned ignorance, he says he has to do so in *writing*, precisely, after the death of his mother, over whom he does not deplore the fact of not having wept, not that I dare link what he says about confession with the deaths of our respective mothers, I am not writing about Saint Georgette, the name of my mother, whom her brother sometimes used to call Geo, nor about Saint Esther, her sacred name, the one not to be used, the letters of the name I have used so much so that it might remain, for my mother was not a saint, not a Catholic one in any case, but what these two women had in common is the fact that St. Monica, the name of the place in California near to which I am writing, also ended her days, as my mother will too, on the other side of the Mediterranean, far from her land, in her case in the cemetery in Nice which was profaned in 1984, and the son reports her wishes *nos concurrimus, sed cito reddita est sensui et aspexit astantes me et fratrem meum et ait nobis quasi quarenti similis: "ubi eram?" deinde nos intuens maerore attonitos: "pontis hic" inquit "matrem uestram." Ego silebam et fletum frenebam,* ["We hastily gathered around her, but she returned to consciousness quickly and looked at me and my brother as we stood by. Rather like a person in search of something, she said to us: 'Where am I?' Then, seeing that we were overcome with grief, she said: 'Bury your mother here.' I remained silent and restrained my tears." (IX, xi, 27) sentences I quote in Latin, I have taught a lot about these subjects, and if I must not continue doing so here, I owe it to autobiography to say that I have spent my life teaching so as to return in the end to what mixes prayers and tears with blood, *salus non erat in sanguine. (Circum.*, 15–20)

The figure of the trinity that will configure the text of *Circumfession* is now assembled: Isaac, son of Sarah; Augustine, son of Monica; Jacques, son of Georgette. Over all three a knife is poised; before all three opens the same hope.

Dante too finds himself in a similar bind as he concludes the *Vita nuova* with the promise that is already inscribed in the flesh of his heart, the same heart that has been cut out and given to his lady to eat. When he promises that he will write of her, in the face of her death, what has never been written in verse of woman before, he identifies himself with the future occurrence of an absolute singularity. It is an absolutely impossible, impossibly prodigal promise, like all promises; a promise born of a dream, a very bad dream, which ends badly, though Dante manages to repress the bad memory for a time. The parallels with Isaac/Derrida are too disturbing not to mark: translated and transcribed, Dante's dream would be the equivalent of the unspeakable demand that mother Sarah/Georgette swallow the severed, bloody foreskin of her son's circumcision. Unspeakable; but it happens. It is an archetype, everybody's bad dream, the particular form, in this style of piety, of the blood sacrifice and consumption that is the signature of divine violence written into every religious covenant in one form or another. Disturbing; but strictly necessary, or so it seems. The promise of the father, the absent God of empty promises, means present death for the son of that promise, for the son of the mother who must swallow it—hence the son of these tears. Promises tend to the ambiguous—they are prayers of hope; they are usually written in tears.

## CHAPTER TWO

# Inferno: The Aporia of Forgiveness

Chapter 2 continues the reading of *Circumfession* as a confession of Derrida's conversion in writing, now read alongside the text of Dante's *Commedia*, beginning with an interpretation of *Inferno* as another conversion story. That story opens with a call for Dante to begin again, differently, the journey of constant conversion which the *Vita nuova* first traced, wherein the Secret promise of writing appeared as the seal on the ambivalent covenant among Dante, Beatrice and the god Amor, just as the Secret promise at stake in Derrida's writing of *Circumfession* sealed the equally ambivalent covenant among himself, Georgette and Abraham, the mark of which he bore written in his flesh.

The first section of this chapter examines the first three Cantos of the *Inferno*, which make evident the differential pattern at work in the confessional testaments that bind together certain writings of Augustine, Dante, and Derrida: each experiences a call to conversion and repentance in the face of the death of the Other/woman, Monica, Beatrice, Georgette. This call to repentance is experienced as a turning into exile. Exile is both a situation and an identity. It is the condition in which one always comes to find oneself again and again (*ritrovai*). For Dante, the place of exile is the Dark Wood, where the "direct way" has vanished; for Derrida, it is Khora, the place that "exappropriates." For both, it is a place of ambiguity and impropriety, a place of irony and imagination, of difficulty and unrelenting, remorseless opposition. For both Dante and Derrida the identity of exile is the experience of conscience, of being cut-off from life by death, and equally, from death by life. It is the situation of separation from all that is "proper" to oneself. It is the experience of being identified by responsibility for the question, "Who am I," in the face of the "Other" who is absolutely necessary, necessarily absent, and whose arrival brings death, the death that is uniquely mine but is my absolute Impossibility. Exile is the time and place of memory and mourning, the situation of being lost, of having lost one's proper time and place, a time and place that now is past and closed, not present, but a time and place for which one cannot help but hope that it might come again. Exile takes place as the space of separation across which life and death call each other into question. "Aporia" names the topography, the terrain of exile.

The center through which these texts of Dante and Derrida both pass in this reading of exile as situation and identity is the figure of Abraham, or rather a certain figure of Abraham—Abraham turning into exile, Abraham as the father of Isaac, Abraham as the "father of faith," Abraham in the instant of decision regarding how to keep the secret promise of the covenant in the face of the Other's demand for sacrifice. The second section of this chapter traces the figure of Abraham as the gate through which the journey of conversion must pass. For Derrida, the fear and trembling that the figure of Abraham provokes opens up the possibility that the turn into exile can be crossed by the turning of faith, which keeps the Secret of broken promises, into the hope of a responsibility that passes over the aporia of sacrifice in favor of an impossible forgiveness that is yet to come. For Dante, terror at the experience of exile precipitates the descent into the depths of conscience where alone conversion must and can always begin again with the recognition of the need for forgiveness. His journey through Hell ironically traces the growth in conscience of the recognition of the need for forgiveness in the revelation of a different figure of religious responsibility than that of Abraham. In the sign of the Cross of Jesus, this reading of the *Inferno* discerns within Dante's text a *différance* that appears when it is read alongside the text of Derrida's third essay in *The Gift of Death*. There, in Kierkegaard's version of the Abraham story, Derrida traces the necessary self-deconstruction of every story of fathers and sons that is inscribed within the figure of the paternal demand for sacrifice, even when that demand is dispensed by placing in suspense the question of who shall bear the responsibility to provide the victim. In the Ugolino and Satan episodes that conclude the *Inferno* Dante figures the Cross of Jesus differently than as a structure of economical redemption of the debt of sin through the token of sacrificial victimization. Rather than as a reversal of the circulation of sacrifice, dispensation and redemption that passes through the gateway of Abraham's faith, Dante portrays forgiveness as an altogether different pattern of the parental relation of feeding than the father's economical provision of the victim, which only substitutes one death for another. In contrast, Dante lifts the repression under which all the religious traditions of the children of Abraham labor, the repression of the mother's way of feeding, which is not by provision but by nutrition. Nutrition is an-economic in that the mother feeds the child without substituting the death of another for her own death; she feeds the child through the transformation and expression of her own body, which passes over and becomes the body of the child. This new crossing converts the aporia of sacrifice into the aporia of forgiveness, understood not as sacrificial consumption of the victim, but as the eucharistic communion of life and death.

## WRITING IN EXILE

No point going around in circles, for as long as the other does not know, and know in advance, as long as he will not have won back this advance at the moment of pardon, that unique moment, the great pardon that has not yet happened in my life, indeed I am waiting for it as absolute unicity, basically the only event from now on, no point going around in circles, so long as the other has not won back that advance I shall not be able to avow anything and if avowal cannot consist in declaring, making known, informing, telling the truth, which one can always do, indeed, without confessing anything, without *making* truth, the other must not learn anything that he was not already in a position to know for avowal as such to begin, and this is why I am addressing myself here to God, the only one I take as witness, without yet knowing what these sublime words mean, and this grammar, and *to,* and *witness,* and *God,* and *take,* take God, and not only do I pray, as I have never stopped doing all my life, and pray to him, but I take him here and take him as my witness, I give myself what he gives me, i.e. the *i.e.* to take the time to take God as a witness to ask him not only, for example, like SA, why I take pleasure in weeping at the death of the friend, *cur fletus dulcis sit miseris,* and why I talk to him in Christian Latin French when they expelled from the Lycee de Ben Aknoun in 1942 a little black and very Arab Jew who understood nothing about it, to whom no one ever gave the slightest reason, neither his parents nor his friends, but why do I address her like him, my God, to avow, while he is the very thing who, I know nothing else about him when I prepare for avowal, must already know, and indeed he knows that very thing, as you well know, *cur confitemur Deo scienti,* . . . and for years I have been going around in circles, trying to take as a witness not to see myself being seen but to remember myself around a single event, I have been accumulating in the attic, my "sublime," documents. . . . about circumcisions in the world, the Jewish and the Arab and the others, and excision, with a view to my circumcision alone, the circumcision of me, the unique one, that I know perfectly well took place, one time, they told me and I see it but I always suspect myself of having cultivated, because I am circumcised, *ergo* cultivated, a fantastical affabulation. (*Circum.,* 11, 56–60)

As Hippolytus departed from Athens, by reason of his pitiless and perfidious stepmother, so from Florence must you depart. So it is willed, so already plotted, and so shall be accomplished soon by him who ponders upon it in the place where every day Christ is bought and sold. The blame as always, will follow the injured party, in outcry; but vengeance shall bear witness to the truth which dispenses it. You shall leave everything beloved the most dearly; and this is the arrow which the bow of exile shoots first. You shall

come to know how salt is the taste of another man's bread, and how hard
the path to descend and mount by another man's stair. And that which shall
most weigh your shoulders down will be the evil and senseless company with
which you shall fall into this vale; which shall then become all ungrateful, all
mad and malevolent against you, but soon after, their brows, not yours, shall
redden for it. Of their brutish folly their own conduct shall afford the proof,
*so that it will be for your fair fame to have made you a party by yourself.* (Par., xvii,
46–69; emphasis added)

> The Lord God said, "behold, the man has become like one of us, knowing
> good from evil; and now, lest he put forth his hand and take also of the tree
> of life, and eat, and live forever"—therefore the Lord God sent him forth
> from the Garden of Eden, to till the ground from which he was taken. He
> drove the man out; and at the East of the Garden of Eden he placed the
> Cherubim, and a flaming Sword which turned every way, to guard the way to
> the tree of life. (Gen. 3: 22–24)

There is a time and a place for exile. Exile is necessary, akin to the harsh
necessity that keeps both the Secret and the Promise—the necessity of death.
Death is necessary in order to keep the Secret and the Promise. This death,
keeping the secret, is the necessity of responsibility, the necessity of religion as
the history of responsibility, as the history of the necessity of bearing witness.
Taking God as witness of the necessity of avowing and confessing, this necessary history makes the truth without knowing or telling the truth that God
has always already known and told. This history is traced in the flesh, making it flesh, circling us around, cutting us off, making us true by witnessing us,
witnessing to us, beholding us, holding us in his sight. By having (us) in-sight,
knowing the truth he has made and calling to us, we who avoid being seen,
who hide being naked, calling to us to take God as our witness, who witnesses
and knows, we avow the truth that we do not know by taking as our witness
him who always already knows us, who always holds us in his sight and calls to
us as our witness, calls us by witnessing, from whose call we hide by going in
circles to avoid being beheld, naked, to avoid being witnessed naked, showing
the trace of having been marked, held in sight, and re-marked, encircled. We
repeat the trace with which we have been remarked, and by repeating the figure
of having been known, we remain without—"you were within, but I was without"—without a witness, so that we continually, of necessity, must *take* God
as witness, take, as if witness had not always already been given, as a gift, take
God as witness, take God, as if God had deserted us, left us alone, bereft like a
child whose beautiful mother had disappeared, had absconded without a trace,
deserted the child and left their world, left it a desert. It would be as if her
passing away, leaving only a trace, her death marked and re-marked in the flesh
of the child, had become the cause of the child's exile, its expulsion from the
familiarity of home, its being sent out, deserted, into the desert, unwitnessed, so
that of necessity the deserted child must take God as a substitute witness, must

take a substitute witness who had always already been a witness, substitute for the witness who had left the child deserted, in exile in the desert. The circle of life closes on itself—the circle in the flesh, of the flesh cut off, going around in circles, re-marking, remaking the cut which cuts it off, the trace-mark of the Promise of a witness, the mark in the flesh of the Promise of a witness, of a cloud of witnesses, a great nation of witness; the promise always to be witnessed, always to have already been witnessed and called and avowed.

Yet at the same time and in the same place, in the same figure of place, a naked hiding and a patent substitution, taking God as absent witness for the present witness who has deserted it, circling around without a witness, forced to take a witness who cannot be taken, cannot be present, cannot be made a present of, whose absence must be pardoned, the great, singular pardon, pardoning the present for the witness it cannot give, pardoning the failure of the witness to be present, pardoning death for keeping the witness who once was present from being present again, because the witness is within and "I" am without, circling around because the door, the Gate, is barred and blocked by a flaming Sword that cuts in every direction. Having been exiled, marked and re-marked, cut off and inscribed with the trace, we take God as our witness, in substitution for the witness whose presence failed us and who deserted us leaving only a trace, leaving us in exile awaiting pardon. This pardon allows us through the Gate, allows us to pass, to pass over the failure of the present witness that forces us to take a substitute, allows us to pardon the death of the needed witness, to pardon both the death of the necessary and the necessity of death. It allows us to pass, to be pardoned and passed over, to be allowed to pass over from exile in the figure of the deserted present into the gaze that has always already promised to behold, promised to witness, promised to avow; to be allowed to pass, through death, to be allowed to return, to be pardoned and passed over through death given as gift, a gift which need not be present.

## Turning into Exile

Dante's *Commedia* was written in exile; it is the gift of writing in exile. It is the story of his being led out of exile, just as Israel was led out of slavery in Egypt.[1] Dante was not pardoned during his lifetime nor allowed to return to Florence, but during the time of his exile Dante found his way to pardon for the prodigality of his promise made at the end of the *Vita nuova*. He found, or rather, was shown, a way to keep the Secret and keep the promise of the beginning of his new life in writing, and in so doing was shown a way to write a pardon for his exile, if not for the city and the citizens who imposed it. His exile was pardoned in writing, in the writing of the poem. The poem is the gift of pardon, given *par don*, given in exile, by exile, to exile. But exile is a figure of death, it is a way that death begins to take place in life. Exile is a way for death to begin to find its way in life. So it can be said that in being shown a way to pardon for his exile, by learning to write in exile, Dante was shown a way in which he could give himself the gift of death as the gift of pardon for his exile, both gifts, the gift of death and the gift of pardon, being one gift, given in writing: three in one, one in three.

Dante's *Commedia* begins in exile; exile is the time and place of its beginning. The beginning of the poem takes place in exile, in the desert of exile, in the deserted place, the unwitnessed place, the Dark Wood where Dante is alone and cut off. How does the beginning of the poem take place? What is the Secret of its beginning? How can its beginning be located? How does the history of its writing in exile begin? Where, when does it begin? *Nel mezzo* . . . "nel mezzo" marks the keep of the secret; it marks the spot of the beginning and, let it be remarked, of the end of the writing:

*Nel mezzo del cammin di nostra vita*
*mi ritrovai per una selva oscura*
*ché la diritta via era smarrita.*
"Midway in the journey of our life I found myself in a dark wood, for the straight way was lost." *(Inf.*, i, 1–3)

What could it mean to keep an impossibly prodigal promise? How does one keep what is, twice over, not one's own, what has been received and promised as a gift? This remains a question, necessarily. Sometimes a promise can be kept only by letting it turn itself into a question. The question marks the spot where the secret of the beginning, already marked with the promise, is kept by remarking it as a question, by its turning into a question. The question marks the turning point, the point of conversion, where conversion marks a new beginning, taking a turn into a new direction, a new way of going on, a different journey. The question is a way of taking responsibility for keeping the Secret and the Promise when one has no other way of going on, when the direct way, the straightforward way, has disappeared. The question is itself an expression of hope, the hope of opening up a new way of keeping to the way that has disappeared, a way of going on without knowing. Turning into question is an inscription of freedom; it marks the spot differently, and as such it opens up a new way of taking responsibility.

The question creates a new world. The turning into question sheds new light on what had been dark. It reveals new possibility. It marks a difference. The question opens up a new space and new time; it gives space and time by suspending them, suspending the journey by taking it out of space and time. It short-circuits the going around in circles, by relocating its point of perspective from the circumference to the center. *Nel mezzo.* In the question, one finds oneself again (*mi ritrovai*), but finds oneself different, converted, because one finds oneself differently. This difference is inscribed in the poem as the difference between Dante the pilgrim, who finds himself lost in the writing, and Dante the poet, who is beginning to come to himself again in the writing, seeing himself beginning, and seeing the end in the beginning. Ironically, the poem ends where it begins, *nel mezzo,* and the poet sees himself ironically there, now, suspended between beginning and end, suspended in time and space, located in the middle but also at the center, in question.

And so the poem begins ironically. Irony is its way of beginning, its way of going on, and its way of ending. Every question is ironic, not occasionally or circumstantially, but always, of itself. The question reveals freedom as the possibility of difference, of being different, of seeing differently, of conversion, of turning into a different way, of coming to oneself again with a difference, with a changed mind (*metanoia*), a different consciousness, in a new light. The poem keeps the beginning, and the end together and in so doing keeps the secret of an impossible freedom. This freedom allows difference, gives space and time for difference, allows the irony of the question that knows that it does not know, allows responsibility to be in question, allows doing the truth without knowing the truth or telling the truth, allows for keeping what is not one's own, what one does not have and therefore cannot give; it allows for keeping oneself in secret and keeping one's promises although they are already broken, allows one to ask, deserted, "Who am I?" and to be identified by a witness who cannot be present but whose absence is kept in secret and promised in the hope of the question.

"*Nel mezzo*" marks the spot of the poem's beginning; it gives the poem its where and when, its space and time, locates it in the history of freedom as responsibility. It marks the point of the style of its writing, of its auto-deconstruction, inscribing itself in the space and time that allow difference, in the desert that Derrida calls "Khora," and says is the "other" identity of *différance*, the "surname of *différance*." All that is inscribed "*nel mezzo*" is written in the place, the time, and space, of exile. It is written in the no-man's land, the in-between of the middle that is always also the center, the point where one is identified by a witness, God-or death[2], who cannot be taken in the present moment because God-or death has always already given witness, has always already held us in its gaze, in sight, known us and seen into us, seeing into the mother's womb, the secret place of that other witness, who has also always already known us and held us in secret. The whole story takes place in the "soul," the no-place where one cannot escape being seen by God, the secret place where one cannot hide, where God sees without being seen, because we have been expelled from the place where he still holds and beholds us, from the center, which is the garden where the tree of life is planted, exiled to the circumference, the place of going around in circles, the desert where we find ourselves deserted, except for the impossible freedom of a calling, a voice that wakes us from sleep and calls us to ourselves again, calls us into question, calls us into the irony of the question, "Who am I," so that we do not know whose voice it is that calls, whose name it is calling and calling for, who is to witness and who is to be identified.

Not surprisingly, with this question Dante's journey joins the track traced out by the ironic ambiguity of the question that Derrida takes from St. Augustine, "What do I love when I love my God?" Most styles of piety hold that faith, hope and love belong together, so we might seem to be on the right track. In fact, it seems that keeping a promise means following the trace marks, being on the trail of a doubly impossible destination, the impossibility that is the bond of secrecy shared between "I" and the "Other." The questions Who am I? and What do I love when I love my God? both point out the path of a journey to be taken that necessarily leads into exile. The place of exile is the place of an absolute separation that occurs in these two questions, cutting off "one" from every "other." The place of exile these questions cut off can only be traversed by following the traces that they leave behind as they pass, the marks of their passing, the trace of the questions passing away, trailing off, leaving us behind but calling in passing, calling for a response, the call that marks the passing of the question Who am I? with the response that gave Abraham his new name and new place, "Here I am! Ready to follow . . . into exile." One finds one's place and one's way in exile only by following the traces that mark the way of a faith that entrusts itself by responding to the call of an unseen witness who keeps passing away, who keeps to absolute secrecy by keeping to the passing way, leaving behind only the call to follow in the hope of beholding again the "lost" face, the lost face that still beholds without being seen, that still calls, leaving a trace, only a trace, behind, the face of love, of desire, of need, the face that keeps the secret of passing on, of passing over, of beginning again.

Derrida's question in *Circumfession* is also Dante's question in the *Commedia*—for each, writing is his way of keeping faith with and entrusting his way to his impossible promise. Both get their question directly from St. Augustine: "What do I love when I love my God?" Augustine's *Confessions* inspired Dante's *Commedia* just as directly as it did Derrida's *Circumfession*. The first words of the poem tell us that clearly: *Nel mezzo del cammin di nostra vita. . . .* "In the middle . . ." It all begins in the middle. Literature, and life, has always already happened. It is a journey, *cammin;* mysterious, without beginning or end. And it is "our life," always "mine" for all of us; it never happens any other way. We all belong to this tribe, necessarily: Everyman and Everywoman. But the beginning of this journey is not promising because Dante says he is lost; the direct route (*via diritta*) has vanished. Perhaps we are as surprised to hear that there is a direct route for this journey, a right way of keeping prodigal promises, as Dante seems to be to find it disappeared. Dante got it directly from St. Augustine, "I was without, but you were within." *Nel mezzo*—within; at the center, the necessary, impossible starting point which makes all the circumstantial, circumferential points possible. The direct(-ion of the) way. The center is the secret point that can be measured only by the number/name that cannot be spoken or written.[3] The center point is the point on which everything else turns; it is the crucial point, the critical point, the point where the point enters and begins to make the cut, the decisive cut on which depend life and death.

This is the point at which Dante finds himself, or more accurately, re-finds himself, *"mi ritrovai,"* comes to himself again, wakes up. He says later he was full of sleep when he strayed from the path. He further says that he wakes up to find himself again, *per una selva oscura*, in a dark, obscure wood (literally, *per:* through, in the midst of, through and through, thoroughly; but also, by means of and for the sake of). In and through, by means of, the journey through the dark wood he finds himself differently. The wood: the forest/desert; the place of exile; paradise lost; original sin: the uncanny place where one cannot be at home; the un-Promised Land. He *found himself* there again. Always there, in the middle, at the center. Dante got this as well from St. Augustine, *factus sum mihi terra difficultatis et sudoris nimii*, "I have been made for myself a land of difficulty and of great sweat and tears." He found the center of himself—his identity, the "truth" toward which the question of human identity, Who am I? directs all persons. *"Quaestio mihi factus sum."* He found his "soul" there, which he had all but lost, by tracing back his steps to where he went astray, where he got cut off. The soul is the starting point of every pilgrimage, of every human journey whose divine origin and destiny is taken seriously. It is the center, the point where the point enters, where the cut originates. The soul is the slit: it is the eye through which one sets one's sights, the ear to which the silence of divine mystery addresses itself, soliciting a response, inviting us to tell the story of who we have become on the way to making the truth of ourselves through our journey to God-or death. Dante puts it thus:

> Ah, how hard it is to tell what that wood was, wild, rugged, harsh; the very thought of it renews the fear! It is so bitter that death is hardly more so. But, to treat of the good that I found in it, I will tell of the other things I saw there. (*Inf.*, i, 4–9)

From the beginning the journey is taken in the face of death—a difficult friend, rude, rough, stubborn. From the beginning, the journey has the whiff of death about it and awakens fear and trembling, "in the blood." Yet the starting point, in the center/soul of himself, is where the highest good begins to shine forth and reveal itself in the telling of the tale (*Inf.*, i, 12–18), a tale told through the tangle of writing. Here Dante, like Derrida, acknowledges the Augustinian doctrine *"facere veritatem in amore,"* to do the truth in love. This is also the doctrine of freedom, *"ama, et fac quod vis,"* love, and do what you will. The journey is taken in the face of God-or death, or love. The trick of three: these three are one—the other, the self, and the exchange of gifts between them. Identity and freedom are the path their journey traces, its question marks.

This is why Caputo says of Derrida's *vademecum*—"What do I love when I love my God?"—that in the articulation the emphasis falls on the "my." The love of God reveals itself beginning with the coming to himself (always again) and the response of "Yes! Come! God-or death; Yes! *My* truth!" This love reveals itself again in the freedom to do the truth by expressing it in the writing of the story. God becomes incarnate in the word of a personal story of a poetic pilgrimage. The parallel with the case of Derrida seems straightforward.

He comes to himself again in Paris, in the middle of his exile/flight from El Barib. He has left behind the land of the broken promise and the death of its God. He has followed a different path, a path that went astray and now he finds himself lost in the thicket/desert/Khora of deconstructed stories. *Différance,* the path that strays. But, at an uncertain time, he stops and turns to face that death, or God, or his lady-mother, or himself, the truth/soul of who he has made himself in writing, and he takes his stylus in hand and rewrites the journey differently. In an apparently newly pious style, he tries to tell of the good (God) that has always been inviting, calling, promising, hoping, sighing, dreaming . . . and which he found there in the dying/writing of the old story of the "new life." This new story is a story of a journey, a tale told in prayers and tears, which is why Derrida says that it has been understood less and less well. Apparently, the further he journeys, the less well marked the trail becomes, the harder he becomes to trace—at least for some. Just like Dante, Derrida writes differently when he catches the whiff of death and feels the fear of it in his blood—his death, God's death, his lady-mother's death.[4] For both, the story begins with a gesture of fidelity, of keeping faith in the promise of writing, a coming to oneself again in the face of death in an act of trust that there will be a way out, a way to go on writing the good that one finds there *nel mezzo.*

## CRYING IN THE WILDERNESS—WRITING IN TEARS

Chance or arbitrariness of the starting point, irresponsibility even, you will say, inability I still have to answer for my name, even to give it back to my mother, remains (the fact) that I am here now, let us suppose, for I shall never be able to demonstrate the fact, the counterexample in a series of what I might have written or what G. might know about it, and the fear that has gripped me since always, for to that at least I am faithful, discords with itself, threatens itself from two apparently contradictory imminences, that of the writer who is afraid of dying before the end of a long sentence, period, without the signing counterexample, and that of the son who, dreading seeing her die before the end of the avowal, for this confession promised unto death, trembles then too at the thought of departing before his mother, this figure of absolute survival he's talked so much about, but also the one who literally could not weep for him, it would be an excess of suffering for one who has already lost two sons, one before me Paul Moises, who died in 1929 when less than one-year-old, one year before my birth, which must have made me for her, for them, a precious but so vulnerable intruder, one mortal too many, Elie loved in the place of another, then the other after me, Norbert Pinhas, dead age two when I was 10, in 1940, without the least image of his circumcision that I nonetheless remember, and I saw then the first mourning as the mourning of my mother who could not, then, literally weep for me, me the sole replacement, weep for me as my sons will have to, whereas my sole desire remains that of giving to be read the interruption that will in any case decide the very figure, *this writing that resembles the poor chance of a provisional resurrection,* like the one that took place in December 1988 when a phone call from my brother-in-law sent me running for the first plane to Nice, tie, dark suit, white *kippa* in my pocket, trying in vain not only to cry but, I don't know, to stop myself crying, *et fletum frenebam,* to get myself out of all the programs and quotations, when the unforeseeable did not fail to happen, surprising me absolutely but like what goes without saying, inflexible destiny, i.e., that having been incapable of recognizing me that evening and, according to the doctors only due to survive a few hours, in the early morning at the moment when, having slept alone in her house, I arrived first in the white room at the clinic, she saw me, heard me and, so to speak came round, as though immortal, SA also had this experience, went through it, was its *Savoir Absolu,* SA tells us, and *I write between two resurrections, the one that is given then the one that is promised,* compromised to this almost natural monument which becomes in my eyes a sort of calcinated root, the naked spectacle of a photographed wound, the bedsore cauterized by the light of writing, to fire, to blood but to ash too. (*Circum.,* 10, 50–54; emphasis added)

Confessions are stories of conversion; one confesses the truth that one has done when one reached turning points. Augustine identifies three turning points in his journey. Allegorically, each of the three stages of Dante's journey through the "afterlife" (after death, after facing death), *Inferno, Purgatorio,* and *Paradiso,* unfolds in the direction of a conversion episode that initiates his movement into the middle of that "region," where the region itself opens up as a distinct perspective from the one central point of the soul. A conversion is a *metanoia,* a change of "mind" or attitude, a new bearing or stance or posture of freedom. In the present context, the relevant fact is that for Augustine, Dante, and Derrida, the turning points are marked by the call of a beloved lady, the god-bearing image, and the efficacy of the call has much to do with fidelity; it is the constancy of the calling that supports the keeping of the promise in the face of death. For each man, the promise is in the keeping of a woman whose face brings them face to face with death, and so turns their face in a new direction on the journey of life.

Canto i of the *Commedia* anchors the poem as a whole. There are exactly 100 cantos in the poem: thirty-three devoted to each of the three movements that together constitute but one movement of Dante's conversion, the process of his "change of mind," his change of identity. Canto i marks the spot where each of these three different movements occur and form one movement of identification. Canto i marks the spot, the place, Khora, where the story of freedom's journey takes place.[5] It identifies the center from which each of the movements originates and through which each passes, intersecting the others. Canto i anchors the poem in its proper place, allowing it to journey along the path that turns, the path that is not the *via diritta,* the path that has disappeared and been lost, the path that differs and defers, the improper path, the path that is three—Inferno, Purgatorio, Paradiso—yet one. Canto i marks the spot of the beginning and the end, the place where Dante always finds himself again, at the beginning and at the end, always the same, always different. This site, the situation in which freedom takes place, a movement that centers itself through the orbits it performs, this taking place of freedom, this Khora, which is exiled, removed, and withdrawn from all locations and all traces and inscriptions, all place markers and way stations, this is the place of the anchor, the place of the one who anchors, the anchorite, the one who goes into exile in the desert, who withdraws from all inhabited, inscribed, and well-marked places, who solicits, invites, and suffers the disappearance of the *via diritta,* so as to orbit in movements of free variation around the center. Dante finds himself again, transported, as if in a dream, while asleep, no accounting for it, ir-responsibly, retracing his steps back to the place where he went astray: "I cannot rightly say how I entered it; I was so full of sleep at the moment I left the true way" (*Inf.,* i, 10–12).

To be clear: all these places, the Dark Wood, Inferno, Purgatorio, Paradiso, the city of Florence during Dante's lifetime, all the places around which Dante orbits are one place, the place that differs and defers, the one place, the center, Khora, in which all times and places are inscribed, improperly. Nothing belongs there properly, so everything may take place there, improperly, without belonging there. To abide there in the desert, in exile, things and events, and especially persons, must have an anchor. They must take and hold an improper place, they must have a placeholder, an instrument that marks and incises, bites into the shifting sand of the desert and holds—a bit. The writing of Canto i anchors the movements of the poem as a whole and allows its diverse movements, the movements of its different orbits, different improper times and places, to situate Dante the pilgrim-poet in the place where the path turns, and turns differently along the way that strays, the necessary path of conversion.

In Canto i the anchor, the one who holds Dante in place as he strays, undergoing the anchoritic variations of conversion, is Virgil. Virgil holds Dante fast; he is able to take hold of Dante because his writing has also been inscribed in Dante's heart, or rather everything that has been inscribed in Dante's heart has been transcribed into and through Virgil's style, the style that makes the *epos,* the song in praise of a different dream, and the different style of writing dreams and visions than the one that marked the dreams and visions that troubled Dante's sleep in the *Vita nuova.* Here in Canto i, Virgil takes the place of the god Amor, the idol of Dante's love writing in the *Vita nuova,* and becomes Dante's new "lord," the dominant style of his writing as it turns through all the movements of his journey of conversion. Dante takes Virgil as his new "master and author," Virgil, "that font which pours forth so broad a stream of speech. . . . You alone are he from whom I took the fair style that has done me honor" (*Inf.,* i, 79–80; 85–87). A new pattern of substitution replacing the old, the beginning of a new style of writing, acknowledged by Dante, "my brow covered with shame" (*Inf.,* i, 81).

Dante accounts for the substitution of this new substitute, this new style of marking his place, taking a new anchorite as lord, this recognition of a new propriety and decorum by stating:

> O glory and light of other poets, may the long study and the great love that have made me search your volume avail me! . . . See the beast that has turned me back! Help me against her, famous sage, for she makes my veins and pulses tremble. (*Inf.*, i, 82–84; 88–90)

"The beast that has turned me back," the she-wolf, the last of the three, leopard, lion, wolf, the allegorical trinity of the movements of sin: incontinence, pride, and the all-consuming hunger of malice. These three mark the place where his way has been blocked, where the journey he had hoped to take to the summit of the hill, the high place of vision appears impossible. "There at the end of the valley that had pierced my heart with fear, I looked up and saw its shoulders already clad in the rays of the planet that leads men aright by every path" (*Inf.*, i, 13–18). The three that are all beasts in one; all the beasts that Adam had named while the garden was still his home, but among which he found no "proper" companion, so that God took him out of himself and made of him an other, the other with whom he was expelled from the garden, and so that now he is separated from the beasts, as he is from her, and from God, and from all others. It is the she-wolf that finally turns the pilgrim back:

> . . . a she-wolf, that in her leanness seemed laden with every craving and had already caused many to live in sorrow: she put such heaviness upon me with the fear that came from sight of her that I lost all hope of the height. And like one who is eager in winning, but when the time comes that makes him lose, weeps and is saddened in all his thoughts, such did that peaceless beast make me, as, coming on against me, she pushed me back, little by little, to where the sun is silent (*dove'l sol tace*). (*Inf.*, i, 49–60)

The she-wolf is the third of the trinity of beasts, but it also figures another third: one of the trinity that identifies the situation that anchors the poem. The she-wolf is Beatrice for Dante in this situation; the wolf is all that Beatrice had become in his writing, along the way of his writing, all that is left of the promise, the transcription of the promise that has long slept, the encrypted secret of the tomb. The she-wolf is the de-formation of the one who, when she and he were nine, caused "the vital spirit, the one that dwells in the most secret chamber of the heart, [to begin] to tremble so violently that the least pulses of my body were strongly affected; and trembling, it spoke these words: 'Here is a god stronger than I, who shall come to rule over me" (*Vita nuova*, ii). He recognizes her in the pattern of the blood pulses, the frantic strokes of blood-writing on his heart. Beatrice: the heart-eater, the vampire returned from the tomb, the de-formed trace of the encrypted secret promise of writing, now turned monstrous and beastial under the enforced diet of blood-drinking and heart-eating, so that his blood forever resonates her presence and is re-pulsed by the hunger that cannot be satisfied. All three, Dante, Virgil, Beatrice, are united here in this no-place at the center of all times and places, where their way must take a different turn. Virgil to Dante: "'It behooves you to go by another way if you would escape from this wild place,' he answered when he saw me weep . . ." (*Inf.*, i, 91–93).

Virgil's dominion over Dante takes a different turn than did that of the idol, Amor. Present in the image of the she-wolf, there echoes another story of beginning, another ambiguous destiny that opens a new horizon on the situation of this new beginning; another story of lupine feeding that reverses the pattern: the she-Wolf who suckles and satisfies Romulus and Remus, dispensing a new destiny and a new order, that of empire.[6] Virgil for Dante is the poet of the dream of empire, the earthly image of the dream of the Empyrean, another substitution, another turn in the way through which conversion must pass. It is a dream not without its own ambiguities, to be sure, that will continue to play and resonate down through the whole poem to its end where it began, something unthought, another pattern of substitution not unlike those that structure the *Vita nuova,* but with a difference, one that Dante takes here as authoritative in a way that replaces the authority of Amor. Taking Virgil as his anchor and master-author, Dante substitutes the authority of Virgil's dream for his own in the *Vita nuova,* and in so doing "changes his mind"; the change opens a new horizon, spreads out a new vista within the Khora, a new hope in exile substituting for the one lost in the ruining descent (*rovinava in basso loco*) that dislocated and deranged him in the face of the wolf. It is a vision of salvation rescripted for him by Virgil in the promise of a savior to come here, to Italy, to Rome's empire:

> He will not feed on earth or pelf (*peltro*), but on wisdom, love, and virtue, and his birth shall be between felt and felt. He shall be the salvation (*salute*) of that low-lying (*umile*) Italy for which the virgin Camilla and Euryalus, Turnus, and Nisus died of their wounds (*Inf.*, i, 103–108).

Virgil's dream of empire as inscribed in the *Aeneid* substitutes for Dante's dream gone bad in the *Vita nuova,* or rather reinscribes and redoubles the ambiguity of that dream, promising more than, in and of itself, it can offer. More precisely, one style of writing, Virgil's epic of imperial destiny, reconfigures the khoral space of another style, the Courtly Love songs of the troubadour tradition, transcribing and transfiguring the figure of their praise, reconfiguring their trinity into that of the dominion of Rome, that capital in exile for the new Jerusalem, and indeed the new Troy. This pattern of capital substitution, this shifting of headwaters and headquarters set in motion by Dante's consciously taking Virgil as his master-author is itself destined to be reconfigured again through another substitution, of which Virgil is already conscious and which he acknowledges prophetically. Virgil thus takes his stand as authoritative witness to a "wisdom, love and virtue," not his own but which he serves:

> Therefore I think and deem it best that you should follow me, and I will be your guide and lead you hence through an eternal place, where you shall

hear the despairing shrieks and see the ancient tormented spirits who all bewail the second death. Then you shall see those who are content in the fire because they hope to come among the blessed, whensoever that may be; and to these, if you would then ascend, there shall be a soul worthier than I to guide you; with her I shall leave you at my departing. For the Emperor who reigns there-above wills not that I come into his city, because I was rebellious to his law. In all parts is His empire, in that part is His kingdom, there is His city and His lofty seat. Oh, happy he whom He elects thereto. (*Inf.*, i, 112–129)[7]

Virgil's dream of empire and the authority of divine law must necessarily be sublated and transcribed into another khoral movement by another scribe worthier than he. The ambiguity of his epic style must be redeemed because, on his own authority, it is rebellious to that promise which is higher, which promises more and is more promising than his imagination can hold anchored in the desert, than he can witness to and stand warrant for. But he is conscious of the substitution and will reveal the one who in turn anchors his place as witness and guide to Dante, the other anchorite who authorizes his temporary authority, who authors the visions of hope that he transcribes and transmits as messenger, as *angelos,* the trace of a different promise in a different writing. The limit of Virgil's horizon, a horizon still new and different to Dante, open and broad enough to accomplish these first turnings of conversion, is nevertheless circumscribed in the writing style of the *Aeneid* by the epic tension of heroic destiny achieved at the cost of tragic loss, of "wise, loving, and virtuous" deaths which, in the figures of "virgin Camilla and Euryalus, Turnus and Nisus," present themselves as sacrifices unredeemed by any gift, but paid as the necessary price in exchange for Aeneas's arrival at his destination and destiny. Virgil's authority inscribes a vision that is the ambiguous dream of the City of God to which Virgil does not know the way, and from which he must remain in exile, just as Dante is in exile from his city, Florence, because both he and the city are separated from themselves, on the way to the identity behind all "capital cities," the new Jerusalem. Yet, knowing that he does not know, Virgil can still witness effectively to another authority, in yet another style that he did not know, but which in wisdom, love, and virtue, he learns to transcribe so that it might speak to Dante and reveal the anchorite who anchors both of them. Virgil is the poet of the dream of empire and of the law that promises what it cannot deliver, master-author of those who serve another whom they do not know, who serve knowing that they do not know, "virtuous pagans" who must remain in exile in the place deserted by the final witness, Virgil whose voice witnesses to the absence of the final witness, who witnesses in secret, who necessarily must remain unknown. Here Virgil is the one who witnesses to the necessity of sacrifice as the way through which Dante must pass so as to see another vision through other eyes. O father Virgil, O father Abraham, you who know how to journey and find your way through all those places unredeemed from sacrifice—"he set out, and I followed him."

## "I am not Aeneas; I am not Paul."

Already in Canto ii of the Inferno, Dante discovers that the journey of conversion leads along a path that is not straight, that turns again and again,
beginning anew, a constant conversion, constantly turning in new directions.
Dante's discipleship, his resolve to follow, quickly slips all the traces of Virgil's
discipline. The anchor does not hold. The old ambivalence engraved in the
patterns of substitution that the *Vita nuova* records reawakens again now too,
jogged in memory by the call of writing. The terror of the no-place and the
monsters of desire that prowl through it reawaken the question that gnawed
at Dante as Beatrice ate his heart in the dream that dissembled the original
terror: "Dare I? *Who am I* to do so?" Who will take responsibility for my daring the journey in writing in another way, to another place, to an other's place,
to where the other takes place?

> Like a swimmer, cast off in the endless churning sea, going under, already
> gone under for the third time, who has, he does not know how, been spat out
> of the churn gasping on the shore . . . (*Inf.*, i, 22–27)

Dante now finds himself casting off again, making another profligate,
prodigal promise to keep the secret of the necessity to begin, the need of all
beginnings, all that begins unjustified, without cause, without reason; to begin
the journey that gives the gift. "I began: Poet, you who guide me, consider if
my strength is sufficient, before you trust me to the deep way" (*Inf.*, ii, 10–12).

It is the pattern of substitution that must undergo conversion; Dante's trust
of Virgil is genuine enough to allow him to show the scarred-over love wound
that had become infected by the substitute writing of the substitute desire in the
first dream, and now Dante flinches as Virgil makes to touch the scar. Dante's
spoken question, "Consider if my strength is sufficient?" substitutes for the
other, unspoken one in his heart, "Consider if *your* strength, the strength of your
hold on me, is sufficient? Are you the one who will anchor me in the desert
which erases all traces, closes over every mark like the ocean waves, where all
goes under? If we go under now, can your lines hold?" It is simply a matter of
trust, a commitment that Dante has from the beginning evaded through substitution, seeking to evade the sheer terror of being held by the desire of the Other.
He tried from the beginning to leave behind him a trace in writing of the path
he was being solicited and seduced to take by the god who dominated him, like
poor Hansel (and his Gretel) who tried to leave a trace behind himself as well,
but the birds of desire, harpy-like, came and ate, consuming their memory's
mark. Now he remembers that he himself has tried to take the epic turn, has
tried to turn a verse in praise of Beatrice, but it did not seem to take. Is Virgil's
authority sufficient to authorize Dante to go farther on this path?

> "But I, why do I come there? And who allows it? *I am not Aeneas, I am not
> Paul;* of this neither I nor others think me worthy. Wherefore, if I yield and

come, I fear that the coming may be folly. You are wise; you understand better than I explain it." And like one who unwills what he has willed and with new thought changes his resolve, so that he quite gives up the thing he had begun, such did I become on that dark slope, for by thinking on it I rendered null the undertaking that had been so suddenly embarked upon. (*Inf.*, ii, 31–42; emphasis added)

If Dante suspects that Virgil's authority cannot be altogether trusted here, it is because Virgil wrote the song of *"pius Aeneas,"* the hero of piety, the ready pilgrim, strong enough to carry others on his back. Can Virgil rescript the story, write into it a new identity, transcribe and recast the role of hero for one who is no hero, one who is not singular. Will Virgil tire of speaking vernacular Italian to a Florentine Everyman, instead of imperial Latin? What if Dante cannot find himself in Virgil's tall tale; what if he does not measure up to the epic proportions of Aeneas, and finds himself again abandoned, deserted, unwitnessed? "Can I entrust myself, the question of who I am, to you, since I am not Aeneas? Do I entrust myself to that journey with you, whose lines don't seem to hold me in their trace? Neither do I belong to that other empire of heroes you unknowingly foretell. I do not recognize myself in Paul's vision. It was not Jesus who spoke to me and asked me why I persecuted him. I have nothing to do with Jesus; I do not know the man! Why should he call to me, name me, knock me off my horse, convert me and send me on a different road, out into the desert, make me go under, go down without a trace, require that I write things I never dreamed of. I am not Paul."

This new moment of crisis is important to an understanding of the human journey through freedom to identity. First, despite the ambivalence, it is a step forward, a step toward greater consciousness and more authentic self-knowiedge. Furthermore, it is a necessary step; necessary not just because the pilgrim happens to be fearful and hesitant, but because ambivalence, fear, and irresolution belong to the structure of freedom itself. Freedom first arises as the question of personal identity, Who am I? Because it is genuinely a question, it is open to two genuinely different possibilities, a "yes" of trust in relational identity and a "no" of refusal to allow the Other to enter within the boundaries of the individual self.

Of course in one sense, this refusal is illusory because the experience of divine mystery always finds the Other already "within," surrounding and penetrating every situation of existence. Yet, the "no" is real because, at least in the Judaeo-Christian-Islamic tradition, "creation" means that God allows the freedom of the human person to be an authentic reality that makes a difference, indeed an absolute difference that has cosmic and eternal consequences that even God itself is committed to endure. To say it clearly: in Dante's imagination, radically orthodox as it is, freedom is the sole source of both reality and meaning. Both arise originally and are finally determined in the mutual relations of personal freedoms. This is certainly not to conflate divine and human freedom; the structure of mutual free relation is hierarchical in this specific sense: the initiative in the relation always remains with the divine, "All is grace"; and "in the beginning was the Word, and the Word was with God and the Word was God." That Word is "Love," the Love of a gift offered freely, without cause or reason. Nevertheless, the meaning of the gift offered necessitates a response of either acceptance or refusal. The divine offer of the mysterious gift of existence as freedom for personal identity in a relationship of love would be both unreal and meaningless without the mutuality of an equally real possibility of a properly human choice to say yes or no. Since this possibility is there from the beginning to the end, the journey in freedom is the journey into fully conscious identification with this necessarily ambivalent situation. This is the ambivalence that Dante now experiences and expresses in his hesitation to undertake the "hero's journey," which, ironically, he has yet to learn is the journey of Everyman.

What makes the decisive difference in the pilgrim's moment of need, allowing him to resolve his ambivalent fear of going on, at least for a time? It is the name of Beatrice, his beloved, his poetic muse, his sign of grace. Virgil relates the story of Beatrice's love, enduring and effective despite her death, which makes clear that the act of trust the pilgrim is being asked to make is not primarily in the authority of the figure of Virgil, either as poet/mentor or even as the allegorical voice of sound reason, but in the one who has commissioned him as her emissary. The narrative of *Inferno* ii establishes Beatrice's metaphoric identity in the poem as Dante's "god-bearing image," to use Dorothy Sayers's term. The figure of Beatrice and her metaphoric identity in the poem becomes progressively the focus of the poet's powerful act of imagination whereby he establishes for himself and the reader the meaning of the doctrine of Incarnation in the specifically Christian understanding of human freedom that his journey will map.

Beatrice's identity and role in the journey are not, however, simply a repetition of the standard meaning of "incarnation" in the Christian tradition, applied specifically and uniquely to Jesus as the Messiah and later, as the second Person of the Trinity. Dante expands the range of meaning of what he takes to be the secret truth kept hidden in the cryptography of the doctrine by applying it to his own experience of grace, sin, and forgiveness on an individual level, and to the way in which that individual experience was shaped and mediated by a historical, cultural event that allowed the power of the truth claim that the doctrine expresses to reach him and become effective in his life. This event is Dante's identification of himself as poet with the style of poetry that emerges in the Provençal Troubadour movement of the 12th century and the secular doctrine of Courtly Love associated with it. It is the combination of these two "doctrines" and the tension between them that merge in the figure of Beatrice and give her metaphoric identity the power to become the living center of the poem.

The *Vita nuova,* Dante's work of poetic apprenticeship and spiritual novitiate, serves as his first expression of the fusion of horizons between the Christian and secular inspirations of Dante's "way." It provides not only the relevant autobiographical background for Dante's journey in the *Commedia,* but something more important as well: the challenge to understand realistically whether Dante's claim for the significance of Beatrice's love for him, as well as his for her, which is the premise for the entire poem, is humanly credible and capable of supporting the truth claim the poet makes for it in his experience of conversion and fulfillment through the rest of his journey.

Dante the poet, who writes "from beyond" the journey, that is, from the perspective of the final vision, the end of which is joined to the beginning *nel mezzo,* rescripts Virgil's authority and rewrites its figure, inscribing it here into his own beginning, recasting Virgil as himself in a reenvisioning of the original dream of the *Vita nuova.* Virgil responds to Beatrice's solicitation as the poet would now wish to have responded in writing to that first beginning, and in so doing transcribes it differently. The difference is plainly marked:

> "If I have well understood what you say," the shade of that magnanimous one replied, "your spirit is beset by cowardice, which oftentimes encumbers a man, turning him from honorable endeavor, as false seeing turns a beast that shies." (*Inf.,* ii, 42–48)

The poet confesses himself *in writing,* as he knows himself to have been *in writing,* by having Virgil show him as he now is in writing, the pilgrim who has just been turned by the beasts, himself turned into a beast that shies, resisting the reins, tugging at the traces. So as "to free you from this fear," Virgil goes on to reveal more of the story, the story of the person(s) behind his voice: a feminine trinity of heavenly women—Beatrice, St. Lucy, and the Virgin Mary, the universal mother and "mediatrix of all grace." Writing in the provenance of the Courtly Love tradition, Dante casts Virgil as the chivalrous courtier who cannot refuse anything to a woman of noble virtue, especially when that virtue is exponentially raised to the perfect power of three, reaching to the very limit of the silence of divine mystery. Virgil tells the story of his sending as a mirror image of the story of another calling, the Annunciation of the angel Gabriel to Mary, who is in her turn now the initiator of the vocation that reaches Dante through Beatrice and Virgil and begins to turn him in a new direction. Virgil, recounting his solicitation by Beatrice, explains:

> "When she had said this to me, she turned her eyes, which shone with tears, making me the more eager to come; and so, even as she wished, I came to you and rescued you . . . . What, then, is this? Why, why, do you hold back? Why do you harbor such cowardice in your heart? Why are you not bold and free, when in Heaven's court three such blessed ladies are mindful of you, and my words pledge you so great a good?"

As little flowers bent down and closed by chill of night, straighten and all unfold upon their stems when the sun brightens them, such in my faint strength did I become; and so much good courage rushed to my heart that I began, as one set free, "oh, how compassionate was she who helped me and how courteous were you . . . By your words you have made me so eager to come with you that I have returned to my first resolve . . . Now on, for a single will is in us both; you are my leader, you my master and my teacher." So I said to him and when he move on, I entered along the deep and savage way. (*Inf.*, ii, 115–142)

The image literally speaks out of the earth, the oldest of the old, but speaks from beyond the earth at the same time. It does not only speak of the "cycle of life," of day and night, or of seasons where there is no real death or life but just the play of forces, just alternation and alteration. Here there is also initiative and transformation, conversion, a new direction resolved. "Oh, how compassionate was she who helped me." The gift of the other, given after death, through death. This line refers to Beatrice who voluntarily descended all the way into Hell, from a place of joy to a place of sorrow. This is St. Paul's theme of *kenosis*, an "emptying" or a "pouring out," the occurrence of an expropriation. St. Paul uses it with regard to the process of incarnation, and that reference is important here. In the event of incarnation, the Christian imagination envisions the divine "emptying" itself of that mystery which is its divinity and "pouring" itself out into history, by occurring and taking place in history, by taking on himself the form of a "slave" for the sake of other human beings. Beatrice's condescension here, her descent into hell, voluntarily surrendering joy for the sake of another, mirrors the redemptive act in the Christian tradition, which God enacts through the incarnation. She is mirroring this event in the Christian story wherein the divine takes on itself the figure of a human being. To be human is to be enslaved to death; thus, in entering into history, the divine takes on itself openness and vulnerability to suffering, to having something happen to it, to the "other" happening to it, and thus, to dying. Through incarnation the divine passes over into the need, and thus into the passion, the desire of the other. Beatrice willingly takes the risk of being in need, following the necessary pattern of love: to love is to be compassionate (com-passion: suffering with/from another), to identify oneself with the need of the other through suffering. It is the essence of a loving personal relationship to share suffering. Not only to share the suffering of another, but to share one's own suffering, to suffer together. This gesture of compassion on Beatrice's part, Virgil tells Dante, was initiated above and beyond her, by Saint Lucy, his muse or patron saint in the Christian sense. This is probably because she is the Saint of Sight. She is the patroness of eyesight, as she was martyred by having her eyes gouged out. Those who fear for their physical sight go to her, but she is also the patron saint of spiritual insight-inspiration, vision of the soul. Thus she is the Christian muse of the poet. She is his patroness in that regard. She was the one who pointed out to Beatrice that Dante might well wonder where she had gone and what happened to her, why she was not helping him in his need, especially since he had tried to be as loyal to her as he could. This suggests that St. Lucy needed to urge Beatrice to act; although she is Dante's destiny, Beatrice is just another person, still a human being though now dead. Furthermore, the shove delivered by Lucy was initiated by Mary, mother of Jesus. Here an image recurs that was idealized in the *Vita nuova* iii: a feminine trinity as the configuration in Dante's experience of the way in which the divine reveals itself as love. A feminine trinity, three women, who are, in a fashion, the chain of signifiers through which the ultimate Mystery of divine love gradually becomes inscribed in the heart of Dante the man. Virgil is the only one now who can speak to Dante, because Dante has totally lost his sense of who he is except for that last vestige of memory: the promise of writing that had long lain sleeping sealed, as in a tomb. He is a poet. Virgil is his living but spectral connection to the promise of writing, but Virgil's poetry can only speak because of a larger dynamic that connects Dante to another human being he trusts, Beatrice, and Beatrice to God via Mary. In sum, the vocation is from God through Mary, St. Lucy, and Beatrice to our poet.

This evokes one of the most purely poetic sequences of lines in the poem. When Virgil has finished telling the story of how he came to be there, he asks Dante:

> "What is it then? Why, why do you resist? Why does your heart host so much cowardice? Where are your daring and your openness as long as there are three such blessed women concerned for you within the court of Heaven and my words promise you so great a good?" (*Inf.*, ii, 121–126)

Thus he gives Dante two reasons to follow: the love of the three women and his own spectral words as a token of the promise of writing. Then Dante says:

> As little flowers bent down and closed by chill of night, straighten and all unfold upon their stems when the sun brightens them, such in my faint strength did I become; and so much good courage rushed to my heart that I began, as one set free, "oh, how compassionate was she who helped me and how courteous were you . . ." (*Inf.*, ii, 127–132)

Freedom is the capacity to have an identity, to make the journey to identity. The sun, the same sun that shone on the hill that first gave him hope, becomes instrumental here in revealing a different possible signification, indeed a different possibility of signification. The flower that opens at the touch of the sun signifies the "Yes" by which Dante is enabled to walk in the direction to which he has been newly converted, accompanied by Virgil. That "Yes" signifies both the necessity of the gift for the possibility of signification: he will go on this journey *because* he has been called. Dante says, "I began, as one set free, 'O, how compassionate was she who helped me . . .'"

Here is the whole dynamism of Dante's view of freedom as responsibility. Freedom is a gift that another gives. This implies neither passivity nor magic. Rather, it recognizes the human necessity that no gift can be given unless it is accepted. In Dante's radical orthodoxy of Christian imagination, he gets to the heart of the matter. One of the clearest expressions the voice of human freedom can articulate is the response of gratitude. Gratitude is the freest gift that human beings can offer in return for the gift of life, since human existence is always in need, always in the position of depending on help in the form of the gift of the other. But, at the most basic level, gift and gratitude articulate the inescapable aporia that mark the place of Dante's present situation: both gift and gratitude are equally and ultimately impossible. They cannot *be;* yet they are absolutely necessary to the very possibility of responsibility in the mutuality of free relationship. They can only occur *in passing,* in the "passing over" that is the *via diritta* of personal existence, the "straight and narrow" of responsible freedom, the passing over that forgives the Gift of Death, of which writing is not simply the memorial, but memory itself. Human beings do not bring themselves into existence nor do they control the path of existence. If one believes that existence is basically good, then that goodness is accepted as a gift received for which gratitude is the first and the final expression. At the same time, both the gift and the gratitude remain ambiguous and ironic. If Dante speaks here as one who "has been freed," and so speaks of gratitude to the one who helped him, this can be so only in the light of what is yet to come, only in the light of the place of darkness and exile into which he must now enter. So now, free, Dante is free precisely for the taking place of responsibility, which takes places in, as the Inferno, that "land of difficulty and great sweat and tears," which Derrida calls Khora, the place of exile constituted by the not yet of an impossible freedom, which cannot be, but must be forgiven. And so he continues on his journey in the hope of a freedom and an identity for which he will be responsible.

The movement of Canto ii suggests that this relationship between Beatrice and Dante with its intermediary Virgil, and between Beatrice and God with its intermediaries Lucy and Mary, must be read from the perspective of Dante's experience of the existential truth claim that is signified by the Christian theological doctrine of Incarnation. At the same time, without minimizing the power of the truth claim of the particular messianic faith undeniably at work in Dante's poem, it is also possible, perhaps necessary, to respect the radical originality and finality of the freedom that imagines, not simply differently, but as necessarily different in the occurrence of an impossible faith, hope, and love, which can occur only in the process of constant conversion, that is, always only by beginning again. It is therefore necessary that because of Dante's history, and particularly his history as a poet, Virgil's speech here must be read as a chapter in Dante's personal scripture—his testimony to the way in which divine mystery has revealed itself as love occurring in his life. Virgil's story is a revelation, following the metaphoric pattern that recurs in similar fashion within the scriptural traditions of Judaism, Christianity, and Islam. The scriptures are viewed as the telling of a story that reveals God's action in history to make real His love for human beings. The speech by Virgil reveals to Dante *how* God's love is acting in his life: it is acting as a pivot point that passes through Beatrice, beyond her to him, as forgiveness. The journey through the Inferno reveals how that passing over can happen.

## "I DESIRE MERCY, NOT SACRIFICE."

### "I AM NOT ABRAHAM."

*Leave nothing, if possible, in the dark of what related me to Judaism, alliance broken in every aspect (Karet), with perhaps a gluttonous interiorization, and in heterogeneous modes: last of the Jews, what am I [. . .] "the circumcised is the proper" (12–30–76),* that's what my readers won't have known about me, the comma of my breathing henceforward, without continuity but without a break, the changed time of my writing, graphic writing, through having lost its interrupted verticality, almost with every letter, to be bound better and better but be read less and less well over almost twenty years, like my religion about which nobody understands anything, any more than does my mother who asked other people awhile ago, not daring to talk to me about it, if I still believe in God, . . . but she must have known that the constancy of God in my life is called by other names, so that I quite rightly pass for an atheist, the omnipresence to me of what I call God in my absolved, absolutely private language being neither that of an eyewitness nor that of a voice doing anything other than talking to me without saying anything, nor a transcendent law or an imminent *schechina,* that feminine figure of a Yahweh who remains so strange and so familiar to me, *but the secret I am excluded from,* when the secret consists in the fact that you are held to secrecy by those who know your secret, how many are there, and do not dare admit to you that this is no longer a secret for them, that they share with you the open secret, letting you reckon that they know without saying, and, from that point on, what you have neither the right nor the strength to confess, it is just as useless to make it known, to hand over to this public notoriety you are the first and only one to be excluded from, properly theological hypothesis of a blank sacrifice sending the bidding up to infinity, God coming to circulate among the unavowables, unavowable as he remains himself, like a son not bearing my name, like a son not bearing his name, like a son not bearing a name, and if, to give rise to this beyond the name, in view and by reason of this unacceptable appellation of myself for my mother has become silenced without dying, I write that there is *too much* love in my life, emphasizing *too much,* the better and the worse, that would be true, love will have got the better of me, my faithfulness stands any test, I am faithful even to the test that does harm, to my euthanasias. (*Circum.,* 30, 153–157; emphasis added)

Undoubtedly, the comparison of Dante's conversion in writing with Derrida's is asymmetrical. Nevertheless, it is contended here that the comparison is not disproportionate; as religious converts, Dante and Derrida belong together familiarly, familially, even though their relationship is improper, as are all familial relations. The poetic style of the *Commedia* is tightly allegorical in the sense that all the dimensions of its figurative, metaphorical meaning are closely disciplined to attend on the apparent chronology and programmatic structure of the pilgrim's narrative journey. Everything that Dante the poet writes is written from the perspective of the vision to which he finally attains (whatever that vision might mean; indeed, if it can be called a *vision* at all rather than, more properly, a loss of vision, a blindness, an improper vision, or an impossible vision, or better still, a vision of the impossibility of vision, the death—and resurrection—of vision). Such vision can only be written into the body and blood of the narrative account in words that trace the figure of the pilgrim's journey. Pilgrim and poet: different, yet they find themselves together, they exist together *nel mezzo*, and exist only there, at the center of all the circular orbits that together they describe around that center: Inferno, Purgatorio, Paradiso, all orbits of freedom around the center of identity through which all relations of freedom must pass, and in so doing must inscribe themselves ironically in relation to all of the possibilities, differing in their sameness, figuring the differing, performing that differing, different in the possible identities they inscribed in the place of *différance*, the Dark Wood, the Khora, which is no place and all places, the very possibility of taking place, and its impossibility as well.

The figure of Derrida's conversion in the writing of *Circumfession* apparently lacks the strict symmetrical discipline of Dante's tight allegorical structure. Yet it remains proportional to that structure in the figure it cuts and traces in the irony of its being structured *nel mezzo*, between two resurrections, between two witnesses, Geoff and Georgette. It also remains proportional in its being centered around a cut in the flesh and blood of his body and of his writing, his circumcision, which is the mark of separation, of being separated, set apart, excluded, deferred, cut off, from the secret of one's self and of one's name, by which one is identified by the Other, to the Other, for the Other, with the Other. It is around this circumcision that the writing of *Circumfession* circulates, circum-navigating this circumference in the name of three *topoi* that keep inscribing themselves in the sands of the desert of Khora, crying in the wilderness for the name which is lost in the secret which is open to all and from which he is excluded, the secret of the beginning of being chosen for and promised to the impossible. The secret separates; the promise keeps the separation, and death is the keeping of the promise, the crypt of the secret, the irony of cutting off from itself by inscribing itself as the writing of the history of separation.

The irony of *Circumfession*, strictly proportionate to that of the *Commedia*, is that in tracing the history of separation, which is a history of cowardice, of nursing the wound, of trying to keep the secret hidden even though it is a secret open to all the others that must be kept from oneself, by oneself alone: the secret that I am Abraham. This secret is the history of hiding, of cowering and disguising, of deferring the revelation that no one could understand because it is the secret of separation, the secret of secrecy, which cannot be kept: I am Abraham, I am in the name of the Father, I am in the name of the Son, and I am in the name of the Other, the name of the (m)other. I am in the name of the Spirit, the spirit of secrecy, the Holy Ghost, the spectral appearance, the haunting of the desert place, the turning into a ghost of one's self, the going into exile.

The writing of *Circumfession* is the history of cowardice inscribed in the denial of the name of the father by the son: I am not Aeneas, I am not Paul, I am not Abraham, I am not the child of the Secret, nor of the Promise, nor of the sacrifice required to keep the promise, of the sacrifice of being cut off, put to death; I separate myself from all that cuts and separates, so as to keep the secret and the promise, performing in the sacrifice by hiding that I am the son of the father, and hiding especially from the (m)other, Georgette, and Geoff, hiding in the writing until the time when, in the end, it can be confessed and done differently, be forgiven, in writing:

> **Dante:** Ah, how hard it is to tell what that wood was, wild, rugged, harsh; the very thought of it renews the fear! It is so bitter that death is hardly more so. But, to treat of the good I found in it, I will tell of the other things I saw there. (*Inf.*, ii, 4–9)

> **Derrida:** . . . and the fear that has gripped me since always, for to that at least I am faithful, discords with itself, threatens from two apparently contradictory imminences, that of the writer who is afraid of dying before the end of a long sentence, period, without signing the counterexample, and that of the son who, dreading seeing her die before the end of the avowal, for this confession promised onto death, trembles then too at the thought of departing before his mother (*Circum.*, 10, 50–51) . . . and if . . . I write that there is too much love in my life, emphasizing too much, the better and worse, that would be true, love will have got the better of me, my faithfulness stands any test, I am faithful even to the test that does harm, to my euthanasias. (*Circum.*, 30, 157)

In *Circumfession*, Derrida mirrors in reverse Dante's image of himself as a "little flower" that opens on its stem at the touch of the sun, in the light of Virgil's revelation of the constancy of Beatrice's love when he recalls a scene of his mother, "she was holding my hand," on the way to nursery school, and wishing to stay with her, he invents an illness, but is left nonetheless:

> . . . whence the tears when later in the afternoon, from the playground, I caught sight of her through the fence, she must have been as beautiful as a photograph, and I reproached her for leaving me in the world, in the hands

of others, basically with having forgotten that I was supposed to be ill so as
to stay with her, just according to our very alliance, on of our 59 conjurations
without which I am nothing, accusing her in this way letting me be caught
up by school, all of those cruel mistresses. (*Circum.*, 51, 272)

Derrida, but also Dante, bereft by Beatrice's death in the *Vita nuova*, lost
and abandoned in the Dark Wood before Virgil's revelation of her call. Abandonment and Call: opposite experiences to be sure, but only possible within
the same relationship. Possible only where both abandonment and rescue are
real possibilities; only where there is love, which is of course impossible. The
constancy of the call that keeps the promise is the voice of the Other/woman
who speaks in memory and beckons to turn around and remember again in
a new way. "The voice of one who cries in the wilderness," of one and the
other who cries tears in the desert of abandonment—the *topos* of exile, the
Khora that is nowhere and everywhere, the place of separation and of difficulty, of fasting and of the salt bread of another's hospitality and help. "Make
straight the way" is the call to turn back, to convert, to take another way, to
take another's way, to turn back and make straight the way for the Other, to
make straight for the place of the Other, the one who waters the desert with
her tears and makes of it another place, who lets love take place, who lets love
get the better of me—the other me, the secret of me.

## "Mɪ mɪse dentro le segrete cose" (*Inf.*, iii, 21)

> Such is the secret truth of faith as absolute responsibility and as abso-
> lute passion, the "highest passion" as Kierkegaard will say; it is a passion that,
> sworn to secrecy, cannot be transmitted from generation to generation. In
> this sense it has no history. This intransmissibility of the highest passion,
> the normal condition of faith which is thus bound to secrecy, nevertheless
> dictates to us the following: we must always start over. (*GD*, 80)

The inscription by Dante the poet of the whole the pilgrim's journey of
conversion *"nel mezzo,"* the circum-scription of the end back into the beginning, is an artful way of making a narrative out of an event that has no history,
which happens "in an instant." The fictive time of the narrative is seven nights
and days, the same fictive time as the Genesis narrative, the allegorical figure
of the secret time of beginning. The seven days also figure the time of the
event of another beginning, the Paschal mystery, the Christian *mysterium tre-*
*mendum,* the mystery that makes one "fear and tremble," the passion and resurrection of Jesus. Dante goes to great lengths to punctuate quite precisely the
fictive time-sequence of the pilgrim's journey in order to heighten the irony
of a movement that takes no time and goes nowhere and yet centers all its
circumstantial episodes. The passage through Hell traces the steps of one of
the epicycles of that movement. It marks the passing through the center of the
personal narrative history that deconstructs both of the cosmic narratives that

circulate together with it in distinct orbits around the secret point of intersection of three diametric questions: Who am I? What do I love when I love my God? and Who is Jesus? Hell is the place where the story that Dante has written of himself in *Vita nuova* unravels itself and comes undone and then begins its conversion into another story. It is also the place where the story of Abraham dissolves into the unspeakable paradoxes of faith that must always begin again. Finally, Hell marks the place where the secret of the double gift of death given by Jesus is encrypted in the tomb that refuses to give up its dead. The passage through Hell traces the death-spiral downward into the maw of Satan, where the secret of beginning is consumed and digested, disappearing without a trace, finally frozen over in the icy depths of the un-center in which all fire of passion has gone out, the black hole of un-beginning. "Abandon all hope who enter here," where the secret promise of the gift of death is kept by its refusal, by refusing to begin again, by refusing to pass on, by refusing to pass over into an Other way of keeping the Secret of all beginnings. Hell is the place where the finality of a decision made "in the instant" deconstructs itself into all the twists and turns of the city that refuses God-or death.

The third of the four essays which comprise *The Gift of Death* returns to the point where the history of religion as responsibility that Patočka traces broke off at the end of the first essay. Here we return to the story traced by Patočka of the incorporation and repression by the Christian *mysterium tremendum* of the forms of mystery designated by the orgiastic impulse toward fusion and the Platonic discipline that releases the immortal soul from its incorporation in the tomb of the body.[8] Following the text of Kierkegaard's *Fear and Trembling,* Derrida traces the *mysterium tremendum* back to its beginning inscribed in the story of Abraham. Trembling, he says, is a symptom of secrecy: of being "in secret," being in on a secret, being already overtaken by one does not know what, and of which one does not when, where, how, why or, most terrible, even whether it will come again. Trembling reveals the secret of time and also the time of secrecy. Trembling registers both the past and the future of the secrecy with which human existence is always concerned: the secrecy of the impossibility of all its possibilities, the secrecy of death:

> I tremble at what exceeds my seeing and my knowing although it concerns the innermost parts of me, right down to my soul, down to the bone, as we say. In as much as it tends to undo both seeing and knowing, trembling is indeed an experience of secrecy or of mystery, but another secret, another enigma, or another mystery comes on top of the unlivable experience, adding yet another seal or concealment to the tremor. (*GD,* 54)

What makes us tremble in the *mysterium tremendum,* Derrida says, is God-or death. God-or death: both name, in the form of a signature, the final necessity of the Other, the need of the Other that is inscribed in the heart. Trembling is the registration in the heart of the need of the Other, the necessity of being cut off from the Other. God-or death both attest to the singularity of

every person, to the impossibility which is inscribed into the identity of each
person, to the need for one's living to be witnessed and the necessity to die
alone. Together these finalities form the polarity of existence, separated from
one another by nothing, correlating with one another in the mirrors of time and
space, in the khoral-play of the no-place where all takes place and is inscribed,
recorded, remembered.

Derrida, however, names a third, more proximate cause of the double seal
that trembling places on the secret it conceals, the infinite gift of love:

> the dissymmetry that exists between the divine regard that sees me, and
> myself, who doesn't see what is looking at me; it is the gift and endurance
> of death that exists in the irreplaceable, the disproportion between the infi-
> nite gift and my finitude, responsibility as culpability, sin, salvation, repen-
> tance and sacrifice . . . We fear and tremble because the inaccessible secret
> of a God who decides for us although we remain responsible, that is, free to
> decide, to work, to assume our life and our death. (GD, 55–56)

Trembling registers in time and space the distance, the openness of the
love which takes place as absence. "Without knowing from whence the thing
comes and what awaits us, we are given over to absolute solitude" (GD, 57). In
this solitude, Derrida says, no one can speak with us or for us; we must take it
on ourselves in the way that Heidegger speaks of the necessity to take on oneself (sich aufnehmen) the necessity of the death that must be "my own," to take
responsibility for the impropriety of death, the taking away of all possibilities,
the expropriation that is most properly mine, my own wholly Other.

The sacrifice that God asks of Abraham on Mount Moriah situates the
experience of Fear and Trembling. Mount Moriah is the apex, the acuity, the
peak experience of the secret for which Abraham becomes responsible in the
name of God, in the face of death, in the boundless openness of love. Mount
Moriah is also the hill that Dante fails to climb in the opening canto of the
poem; it is the inverted mountain into which Dante and Virgil descend in
the death spirals of Hell; it is Mount Purgatory; it is the double inversion of
the spheres of Heaven that mirror the circles of Hell, reaching outward to
the beyond of the Empyrean that reverses the movement yet again toward
the inaccessible secret of the center. All are the one mountain that must be
climbed to the peak of passion at which occurs the instant of decision around
which the possibilities of finality circle, depending on the singularity of a "Yes!"
or of a "No!" In the instant of decision regarding the acceptance or refusal of
the need of the Other, the decision that can only be taken in the face of the
Other, all patterns of substitution are finally canceled:

> . . . sacrifice supposes the putting to death of the unique in terms of its
> being unique, irreplaceable, and most precious. It also therefore refers to the
> impossibility of substitution, the unsubstitutable; and then also to the sub-
> stitution of an animal for man; and finally, especially this, by means of this

impossible substitution itself, it refers to what links the sacred to sacrifice and sacrifice to secrecy. (*GD*, 58)

It is the impossibility of substitution that implies the necessity of the suspension of the ethical order, at the same time that and on the same authority by which it enjoins faith to solitude and silence. Giving reasons, offering an account for one's actions, being accountable, speaking at all of the need for sacrifice involves the singular in the field of generality, there to be lost. King Lear says to his ungrateful daughters, "Reason not the need." But having already spoken, now speaking with them again, he dissolves the imperative of his command, cancels its authority, and necessarily slips into the pathos of tragedy. Sacrifice cancels tragic pathos in a higher, more acute passion. For Derrida, this is the aporia of responsibility:

> One always risks not managing to accede to the concept of responsibility in the process of *forming* it. For responsibility (we would no longer dare speak of the "universal concept of responsibility") demands on the one hand an accounting, a general answering-for-oneself with respect to the general and before the generality, hence the idea of substitution, and, on the other hand, uniqueness, absolute singularity, hence non-substitution, non-repetition, silence, and secrecy. What I am saying here about responsibility can also be said about decision. The ethical involves me in substitution, as does speaking. Whence the insolence of the paradox: for Abraham, Kierkegaard declares, *the ethical is a temptation*. (*GD*, 61)

Here Derrida's way of writing takes a turn into what Caputo refers to as "the quasi-transcendental."[9] This means that what Derrida refers to here as "absolute responsibility" reflects the aporetic structure of the experience of which it tries to speak. Absolute responsibility cannot be derived from a concept of responsibility, so it must remain inconceivable and even unthinkable. Therefore, it cannot answer for or explain itself; absolute responsibility undergoes the humiliation of being unable to take responsibility for itself, and so necessarily appears as irresponsibility. Nevertheless, what cannot be thought here still can and must be done. The impossible idea becomes a necessity about which Abraham has a choice, a possibility about which he alone must decide. Responsibility does not exist as a being or as Absolute Being; absolute responsibility is a real possibility only in the moment of decision. This turn, this conversion in Derrida's way of writing, which for a long time had insisted on the impossibility of finality, the impossibility of the absolute occurring in writing, insisted on writing as the trace of the cut that separates and cuts off writing from ever reaching its end, its *finis*, now points toward and remarks a finality that marks "the instant" of decision, the absolute responsibility for keeping the secret of the end that is inscribed in the beginning.[10] This insistence marks the confessional turn that Derrida has taken in following St. Augustine in *Circumfession*, understanding "confession" as the imperative, the

divine command, the necessity to testify, in writing, to the absolute responsibility "to do the truth in love." Absolute responsibility to the absolute Other,
God-or death; the absolute, final truth of love that cannot be thought, must be
thought impossible. With God-or death, all possibilities become impossible;
yet with God-or death, the Impossible, all things are possible.

This conversion that transpires between the impossible and the possible
at the inspiration of love also comprises all the other elements of the sacrificial
structure of the *mysterium tremendum,* all that comes to tremble at the spectacle of sacrifice. Love inspires this absolute mutuality of exchange and gra-
tuity of gift-giving and receiving that flows in excess between the divine and
the human, between the temporal and eternal, between the living and the dead,
between presence and absence, and even between love and hate. In another
idiom it might disseminate itself in the field of meaning that St. Paul designates
with the notion of *kenosis.* This form of excessive exchange and absolute conversion institutes a new order, a new form of imperative, a new imperium, a new
authority, command, reign—later to be called the Kingdom of God on earth—
an order that commands a time and space structure different than that of orgiastic fusion or the disciplined economy of ethical exchange with the accrual of
interest credited as immortality. Its space is khoral, difficult terrain, here in the
figure of the mountain rather than the desert; its time is kaironic, the time of
the *kairos,* the instant of "grace," or "gift," the temporality of the "peak" moment,
the uniquely, absolutely right moment, where "right" signifies the hyperbole of
any calculated, relative order of validity or justification. It is in the sense of this
"peak moment," that Kierkegaard and Derrida account for contradiction, the
countermanding of all commands, including especially the commands of ethical responsibility and duty, in favor of the order of the singular and unique, the
order of time and space instantiated in an "instant." Kierkegaard says:

> . . . for it is indeed this love for Isaac that makes [Abraham's] act a sac-
> rifice by its paradoxical contrast to his love for God. But the distress and
> the anxiety in the paradox is that he, humanly speaking, is thoroughly inca-
> pable of making himself understandable. Only *in the instant* when his act is
> in absolute contradiction to his feelings, only then does he sacrifice Isaac, but
> the reality of his act is that by which he belongs to the universal, and there he
> is and remains a murderer. [74, translation modified—DW] (*GD,* 65)

And Derrida adds,

> "The instant of decision is madness," Kierkegaard says elsewhere. The
> paradox cannot be grasped in time and through mediation, that is to say, in
> language and through reason. Like the gift and the "gift of death," it remains
> irreducible to presence or to presentation; it demands a temporality of the
> instant without ever constituting a present. (*GD,* 65)

In the order of "the instant," all trembles in suspense and enters into a
suspension of all standing orders, including that of the ethical imperative,

the universal order. This is what Derrida signals with a reference to "absolute responsibility": not simply a responsibility that has been absolved from conditions, but rather the "dissolving" of the impulse toward fixity of conditions, "absolute absolution," the absence of all "solution," the acknowledgment of a movement and moment of dis-solution, the suspension of all standing orders, which leaves them standing while accepting their powerlessness to take hold, to provide a foothold in the difficult and unknown terrain of Mount Moriah. The instance of decision and absolute responsibility constitutes the "leap of faith," the instant of suspension in the abyss of singularity, silence and solitude, catalyzed by the contradiction of two loves, the contradiction that converts love into hate, the conversion that sacrifice requires:

> The contradiction and the paradox must be endured *in the instant itself.* The two duties must contradict one another, one must subordinate (incorporate, repress) the other. Abraham must assume absolute responsibility for sacrificing his son by sacrificing ethics, but in order for there to be a sacrifice, the ethical must retain all its value; the love for his son must remain intact, and the order of human duty must continue to insist on its rights. (*GD,* 66)

Here Derrida reestablishes contact with the first essay of *The Gift of Death,* where he engaged Patočka's rendering of the history of religion and the history of Europe as a history of responsibility that, because it is history, remains open. Therefore, it is history that has not altogether been thought through, because it cannot be thought through, not through and through. It is a history that remains in suspense, a history yet to be decided, and in the third essay of *The Gift of Death,* Derrida seems to be suggesting that precisely what remains to be thought through, despite the impossibility of doing so, is the relation of responsibility to sacrifice. Abraham is a gate through which the history of European religious responsibility has passed and must always pass through again anew (*per me si va*). Indeed, the story of Abraham retells in a different way what Dante's pilgrim reads inscribed on the Gates of Hell: "Through me you pass into the instant of decision, which is absolutely final, authorized, and commanded by the love whose justice is impossible, but which must be done nevertheless. Abandon hope who enter here." But Virgil-Derrida immediately adds: "Have faith!" The inscription can be read in yet another way: Hell is the story of Abraham read without faith, without Abramic faith, without faithful reading, and so refused—and rightly so, responsibly and ethically refused, for in general and for the generality the story is impossible. Hell is the instant of the refusal of sacrifice, a refusal to be in *Fear and Trembling,* a refusal to pass through the Gate of Abraham, the Gate of sacrifice, "while living" in the instant of deciding to live by giving the Gift of Death. To enter through the gates of Hell is to pass beyond the grasp of ethics and the just, to pass beyond reading the world in that way, and thus to be in need of another reading. Indeed, in the ironic vision of the poet, who sees differently than does the pilgrim, Abraham himself is the Gates of Hell through which one must pass in faith or else abandon hope, finally and absolutely. By refusing the instant decision to give the gift of death through sacrifice all hope is lost that in this instant Issac will be restored by virtue of the Impossible, as the Gift of Death. So sacrifice must not be refused, not done away with, not yet, not by Abraham. For the demand for sacrifice came from God, so it must not be refused or simply postponed through substitution; it must be withdrawn, absolutely. This gate must be entered because it leads to another passage, tremendously distant in nontime and nonspace, another trembling at another secret, another sacrifice, another way of making holy, sacrifice and secret redoubled, hyperbolically hidden and encrypted beyond sacrificial murder in the return of the incorporated and repressed. Beyond Abraham, beyond the beginning, there awaits Another, the oldest of the old, at the center, at the turning point, in the instant of conversion. There the secret seal of sacrifice must be broken to reveal its empty truth, its empty tomb.

Hell is the place of refusal to give the gift of death as the absolute responsibility of freedom, opened up by the need for sacrifice—a divine need, the need of the divine. If Yahweh's command to sacrifice Isaac does not originate in need, if it is not strictly and absolutely necessary, if it is not already contained in the Secret of beginning, then it is arbitrary, capricious, the need of a goat or ram, a bull or a pigeon-dove, a bestial need, sheer brutality and cruelty. If the command to sacrifice his son does not find its necessity and authority in the need of love, if it is not itself a gift, then it cannot occasion the ability to respond with the offer of a gift. It cannot then evoke and reveal the possibility of an impossible hope of an impossible justice; it cannot open up the possibility of doing justice to love, of doing the truth in love. If the sacrifice of human life is not a necessity born of divine need, then there can be no responsibility in offering the gift of death, there can be no real choice, no possible refusal and no freedom. But then too, the covenant between God and Abraham, the vocation to which it is the calling, can hold no promise, and the circumcision that is the mark of the covenant traced in the flesh cannot be read as the inscription and circum-scription of an absolute alliance in which freedom takes the form of a ring, of a reciprocity and circularity that is neither economical nor equal, neither fair nor right, but nonetheless faithfully keeps the secret promise of beginning, which is always excessive, always exceeds the resources of what already is, of whatever is present, present at hand and ready to hand. The ring of the alliance, drawn in the flesh as the mark of the covenant, is the signature of a necessary withdrawal, an overdraw, a promissory note that admits the need of supplement. If the authority of the divine command does not lie in the humiliating acknowledgment of a debt that exceeds the resources of the one who withdraws to presently make good; *if, in other words, Yahweh's command itself is not absolutely irresponsible, then Abraham's faith is in vain.* It remains faith in an alliance that lacks the legitimacy of paradox, lacks the authority of the full faith and credit of one who seeks credit to cover an excessive withdrawal for the sake of a velleity, a need which is not absolutely necessary, to comply with an imperative that is merely hypothetical, not categorical. Obligation can be "justified" only by a need that cannot be covered, by necessity that cannot be canceled. Love names the excess of need which is the secret promise of beginning, the secret that the promise of all beginning is empty, overdrawn, excessive beyond all hope of justification, so that the secret promise of the beginning can only be sustained by an alliance of mutuality in gift-giving that gives full faith and credit where none is due, but is, nonetheless, absolutely necessary. Faith is not faith unless it is faith in the impossible and a doing of the impossible truth in Love. The faith of love requires passing through the gate of sacrifice, giving the gift of death, in order to give credit for the gift of life, which is always excessive. As such it gives and takes nothing except what is necessary, what originates in a need that makes necessity and opens up the originally impossible possibility of a freedom that is not merely optional, a choice where acceptance or refusal makes the real difference. The choice of a faith that must pass through the Gate of Abraham, the gate of sacrifice, must pass through in order to pass beyond it, must do so because the demand for sacrifice must be passed over so that it can pass on to forgiveness: Yahweh must be forgiven the absolute irresponsibility of the demand for human sacrifice, the sacrifice of the beloved son, of (all) the other Others.

Derrida identifies the necessity of excess as the condition of absolute responsibility by recognizing the way it is inscribed in and circumscribes the structure of relational identity as a whole, an integrity that constantly exceeds its own capacity, and so can never take account or give account of itself, except by faith, extending credit to the insolvency of the Other, except by entering into the "absolute absolution" of the other, the double genitive of absolving:

> Duty or responsibility binds me to the other, to the other as other, and ties me in my absolute singularity to the other as other. God is the name of the absolute other as other and as unique (the God of Abraham defined as the one and unique) . . . But of course, what binds me thus in my singularity to the absolute singularity of the other, immediately propels me into the space or risk of absolute sacrifice. There are also others, an infinite number of them . . . I cannot respond to the call, the request, the obligation, or even the love of another without sacrificing the other other, the other others. Every other (one) is every (bit) other *[tout autre est tout autre]*, everyone else is completely or wholly other. (*GD*, 68)

Because the simple concepts of alterity and singularity constitute in themselves the structure of responsibility, obligation, and decision, the structure is absolutely ringed around and hemmed in, circumscribed by "paradox, scandal and aporia" (*GD*, 68). This is itself a revelation about sacrifice as a style of love: sacrifice is a way of writing in blood, of inscribing in the flesh and on the heart, in the mind and on the lips, the name of the Other, which must not be written or spoken more casually. Sacrifice is the signature of the Other as other. Sacrifice reveals the limit, the front, the contested borderline between what cannot be said or thought and what must be done (*GD*, 68). Sacrifice is the revelation of the mutuality of need arising from the excess of the gift to which all are party, divine and human and world, a mutuality of the need that all are covenant bound to sustain and uphold, an alliance of freedom which is so absolutely necessary in its mutuality that, whether the gift-giving is accepted or refused, it identifies each one always and everywhere by its mark. Abraham's story is the Gate to the place of final refusal, where that refusal identifies each one through their "countersignature," the "No!" by which each signs him- or herself as the bond of the need of every other, the stoke that marks the refusal of what is necessary:

> Day and night and every instant, on all the Mount Moriahs of this world I am doing that, raising my knife over what I love and must love, over those to whom I owe absolute fidelity, incommensurably. Abraham is faithful to God only in his absolute treachery, in the betrayal of his own and of the uniqueness of each one of them, exemplified here in his only beloved son. He would not be able to opt for fidelity to his own, or to his son, unless he were to betray the absolute other: God, if you wish. (*GD*, 68–69)

What Derrida does not say here, nor does Kierkegaard, though they both point emphatically in that direction, is that what binds Abraham to his covenant with Yahweh, also binds Yahweh to Abraham as well, even if it binds them differently. As a result, the essay concludes with several gestures of indirection, several different ways of not saying directly what remains unsaid, necessarily so, because it cannot be said directly, even paradoxically, hyperbolically or aporetically—but nonetheless must, and therefore can, be done. What must be done and can be done in love is possible, and as possibility contains within itself a difference, a way of differing and of deferring, an ambiguity and ambivalence about going on. Heaven and Hell for Dante named the ambivalence of freedom that allows difference, allows Yes and allows No in the absoluteness of the need of the Other.

In considering the possibility that God suspends the command to sacrifice Isaac because God is satisfied with the terror that the command has provoked in Abraham—"I know now that thou fearest God, seeing thou hast not withheld thy son, thy only son from me" (Gen. 22:12)—Derrida sees another possible reading:

> But it can also be translated or argued as follows: I see that you have understood what absolute duty means, namely how to respond to the absolute other, to his call, request or command. These different registers amount to the same thing: by commanding Abraham to sacrifice his son, to put his son to death by offering a gift of death to God, by means of this double gift wherein the gift of death consists in putting to death by raising one's knife over someone and of putting death forward by giving it as an offering, *God leaves him free to refuse—and that is the test.* (*GD*, 71–72; emphasis added)

God acknowledges the mutuality of the need for the gift of life to be sealed and countersigned by leaving Abraham free to refuse and so free to accept. In dispensing the sacrifice, God acknowledges that Abraham has, in the instant of the decision, already sacrificed Isaac, and in so doing has returned God's prayer back to him, asking a gift of death, making a prayer that God do the impossible in love (*GD,* 72).

Derrida makes the first of the gestures of indirection with which he concludes the essay by calling attention to the "absence of woman" in the Abraham story; Sarah, the mother, is precisely the one to whom nothing is said (*GD,* 75–76). The sacrificial structure is configured among and by males alone: God the Father, Abraham, Isaac. Would it make a difference in the sacrificial logic of the covenant if another other, one of the others, were to be inscribed into the story and allowed to deconstruct that logic by allowing a different style of writing in the flesh to occur? What difference would such a difference make? Derrida asks:

> Does the system of this sacrificial responsibility and of the double "gift of death," imply at its very basis an exclusion or sacrifice of woman? A woman's sacrifice or a sacrifice of a woman, according to one sense of the genitive or the other? Let us leave the question in suspense. (*GD,* 76)

The reference to the double sense of the genitive here raises the question, though only in suspension, of a conceptual grammar and seminal semiotics that is other than the conceptuality and semiotics of the general and the universal, a conceptuality and semiotics of the unique and the singular, of the singular person and of the beginning of the history of persons and therefore of freedom, responsibility, and religion. By raising and suspending the question of the difference it might make to the consideration of absolute responsibility to introduce a maternal rather than a paternal genitive, a maternal story of genesis, a woman's way of "making holy," which differs from and defers the paternal way of sacrifice, Derrida's account turns itself into an account of the irony of Abraham's style of responding and taking responsibility, an irony that suggests something both other than and more than it says or even could say. Irony is another way of keeping the secret promise of beginning. Referring to Kierkegaard's treatment of Socratic irony in *The Concept of Irony* as dissimulation, as questioning by declaring ignorance, Derrida quotes Kierkegaard in *Fearing and Trembling:*

> But a final word by Abraham has been preserved, and in so far as I can understand the paradox, I can also understand Abraham's total presence in that word [*"God himself will provide the offering."*]. First and foremost, he does not say anything, and in that form he says what he has to say [he leaves God free—to refuse]. His response to Isaac is in the form of irony, for it is always irony when I say something and still do not say anything. (Quoted in *GD,* 76–77; emphasis added)

Derrida then goes on to suggest: Perhaps irony would permit us to find something like a common thread in the questions he has just posed regarding maternity and sacrifice and what Hegel said about woman: that she is the "eternal irony of the community" (*GD*, 77).[11]

The question of irony unites the question of woman and the question of God. The absence of woman in the story and the irony of Abraham's response to Isaac, "God himself will provide the offering," leaves in suspense the question of how God will provide, not the substitute offering of the ram that takes the place of the Isaac, a substitution that suspends and postpones the question that Abraham by his decision has turned back toward God, returned to God what God has already given him, prior to God's request that he give Isaac the gift of death and give to God the gift of Isaac's death, prior even to the gift of Isaac himself, who embodies the gift of the promise of the covenant. Rather, prior to all these gifts and to the whole history of that covenant, as the condition of its having a promising history of gift-giving, is the *risk* of freedom: the possibility of giving or withholding, accepting or refusing, all gifts whatsoever. The original possibility of either a gift of death or a gift of life lies in the ambiguity of freedom. Freedom is the Impossibility that is before the Gift, and it is that Impossibility that the story of Abraham keeps as its secret. It is this ambiguous impossible possibility of freedom that Abraham now returns to God in the irony of his response to Isaac by leaving to God whether to accept or refuse his decision, thus turning it ironically into a question, *How* will God provide the offering? How will the offering pass on and pass over and always begin again? "The decision," Derrida says, "is always a secret." That is to say, it is always involved with the secret of beginning, which is history, the need to begin again, to begin the gift-giving again in a new gift of excess that renews the emptiness of the secret that can sustain itself in no other way. This prompts Derrida to suggest that perhaps what we share with Abraham is precisely this secrecy, this freedom, this secret of freedom.

But what does it mean to share a secret? It cannot mean to know anything, for Abraham doesn't know what God will do, and he goes on not knowing even after the dispensation of the sacrifice. Faith is not faith if it is sure of itself, which is to say, when it is sure of the other: not just whether, but even more, *how* the other will be faithful to the promise; how the other will do the impossible or how the other will ask that one be faithful, even if that too is impossible. Hence the need always to start over; that is, to begin again, to remain, to keep, to be in secret:

> Our faith is not assured, because faith can never be, it must never be a certainty. We share with Abraham what cannot be shared, a secret we know nothing about, neither him nor us . . . To share a secret is not to know or to reveal the secret, it is to share or know we know not what: nothing that can be determined. What is a secret that is a secret about nothing and a sharing that doesn't share anything?

Such is the secret truth of faith as absolute responsibility and as absolute passion, the "highest passion" as Kierkegaard will say; it is a passion that, sworn to secrecy, cannot be transmitted from generation to generation. In this sense it has no history. This untransmissibility of the highest passion, the normal condition of a faith which is thus bound to secrecy, nevertheless dictates to us the following: *we must always start over*. A secret can be transmitted, but in transmitting a secret as a secret that remains secret, has one transmitted at all? Does it amount to history, to a story? Yes and no. The epilogue of *Fear and Trembling* repeats, in sentence after sentence, that this highest passion that is faith must be started over by each generation. Each generation must begin again to involve itself in it without counting on the generation before. It thus describes the nonhistory of absolute beginnings which are repeated, and the very historicity that presupposes a tradition to be reinvented each step of the way, in this incessant repetition of the absolute beginning. (*GD*, 80; emphasis added)

History must begin again anew with each new generation. History is the movement of new generations, new stories of new generations, different ways of generating new generations, different stories of genesis, different stories of different ways of giving birth (the gift of life) and of giving death (the gift of death).

Derrida says that *Fear and Trembling* "hesitates" between three generations in the lineage of the so-called religions of the Book: Jewish, Christian, and Islamic. Derrida notes that as a Christian writer, Kierkegaard ends *Fear and Trembling* by reinscribing it within a space that seems, in its literality at least, to be evangelical. This does not by any means exclude a Judaic or Islamic reading, but it does, precisely in its "literality," gesture toward a different generation and a different story of generation, a different way of beginning again. The evangelical text that Derrida thinks is orienting Kierkegaard's interpretation of the Abraham story is not cited by Kierkegaard; it is simply suggested, "but this time without the quotation marks, thus being clearly brought to the attention of those who know their texts" (*GD*, 81). The smallest gesture, a slight change of direction, the removal of the quotation marks, which are themselves the mark of a suspension, a change of voice, this suspension of a suspension, marks in Kierkegaard's text a gesture toward a new style of storytelling and of generation. Derrida locates the origin of his suspicion of a suspension occurring in the text of *Fear and Trembling* precisely where Kierkegaard says:

But there was no one who could understand Abraham. And yet what did he achieve? He remained true to his love. But anyone who loves God needs no tears, no admiration; he forgets the suffering in the love. Indeed so completely has he forgotten it that there would not be the slightest trace of his suffering left if God himself did not remember it, *for he sees in secret* and recognizes distress and counts the tears and forgets nothing.

Thus, either there is a paradox, that the single individual stands in an
absolute relation to the absolute, or Abraham is lost. (Quoted in *GD*, 81;
Derrida's emphasis)

Either/or—the paradox. Either God sees in secret or Abraham is lost.
What God sees in secret, we do not know, except he recognizes distress, presumably by "counting tears." God reads the text of tears, the writing in water,
that traces Abraham's figure among the secret things (*le segrete cose*) and saves
him from being among the lost, among those lost for refusal of the gift of death
given as the need for love, the need for love to begin again, to be converted by
passing through the gate of sacrifice into a new beginning. God witnesses in
secret and keeps in mind the secret of those who keep faith in the promise that
is written in their flesh, written as flesh and blood and tears. Death is rewritten
as trans-mission: passing on, passing through, passing over. "Do not hinder his
fatal (*fatale*, literally 'fated') passing on; thus is it willed over there where One
can do what one wants; and ask no more." (*"Non impedir lo suo fatale andare;
vuolsi così colà dove si puote ciò che si vuole; e più non dimandare."* *Inf.*, v, 22–24;
my translation)

The pilgrim Dante's passage through Hell is written as a deconstruction
of death. It deconstructs a certain reading of death as loss, final loss, the loss
of death as the gift which supplements the gift of life that allows the secret
promise, the covenant, which binds the two together, as if they were divine
and human, Abraham and Elohim, to be transmitted, passed on ironically,
as if they were and were not a history, a story. It is a deconstruction of a
certain story of Hell—Hell is, after all, a story—the story of Hell as a punishment imposed by divine power. In the *Commedia*, Hell is structured as a
narrative, an interpretive narrative: as the place of damnation, of malediction,
the hard, harsh saying that is inscribed its gates as a condemnation that
predicts and prejudices, that verdicts and contradicts the hope of the future
absolutely, finally closing off the secret promise of beginning, of finally beginning, beginning and always beginning again. But the malediction of Hell is
contained in the narrative that each of the damned speaks for him- or herself.
Hell's malediction lies in the story by which each identifies him- or herself.
The malediction of Hell is the last word of the form of writing in flesh and
blood and tears that calls in the wilderness, the calling for the future, calling
for the future to come as judgment, to come ironically as "Yes!" and "No!" to
come as freedom; to come from over there, where one can do as one wills, to
right here, where justice must be done here and now, in the instant, in the
time without time and in the space without space, in the time and space of
the decision that is final because it has always already done what it is ready
to do. The instant of decision, where and when *to will* and *to do* are one and
the same, is the place where all history takes place, the absolute place, for
which Dante's realms of the "afterlife," Inferno, Purgatory, and Paradise, are
truthful metaphors. In the instant of decision, the divine and human are one

in a mutuality and reciprocity that is absolute necessity and absolute freedom together, absolute responsibility, an exchange of gifts in the form of the promise to keep the secret of all stories of beginning, to keep the secret by remaining in secret, to identify with the secret, through the secret, by passing on the secret, by passing judgment on the secret, by passing the secret on, transmitting it in the judgment of identity, doing justice to the one, the one who is to come, prophesying the future by witnessing to the need to do justice, to do the truth in love and take absolute responsibility, to see in secret and be seen in secret, to see face-to-face, to know and be known, to be called by name and to respond, "Here I am; Ready!" Ready to be named, to be identified, finally, for all new beginnings, ready to start over, to keep passing on; ready to prophesy, to write judgment in flesh and blood and tears, ready for the one who is to come.

As a text, the *Inferno* deconstructs death, or at least one story of death, one of its possible readings: death as the judgment and punishment of sin, death as damnation. As such, it can be read straightforwardly as tracing the figures of prophetic judgment and messianic justice that Caputo identifies as characteristic of Derrida's religion without religion. The literal level of the Inferno's narrative, however, which recounts the progress of Dante the pilgrim through this narrative of judgment and justice has written into it a structural irony that requires that the narrative be read as having another meaning, a level of "other-meaning," which is itself three levels of meaning in one: the allegorical, the moral, and the anagogical.[12] Through this formal structure of interpretation, which already had 2,000 years, at least, of tradition and sophistication concentrated within it, Dante the poet is attempting to write the narrative of Hell in another way, *in alleon,* in a way in which Derrida might interpret as writing in the way of the Other, writing the Other of the literal way, but also as the writing of the Other, the way the Other rewrites the pilgrim's way, the conversion of the pilgrim's way into the Other's way. Indeed, from a perspective like Derrida's, the possible plays of irony opened up by this double interpretive structure, itself containing a tripling turn could come, symbolically at least, to be thought of as extending without limit. Of course, in one sense it would be true for Derrida that any important text contains within itself dynamics of auto-deconstruction, traces of other ways it could be read that are, in their impropriety, as truthful as any of its possible "proper" readings. It might well be that the *Inferno* is a deconstructive reading of the received medieval tradition of Hell and damnation, of the final judgment and punishment of sin, but this would not be the same as a deconstruction of that deconstructive reading, for as Derrida would no doubt observe, *"tout autre est tout autre,"* or loosely rendered, "every other (story) is another whole story," and would itself require (of itself) deconstruction. Nevertheless, *différance* should make a difference, at least with regard to deconstructive reading. Texts that write out a deconstruction of other texts, "right out in the open," so to speak, might well auto-deconstruct themselves differently than other texts do. Furthermore, even this is to view deconstruction in terms of generality, texts in general, deconstructive texts in general instead of as the singularities, unique and irreplaceable.

In short: Dante's poem as a whole, his *Commedia,* and for the moment, in the instant, the *Inferno* in particular, is a singularity; it is altogether, irreplaceably Other. Among the characteristics of this singularity is the peculiar irony of its allegorical style, the irony that is written into its narrative structure by the double genitive of that structure, the way of the pilgrim and the way of the poet, who are genuinely other to one another, *"tout autre est tout autre."* The irony of the allegorical structure makes the poem singularly "modern" in its resulting concern with the issues of personal identity and freedom, and singularly "postmodern" in its awareness not simply of the need for deconstructive reading(s), but much more in its adeptness at making those gestures of indirection by which it converts itself, changes direction, gives itself a new heading and acknowledges the need of faith to go on, to start over, to begin where one ends and end where one begins, *nel mezzo.* By inscribing its narrative structure into the "instant" of the allegorical temporality of liturgical commemoration of the Paschal Mystery, of the Jewish feast of Passover and the Christian feast of the Passion and Resurrection of Jesus, as well as mirroring the seven days of Creation in *Genesis* in the seven days of the pilgrim's journey, the structure of the *Commedia* as a whole fictively transcribes the ironic structure that Derrida finds written into the story of Abraham. Both stories figure forth the time-space of freedom, and therefore of history, of how history takes place, of how it happens that there occur decision, responsibility, and religion.

Derrida is pre-figured in the writing of the *Commedia* in another way as well. In *Circumfession,* Derrida stylizes his confession by writing it toward his mother, his lady, his feminine Other, the other woman, woman as other, using the style of confession as a way of keeping the question of woman in suspense by relating it to the question of sacrifice. In fact, *Circumfession* keeps both the question of woman and the question of sacrifice in suspense, although differently than the way they are suspended in *The Gift of Death.* By writing his confession toward his mother, and therefore to his mother, for his mother, through his mother and from his mother, by writing it in the face of his mother and in the face of death, Derrida inscribes his confession into an ironic structure that resembles that of the narrative way of the pilgrim and the poet in the *Commedia.* Both confess that they recognize themselves in the face of the other; they recognize themselves in the other and the other in themselves. For Derrida that self-recognition in the face of his mother is the confession of the pilgrim way that he has traveled and continues to travel in his own texts, texts that encounter other texts along the way much as Dante the pilgrim encounters souls along the way in the *Inferno,* as well as in *Purgatorio* and *Paradiso.* These deconstructive encounters, structured and guided by the mastery of the text's auto-deconstructive dynamics are confessed by the writing of *Circumfession* to be the markers of his own path of conversion in writing, the testaments and testimonies of his own religion without religion, that have been "read less and less well over almost twenty years now" (*Circum., 154*). Dante's poem too speaks of "his religion," which had been read less and less well over more than thirteen hundred years, and which always needs conversion to start over again in faith. Just as he stands in need of conversion and starting over, in need of keeping faith with the alliance that has been written into him and misread and misunderstood by him "for more than twenty years now," the alliance made through his lady, toward and for and from her, as recounted in *Vita nuova*.

When Derrida exhibits in writing the circumcision that marks in the flesh of his penis the bond of the covenant between God and Abraham, he, in the name of Isaac, shares with his mother the secret that Abraham kept from Sarah. He transmits the secret that he is cut off from her, his own other, and all others, cut off from the mother by the writing of the father and the father's father in his flesh. He transmits the secret but necessarily remains in secret, shares the secret without saying anything, shares it by saying nothing, confesses the secret by doing the truth in love, by doing the truth in love in the way he has been doing it already for a long time, in writing, without saying anything, while still keeping the secret and keeping its promise.

If it is possible in any sense to regard Derrida as a sort of Virgil figure in reading Dante's poem for ourselves, that sense will largely be determined by the historical situation in which that reading necessarily must occur. Virgil is for Dante a kind of structure, one that moves with him and through which he moves over and over again. Like Abraham, but in a different sense, Virgil is a pass, a structure that allows passage, allows one to pass through, pass on, pass over, to begin and to continue to begin. Virgil's poem, the *Aeneid*, is Dante's pass into the time and space of epic, which is the realm of the hero and so an opening onto the scene of tragedy, a passage of which he knows himself to be unworthy ("I am not Aeneas; I am not Paul"), and yet, ironically, one through which he knows that he must pass, even though he knows it to be unworthy of the secret hope and promise of his writing. Virgil's poem is also a bridge between the realm of epic, heroic destiny and the tragedy that inevitably accompanies it, the realm of the Roman Empire, and the other realm of destiny with which Dante is concerned, the Holy Roman Empire, the Roman Catholic Church, which shares the destiny of Rome.

But Virgil is a pass in still another way: he is the pass through which the words and tears of Beatrice reach Dante and begin to touch and soften the scar of the wound made in his heart by its first being incised and then excised by the god Amor, the god of the love wound and love sacrifice, the god who requires that the beloved lady swallow the heart that he has incised and excised. Virgil is a pass in the sense of being a transmitter of the secret that Beatrice has been keeping for Dante, in holding it in safekeeping in the crypt of her heart, in the crypt of her death, as the encrypted secret of the gift of her death, which Virgil now shares with and transmits to Dante in a style of writing other than Virgil's own. When Virgil speaks in Canto ii, it is in the style of Courtly Love. As transmitter, Virgil allows a style of writing other than his own to reach Dante and allows Dante to begin to superscribe his confession over the epic structure of the universe, the universe of empire, the universe of Church, the universe of nature. Virgil passes on and shares with Dante the secret of *différance,* of necessarily writing differently, without Virgil's knowing anything or saying anything of himself. Virgil transmits the secret by leading Dante, in writing, among *le segrete cose,* by revealing that Dante must write from the Other in the style that is witnessed and beheld by the Other who sees in secret, who sees without being seen except in the trace of the writing.

Virgil's identity for Dante is as the one who shows him how to *pass on* along his way. Virgil is the transmission of Dante's journey, the one who transmits the secret that absolutely empowers Dante's journey, the secret that necessitates and enables Dante's way both as pilgrim and poet among *"le segrete cose."* Virgil transmits the secret of beginning and ending and starting again, the secret of being *nel mezzo,* in the instant, without knowing the secret or telling it, the secret that cannot be known or told because, as beginning and end, it is empty. Virgil's identity in secret transmits the secret, opening the way for Dante's passing on through the "secret things," opening the way in writing of the pilgrim and the poet, opening the way for Dante's journey to find himself again, in the instant of decision that finally decides his responsibility for the question "Who am I?" The moment in which he responds, "Here I am! (All!) Ready!"

Virgil traces out the pilgrim's path and shows him how to pass on along that path in different ways throughout the journey. One of these ways is via the formula that Virgil uses as a password to suspend the opposition posed by the monstrosities who block the way through Hell, refusing passage to him and Dante: Charon, Minos, Cerberus, and the demons. The password is a word of power that evokes the secret of beginning. It articulates the ironic power of the double negative, the power of refusal in the face of refusal, the "divine" power to do what one wants, *"si puote cio che si vuole,"* the same power St. Augustine references in his imperative *"Dilige, et fac quod vis; Love, and do what you will,"* the power that writes the name of the Divine as Love, the identity of Truth, Freedom, and Love as Three in One. The monstrosities of Hell are all the forces of premature ejaculation, the voices that cry out in the wilderness for untimely endings, for cutting things off short, all the sounds of weeping and wailing and gnashing of teeth against the necessity of passing on, of not judging (the other) lest you be judged (by the other), the necessity of "passing judgment" so that one can pass on. Virgil shows Dante the way through judgment, the way to pass judgment, to judge by passing on. It is in this way that one might recognize in Virgil the figure of deconstruction, perhaps even the face of Derrida.[13]

The first occasion that tests Dante's responsibility to pass on judgment occurs in Canto V of the *Inferno* in his encounter with Paolo and Francesca. In hearing Francesca tell her story, he is required to give prophetic testimony to the messianic structure of justice, the Justice that is not yet come, the Justice that comes only by passing on judgment so that judgment might be passed in an Other's way. This episode sets the pattern and marks the direction along which the entire journey through Hell must go. In each encounter, Dante must see in the damnation of the others the possibility of his own damnation. He must recognize in himself the reality of his freedom: the real possibility to choose to identify himself with their refusal to read the text written by their sin in their flesh, the meaning of the decision with which they have chosen to identify themselves as it appears now in the imaginative interpretation of the poet and therefore in the eyes of the pilgrim as their "souls." The pilgrim must learn to interpret the dissimulated text of their identity, the secret that the story they tell keeps secret, of the real possibility of his own refusal, like theirs, not merely to refuse sacrifice, but decisively to refuse responsibility for that refusal. They refuse to seek forgiveness for their sin by refusing to take responsibility for their need of an Other to rewrite the meaning of their doing, their need of a supplementary meaning for what is written in doing without love, for what is done without the truth of love. This explains why the *Inferno* must not be read as a story of damnation, but of the prophetic structure of judgment and the messianic structure of justice, a judgment and a Justice for which responsibility is taken by a response of "Yes! Come!" This is a response that allows the journey to continue, as it must, to pass beyond each occasion of the cry for judgment and Justice, to let judgment and Justice happen differently than they do in the abortive desire of the sinners who stop short of the desire and love of the Other. The meaning of the Inferno lies along the path of the pilgrim's growing recognition of his own need for forgiveness for all the possible judgments of identity, all the possible ways of doing justice to the responsibility for sacrifice that the Other's need demands, which fall short of the responsibility that says "Here I am! (All!) Ready!" None of the souls in Hell are without hope because of what they *have done;* they suffer there from the hopeless refusal of the possibility of forgiveness, the possibility of every other possibility, the absolute condition of possibility. They refuse to recognize the absolute necessity of forgiveness; they refuse to identify themselves with forgiveness as the absolute responsibility of love.

In the journey through the Inferno, Dante the poet captures in all the twisting, turning ways of refusal that the pilgrim's encounters with the sinner-citizens of Hell serialize, a profoundly rich psychological study of the progressive dynamics of what Christian theology would diagnose as the hierarchy of sin, the sins of the leopard, the lion, and the wolf. These are not a mere classificatory display, but a genealogy, the genetic study of the growth of sin. It traces the symptomatic pathologies of psychological character development and the failure to achieve self-identity, the failure of what in such a framework might be termed "self-actualization." Dante argues for a certain organically pathological growth of sin, admittedly highly formalized and allegorized, as a kind of cancerous development of personal identity in relation to the need of the Other; it is a cancer of freedom, in other words. In the pilgrim's journey through Hell, he traces the growth of sin, the way one thing leads to another so that one sees amid the episodic series a strong organic progression from one to the next, a restless impulse to go on that deforms the organicity of health into disease, the mysterious self-contradiction of the body that figures so centrally in Plato's reading of justice in the *Republic*.

This begins to account for the situation of Paolo and Francesca as the first encounter that marks the pilgrim's way of conversion. The movement of conversion rewrites the history of sacrificial substitution without revision. It reinterprets the literal meaning of the history of texts so as to see in them other possibilities of meaning. It seeks forgiveness. It opens itself to a for-giving that turns again to the original temporality and spatiality of the situation, to the time and space of the instant that decides the direction, and then redirects it with a new orientation toward the Other, a direction that comes from the Other differently. It takes a new path for the Other, passing through the Other's way of giving differently. It rewrites the double genitive of the Other, giving it a new meaning for the relation, giving a new beginning. Forgiveness is above all else a new giving of the secret of beginning, a new beginning in secret, a new way of seeing in secret.

In the scriptural tradition of Dante's religion, all sin is idolatry, the worship of "strange gods," other gods, the gods of others, instead of the God who is Other. Idolatry is a sort of insistent errancy or errant way of reading the ambiguity of all writing insofar as it transcribes and transmits the Other, who is in secret, by means of necessary substitution. Idolatry misreads the necessary ambiguity of substitution that is the pattern of all writing and insists instead on blocking the dissemination of signifiers. Idolatry is the refusal to allow difference; it refuses to do justice to the demand for substitution inscribed in writing as its *différance*. "*Tout autre est tout autre.*" Every other is disseminated in all the others, so that there is no way to deal with the Other except through substitution, so that no other can be worshiped as the Other. The name of God cannot be named; every name is strange to God. Every name names one of the other(s) who is an other for the Other. All of Dante's sinners violate this prohibition in one way or another. Among those identified with the sins of the leopard, this violation comes in the form of "incontinence," the unwillingness to limit desire that gradually grows toward the insistent refusal to economize on desire, to recognize the necessary economies of desire that are inscribed as law into all the circulations of credit and debt that are substitutes for the open excessive flow of sacrificial desire. The sins of lust, gluttony, profligacy, and wrath are idolatry in the figure of addiction, the insistent errancy of a purely formal ascription to the other(s) of one's total responsibility to the Other.

Paolo and Francesca are caught in the howling, frigid circulation of a spiration that is not divinely inspired, a movement of passionate desire that is unwilling to risk the absolute passion of sacrifice and insists on a pattern of substitution, the effect of which is to economize on desire, to insist on closing the circle of desire and to make a god of another, not identified as absolutely Other, and therefore not in excessive need. The excessive need of the Other that demands sacrifice lies concealed in the murder of Paolo and Francesca by another, sealing the encryption of their sin in the tomb of words by which she seeks to refuse responsibility. Their addiction to the economy of mutual but exclusive passion binds them to one another in the refusal of the Other whom they insist on cutting off. Their sin and the finality of their judgment in the instant of decision takes flesh in the words by which she tells their story to the pilgrim, the words the poet chooses so as to express in their figure the possibility he has found in himself to refuse to pass beyond a desire of the Other that is only economical.

It is Francesca who speaks to Dante. The poet chooses to let the woman speak. But in speaking, Francesca insists on maintaining a pattern of substitution that idolizes an economy of passion, putting it before the excessive need and sacrificial desire of the Other. In letting the woman speak, the poet recognizes in himself a possible scripting of woman that situates this encounter by reinscribing it in the scripting of woman in the first dream of the *Vita nuova.* The poet now recognizes the necessity that he take responsibility for this dream in order to pass through it and begin again as the pilgrim does in the narrative. This situation is reinforced by Francesca's triple invocation of the name of the god Amor (*Inf.,* v, 100–108) as the first word of the first line of each of the three tercets that lay out the grounds for their putative exculpation. In this way, she assigns the responsibility to the god who sacrificed them through the hand of her husband, his brother, whom they now judge and condemn as a murderer. The poet clearly convicts these two of idolatry through her words, which figure Amor in parody of the trinitarian divinity of Love. Amor is external to their relationship and works on it, leaving them in the end abandoned to one another. This disfigured image of God accounts for her perception of the "King of the universe" as being "unfriendly" toward the two of them and as being closed to prayers from them on Dante's behalf, as if to say they would pray for him if God did not refuse to hear. The irony of judgment lies in this refusal of responsibility. The pattern of substitution expresses itself in Francesca's self-scripting as passive and victimized by forces external to herself, as incapable of responsibility, a self-scripting that amounts to a refusal of responsibility.

The Francesca who speaks here speaks in the voice of the Beatrice whom Dante scripted into his dream of heart-eating under the domination of Amor. Dante the poet here allows Francesca to speak out the script he wrote for Beatrice to play out cryptically under the erasure of his own signature in the name of Amor, and in so doing, allows himself to recognize the victim's identity that he had ascribed to her and to himself by assenting in writing to the perversion of sacrifice demanded by the god Amor in the dream. The pilgrim, however, who hears these words with bowed head, hesitates while regarding their meaning, caught between romantic insistence on sweet thoughts and great desire on the one hand, and the "woeful pass" to which such thoughts and desires have led this pair. Now he is caught, like they are, in a closed circle of spiration, aspiration and conspiracy. Virgil's question, "What are you thinking?" interrupts that circuit at least enough to prompt him to ask his own question of them, allowing the story to pass on to its denouement: "How did Love grant you to know the dubious desires?" (*"Come concedette amore che conoscete i dubbiosi disiri?"* [*Inf.*, v, 119–120]). Desire riddled with the ambiguity of the disseminated substitution of *"Tout autre est tout autre"*; undecidability that must be decided without authority, without the authority to insist on judgment in the instant, to insist that judgment not be fixed in addiction, which puts an end to questioning and to passing on, which refuses dissemination and brings reading to an end as it did for Paolo and Francesca:

> But if you have such great desire to know the first root of our love, I will tell as one who weeps and tells. One day, for pastime, we read of Lancelot, how love constrained him; we were alone, suspecting nothing. Several times that reading urged our eyes to meet and took the color from our faces, but one moment alone it was that overcame us. When we read how the longed-for smile was kissed by so great a lover, this one, who never shall be parted from me kissed my mouth all trembling. A Gallehault was the book and he who wrote it; that day we read no further in it. (*Inf.*, v, 124–138)

The story of Paolo and Francesca's reading of the book, told under the fiction of her own narrative to the pilgrim, but scripted by the poet who stands in the instant, *nel mezzo,* and transmits the secret without knowing it or telling it, allowing the woman to speak in the words he has written for her, illustrates the ironic structure of prophetic judgment and messianic justice in the *Inferno.* Caught in the scripture of the courtly love tradition, ushered into the presence of its own blessed trinity, Lancelot, Guinevere, and Arthur, the trinity that Paolo, Francesca and her husband Gianciotto parody, they are "constrained" (*strinse*) as Lancelot was.[14] "We were alone and suspected nothing." Original innocence, untaught by experience; Adam and Eve alone in the garden, forgetting the Other, insisting on presence as the condition of responsibility, erring in their reading of the Other's absence, "suspecting nothing," failing to see beneath and behind absence their responsibility for the empty Secret of the Other who sees in secret (whatever that might mean). In this state of half-consciousness, as in a dream, as in the dream of *Vita nuova,* iii, they portray in the figure of the kiss, into which they now read themselves, the "heart-eating" that was the substitute consummation of the script of Dante's dream. This kiss, the kiss that stops the mouth of the other, the kiss that opens the way to the heart, eating the mouth of the Other on the way to eating the heart of the other, the first taste of forbidden fruit, the first faltering step toward consummation, toward consuming, toward eating the heart of the other, eating the secret of the other, toward Satan who waits beyond—(All!) Ready!—to consume.

Clearly their adultery does not explain their damnation. Lancelot, after having separated from Guinevere following the death of Arthur and retired each to a penitent life, ended his days with a smile, laughing. In contrast, Paolo and Francesca are damned by their refusal of responsibility for the final expression of their mouths, for their kiss, insofar as it marks the place where they stopped, where their freedom went no further, beyond which they read no further into their responsibility to the Other of their each-other. Their refusal to allow the meaning they had read into the story of Lancelot and Guinevere to deconstruct itself, to allow the unsuspected Other of the story to speak to them and interpret their own story differently constitutes their damnation. They lose themselves, their freedom, to themselves and one another by refusing to read on and risk *différance*. Hearing their final word to him, "that day we read no more," the poet describes the pilgrim's response, "While one spirit said this, the other wept, so that for pity I swooned, as if in death, and fell as a dead body falls" (*Inf.*, v, 139–42). Paolo and Francesca fell asleep in each other's arms and were murdered by her husband, his brother. Dante, like them, falls into something like sleep, something like the state of reverie into which he fell in his room the night he dreamed of Beatrice. Shocked by the finality of God/death's judgment on these two, he is set back almost to where and whom he was when he came to himself again to find that he was lost in the Dark Wood. In them he finds himself—lost. To stop reading now in the moment of judgment, in the instant of decision, to refuse to allow the Other of the story to tell one's own story differently, to close off the meaning of the journey in writing: this would be to choose death prematurely, a kind of premature ejaculation of death, a refusal to receive and give the Gift of Death, to take one's death upon oneself *as it comes from the Other*. The result of this refusal would be that death becomes Hell, leaving no exit from ourselves or from the Other who is finally refused. "That day we read no more." With these words, the poet marks the ironic climax of the story, a revelation that the pilgrim receives in exactly the same way he received the revelation of the dream of heart-eating, that is, as one seized by sleep. Revelation reveals ambiguity through which one must pass. Here Dante the poet passes through the ambiguity of Francesca's "we read no further," differently than does the pilgrim whose weight of responsibility must still be born by another, Virgil. But the poet inscribes his prophetic testimony to judgment and the call he hears in these words to a justice yet to come by heightening their resonance, allowing it to reverberate through another scripture of testimony and conversion: St. Augustine's testimony to the decisive instant in his own journey of conversion, which also turned on a reading:

> I was saying these things and weeping in the most bitter contrition of my heart, when suddenly I heard the voice of a boy or girl—I know not which—coming from the neighboring house, chanting over and over again, "Pick it up, read it; pick it up, read it." So damming the torrent of my tears, I got to

my feet, for I could not but think that this was a divine command to open the Bible and read the first passage I should light upon. So I quickly returned to the bench where Alypius was sitting, for there I had put down the apostle's book when I had left there. I snatched it up, opened it, and in silence read the paragraph on which my eyes first fell: "Not in rioting and drunkenness, not in chambering and wantoness, not in strife and in envying, but put on the Lord Jesus Christ, and make no provision for the flesh to fulfill the lusts thereof." *I wanted to read no further, nor did I need too. For instantly, as the sentence ended, there was infused in my heart something like the light of full certainty and all the gloom of doubt vanished away.*" (*Confessions*, Book VIII, xii; emphasis added)

In the instant of revelation and decision, finality unites the end to the secret of beginning. Conversion—allowing the story to go on absolutely differently. Coming to himself again, the pilgrim begins to understand how he is to read the ironic text of judgment and how to go on in writing with his own judgment. Judgment is finally for the Other, comes from the Other, comes by going on through and for the Other. Now he has begun to let go of his suspicion and mistrust, let go of his conscious resistance to trusting the other, begun to let Virgil bear him on and through, and in so doing has begun to understand Virgil's prophetic words as they stood before the Gates of Hell, "We have come to the place where I have told you we will see the wretched people who have lost the good of intellect" (*Inf.*, iii, 16–18). For the good of intellect is judgment, knowing how to use the "Yes!" and "No!" that are the punctuation marks of history, the history of freedom. Derrida, in the role of Virgil, might recognize in the story of Paolo and Francesca the desperate bind of another pair of lovers: Abraham and his God, whose story, like that of Paolo and Francesca, must be interrupted and supplemented, by passing through an other.

Going on from here, the stories of prophetic judgment continue to bend and twist and writhe, descending into the abyss of freedom as the pilgrim goes on recognizing himself in the other, the other in himself, more consciously as he journeys on cataloging in his unapologetically scholastic way the full range of impossibly possible ways that hope can be finally lost. The sum of these recognitions is that Hell is the place of refusal. Refusal of the Other certainly; but refusal in a most precise sense, through all its modalities: the final refusal of the Other is the refusal to seek the possibility of forgiveness, which can only be reached by passing through acceptance of responsibility for the demand of sacrifice. This sense of the absolute finality of damnation in Dante's Inferno intersects the trajectory of Derrida's tracing out of absolute responsibility in the instant of decision. Derrida interprets the divine command to give the gift of death as sacrifice as the prayer of God calling on Abraham to consummate the covenant between them by responding to the divine excess of need, the absolute necessity of the promise of the covenant, which is its empty secret, the secret that is betokened by the flesh of Isaac. There is no covenant, no promise, no secret—all are empty, but for Isaac. Abraham and God cannot both have him, however. He is a secret they cannot share. God asks Abraham for the promised flesh of Isaac, asks that Abraham give death to Isaac and to God. God requests that Abraham let flesh be consumed in the fires of sacrifice, let it be transformed in the heat of the passion that is all-consuming, meet the absolute need of a love that keeps its promise in secret in the empty secret of beginning. The secret is held without reserve, without withholding.

The intersection of these trajectories, the pilgrim's journey to the center of gravity marked in Cocytus by the figure of Satan, and Derrida's tracing of the journey of Abraham to the peak experience of Mount Moriah maintains their inverse symmetry through the elasticity of the religious metaphor of sacrifice. Sacrifice plays entirely on the ambiguity of life and death when they become caught up in the absolute responsibility of the Gift, an aporia that contains within itself as its empty secret promise the necessity of its own dispensation. Sacrifice reveals "de-pendence," a weighing out as if by the hanging in the balance of "Yes!" and "No!" Here, the common stock or reserve is portioned out, which also reveals the inner relation of sacrifice to the Greek sense of the law, *nomos*, which has its origin in the verb *nemein*, the dispensing or portioning out that is fundamental to the law of the household, *oikoinomia*, the portioning out or dispensing of necessities: the necessities of life, food, drink, and shelter and all the goods of familial hospitality.

But *nemein* is also immediately related to another sense of portioning—portion as limit, as in *moira*, fate, the allotted portion, related also to Nemesis, the avenging necessity of retribution that rectifies transgressions of the allotted distribution of portions. When God dispenses with the sacrifice of Isaac that he had demanded of Abraham and allows the substitution of the ram, by that dispensation God becomes involved in another dispensation and in another pattern of substitution, another way of portioning out the world and time and space and history, another way of dealing with the necessities of life and death, the pagan dispensation (whether Greek, Roman, or Canaanite), the "other" way, the way of the "others," the way of the strangers who have strange gods. This is the abiding ambiguity and ultimate risk of the covenant between Elohim and Abraham: it puts in question the pagan economy of ritual sacrifice, especially human sacrifice, as a form of retributive justice, the Justice that is dispensed to redistribute life and death according to its original necessarily fated and fatal portioning, its *moira*, which is always in contradiction to itself, as the thread that is always cut off in the giving. But this portioning is done without justice, without being able to account for how it will do justice to the absolute dispensation of all economies of dispensation and distribution, a dispensation that is without scale and so without measure, and therefore without justice, an economy without promise, without the promise of inscribing the end back into the beginning. The empty secret is the promise of an impossible justice, a justice which cannot be done and so must always be dispensed.

Dante's pilgrim journey through the Gate that is Abraham passes on until it reaches the necessary final turning point of Abraham's story, the story of how Abraham's "God himself will provide the offering" turns everything around, converting the movement and meaning of the story by putting it into suspense: the suspense that awaits the impossible justice, the dispensation of God's impossible justice, the Kingdom of God on earth, and of the one anointed to do the impossible—bring the justice that must come because it has been promised, promised because it is absolutely needed. Abraham's ironic response to Isaac's question, "Where is the lamb for the sacrifice?" is "God himself will provide the lamb, my son." His response allows Abraham to speak, according to Derrida, to respond without saying anything, without having anything to say, without having to say anything. It allows him to respond, to take responsibility while keeping the secret of the covenant-promise that binds him alone to God and God alone to him. Abraham's responsibility binds God to the secret demand of sacrifice; Abraham's binding of Isaac binds God to absolute responsibility for the need of sacrifice, the need to make a gift of death and to make death a gift. It binds God to keep the secret of the promise and the binding cord is the line of the story: God must keep the secret of the promise that Abraham passes on to God, turning the line of the story in a new direction, converting the story line into the demand that the promise of the secret be kept in and through taking responsibility for sacrifice by dispensing it, and so putting the demand for sacrifice into suspense, meeting the demand with a new form of responsibility. The conversion of the story into a new line calls for a divine initiative in response to Abraham's responsibility. It calls for divine responsibility to provide an offering, a substitute sacrifice, or perhaps a substitute for sacrifice, a token of sacrificial substitution, to dispense with the demand for sacrifice addressed to Abraham, by dispensing an offering, the offering of the Other, not a pagan offering, one that is always strange and unfamiliar because it is the offering of the "others," but an offering that is familial and therefore familiar, recognized as one's own, recognized as responsible because the response is recognizable, already known, instantly, as one's own story through which one has already lived. By dispensing Abraham from the demand to sacrifice his son, God allows the story to continue by taking responsibility to provide a victim that is betokened by the substitution of the ram, a new dispensation that keeps the secret of the promise, allows the story of promise-keeping to pass on, to be transmitted and transmuted, to be kept in secret in a different way, a way that Abraham and all who remember Abraham's story will immediately, in an instant, recognize, because the story is familiar. It is Abraham's own story—the story that answers to the question, "Who am I?" with the affirmation "Here I am! (All!) Ready!"

The dispensation of the demand for human sacrifice is the demand for a new dispensation, the demand that God take responsibility for keeping the empty secret of the (empty) promise in a different way, for turning the story of secret/promise keeping in a new direction, converting the binding story by allowing it to bind differently and to bind a different victim. The story of Abraham and Isaac can go on only by adhering to the strictest irony, the irony of inversion, of complete and final conversion. *God's demand for human sacrifice necessarily turns into the human call for divine sacrifice.* A voice is heard calling in the wilderness of Khora, the voice of need,

> *calling for an impossible justice to be done so as to keep the impossible secret/ promise/covenant from finally coming to an end,*
>
> *from falling into the un-gift of death, the death of the word that meets with no response, that meets with the response of No!*
>
> *the final refusal to respond, the No! that refuses dispensation, that refuses to provide a victim for sacrifice in response to the responsibility of the Other,*
>
> *the refusal to for-give the Other for the love that takes absolute responsibility for the need of the Other by giving the gift of death in forgiveness,*
>
> *in dispensation of the necessary demand for death as sacrifice, thereby making of death a gift, a more terrible gift,*
>
> *a gift that causes one to tremble even more violently because it does greater violence, transgresses the limits of necessity, the fate of fatality, even more violently than the demand for human sacrifice,*
>
> *the gift of divine responsibility to give the gift of death in the face of the readiness (Here I am!") of the human to take absolute responsibility for keeping the secret promise from meeting the death of refusal,*
>
> *the final refusal which prematurely gives death to the passing on of the story of the secret promise of beginning, by refusing the final responsibility to begin again, anew, differently,*
>
> *to dispense the story in a new way, to keep the story in suspense through the irony of a conversion which inverts the story so as to take responsibility in a new way,*
>
> *to provide and fore-see the keeping of the secret in the passing on of the story that always takes responsibility, takes absolute responsibility for a new beginning,*
>
> *the one prerogative of the divine, from the beginning, to be in the first place, to have the initiative—to begin and to be able to do whatever it wishes, "vuolsi così colà dove si puote ciò che si vuole,"*
>
> *to keep the terrible secret of divine power, to be absolutely responsible, to be able to begin a new without end,*
>
> *not simply the power to give the Gift of life, but the power to forgive the Gift of Death.*

The story of the sacrifice of Jesus is the story of the Other's responsibility for the dispensation by substitution of the sacrifice of Isaac. The secret that both stories keep in the strict irony of their inversion is the secret of the conversion of one story into the other story. That secret is kept and passed on without knowing or sharing anything through the complete inversion of the secret of woman, the per-version, if you will, of the secret of woman, the secret kept by woman, the secret of woman; the woman who keeps the secret differently than the man, the secret of how the woman gives the Gift of Death differently than the man, the woman as the Other of the secret and of the Gift, the woman as the secret and gift of the Other. The work of the man is to provide; dispensation is the work of the woman as other to man, as the other Other. For the woman,

> to dispense is to provide differently than the way the father provides, to portion out differently, to do justice differently to the familiar needs of life;
>
> to dispense is to do what is necessary for life, to apportion, not what has been provided by another, by the man, the father, but to portion out one's own stores of life without reserve or substitution,
>
> as in the story of the widow, who is all women who must do without the man, the father, who are excluded from the secret kept among men;
>
> to give life by sustaining the needs of life with one's own flesh, to let life feed on one's own flesh and blood, to give one's own flesh as food and one's own blood as drink,
>
> to dispense without end and without reservation, to generate and regenerate as nutrix, as nurse and as wound, as Khora, the barren place that allows all to take place within it, the place that sustains difficulty, the difficulty of life, and as womb, where the empty secret always begins again.

It is not women who feed; rather, it is in the feeding that there occurs the *différance* that is woman. Feeding dispenses the need of the Other differently than does the provisional sacrifice of man. Feeding dispenses the need for sacrifice differently than by substitution. Woman is the other Other, the feeding which is no man, no god, the third who lets man be man, and God be God. The feeding which is woman saves the name of the father and the Father, saves face for the father and every father's son; woman as the saving face. This is the empty secret kept secret by the story of Abraham, in which Sarah is not mentioned, the secret that is "revealed" by being passed on, transmitted without saying anything or having anything to say except the double turn in the story. It is the double turn of a conversion to a different absolute responsibility, a different way of being absolutely responsible: a turn to woman, and a turn to a "more divine" dispensation of sacrifice.[15] Both are ways of doing an impossible justice, of pronouncing a prophetic judgment on the refusal of the covenant, the promise of absolute responsibility, the double revelation of the need of the Other so as to for-give the story of Abraham, to allow it to pass on, in suspense, to keep the secret even more secret, to tell the story differently so as to provoke an even more terrible trembling, to keep the secret even more secret, to apply an even greater force by virtue of the power that can do whatever it wishes to repress the mystery that the Greek dispensation incorporates without adequately concealing, to drive the mystery of the orgiastic desire for fusion, the desire to be one with the Other, to drive it back completely and finally into the flesh, to encrypt it in the flesh, with the flesh, through the flesh, to seal it finally by pressing it back into the flesh, to mark and memorialize that repression of the *mysterium tremendum*, with the Gift of Death, the absolute finality of the flesh given as the gift of absolute responsibility and the absolute need of the divine for the human and of the man for the woman, the absolute responsibility of the Other to all the others—*tout autre est tout autre.*

## . . . AND IF YOU WEEP NOT, AT WHAT DO YOU EVER WEEP?

Dante keeps the secret of the double conversion of the story of Abraham, the dispensation of the demand for human sacrifice, by encrypting it in the pilgrim's story, by writing himself into the stories of Ugolino and of Satan. Ugolino's story is the dramatic peak of the pilgrim's journey through the Inferno, even as it leads to the perverse nadir of sin; it is the doubly inverted image of Mt. Moriah in Abraham's story. It calls for a closer look.[16]

The encounter with Ugolino is the last major scene before Dante and Virgil reach Satan. The scene parallels the scene with Paulo and Francesca, and the growth of sin that began with the two lovers comes to fruition with Ugolino. In Canto xxxii, 133–139, Dante encounters Ugolino locked in ice, showing the depths of Hell as absolute frigidity, absolute zero, the absence of motion, activity, dynamism, and thus of all vitality. It is symbol of sterility, the absolute absence of all meaning because it is the absolute absence of all relation. Yet at the last step before encountering Satan, we also encounter the last figure Dante tries to give us of the human face and incarnation of evil and sin, the text of refusal written in the flesh by what is done without love.

Dante presents us with the image of Ugolino, his jaws locked onto the neck of Archbishop Ruggieri, the only movable part of his body as the rest of the pair is locked in ice. He is gnawing on the back of his neck. Dante asks Ugolino to tell his story, promising that if his hatred is justified the poet will let others know how Ugolino was wronged through the poem. We see that Dante has unabashedly mastered the strategy of playing on the perverted desire of the sinners to be known by the community of the living—to still be recognized by the Other, even though they have identified themselves with the refusal to be identified with the suffering of the Other. They cannot escape their desire to be recognized, though they refuse to offer recognition. The poet plays on that desire to call forth the word of their stories, by which they identify themselves, and in so doing, confess who they are and the sin with which they have become identified.

In Ugolino gnawing on the head of the Archbishop, we see the image of consumption and predation—the act of preying on, in the literal sense that animals have prey. That is the significance of the "bestial sign" to which Dante refers, the act of consuming another human being to feed Ugolino's hatred, specifically his desire for revenge. It was Ruggieri who betrayed his compact with Ugolino to betray their city, Pisa, and that is what Ugolino holds against him. It was that double betrayal that caused Ugolino to suffer the death in the Tower with his two sons and two grandsons. The notion of the beast, or three beasts, within us that represent the three classes of sins, symbolizes a view of human nature in its basic ambivalence reflected by the standard Renaissance idea that human beings are situated halfway between the angels and the beasts. To be human is to half angel, half beast. To refuse the need of the Other is to identify with the beast within us, and the ultimate characteristic of the beast as it symbolizes sin in the wolf, is this predatory quality—living through preying on other life. It is also worth noting that the predatory character, is, like the "yes" and "no" of freedom, not a simple either/or choice but a fundamental ambivalence that is inscribed in the flesh of our existence as human beings. Unless one is a vegetarian, one lives by eating the flesh of other living things, and even if a vegetarian, one still must eat life in some form or other. It is the very essence of our existence that we must devour to grow, that we must feed and prey on life to nurture life. The transition that Dante is symbolizing in Ugolino is one where predatory feeding on life specifically is focused in sin on other human life.

Ugolino lifts his head, and then wipes his lips on the hair of the head he was feasting on. He then tells Dante that to recall his story will cause him great pain. This parallels Dante in the beginning of the poem (*Inf.*, i, 1–12), saying that even in recall it renews his fear to recount the journey, yet to tell of the good he found through it will relive the terror of the rest. In a basic sense, the whole poem consists in Dante doing that which he now asks of Ugolino. He is recounting his story, recounting his encounter with sin, and renewing and living again the fear and terror and threat of death in doing so. In that semantic and poetic parallel Dante is already strongly identified with Ugolino. When Ugolino speaks, Dante will see himself in Ugolino, because what Ugolino is doing is not just recounting the story of particular sins, but doing what all human beings do—giving flesh as word to the identity that they form by the choices that they make about their relationship to the Other.

Ugolino then says "But if my words are seed from which the fruit is infamy for this betrayer . . ." Another food image here where Ugolino thinks of planting a seed that will grow into infamy. We are also reminded of the trees of the Suicides, the Tree of Adam and Eve, the apple, the fruit, all echoing through this image. The imagery of the Canto is particularly dense because this is Dante's final and most difficult challenge in the *Inferno,* and he must marshal all of his poetic resources to try to deal with it. Ugolino then says he will speak and weep at once, and this is a cue to pay attention to the presence and the absence of speaking and weeping throughout the story.

Ugolino recognizes Dante as a Florentine by his accent, and then tells that he is Count Ugolino and the soul next to him is Archbishop Ruggieri. Many commentators have made much of the fact that we have a bishop and a count. This is not just the story of two individual people but the relationship between church and state, and in the Augustinian political sense, Dante is also reflecting on the very structure of society itself. He is reflecting on how the two parts of society, the secular and the ecclesiastical and spiritual feed on and betray one another in the context of the Holy Roman Empire. Ugolino then says he will proceed to explain why Ruggieri is his neighbor (*vicino*). This is an irony, for though he is next to him, he is anything but his neighbor in the scriptural sense of the word, or even simply in the sense of human decency and human relationship. Ugolino then says he will not say why he is here in Hell, for we know it is because he was betrayed in the plot to betray his city. That is neither the sin Dante the poet is interested in nor what Ugolino tells the pilgrim he should be concerned with but cannot know because it is a secret locked away with Ugolino in the keep of his prison tomb. Ugolino believes that what happened in the "Hunger Tower" where he and his children were starved to death on Ruggieri's orders will prove him more victim than victimizer, but Dante wishes to show us something else. The tower is like the secret garden of Paulo and Francesca, something that happens behind closed doors and has to be revealed. It is through what is revealed that Ugolino will show who he really is, not in the story of the failed plot. Ugolino died in the tower because he trusted Ruggieri, echoing the occasion when Virgil told Dante at the Gates of Hell he had to trust in contradiction to the epigraph on the gate that said "Abandon Hope." Virgil said you have to trust me, you have to trust God, you have to trust Beatrice, because all the way through there is a relationship between us and each of the others, and the foundation of that relationship is trust. Yet Ugolino trusts Ruggieri in a plot to betray trust. Now, Ugolino says that Dante will find out if Ruggieri wronged him by learning of the cruel death the Archbishop devised for the count. Ugolino first mentions the cruel death devised for him, rather than mentioning his sons who die with him. The story shows not how Ugolino was wronged by Ruggieri, but how the Count wronged his children.

Ugolino misinterprets the dream that he has, and the other signs he will be given in the tower through his children. By misreading, he misses the real issue with which his story is concerned. In his dream, Ruggieri appears as lord and master, echoing the time Love appears as lord and master to Dante in the *Vita nuova*. Then the man hunts the wolf and its whelps, which are Ugolino and his children. Ruggieri sends hounds after them, and in the dream Ugolino sees the wolf and its cubs are weary, with their flanks torn by sharp fangs. Ugolino is the wolf, and we are in the place of the sins of the wolf. If Ugolino were keen to the reality of sin and the symbolism of the wolf, he would see that in the dream he is father to his sons in the form of a wolf, and in the end he is the father who will ultimately devour them in one way or another. Instead, Ugolino misinterprets the dream, seeing himself as victim in the form of a hunted beast pursued by dogs that rip his flanks, bringing back the image of predation in parodic form . . . He then awakes, and he sees that his children are shedding tears in their sleep, asking for bread. It is they who are weeping. This echoes the scene of Pier della Vigna in the circle of the suicides, where, in order to speak, the tree must weep the blood sap. Thus, at this point in the story, weeping is associated in ironic anticipation with speaking and giving one's identity to be heard, to be seen.

Ugolino next tells Dante that he would be cruel if he could see what the Count's heart foresaw yet did not grieve. He then says, "If you would not weep now, when would you weep?" That line hangs over all else that he says as a kind of specter, a specter of self-judgment that he refuses to acknowledge but that his story passes on him nonetheless. Though they know they should be fed around that time, the prisoners hear instead the nailing shut of the tower door. Ugolino then looks into the faces of his sons without a word. He did not weep; he says that within he turned to stone. The Count's words attest that he has already fully mastered, or been mastered by, that growth of sin that occurs up to the gates of Dis, guarded by the Medusa that turns the heart to stone. It is that guilt which he thinks he can master by not looking at it, appearing now in the faces of his sons where he says he sees his own face reflected. He is guilty at the very least of putting them in this situation by the original plot. The children weep, and Anselm says "Father, you look so . . . what is wrong with you?" Ugolino sheds no tears and does not answer until another son falls to the earth. He withholds word and tears, stifling the two expressions of the soul that should be pressed out by the weight of what he is suffering, which is the necessity to witness the innocent suffering of his beloved sons. But nothing is pressed out, like squeezing a stone. One cannot get either blood or water from a stone; nothing will express itself. Then, when a thin ray of sunlight makes its way into the tower, Ugolino sees the faces of his children and sees his own face in theirs, he bites at both his hands, in a gesture of frustration and rage, but also to block the passage of words or tears with pain. The gesture of eating himself, eating his own flesh, says something is eating away at him inside, and the gesture is the externalization, the expression of that inner gnawing hunger of hate, an act of symbolic cannibalism. The act is similar to his consuming of Ruggieri. In both instances, the anger and desire for revenge is eating away at him, and he expresses that through this desire to eat living flesh, so as to feed the hunger that won't be satisfied within himself. In that way, he would try to metabolize his enemy, to digest the enemy by turning him into himself.

His children, who believe he bit his hands out of hunger, tell him that it would be far less painful for us if he ate of them; since it was he who gave them flesh, it is he who has the right to despoil it. They are saying that when they watch him suffer, they would rather die for him, would rather have him feed on their flesh than on his own. The reference is not meant to be literal, although the echo of the literal cannibalism hangs over the whole story, but what they are suggesting is that they want to feed what is eating away at him and alleviate that hunger. But Ugolino refuses to be fed, refuses to see a meaning in what they say to him that could give a new meaning to their situation. To give a new meaning to events is not to change them, but to give the events a new significance, a saving meaning within their relationship. Their offer of their flesh to eat is an offer that they are extending to him to make him see that if only he would somehow or other let them alleviate his suffering, they could die together. Not just physically together, but that he could see in this last act of love on their part a meaning that could perhaps redeem the physical death that is going to occur. His soul, if it is willing to be fed by them, need not endure the torment of feeding fruitlessly, futilely, on Ruggieri forever. They can give a new meaning to his sense of being victimized, and the desire for eternal revenge that it breeds, and his allowing them to feed him could become a communion of love. As references throughout the text make abundantly clear, Dante is evoking figures of the Christian sacrament of Eucharist: Jesus offering his body and blood as food and drink for human beings in the sign of the forgiveness of sins. Dante the poet here uses the story of Ugolino to offer an insight into the human existential meaning of the sacrament of Eucharist, as an enactment of something that is supposed to take place not only ritually and liturgically, but in the communion of the human family, among human beings who are all "children of God." Jesus offers his flesh and blood as food and drink, and by so doing, those who partake of it have life to give to others, by feeding them as they have been fed. The dynamic of feeding and being fed by is a sacramental dynamic, in the sense that the bread and wine symbolize a food, but a food that is not material and physical. Ultimately that food in the Eucharistic image is the flesh and blood of Jesus. Following Dante's logic and the way in which he interprets Incarnation in the poem, that flesh and blood, no matter whose flesh blood it is, is the formula of word made flesh, flesh made word. Through words of love, we feed one another so as to have life within us, a meaning or identity to our existence that is not bound by, not devoured by death.

Ugolino then grows calm to keep his children from more sadness, not recognizing what they need is not stoic calm, or the absence of sadness, but that they need something to be joyful about, something to feed the possibility of a meaning being resurrected from their death, despite the loss of life. He then asks the hard earth, "Why did you not open up?" This is ironic, for he is truly speaking of his own heart, which has turned to stone. His heart is the hard earth that does not open up, but he does not recognize that this is a comment on his own identity because he fails in self-knowledge, blind to all that speaks of his failure of responsibility. This echoes and parodies the earthquake following the Crucifixion, when the veil or curtain of the temple was rent and the inner sanctum was revealed, just as the inner truth of what happened behind the nailed door of the tower is shown here. Then, on the fourth day, Gaddo implores his father, saying, "Father, why do you not help me?" and then dies. He is asking why his father is silent and will not give a sign. This echoes the imploring of God the Father by Jesus on the Cross, but in Psalm 22 that expression of abandonment is turned back to hope. That would be relevant here, just as it was for Paulo and Francesca: because they read no further they do not discover the whole meaning of their own story. Just as they missed the point, so does Ugolino. Then the other three children die, and Ugolino, now blind, gropes over each, and too late, begins to call for them for two days. He calls them by name only after they are dead. Then he says "fasting had more force than grief." There is an undecidable debate among scholars as to whether these last lines mean that fasting killed him when grief should have killed him long before, or that Ugolino cannibalized his children out of hunger, where the image of him eating his children would connect well with his gnawing on Ruggieri in Hell. Dante intends the ambivalence of both meanings: Ugolino has already consumed them through his hardness of heart, through his failure to give a meaning to their death by not responding to their offer to feed him. Thus the actual cannibalism is irrelevant except in so far as it is the suggestion of a possibility that would only be the literal sense of what he has already done without love.

Dante is interested in what it is that could cause a human being to betray another human being, especially those closest to him. This is the last revelation; it is as far as the poet can go in trying to fathom that depth of evil that in the next Canto will be symbolized by the purely unimaginable, horrific, monstrous figure of Satan. The vision of Satan is an anticlimax, however, as Satan is just a stepladder, a structure, an encrypted cipher. The movement of the *Inferno,* and with it Dante's human concern reaches its true climax here in the Ugolino episode. Ugolino's story is not meant to show us that he is in Hell because of what he did to his children. Rather, it reveals to us the secret of betrayal, and also, through inversion, of fidelity as well, what it is to keep faith, to keep the secret of faith. Ugolino is a betrayer, not of his state, but of the bonds of intimate human trust. The closest Dante can come to imagining the full reality of sin that is encrypted in the figure of Satan is to make visible the possibility of how one human being can betray another human being within the bonds of a relationship of trust and love, a person-to-person relationship. The larger structure of the poetic insight reveals itself very quickly once we remember that we rediscover what the poet has recognized in himself in what the pilgrim sees; Dante is learning something about his own need for forgiveness. Dante, like Ugolino, had four children. (Actually, Ugolino only had two children and two grandchildren. Dante rounds the number to four, according to one interpretation, because in some very specific way Dante is reflecting on his own life.) He is reflecting on the fact that it was his own involvement, perhaps not altogether innocent at least in regard to the maturity and integrity of his judgment, in a political debacle in which one party betrayed the other party, his own, and thereby caused his exile, that was the cause of his being separated from his family and excluded from the upbringing of his children. He is recognizing his need for forgiveness for the way in which his situation, guilty or not, and his involvement in the politics of Florence deprived his children of a father. The role of a father is to offer a word of meaning that provides for the nurture of his children, whatever his situation or theirs. Dante is forced to recognize that he is Abraham, ready to sacrifice his children by refusing to take responsibility for the demand of sacrifice that involvement in the covenant of life inevitably and absolutely makes.

There are various biblical images that relate to the scene of this Canto. One is at the Sermon of the Mount where the feeding of the multitudes occurs. The miracle reveals that the limitations of material circumstance are subject to the power of the word and can be given a new meaning, specifically in this case with regard to feeding the need of those who are hungry for a new beginning, such as Jesus has just presented in his vision of the Kingdom. Shortly after this story, Jesus says "Ask, and it will be given; seek and you shall find; knock and it will be opened to you" (Matt. 7:7). This contrasts pointedly to Ugolino's words "Oh hard earth, why did you not open up?" and "If you don't weep now, when would you weep." Jesus then goes on to say:

> "Or what man of you, if his son asks him for bread, will give him a stone? Or he asks for a fish, will give him a serpent? If you then who are evil, know how to give good gifts to your children, how much more will your Father who is in heaven give good things to those who ask him. So whatever you wish that men would do to you, do so to them." (Matt. 7:9–12)

Ugolino did not weep, rather he turned his heart to stone; he gave his children no tear to speak his sorrow and love, yet wants tears for himself from strangers. He wants to feed on the tears, drink the tears as if they were the blood that allows the dead to speak. He does not want to give flesh or blood, to give bread.

In fact the entire Ugolino episode can be seen as a distorted image of the spirit of Jesus' "Sermon on the Mount," as well as being a parody of the of the Eucharist. When, for example, Jesus teaches the disciples how to pray, he teaches them to say "Our Father, . . . give us this day our daily bread" (Matt. 6:11) and in another place, "man shall not live by bread alone, but by every word that comes from the mouth of God" (Matt. 4:4). In chapter 18 of Matthew, Jesus says, "Truly I say to you, unless you turn and become like children, you will never enter the kingdom of heaven. Whoever humbles himself like this child, he is greatest in the kingdom of heaven" (18:3–4). "Whoever receives a child in Christ's name receives him, but whoever causes them to sin, it would be better for him to have a great millstone tied on his neck and be drowned in the sea" (18:5–6). As a father, it is necessary for him to provide for and to feed the children and to keep their faith, and Ugolino is guilty of the betrayal of that need. He fails to give them a word, a meaning to their innocent deaths and to their offer of their own flesh to feed him. Now Dante hopes to give bread to his sons, in the form of the poem itself, and by telling this story he is discovering what he can do to give meaning to their innocent suffering of his exile. He can give meaning by writing the poem, and the flesh of his life becomes the word of the poem that he gives to his children. By extension, he gives this bread to all who read the poem.

The poem would also seem to have in mind the story of the Prodigal Son (Luke 15:11–32), who comes back to his father willing to be a servant, having sinned against both him and heaven, but whom the father welcomes with compassion and forgiveness, saying to the unforgiving brother, "It is fitting to make merry and be glad, for this brother of yours was dead, and is alive; he was lost, and is found." The basic image of father, son, and death through starvation configures the text of the Ugolino episode, but in contrast to the Gospel texts it parodies, forgiveness, the recovery of life, and feasting are lacking. The letter of the law kills by starving the spirit. Ugolino wants be judged by the letter of the law, asserting that he was betrayed, despite the fact that he was a betrayer. The spirit of the law gives life, the word that expresses its true meaning. The sons speak for the spirit of the law. "Eat of us, rather than feeding on yourself." That refusal of Ugolino to recognize their offer of forgiveness is the final death, the "sin against the Spirit," for which there is no forgiveness. The fact that Ugolino could refuse the last opportunity to accept the offer of forgiveness to bring the dead back to life, even when it is written in the faces of one's own flesh and blood, reveals the finality of the injunction written on the Gate of Hell. This is what it means finally to have abandoned every hope. It is clear that they are all going to die and that their deaths are ultimately his responsibility, but rather than take that responsibility on himself, rather than owning up to death, Ugolino instead lets them die without giving them the word that gives life. This echoes the Eucharistic discourse in the Gospel of St. John, where the people ask the Lord for the bread that will deliver them from ever hungering again, referring to the manna Yahweh gave to the Israelites. The Lord tells them that he is the bread of life, and those who believe in him will never hunger or thirst. Christ then says that he has come down to do the Father's will. We see in Christ what is revealed about the Father's love through the son, and just as in Ugolino we see what is revealed about the father's lack of love through the sons.

The pilgrim is to see the growth of sin, but the poet is to see the need for forgiveness. These come together in this story, the real climax of the *Inferno*, where the reality of human evil is shown written in the flesh of the sons by a father who withholds the word. Unlike Abraham, who speaks without saying anything, Ugolino fails to turn his flesh into bread to eat and his tears into wine to drink and gladden the heart. This is the reality of one human being, in full knowledge, refusing to participate in the communion of human suffering that binds all persons together in the face of inevitable death and allows them to feed the hunger and thirst for meaning in life by feeding on the word that itself is forgiven, given before every gift, absolute giving that gives nothing but itself. The life that does not end in death depends on whether that life has found meaning in the bonds of relationship with other human beings. The capacity to withhold affirmation of those bonds even in face of the cruelest of deaths is not just death of the body but also the death of the spirit. This is what damns a human existence to the deepest depths of Hell, whatever that mysterious depth represented by Satan is. If anything could rob human identity of life, finally and irrevocably, it is the capacity to say an authentic "No!" in the face of those human beings to whom we are most intimately bound when they ask us to feed them with a word of meaning. The "No" can take all the forms the *Inferno* has cataloged, but in the end, the seed is in that ability to say no to those human beings who have trusted themselves to be fed. To feed and be fed is to forgive and be forgiven, to be forgiveness, of the hunger and thirst of existence in which is written the empty secret and terrible suffering of the Gift of love.

The story of Ugolino is the story of the refusal of the man to recognize the need of the Other, told as the story of the refusal to recognize the need of woman, the woman who is missing from the story: the need for the woman, the woman's need, the need that is woman and that the woman is; the need to feed, to sustain life in the face of death, to give death as the gift that allows the story to pass on by telling it differently, to pass on judgment by telling the story of death differently, to judge death differently and so to forgive death, to give death a different meaning, to take responsibility for death differently and so to do messianic justice to the necessary demand for death by keeping that demand in ironic suspense, waiting for a new way of providing for that death, a new way of feeding life through death and in death, a new way of telling the story of the demand for death, telling it differently according to the need of the Other as the woman who feeds. Ugolino refuses to be mother to his dying children and so refuses their need to be fed, of which their physical starvation is the outward corollary. In the face of their compassion for his face, expressed in the question, "You look so, father; what ails you?" (*Tu guardi così, padre, che hai? Inf.,* xxxiii, 57), he has already turned his heart to stone by his refusal to weep—"I did not weep, inside I turned to stone" (*Io non piangëa, sì dentro impetrai;* ibid, 49). Ugolino, like Abraham, says nothing; unlike Abraham, however, who speaks while saying nothing, Ugolino is as mute as the stone, as silent as the grave. His withholding of words in the primitive form of tears, the withholding of the lacrimation that betokens lactation, enacts a betrayal of the most basic bond that sustains life. His refusal to allow for dispensation even by desperate substitution of the water of tears for the milk of words, this refusal of the responsibility for language as the original form of substitution, the original sin that can never be redeemed, only forgiven, the substitution of the word for the flesh as the victim of sacrifice, opens Dante's text to be read as Hell's last word on the finality of refusal. Ugolino appears as the final image of sin as the betrayal of responsibility, the absolute responsibility to allow the Other to provide the victim of sacrifice by substitution, of word for flesh, of the divine blood made human flesh to substitute for flesh made human word—"Here I am! Ready!" The cross of Jesus marks the forgiveness for the original sin of substitution. The cross of Jesus forgives and connects the original sin of substitution in/to the exchange without reserve, which is love. It turns the story of responsibility in a new direction, into a new way of keeping the secret promise of beginning by forgiving the original sin of substituting the eating of flesh for the keeping of the word, the word of secret promise not to eat except as dispensation, to eat only what is provided, to feed on the flesh provided by the word of God. Now Ugolino refuses to provide the word on which his children can feed, refuses the substitution of word for flesh, and so refuses the substitution of flesh for word that offers itself as flesh—food, "This is my body, this is my blood. Take and eat. He who eats of my body and drinks of my blood shall have life within him and shall never die."

The parody in Ugolino's story of the Eucharistic discourse of Jesus, the final word concerning the sacrificial meal that commemorates the passing-over of another substitution for the sacrifice of the firstborn, encrypts the name of Jesus as the final episode of the story of Abraham in that place where the name of God can be spoken only in suspense, only in *epoche*, only as the circumlocution for the power that can do whatever it wishes, the power that is the power of all transformation, all substitution, all conversion, the power of language to transform the end into the beginning by inscribing both beginning and end in the center of life, the turning point, the crisis point, the point of the cut (*krinein*) that brings judgment in the form of death, and transforms death as endpoint into the gift of a new beginning. In the figure of Ugolino, Dante's poetic imagination recognizes that in order to face up to the final secret of the Inferno, the place of judgment as damnation, judgment as final absolute responsibility for freedom's possible refusal of an impossible messianic justice, he must pass beyond justice without being able to surpass its demand; *responsibility must be converted into forgiveness,* which is to say, responsibility must turn back to its beginning, must begin again differently. Forgiveness occurs as the justice which passes on judgment by allowing faith and hope to substitute for responsibility, a certain sacrificial responsibility, and so become absolute responsibility, absolute absolution. It dispenses the demand for both human and divine sacrifice by converting it into the Gift of Death given as Divine Word made flesh offered as food, the substitution of Divine Word made flesh offered as food to human flesh so that this flesh might become word by feeding on the flesh of the Divine Word—absolute responsibility as the conversion of responsibility back to forgiveness from which it was begotten, not made, as the only begotten son; *tout autre est tout autre.*

But the substitution of divine for human sacrifice, of the woman's dispensation as feeding for the man's dispensation as providing, this absolute dispensation through the complete inversion of dispensations, this conversion of responsibility into the absolute need of the Other, this *mysterium coniunctionis,* which is the complete satisfaction of the demonic, orgiastic desire for fusion, this transformation of magic into religion as the history of responsibility, cannot be completed as a conversion, cannot be told as a completely different story, as the story of the Other, *tout autre . . . ,* without the revelation of a way of keeping the secret promise of beginning absolutely secret, keeping the secret of its encryption in the flesh under the seal of death, revealing the secret of the repression of the incorporated demonic without saying anything about the power that accomplishes the forgiveness of the violence of that repression and the transgression that demands human sacrifice. Satan's appearance in Hell provides this revelation by encrypting the power of the secret's keeping in a figure of the final irony of complete inversion as the structure of conversion.

Satan's appearance is the figural structure of the refusal of conversion as the complete inversion of the Cross of Jesus.

The opening lines of Canto xxxiv of the *Inferno* establish the pattern of Satan as the *structure* of refusal and inversion, the parody of freedom, the parodic ambiguity that is the structure of freedom itself, its essential ambiguity figured in the mirror play of "Yes!" and "No!"[17] Satan's appearance is the figural structure of the refusal of absolute responsibility offered as the mutuality of love as the inversion of the Trinitarian structural image of the necessity of the third, the necessity of substitution as the finality of responsibility and the conversion of substitution into the mutuality of communion, the absolute reciprocity of the need of life to feed and to be fed on itself—*tout autre est tout autre*—the need of the Other recognized as the absolute power of the Other to take absolute responsibility for the substitution of all others.[18] Finally, Satan's appearance is the figural structure of refusal as the inversion of the need of the Other as woman. Satan's three faces, three mouths gnawing at the three embodiments of betrayal—Cassius, Brutus, and Judas—are the final encryption in face-writing, the consummate portrayal of predatory consumption as the final human form of the refusal to feed the need of all the others by the transformative substitution of human words for the human flesh of the Divine Word. Here we see the completion of the inscription of love into the story of the secret promise of beginning. In this image of inversion, Dante portrays the absolute negation of the history of freedom, of responsibility, of religion, that is, religion as the history of responsibility and therefore of freedom. Satan is the inverse image of "salvation history," of the history that is centered on and by the Cross of Jesus, of history "saved" from ending, forgiven as the whole story, the story of the whole, which is only complete in its recognition of the need for forgiveness, the dispensation of all dispensations, forgiveness as the recognition of absolute responsibility for always beginning again, which can occur only through the hope of human faith in the divine power of love to do whatever it wishes and to wish to bind itself to the history of absolute responsibility, to the necessity of the need of all the others. Satan endlessly parodies Ugolino's insatiable predatory consumption of his neighbor, the parodic betrayal of betrayals that endlessly feeds on its own final refusal of the need of the Other. It is this refusal of the need for forgiveness on which Christianity takes the Cross of Jesus to be the final revelatory word of prophetic judgment and the mark of messianic justice. This final word, however, is the revelation of a secret. It is held in suspense for the same three days it takes Abraham to journey to Mount Moriah, the three days that are the instant, the temporal structure of the power of freedom to do whatever it wishes. It is the time of *kairos,* the absolute grace period, prior to every economic demand for every form of substitution, barter, sacrifice, redemption, expiation or retribution, the freedom of absolute absolution for the impossibility of doing justice to the Other and all of the others. Forgiveness is the way freedom does justice to absolute responsibility to the Other through all the others, all the others of the Other through and through, by the power that forgives through the dispensation of every dispensation, the power that forgives the Gift. The Gift is Impossibility itself and so can only be forgiven. It is the silent power of forgiveness that allows the story to transmit the secret promise of beginning again without saying anything, allows the secret to be kept in secret even while it is revealed as story, as history. It is revealed as the mystery of the need of and the desire for the Other incorporated and repressed in the Christian *mysterium tremendum,* the Cross of Jesus that marks the taking place of the final revelation of the story of keeping the covenant, the secret promise kept in the flesh of Isaac. The Cross of Jesus marks the place of death, death encrypted as sin (Golgotha, the place of the skull). The Cross of Jesus therefore remarks the place of original sin with the sign of the encryption of forgiveness as sacrifice, redemption and expiation, thereby marking the truth of sin as the history of betrayal by substitution (all sin is substitution; every substitution is a betrayal) that is encrypted in the absolute non-responsibility of Satan entombed in ice just as Ugolino was. Satan weeps now just as Ugolino demanded that one must weep at the story that brings tears of blood to eyes fed by mouth that consumes human flesh, flesh which has used words to betray all the others universally, all-in-one, Caesar and Jesus; flesh which has through words betrayed the flesh of the Word, betrayed the Gift of the Word made flesh given as the Gift of food—the word that keeps the secret promise, the word that dispenses sacrifice and forgives the refusal to feed and be fed.

When Virgil has Dante cling to his back as together they climb down the hairy scaffolding of Satan's torso to the "center point," the center of gravity of the earth and also of the story, the story of history, the story of freedom, they reach the turning point, the point where the history of religion as the history of absolute responsibility takes a turn in a completely different direction, turns into the story of absolute responsibility for giving the Gift of Death in a completely different way than the way Abraham declares himself ready to give the gift of death to the Other and all the others; their journey turns into the story of an absolutely different absolute responsibility and an absolutely different Gift of Death, given according to the absolutely different need of the Other for all the others, the gift that forgives the necessary sacrifice of all the others to the Other by the sacrifice of the Other for all the others. The story of the Cross of Jesus finally turns around the center of gravity that it marks as the turning in the story of giving the Gift of Death, the conversion of that story into the story that passes on judgment and defers to messianic justice according to the hope that is encrypted in the story of the resurrection of Jesus. Dante's conversion in writing tells the story of the Gift of Death differently than the story of Abraham, according to the different ways of keeping the secret that are revealed by women and by the demand for divine sacrifice that are suspended in the story of Abraham.

Just as a mother carries her child in the womb before it undergoes the conversion of birth, Virgil carries the pilgrim Dante on his back as together they climb first down and then up the body of Satan. In so doing, they pass the navel of the world, pass the turning pint that is the same point at which the story began in the Dark Wood, *nel mezzo,* but now their passing through that point happens differently and becomes a passing over to the other side, the other world, the southern Hemisphere, the other face of the earth, the forgotten hidden face, forgotten and hidden since the beginning, since the time when exile had taken place, where all the same things must begin again, but where they must take place differently. So too with Derrida, here their paths cross. Having past through the ever-narrowing going-around-in-circles of *Circumfession,* after passing through the gate of Abraham, who had left his mark so deeply cut in the writer's flesh that he had feared it had cut him off from his dying mother and his mother's dying, now things begin to happen differently. The *différance* that had always been happening in his writing, which had always been deferring something in his writing, deferring something in writing, now begins to happen again in a new way starting with the fourth essay of *The Gift of Death,* and continuing in the direction of "To Forgive." Derrida, passing through the Gate of Abraham, through Kierkegaard's concluding postscript to *Fear and Trembling* regarding the father who sees in secret, and through the turning point where absolute responsibility undergoes an absolute conversion, the conversion of life into death into life again (and again) absolute forgiveness, and finally passes over into the Gift of Death, or what Dante calls Resurrection.

## CHAPTER THREE

# Purgatorio: Re-turning to the Scene of Forgiveness

Chapter 3 takes up the aporia of forgiveness as the precise "turning point" through which the process of constant conversion must always pass so as to begin again. Dante locates this turning point in the Resurrection of Jesus, the secret encrypted in the sign of the Cross. For Derrida, this figure of constant conversion traces the movement of life passing over into a new beginning by passing through the *Gift of Death*. The *Purgatorio* traces this movement in the ascent of the mountain by Dante and Virgil interpreted as a "school of contemplation," in which the pilgrim learns to sustain the suffering of the arrival of the "Other/woman," the one who is to come, the one whose eyes and mouth, whose face bears the secret promise of the death of love forgiven. In the *Purgatorio*, Beatrice's herself is the mountain, the "high place" of the Other, and the resurrected one who comes again in the peak experience of Resurrection to repeat the experience of Genesis, of always beginning again. She is Eve to Dante's Adam, allowing him to begin again the history of love as feeding and eating and to repeat the history of original sin as substitution with a difference. The poetry of Beatrice's eucharistic encounter with Dante in the Earthly Paradise reveals in writing that with which Derrida concerns himself in the essay, "To Forgive." This essay, read alongside the text of the Purgatorio, configures the aporia of forgiveness in the face-to-face encounter in letters of Jankélévitch with the young German who invites him to face up to the arrival of the other who has recognized the need for forgiveness. This encounter revisits the scene of forgiveness marked out by Dante and Beatrice, Adam and Eve, and reconfigures the encounter of Derrida and Georgette in *Circumfession* within the space of the arrival of the Gift of Death, so as to situate the aporia of forgiveness against the horizon of the question of crimes against humanity as the "Unforgivable," and of original sin as the crime of existing.

## ACCEPTING FORGIVENESS: SEEING IN SECRET
## THROUGH THE EYES OF THE OTHER (WOMAN)

### TEXTUAL REFLECTION

> To course over better waters the little bark of my genius now hoists our
> sails, leaving behind her a sea so cruel; and I will sing of that second realm
> where the human spirit is purged and becomes fit to ascend to Heaven.
> But here let dead poetry rise again, oh holy Muses, since I am yours; and
> here let Calliope rise up somewhat, accompanying my song with that strain
> whose stroke the wretched Pies felt so that they despaired of pardon. (*Purg.*,
> i, 1–12)

The second Cantica begins on Easter Sunday morning, just before dawn,
with a plea and a prayer of hope—for a resurrection in writing! "But here
let dead poetry rise up again!" Having passed through the turning point, the
point of conversion, where death and life hang in the balance, suspended in
the instant of decision, Dante has passed on through poetry and in writing.
Carried through and over and beyond by Virgil, clinging to the back of Virgil,
Dante has passed over the final death promised in passing through the Gate
of Abraham. He has passed through death given as a gift marked in its refusal
by Satan, the structure of the "No!" converted into the ladder of the "Yes!" By
which they now climb up through death, through the turning point where in
death, as death, through death, the "No!" turns into "Yes!" They climb through
the rock, the rock of the heart turned to stone, through the bedrock that supports the sleep of the dead, the rock of the tomb. Having arrived on the shore
of Mount Purgatory, they issue out into a light that is beginning to dawn, a
light that is changing from night into day, the light of the night transforming
itself into the light of the day:

> Sweet hue of oriental sapphire which was gathering in the serene face of the
> sky, pure it even to the first Circle, to my eyes restored the light as soon as I
> issued forth from the dead air that had afflicted my eyes and breast. (*Purg.*,
> i, 13–18)

This is the revelation of the moment, the instant that reveals what happened in secret and now begins to come to light. Here begins the revelation of
the Gift of Death as resurrection, in writing, of another beginning, of a new
life in writing:

> And when the Sabbath was passed Mary Magdalene, and Mary the
> mother of James, and Salome brought spices so that they might anoint him.
> And very early on the first day of the week they went to the tomb when the
> sun had risen. And they were saying to one another, "Who will roll away the
> stone for us from the door of the tomb?" And looking up they saw that the
> stone was rolled back; it was very large. And entering the tomb, they saw a

young man sitting on the right side dressed in a white robe; and they were amazed. And he said to them, "Do not be amazed; you seek Jesus of Nazareth, who was crucified. He has risen, he is not here; see the place where they laid him. But go, tell his disciples and Peter that he is going before you to Galilee; there you will see him, as he told you." And they went out and fled from the tomb; for trembling and astonishment had come upon them; and they said nothing to anyone, for they were afraid. (Mark 16:1–8)

Women tremble too, sometimes. Sometimes women say nothing and keep a secret.

## "*Tout Autre Est Tout Autre*"

Derrida begins the last of the four essays in *The Gift of Death* with the observation, "every other (one) is every (bit) other—the stakes seen to be altered by the trembling of this dictum . . . It becomes the secret of all secrets" (*GD*, 82). Here it is the "dictum" itself that trembles, no doubt the result and the cause of the trembling that Abraham, Kierkegaard, and Derrida himself all undergo. Perhaps too, Dante felt this trembling as he wrote. The trembling of the sentence signals secrecy, the secret of all secrets. It signals not a secret, nor even all secrets, but secrecy itself, the ceaseless, turbulent churning in which each and every secret (other) is every (bit) other secret. The secret is the Other; the secret is in the Other, and so the Other is in secret. Derrida further observes that Kierkegaard's gesture of marking this inscription of secrecy in the trembling that the story of Abraham both describes and makes happen is further remarked by Kierkegaard's transcription of Abraham's story into the story of Jesus' sayings on sacrifice in Matthew 6. Kierkegaard says:

> "But anyone who loves God needs no tears, no admiration: he forgets the suffering in the love. Indeed, so completely has he forgotten it that there would not be the slightest trace of his suffering if God himself did not remember it, *for he sees in secret* and recognizes distress and counts the tears and forgets nothing." (Quoted in *GD*, 120; emphasis added)

The writer of Matthew has Jesus call the God who sees in secret, "Father," referring to a way of seeing in secret that demands and dispenses sacrifice and thereby institutes a conversion, a new covenant. This new dispensation functions according to "heavenly" economy that pays new, better wages in secret, on the condition that one separate oneself from the "hypocrites," those who escape careful scrutiny while appearing to place all under judgment because they are good actors, those who pretend that every transaction should be conducted "under scrutiny" (*upokrisis*) because they have an answer for everything and are trained to be ready with their lines. Like trained actors, they enjoy having everything watched over anxiously and counted up and tallied under the law of parity, the "old" law of the "old" covenant, an eye for an eye and a tooth

for a tooth, while they themselves get on splendidly impersonating or counterfeiting living up to this standard.

Commenting on this section of *The Gift of Death*, Caputo makes it clear
that the writer of Matthew had an ax to grind against "the Jews," and so chose
as the voice of his point of view, a tax collector, a factor of Roman oppression
and injustice in the eyes of the scribes and Pharisees, to promulgate the new
economy of heavenly exchange, the New Deal of the Kingdom for those who
separate themselves yet again from those who were already separated and cut
off from all the others.[1] The violence required by this new economy to repress
the hypocrisy that capitalizes on oppression and persecution demands a separation and cutting off and cutting out that breaks free of the tighter circle of
the circumcision that circumscribed the old economy of the old secret: "If your
hand offend, cut it off; if your eye offend, pluck it out and cast it from you."
Those who break with and separate themselves from parity and hypercriticize
themselves shall be hyperwitnessed by their father who sees in secret. This violence is the endnote to Kierkegaard's *Fear and Trembling*. It takes note of where
the sacrificial economy of fathers and sons is leading, where it must end up.
Derrida notes the heightening of both the violence and the stakes, the risk that
is taken ("the greater the risk, the greater the faith") in Kierkegaard's following out of Abraham's story to its necessary hyperbolic conclusion in the story
of the Father of Jesus. This heightening is marked by the two superscripts to
*"Tout Autre"*: "the danger is so great that I excuse the suppression of the object,"
and " . . . that stroke of genius called Christianity." Both quotations refer to
the heightened risk and promised return predicted for the economic circulation
entered into by the movement from *hypo*-crisy to *hyper*-crisy. For those who
pass on judgment, who pass over judgment and who are above judgment in
comparison to the others because they hold themselves to a higher standard, a
standard that goes beyond equity and parity, these the Other/God who sees in
the secrecy of separation from judgment will reward in secret.

By inscribing the story of Abraham and Isaac directly into the hypercritical story of Jesus and "the Father," Kierkegaard takes the risk of calling
into question whether or not, or in what sense, the sacrifice of Jesus can lay
claim to a power and authority great enough to make good a new dispensation, establish a new Kingdom, the Kingdom of God on earth, a Kingdom in
which sacrifice itself is sacrificed for the sake of a new way of giving the Gift
of Death, a new way of keeping the secret of life, of always beginning again, a
new way of encrypting life and keeping its secret in death and through death.
This claim of power and authority for death, made in the name of Jesus, would
express the sense in which Patočka speaks of the Christian *mysterium tremendum* as having repressed the mystery of the orgiastic that is incorporated in
the Greek style of giving the gift of death, the Socratic style of self-knowledge
and the impersonal Platonic Good that separates the soul from the body by
rendering it immortal. In the claim of power made by traditional Christianity
for the sacrificial death of Jesus, a new form of secrecy is revealed, a secrecy

contained not in the separation of soul from body, but in the reunion of soul and body in Resurrection. This is achieved by the substitute separation of flesh from spirit, where, in the terminology of St. Paul, these two signify the force of sin and the force of love in human existence. But St. Paul is already involved in the risk and suspense of the translation of the story of Jesus the Jew into the language of Greece and Rome, of the "old" covenant into the "new," via the way that leads into and through the "other" kingdom, the Empire. His version of the story of Resurrection, and even that of the writer of Matthew's gospel, intervene within a history that occurs subsequent to the moment in which this decisive turn in the history of "European responsibility" takes place. That moment remains shrouded in the secrecy that precedes the day of Pentecost, the anniversary of the giving of the Law to Moses, that symbolic "day" which is 10 days after the "40 days," the time parallel to the time of Israel's wandering in the desert after the other Passover. On the day of Pentecost, Peter and the other disciples tell their story of the resurrection of Jesus in their own language and it is heard in their own languages by all the others who were gathered in Jerusalem. Derrida indirectly alludes to this dissemination of the mother-tongue by referencing the "trick" of language contained in the formula *"tout autre est tout autre,"* that singularity of expression peculiar to his own language or at least family of languages, the secret of which he is endeavoring to trans-mit in the essay without disclosing it (*GD,* 87–88).

Behind all these stories, all these transmissions of the secret encrypted in the story of the resurrection of Jesus, lies the risk that Kierkegaard ventures, though without taking responsibility for it, encrypting that risk in the story of the hypercritical economy of reward and remuneration that is recounted in Matthew 6, under the seal of the name of the Father of Jesus who sees in secret. Kierkegaard, in other words, enlists the writer of Matthew's gospel as co-conspirator in giving credence to the claim of power which authorizes the new Christian dispensation, a dispensation that exceeds and supersedes the dispensation of the sacrifice of Isaac by father Abraham. Kierkegaard sug-gests, without taking responsibility, the substitution of the Father of Jesus for the father of Isaac, the substitution of the hyperdispensation, in secret, of the sacrifice of Jesus, for the literal dispensation, in the open, of the sacrifice of Isaac. What Kierkegaard does not say, does not risk openly, is the revelation that "resurrection" names the secret of this dispensation of all dispensations, the secret that dispenses with sacrifice, which sacrifices sacrifice once and for all. Resurrection takes place not by substituting one sacrifice, the hyperbolic, an-economic sacrifice by God of his beloved son *in the place of,* as a substitute for, Isaac the beloved son of Abraham, by substituting divine sacrifice for human sacrifice, but rather by forgiving, by passing over, by passing on judg-ment of the entire history of economical exchange that includes sin, debt, retribution, redemption, and remuneration, includes even the notion of sac-rifice itself. Resurrection reveals the death of Jesus to be not in any sense a sacrifice that repays the debt of original sin, but the instant of decision that marks a new beginning, a beginning that is divine as are all true beginnings, the beginning of a new secrecy, the keeping secret of a new creation and a new promise, a moment of decision that begins to be revealed in the resurrection of Jesus, the "first-born of the dead," the first gift of death, the first for whom death has the forgiven meaning of new life, not life toward death but life through death.

The trembling of the dictum, *"tout autre est tout autre,"* with which Derrida begins the essay culminates in the trembling of the suspense into which Nietzsche's remark, "that stroke of genius called Christianity," precipitates the history of religion as the history of responsibility that marks the end of the trajectory which Kierkegaard traces from the sacrifice of Isaac to the sacrifice of Jesus, at least insofar as the latter name is taken to be the signature over which the hypercritical economy of Matthew 6 is written. But as Derrida, following Nietzsche, recognizes the trembling in suspense of this evangelical text signals the violence of the force necessary to accomplish the repression both of the Abraham story, with its promise of the divine victim to substitute for the human victim, and the story of Socrates, with its promise of an immaterial psychic life to substitute for the flesh and blood of human identity. Derrida makes it clear that while the account of the Kingdom of God and the advent of messianic justice promised as the new dispensation for those who allow themselves to be taken into its secret can certainly be taken as a parable of the Kingdom of the excessive love that forgets itself, and gives without counting the cost, *at the same time,* Nietzsche insists on calling the question that articulates the risk of Kierkegaard's faith, the risk without which there is no faith, the risk that hyperbolically heightens the faith, namely, the risk that Matthew 6 can be read as inciting and provoking a new temptation, a new history of substitution and a new economy of exchange at the very moment when the hope of a gift that exceeds all expectation and compensation is raised, at the very moment when hope for the coming of the Messiah and messianic justice seems to take on new life. This temptation, this provocation to transgression, is necessary: it is the signal of the force of the repression necessary to dispense sacrifice, the expression of the violence that is thought of as "the sacrifice of sacrifice," the snare in which the secret promise of the covenant that is transmitted as the rule of fathers and sons is necessarily entangled, when tears are regarded as unnecessary and become only a memory, even when those tears are each counted and treasured away in the chest of the heart.

Derrida introduces this note of Nietzschean suspicion regarding the heart as a secret treasure chest by raising the possibility of reading Matthew 6 in another way:

> In order to eschew idolatrous or iconistic simplicisms, that is visible images and ready-made representations [that is, of "better images" and "greater rewards"] it might be necessary to understand this sentence ("and thy Father which seeth in secret . . . shall reward thee . . .") as something other than a

proposition concerning God, this subject, entity, or X who on the one hand would already exist and who, on the other hand, what is more, would be endowed with attributes such as paternity and the power to penetrate secrets . . . Then we might say: God is the name of the possibility I have of keeping the secret that is visible from the interior but not from the exterior. Once such a structure of conscience exists, of being-with-oneself, of speaking, that is, of producing invisible sense, once I have within me, *thanks to the invisible word as such*, a witness that others cannot see, and who is therefore *at the same time other than me and more intimate with myself*, once I can have a secret relationship with myself and not tell everything, once there is secrecy and secret witnessing within me, then what I call God exists, (there is) what I call God in me, (it happens that) I call myself God—a phrase that is difficult to distinguish from "God calls me," for it is on that condition that I can call myself or that I am called in secret . . . That is the history of God and of the name of God as the history of secrecy, a history that is at the same time secret and without any secrets. Such a history is also an economy. (*GD*, 108–109)

"Such a history is also an economy," a substitute for the economy of sacrifice. Idolatry and sacrifice go together necessarily. Every sacrifice is idolatry; idols by definition demand sacrifice. All self-enclosed systems of Reason for example are idolatrous by virtue of the sacrificial substitution of knowledge for faith: science, a burnt offering. Every economy is a substitute, for economy itself is substitution; every circulation is a substitute for secrecy, for keeping to oneself, for being in secret, for the gift which God-or death gives in secret. The story of sacrifice, the story that culminates with the story of God the Father of Jesus, is a substitute for the story of personal existence which is freed from circulation by the interruption which is the Gift of Death. Derrida's point here, a point he goes on to reinforce with the evidence of the suspicion suggested by the quotations from Baudelaire and Nietzsche that appear as superscripts to the essay, seems to be the constant, necessary danger of idolatry, meaning here the polymorphic danger of everything we are tempted to offer in sacrifice to an other, which substitutes for the Other, who is in secret, unable to solicit or to be solicited, everything we are tempted to offer in sacrifice as a substitute for ourselves. To reduce the Other to an interior witness, to entomb and encrypt, yes—to use Dante's image, to devour, consume, to feed upon and digest the Other, transmogrifying and transmographifying the Other into ourselves—this is the Satanic, diabolical secret of every economy, of every sin insofar as "sin" can be understood as the refusal of the gift. It is the refusal of the giving by which the Other offers itself, the giving that is before every demand and the condition of every demand, the refusal that operates by insisting on substituting an economy of exchange, insists on substitution as the formality and law of every economy under whatever form. This amounts not simply to a foregoing of sacrifice or even a sacrifice of sacrifice itself, but a condemnation of sacrifice, of sacrifice *by itself*, as sin itself, as refusal of the Other through the refusal of the gift of the Other, which is also a refusal of "self," of one's own proper identity, which is necessarily improper because it is identity as the receiving and accepting of the gift of the Other. It is always sin to sacrifice, to sacrifice another, or absurdly, to "sacrifice oneself," which cannot be done, which should not be done, because to sacrifice is to substitute an other for oneself in the face of the desire of the Other, the desire of the Other which is to give, and only to give, to give finally, not to enter into a barter economy of exchange that would amount to a robbery, a rape, the violation and transgression of what ever is "sacred" or "divine," whatever is Other, in that it has the initiative that is absolute, necessary and "perfect" ("be perfect as your Father is perfect"). To the Other belongs the *pre*-rogative of giving. Giving means not to ask in return; giving is a pre-rogative, not a pretext for or solicitation of bartering. It does not ask first if it may give, and it does not ask, after giving, for something in return. Giving is, as Heidegger said, the occurrence of time that gives past (pre) and future (post), and presents the present in the taking place of the gift. Every form of sacrifice is the refusal of the divine Gift, refusal of the divine itself, refusal of the Other, for these three—Gift, the divine (God) and the Other—these three are one, and all three in one are Impossible.

Derrida does not say all of this for himself in the essay. What he does say, over the signatures first of Baudelaire and then of Nietzsche, makes two more specific points relating to the themes of violence (suppression, repression, etc.) and trembling. Baudelaire's mention of "suppression" occurs in the section of his pamphlet, "The Pagan School,"[2] which Derrida characterizes as a condemnation of "counterfeiting" as a type of "paganism," that is, as a type of idolatry that is the necessary concomitant of sacrifice. The idol, only the idol, demands sacrifice. To be the object to which sacrifice is offered of itself constitutes the object as an idol. Counterfeiting, in other words, is a type of substitution, and like all substitution sets up an economy that is both fraudulent and mortally dangerous, *insofar as it operates in secret,* insofar as it opposes one type of secrecy, the secrecy of substitution and hiding, to another, the secrecy of the Gift:

> I understand the rage of iconoclasts and Moslems against all images. I admit all the remorse of St. Augustine for the too-great pleasure of the eyes. *The danger is so great that I excuse the suppression of the object.* The folly of art is equal to the abuse of the mind. The creation of one of these two supremacies results in foolishness, hardness of heart and in enormous pride and egoism. I recall having heard an artist, who was a practical joker and who had received a false coin, say on one occasion: I shall keep it for some poor person. The wretch took an infernal pleasure in robbing the poor and in enjoying at the same time the benefit of a reputation for charity. ("The Pagan School," 77; emphasis added)

Derrida finds in the passage a double image of "counterfeiting" that illustrates the need for a double "suppression" of the object. First, there is the more straightforward counterfeiting and hypocrisy of the one who gives the false coin. But in the identity of this person as an artist, there is the implication of a second form of counterfeiting and a higher hypocrisy, a hyper-crisy, parallel to the aestheticism that Kierkegaard identifies, and which gives for the sake of the enjoyment or pleasure it receives from the giving as the reward of the giving, while still knowing that the object given as gift is counterfeit. Derrida glosses this double suppression as follows:

> . . . as soon as it is calculated (starting from the simple intention of giving *as such*, starting from sense, knowledge, and what ever takes recognition into account), the gift suppresses the object (of the gift). It denies it as such. In order to avoid this negation or distraction at all costs, one must proceed to *another* suppression of the object: that of keeping in the gift only the giving, the act of giving and intention to give, not be given, which in the end does not count. One must give without knowing, without knowledge or recognition, without *thanks* [*remerciement*]: without anything, or at least without any object. (*GD*, 112)

Derrida's identification of the "double" suppression of the object turns on identification of a double "object" of giving: on the one hand, the relative "value" of the gift to the other to whom it is given based on a calculation of that value with the intention of giving "more" than we receive in return, and on the other hand, the absolute value of the gift that lies in the value of "giving" itself, of self-giving, of giving as a way to possess ourselves, and so to deny and betray the Other. In this act of betrayal, we choose to give as a way to possess ourselves in self-knowing and through recognition by the Other. The gift must be without thanks, without return, without any "object" at all; it must be and remain an absolute secret. This constitutes a demystification of the gift in the sense that it unveils a mystery that is without secrecy, a mystery in which the object is "suppressed," or merely hidden, even if violently and doubly hidden, like the orgiastic mystery that is incorporated and repressed by Christianity. Despite undergoing the double operation of separation by which a substitute is created through suppression and kept hidden through the mechanism of sacrifice, this operation only produces a mystery without secrecy. It retains its object in both senses, both values of the giving by keeping them hidden in the hope that they can be seen and enjoyed in "secret"—gnosticism, the mystagogic secrecy of the hidden, that which *is kept* in secret, and therefore not really given. This calculation according to mysterious and hidden values, this substitute for secrecy in which one is not really alone, wherein one is not after all singular, thanks to the presence of one who sees and witnesses in secret, thanks to God, is no secrecy at all. Such giving depends entirely on "values," both relative and absolute, which as values necessarily require calculation, knowledge, and recognition. The demystification accomplished by an analysis of "the double suppression" of "the Pagan School" amounts to a critique of all systems of valuation, a critique of all conspiratorial views of secrecy that substitute shared knowledge of hidden objects and purposes for the unique singularity of the genuine solitude in which one experiences fear and trembling in the face of the demand for absolute secrecy and absolute, resolute responsibility for giving the Gift of Death without receiving thanks, without receiving anything, without any object.

Derrida recognizes in this demystification the precise figure of Nietzsche's critique both of Western morality and Western religion, Christian religion, insofar as both demand and rest on belief in an other who is in on the "secret," one who shares the secret, who witnesses and sees in secret, an other who keeps to him- or herself so as to be hidden, the better to guarantee that she will be able to see what is hidden, one who can guarantee that there will be no real secrecy, no real Other, no real Gift without object. Believing in the other, Nietzsche believes, dissipates the power that makes one fear and tremble in solitude. Believing guarantees that there will always be a return, and hence, that there never can really be a gift. Derrida quotes Nietzsche from *The Genealogy of Morals:*

> The justice which began with the maxim, "Everything can be paid off, everything must be paid off, ends with connivance (*durch die Finger zu sehn*) at the escape of those who cannot pay to escape—it ends, like every good thing on earth, by *destroying itself* [what is translated as "destroying itself" is literally, *"sich selbst aufhebend"* and Nietzsche adds the emphasis: "by raising itself or substituting for itself," Christian justice denies itself and so conserves itself in what seems to exceed it; it remains what it ceases to be, a cruel economy, a commerce, a contract involving debt and credit, sacrifice and vengeance] The self-destruction of Justice (*Diese Selbstaufhebung der Gerechtigkeit*)! We know the pretty name it calls itself—Grace (*Gnade*)! It remains, as is obvious, the privilege (*Vorrecht*) of the strongest, still better, their super-law (*sein Jenseits des Rechts*). (quoted in *GD*, 113–114)

For Nietzsche, "the long history of the origin of responsibility (*Verantwortlichkeit*)," which is also the history of both moral and religious conscience, is a history of violence, cruelty and sacrifice, of fault as debt or obligation (*Schuld*, as the *"Hauptbegriff,"* the cardinal idea of morality). All this, not only moral and religious responsibility and conscience, but the institutionalization of justice as well, in both theory and practice, together with the power of its claim, indeed every claim, of objectivity and authority, Nietzsche inscribes into the circularity of an economy of exchange. He even takes into account the way that justice accounts for the unaccountable, how it has learned to write off bad debts, insolvency and bankruptcy. This accounting is not, however, free of charge; rather it comes at the expense of a force of violence, a suppression of the object—justice—that immolates and destroys it in the extreme exercise of its own power turned against itself, a self-destruction, a self-cancellation (*Selbst-aufhebung*) in the canceling of all debt and guilt and responsibility.[3]

In the final moment, in the instant of *The Gift of Death*'s last words, Derrida suggests that we need to ask about the *Selbst* of this *Selbst-aufhebung* in terms of the constitution of the self in general through this secret nucleus of responsibility. Through the ideas of suppression, the double suppression of the object, and the self-destruction of Justice, on the one hand, and, on the other, the ideas of conscience, responsibility, and a "history of responsibility," accomplished as a history of religion and morality, Derrida returns at this extreme point to what Patočka says about Christianity as repression. He views the idea of the orgiastic mystery incorporated by the Platonic psychic mystery, repressed by the Christian *mysterium tremendum,* as conforming closely to the figure of the "double suppression of the object" and links this figure of power and violence directed against the "Self" (the mechanism of *ressentiment* that is central to the *Genealogy of Morals*) to what Nietzsche calls the "stroke of genius called Christianity." Of this "sacrificial hubris," this hyperbolic, hypercritical economy of excess put into circulation through the sacrifice of Christ for love of the debtor, this economy of sacrifice taken to the absolute extreme, to the point of sacrificing (the demand for) sacrifice itself, Nietzsche exclaims:

> . . . that paradoxical and awful expedient, through which a tortured humanity has found temporary alleviation, that stroke of genius called Christianity (*jenem Geniestreich des Christentum*):—God personally immolating himself for the debt of man, God paying himself personally out of a pound of his own flesh, God as the one being who can deliver man from what for man had become unacquitable (*unablösbar*)—the creditor (*der Gläubinger*) playing scapegoat for his debtor (*seinen Schuldner*) from love (can you believe it? [*sollte man's glauben*]) from love of his debtor . . . (quoted in *GD,* 114)

Caputo comments insightfully (*PTJD,* 217–222) regarding this "instant" in which *The Gift of Death* makes its decision about how to end, how to finish or complete itself, where to situate itself in the end regarding the questions of the gift, responsibility, sacrifice, and the economics of credit and debt. Among other things, Caputo cautions that this final "moment" of the text must be read slowly and carefully, with an eye for what he refers to as "the characteristic reserve of deconstruction which always hesitates before identifying the decisive, exhaustive, final, the central word" (*PTJD,* 219). He points out in particular that Derrida's gloss on Nietzsche's statement begins by conditioning Nietzsche's identification of the "stroke of genius" with the qualifying phrase "if there is such a thing." Caputo also notes that Derrida cautions against too quickly crediting Nietzsche's attribution of this genial stroke to "Christianity," when Derrida again hypothesizes it by saying, "If . . . one were *able* to attribute it *to someone or something called Christianity.*" The point Caputo makes is that Derrida does not assume here that Nietzsche should necessarily have the "final" word about the meaning of his identification of the self-destruction of justice in the form of a hyperbolic economy of sacrifice, or even more important, about the nature of belief, faith, credit or "grace," and love that he himself introduces in the critical discourse on responsibility in *Genealogy*—"can you believe it?" Nietzsche asks. Derrida notes that this rhetorical question itself trembles "suspended" between "the credit of the creditor" ([*créancier*] *Gläu-biger*) and the "credence ([*croyance*] *Glauben*) of the believer [*croyant*]. How can one believe this history of credence or credit?" (*GD*, 115).

This rhetorical question questions itself, calling into question its own claim to be credited or believed. *The Gift of Death* concludes with a cautious "finality" that depends on, hangs in the balance of, the question of belief itself. This question doubles back on itself in the trembling suspense that is the very self of the believer as questioner (Can you believe it?), and also of the questioner as believer (Can you question that you believe?), given that questioning is itself an act of belief. In questioning, we credit the possibility of facing up to the Other as one who could be questioned and who could be questioning. It is then that we can ask: "Who do I love when I love my God?" "Who am I?" "Who is Jesus?" These questions bring one before the possibility of questioning as a question; that is, the possibility of the questioning of belief. Here one must note the double sense of the genitive: every belief can, indeed, must be questioned, but at the same time, every question originates in a believing, in faith in and crediting of every relation of the "self" and Other that can arise only in this way. Such a question implicates both of its genetic elements equally. We cannot help catching the echo here of the formula with which the essay opens, the return to its first word in its final word: "*tout autre est tout autre,*" which in turn echoes the return of another Augustinian formula, "*Credo ut intelligam*; I believe in order to understand," which recognizes and acknowledges the dependence of all selfhood on situating oneself in relation to every other in the recognition of the Other, and which expresses itself as the faith of questioning in the face of the Other. Derrida makes a gesture toward this belief, faith, credence, and crediting that exercises itself as the pre-rogative that comes before all belief and all questions, the power of being in question, which marks the crypt where *The Gift of Death* rests in secret:

> As often happens, the call of or for the question, and the request that echoes through it, takes us further than the response. The question, the request, and the appeal *must* indeed have begun, since the eve of their awakening, by receiving accreditation from the other: by being believed. Nietzsche must indeed believe he knows what believing means, unless he believes it is all make-believe [*à moins qu'il n'entende le faire accroire*]. (*GD*, 115)

As shall emerge, Derrida is making an oblique, anticipatory gesture here in the direction of forgiveness as that which is "before" the Gift. In a sense, he is still on the way toward approaching this Gift face to face. Forgiveness is the pre-rogative of the divine, but not of the divine alone; it is only insofar as the divine is regarded as a person, as having a face on which responsibility can be written, that the divine is involved in the an-economy of forgiveness, the unclosed circle that situates but does not contain the empty Secret of beginning. Faith is impossible, but it occurs; questioning is impossible, but it occurs and continues to occur by always beginning again. Forgiveness seems to have to do with this structure through which the Impossible, in its diverse faces, occurs. Forgiveness is the way in which the Impossible happens.

Caputo rightly registers one facet of *The Gift of Death*'s ending in the question of belief when he observes that *Donner la mort* does not conclude with the dismissal of faith, because "deconstruction, if there is such a thing, means to show that there is never a final word" (*PTJD*, 218). What it accomplishes is rather a deconstructive delimitation of belief as economic exchange, which inevitably leads to its own self-destruction; by that very stroke, it opens up the question of another way of believing, which involves the secret of keeping faith. This manner of keeping the question of belief open, of being able to go on questioning, of keeping in suspense the double genitive that is the genesis of the question, the questioning of belief and the belief of questioning, the question of who it is that questions and who it is that is questioned, is not simply central to deconstruction; rather, it is deconstruction. As Caputo says, deconstruction, if there is such a thing, can never be a dismissal of faith inasmuch as deconstruction is itself faith, even a blind faith. "The point of *Donner la mort* then is not to undo faith but to insist on the an-economic character of faith, that faith is always a matter of the gift and of giving, not a transaction between creditor and debtor" (*PTJD*, 218). This deconstructive delimitation of faith that opens up the possibility of a faith which is an-economic because it is the faith of a giving that keeps nothing for itself, not even in secret, a giving which, like the question, is always already underway, leads us to the question of how this other way of giving, this giving that is always every bit other, this giving of the Other, this giving of the Gift of Death, which is final, takes place in the absolute secrecy of absolute responsibility. How can one accept responsibility for questioning what takes place in absolute secrecy as a giving that has no object and no return?

Still, this is precisely the question of Dante's *Purgatorio:* How does repentance turn into another way of taking responsibility? It is a question of how one finally accepts the gift of love offered as forgiveness. This is a question of another way of giving, the Other's way of giving, giving without return, a giving that forgets itself and so must be remembered by the other and all of the others, a giving that calls for an other way of calling, which we can call forgiving. In Dante's story, and in Derrida's own story in *Circumfession*, this other way of giving, the way of the Other's giving in absolute secrecy without seeing or being seen, is revealed by the giving of the Other as woman, where the "Other" and "woman," the other/woman, is another name for God/death, another name for the way of giving that gives the gift of God/death, for-giving, the for-giving of the Other/woman—in writing. In absolute secrecy, this gift of death is for-given, appearing as the absolute responsibility of faith in the Other/woman's way of giving.

Dante's *Purgatorio* is the place of repentance, that is, of the acceptance of forgiveness, the acceptance of the gift of love offered as forgiveness. Forgiveness is a way of giving that names a way of giving the gift of death other than sacrifice. Specifically, it names another way of giving than by the sacrifice of sacrifice, which is finally the refusal of sacrifice, a turning back and return of sacrifice by its own hyperbolic and hypercritical self-destruction. Repentance names the acceptance of forgiveness as the gift of death given through faith in the resurrection of Jesus. The resurrection of Jesus names the revelation through faith and for faith of a way of giving the Gift of Death other than through the sacrificial economy of fathers and sons. Resurrection names the way of giving of the Other/woman, she who was unnamed in the story of Isaac and Abraham and whose name is the doubly suppressed object, the name that is repressed in the *mysterium tremendum* of the Christian story as well as in the writing of the Jewish and Islamic stories. The *Purgatorio* is Dante's gesture of repentance in writing for the violent force of repression in the *Vita nuova*, which demanded the sacrifice of Beatrice on the sacrificial altar of Amor's demand that she consume Dante's heart. This violence kindles the fires of sacrifice in which all joy and love are consumed. This dream of the sacrifice of sacrifice, of the substitution of her consumption for his refusal of sacrifice, and therefore his substitution of her death for his own, his way of giving her a counterfeit of the gift of death must be rewritten in the *Purgatorio* as another dream, indeed three other dreams, which, through the work of dream-substitution, prepare for what all his dreams dis-place: the face of Beatrice herself.

Beatrice herself is the mountain of Purgatory that the penitent Dante must climb, the mountain that itself is the displaced mass of the pit of Hell. Beatrice must remain in secret until Dante is capable of seeing her face to face, and so she must appear first as the mountain to which he, like Abraham, must journey in fear and trembling and must climb. Beatrice appears as the mountain in the mirror-play topology of the "other" Hemisphere, the Hemisphere all of water, over which the spirit of God still can breathe, as it did in the beginning, and into which the hard-hearted stone of the Inferno has been displaced in the instant of conversion to become the rugged rock of mountain. Beatrice as the mountain of Purgatory is both the dream displacement of the Other/woman who has suffered the violent repression of sacrifice, and the Gate of repentance, figured as St. Peter's Gate, the Gate of "Mother Church" through which Dante must pass in order to pass through the waters of baptism in the two rivers of the Earthly Paradise. There he will be baptized into the death and resurrection of Jesus, baptized into the absolute secrecy of the gift of death, for-given and appearing now as resurrection. There he takes responsibility in writing for himself, Dante, as he is named by the Other/woman. She is empowered to give that name because she takes responsibility for her own name even as she names the other, the one he has sacrificed in writing and in the unkept promise of writing. *Purgatorio* is the place of the displaced Other/woman, Beatrice, who for-gives the unkept promise of writing that had been given in counterfeit. In repentance, in learning to repent, in learning to keep the faith that Beatrice for-gives and to give his promise to Beatrice without being able to keep it, Dante learns to accept the gift that he cannot give himself, the gift that can only be given in another way, in the Other/woman's way, in the way that only God/death can give, the gift that can only be for-given. Love is impossible; no one can give this gift, it can only be forgiven, and accepted as forgiveness. Love is an impossible, empty secrecy that can only be given as forgiveness, the other way of giving, the gift of the Other, God/death, which is revealed as the gift of faith in the resurrection of Jesus, the revelation of a new life, a new way of beginning and always beginning again, a new way of passing on, the impossible finality of the "Yes!" in the instant of responsibility. In the earthly paradise at the top of the mountain Dante identifies himself in fear and trembling with that other way of "refusal," the refusal of substitution, through faith in the Other who never gives, never comes, never does justice, but only forgives, only loves, and who therefore must and can be forgiven.

After Dante and Virgil emerge from the Inferno, after the conversion of their way of going on that occurs on the scaffolding of Satan, the structure of the refusal of sacrifice, the structure of the finality of the refusal of sacrifice, the final "No!" which stops the necessary movements of sacrifice toward its own self-destruction, and at the same time stops the revelation of another possibility of faith and for faith, another way of questioning and being questioned by faith, the conversion of faith in the sacrifice of the Cross into the question of another faith, another way of believing. Christian belief has always insisted absolutely on the inseparability of the Cross and the Resurrection as the one mystery, the *mysterium tremendum,* the single Paschal mystery. Nevertheless, it can and must be asked, Dante's way of writing the poem in fact *does ask* (without here seeking Dante's conscious intention), how faith can sustain the secrecy of the suspense in which these two, Cross and Resurrection, tremble. What is the secret of keeping faith with the other, with each other that is every (bit) other? How can faith be kept with *each other?* How can a man keep faith with the other as woman, and of course with the other woman, each and every (bit) other woman, as well as with the repressed Other as woman? The startling originality of the *Purgatorio* as the heart, the center of the poem as a whole is its centering itself in nothing other than Dante's journey to Beatrice and tracing hers to him, following the movement of love back to its beginning as forgiveness, which is revealed as Resurrection, that is, the gift of God/or death.

## Dante's School of Contemplation: Learning to Suffer

It would be worse than merely anachronistic to fail to see that in many important ways Dante's vision in the *Purgatorio* is deeply traditional and classical, despite the fact that the notion of Purgatory itself, as a theological doctrine and spiritual teaching of Christianity, had only solidified into any truly coherent form during the last 200 years immediately prior to Dante's composition of the poem.[4] It is not primarily Dante's theology or philosophy, his physics or cosmology, or even the intellectual and cultural cast of his mind in general, wherein the genuine and profound originality of his work is to be discovered. It is in his practice as a poet, in his making of art, in his style of writing, though not merely in his "stylistics." Hence it is important to acknowledge immediately that in the *Purgatorio,* Dante's theology of grace, sin, and redemption, in its conceptual structure and content insofar as these could be abstracted from their embeddedness in the poetry, follows lines that, while innovative in some regards for that historical period, could justifiably be viewed as "mainstream," and certainly in all its major points, quite orthodox. For example, the characterization of Purgatory as a "School of Contemplation" implies that along with other, more important merits, this image and its elaboration are noteworthy for the learned way in which they draw on both the Christian and the classical Greco-Roman traditions and integrate the two in an intellectually and artistically harmonious fashion. If, however, there is something uniquely timely to our own historical situation, something genuinely "deconstructive" in spirit about the poem, so that the "spirit" of Derrida would be an apt guide to help us find our way through the poem, we should not seek it in either the theoretical structure or content of the poem, but in its three principal stylistic characteristics that are authentically, perhaps even uniquely, original to Dante *as poet:* his single-minded faith in the efficacy of Beatrice's love in his life; his clarity of focus on forgiveness as the center of the evangelical "good news"; and his inscription of the vast vision of the realms of the afterlife *nel mezzo,* that is, into the momentous "instant" of freedom and responsibility that constitutes the center of human personality, the soul. More specifically, the notion of Purgatory as a school of contemplation is singular in its originality and human appeal for the way it creates a metaphoric embodiment of repentance as Dante the pilgrim learning to accept responsibility for his need of forgiveness to be received as a gift from Beatrice face to face. The *Purgatorio* deploys that singular originality over three stylistic movements, anticipation (the shore and Ante-purgatory), preparation (the seven terraces of Purgatory proper), and consummation (the earthly Paradise), but together they have a single meaning and significance: Dante's experience of "learning," growing, becoming capable, maturing, all through suffering, to take responsibility for "himself," for his identity as one in absolute need of forgiveness, but specifically as "Dante" (so Beatrice names him), the Florentine poet who can live only by accepting forgiveness as a gift, a gift given by God/death, the Other/woman, a gift that can be given in no other way. Consequently if Derrida is to guide our reading, and if our reading of Dante is to help us read Derrida better, it is to these precise elements that we must look in an attempt to recognize how the poetry, how their being written, transforms the conceptual content, for the most part traditional, orthodox, and classical into an absolutely new beginning.

　　Let us put the question of the *Purgatorio* in another form: what more is there to repentance than the recognition of the need for forgiveness. In the *Inferno* Satan embodies this recognition when it has progressed to a full realization of the enormity of sin that lies within the capacity of freedom. The monstrosity of Satan, and particularly the grotesque masking of the Trinity in Satan's all consuming mouths, articulate the enormity of refusal that is necessarily ambivalently contained in the question of responsibility, the necessary risk of faith as a question. But while he is carried on Virgil's back, Satan becomes a ladder for Dante the pilgrim, the structure of possibility for Dante's conversion as he and Virgil pass the turning point of Satan's navel. Schematically, this conversion was from the refusal of responsibility for the very question of forgiveness, to the desire to accept forgiveness as a gift. This acceptance, however, in order to be "free," must be genuinely one's own, that is, forgiveness must be accepted in such a way that one becomes identified as a person by it and with it. For Dante, this will not occur until his face-to-face encounter with Beatrice in the Earthly Paradise after he ascends the mountain. Everything that he experiences on the mountain up to that point has one purpose only: to prepare him for that meeting and his first act of full freedom in accepting the forgiveness that Beatrice offers him, and, in so doing accepting his true identity in relation to her, to his vocation as poet, and to God. Repentance is the necessary preparation required to be able to identify oneself with and through forgiveness authentically. Forgiveness is not a gift; it is the way, the only way, in which the impossibility of the Gift can occur in the history of freedom. Forgiveness comes freely from the Other as a gift of divine grace mediated by human agency, but the acceptance of that gift is one's own responsibility. This responsibility cannot be fulfilled, however, except by one who has learned to see reality as it truly is, in the light of the love which is its original and final meaning. The effect of sin is to occlude this vision; hell is occupied by those who have "lost the good of intellect." For the Christian imagination, this vision of the truth of reality as Love is contemplation. Hence, Purgatory is imagined by Dante as a "school of contemplation," in which the capacity see the truth in full consciousness must be regained, for only when one sees the truth of who one is as a sinful freedom will one both want and be able to take responsibility for that identity by accepting forgiveness.

Dante's image for the rehabilitation of the soul's power of vision is the healing of the wounds of sin, represented by the seven *P*'s carved on his forehead by the Angel of St. Peter's Gate. These scars are the marks he bears of the seven capital sins that remain rooted in the soul even after a genuine conversion has taken place. This is because the capital sins are not simply individual sinful actions or even the cumulative sum of all such actions. They are literally the "root" of all such actions or omissions, the radical tendencies or depositions to sin that are the source of particular sins. This is why they are referred to as "capital," which comes from the Latin "caput," meaning "head" in the sense of source, as in the "headwaters" of a river. For Christianity, sin, like freedom itself, is a reality larger than the individual; this is the significance of the doctrine of "original sin," that as persons we are all implicated in and affected by sin prior to and apart from our individual choices and actions.

The transpersonal mystery of sin means that we remain caught in the web of evil even after conversion, and that mere moral reform of our own liberty is not enough to restore the integrity of our identity. This is also why the suffering of those whom Dante encounters in Purgatory must not be viewed as punishments intended to expiate guilt. Purgatory is in no way a penal colony, where convicts work off the debt of sin that they had incurred. Rather, it is a place of healing and restoration. On the other hand, it is clearly a place of suffering, and the necessity of this healing suffering can be understood only in relation to the primary role of purgatory as a school of contemplation.

The word "contemplation" comes into English as the cognate of the Latin term used to translate the Greek "*theoria*." This word has a complex and rich etymology. The verb "*theorein*" is used in the broad sense as "to see or behold," but originally it had the more technical denotation "to witness as a delegated spectator at the games or festival"; in other words, its root meaning is fundamentally religious in character and has to do with participation in the celebration of the divine mysteries by witnessing a spectacle performed for that purpose. At first this spectacle took the form of athletic contests or an official state embassy to an oracular seat; later it came to include the performances of a dramatic competition staged for a festival. With Plato, its meaning is extended into another technical field, the spectacle of the divine Ideas as they are orchestrated on the stage of Nous or mind. Here we recognize the emergence of the sense of the word "theory," with which we are familiar. In the encounter of Christian religious belief with Greek philosophy, especially in St. Augustine, the sense of contemplation develops as the Beatific Vision, the enjoyment of the vision of the "face of God," the truth of the Divine Being offered to the eye of the soul so as to fully satisfy its desire and thus fully enkindle its love. Even in overview, it is clear that from the beginning the notion of contemplation was associated with the vocabulary of freedom. The games that were the most basic form of festive activity, the liturgical procession of a state delegation to the oracle, the emergence of drama from its earliest association with music and dance in religious rites, all these indicators point to leisure, play, and celebration as the proper context for the "spectacular," that which deserves to be looked at and that which rewards the looking in and of itself, containing within itself its own meaning and significance, thereby revealing the divine and making it manifest in utter freedom of its self-movement.

It is in this sense that Dante's *Purgatorio* might be seen as his way of writing differently the use that Derrida makes of Baudelaire's "The Pagan School." To view the ascent of Mount Purgatory as a school of contemplation is to read this text as another paganism, other than the paganism of idolatry. Rather, it is the "virtuous" paganism of those noble writers whom Dante encounters in the first circle of Hell, those among whom Virgil held preeminence, whose only punishment, terrible though it is, is to suffer desire without hope. They are those who are in suspense, without finality, who suffer from a trembling heart because their hearts are "pure." Kierkegaard said purity of heart is to will one thing. Virgil and his peers will one thing, but without hope. They will the coming of the Other, the Impossible, without the hope of forgiveness for the impossibility of their desire.

The ascent of Mount Purgatory, an ascent which cannot be traced here, is necessarily written by Dante as the history of a certain responsibility, the responsibility of faith to learn to sustain the suffering of hope. Carl Jung has suggested that psychological maturity and human integrity require learning to suffer consciously, to suffer that death which is the desire of the Other always beginning again. In order to be capable of seeing Beatrice again face to face, Beatrice who names him as the one to whom she desires to show her face, the face of death forgiven as gift, Dante's faith must be disciplined to sustain the hope of Resurrection. He must learn to suffer hope for the face of the Other/God/or death, unveiled as the face of the woman whom he has loved and who loves him, who has, through death, through the gift of death, become the Other/woman, the resurrected Jesus.

## FORGIVING GIVES GIVING: PASSING ON THE SECRET

Thus, no gift without forgiveness and no forgiveness without gift; but the two all are, above all, not the same thing. (TF, 22)

Forgiveness as the impossible truth of the impossible gift. Before the gift, forgiveness. (TF, 48)

One always writes in order to confess, one always writes to ask forgiveness; I wrote something like this somewhere, forgive me for quoting myself. (TF, 49)

### PASSING ON THE SECRET

Derrida's lecture, "To Forgive: The Unforgivable and the Imprescriptible,"[5] is a confession, and so necessarily a plea for forgiveness. But a confession of what, and to whom? A plea for what, from whom? Derrida wrote *Circumfession* as a confession and a plea for mercy, forgiveness in the face of death, the death of the Other, his mother, himself. "To Forgive" is the confession of a confession, asking forgiveness for a plea for mercy. It confesses having done the Impossible and identifies the need to be forgiven, the impassioned desire to accept forgiveness for transgressing (again) the limit of the possible and for wanting to do so, for continuing to do so, for needing and wanting to do so again and again.

"Pardon, yes, pardon." The lecture begins by evoking the site and situation of forgiveness as a question, as a problematic expressive of both faith and betrayal, both hope and despair, both love and hatred. Pardon, yes, I am asking, I am taking the risk of trusting you, the other, and all the others whom my prayer might reach, to listen to me confess what I have done, who I am in what

I have done, that cannot be undone and should not have been done; I who am not justified, cannot be justified. I take the risk of saying that I have betrayed you and the others, done that which should not be done and which should not be forgiven, because it should not have been done and cannot be undone and therefore should not be forgiven because it would be unjust and irresponsible to take justice and responsibility from me. So I am taking the risk of asking you (the other[s]) to do the Impossible, which should not be done, in the hope that you will do what is Impossible because it is necessary, it must be done even though it cannot and should not be done. I hope with the passion of the infinite and absolute for the possibility of the Impossible and the gift of the Improper, which must be done because it is absolutely needed, and therefore infinitely wanted, because it has already been done and therefore must be done again, because I suffer from its already having been done, just as you (other[s]) suffer from its already having been done. I hope you will do what has to be done, the Impossible and the Improper, because it has been done, because I suffer from the Impossible, and you suffer from the Impossible, and I necessarily suffer from you to whom it has been done, just as you necessarily suffer from me to whom it has been done. I hope that you will give me again this gift which must be given, yet cannot be given and should not be given, which can only be forgiven, because it has been given, and so is suffered, and should be suffered because it should, it must be suffered.

So I hope you forgive the suffering that you have suffered from me as I have suffered from you, the suffering that was given as a gift and taken as a gift without obligation or guilt, without price or return, which was suffered as a gift and which is needed again, without obligation or guilt, price or return, needed absolutely without end, because it is wanted without end, because it has already, from the beginning, been forgiven without end. It cannot end, it should not end, it must not end, this forgiven gift which has happened, which you have suffered and I have suffered, which has been suffered in happening without responsibility, without justice, without end. I hope you will listen when I ask and not refuse to be compassionate, to suffer what should not but still must be suffered, because it is necessary to be compassionate, to share the gift of suffering without obligation or guilt, without price or return, without end, the gift which can be gift beyond all presentation, calculation and expectation, because it is only suffered and only suffering, it is absolute suffering, absolute need, absolute desire and passion, of the Other—do you hear me?—I am asking pardon, yes, pardon in the name of the Other who suffers, absolutely, who needs and suffers absolutely for no reason, innocent of obligation or guilt, without price or return, suffers for all that has been done, suffers for all to whom it has been done, suffers because it has been done, suffers all responsibility for all to all. I am asking pardon, yes, asking the gift of pardon, which you must give, because I need and want it absolutely and you need and want it absolutely; which must be offered and accepted, and so must be forgiven again without end.

Pardon; yes, pardon. I am trusting you with the hope that you will be compassionate because you must be, you absolutely need to be, be my suffering and your suffering, absolutely without end, to the very end, to the limit of suffering, because your death and my death is absolutely necessary because it is absolutely needed and wanted without end, because death has already happened, it has already been suffered without end. So I am asking you to give me the gift of death, the gift that I suffer from you and that you suffer from me, that gift that is impossible to give, that can only be given by forgiving its giving, forgiving the Impossibility of its giving, forgiving the Impossibility it gives and the possibility of its being given, forgive its already having been given, forgive again by offering and accepting the gift of death that cannot and should not be given, but has already happened through forgiveness and as forgiven. Forgiveness gives giving, which cannot be given in any other way, should not be given in any other way, because it has happened: Forgiveness; before the gift there is necessarily, always, already, again and again, forgiveness. Yes! Come again and again and again. Yes. Come again! Yes, thank you, you are welcome. Yes, just come without needing to ask, without needing to be asked; just come. Come in Justice. Just come; all I ask is that you come in compassion as a companion. Forgive me for asking, just as I forgive you for asking. Forgive me what I need, as I forgive you what you need, what I suffer from you as what you suffer from me. Yes! Come! Forgive what can only be forgiven. Forgive what can only be given as for-given. Forgive all that has happened because it has happened as for-given. All is forgiven. All is already forgiven, so it can only go on and happen again as for-given. Forgive what cannot and should not be forgiven because it has already been for-given.

Suffer all forgiveness in compassion and companionship. Share the bread and salt of the meal of these tears. Sit down at the table to feed on forgiveness, to pass forgiveness around to feed and be fed. Take and eat; to live is to consume. Pardon, yes, pardon. I am trusting you with the hope of being forgiven for offering you the gift of death and accepting the gift of death, for feeding on death as a gift forgiven, because it must be given, and can be given and should be given as forgiveness. Again I ask you, pardon! Yes, pardon; I ask forgiveness for all that has been done. I ask you in the name of Yes, Come! I ask you in the name of death, in the other name of forgiveness, the name that suffers all, that suffers all in the name of all that is Impossible, because it all is already done and must be done again. I ask forgiveness in trust and hope, in the name of "Yes!," the name that I love without end, with the infinite passion that wants to feed and be fed on the gift of death, that wants to love the death that can only be given as the gift that forgiveness gives. I ask pardon, yes, pardon in the Name of the Other, death, from whom I suffer this passion of love.

Only death can be forgiven, because only death is Impossible. Only death can forgive, because forgiveness is Impossible. Only the gift of death offers the Impossible, offers the gift of accepting without end, without obligation or guilt, without price or return, only death offers the possibility of accepting the Impossible, of accepting the Impossible as the unforgivable gift that has already happened, which has already been forgiven and must be forgiven again. To forgive is to love, to love is to forgive. *Amor fati,* the love of what is necessary because it is needed, needed because it is wanted, wanted because it has happened, happened because it has been forgiven. Only death is unforgivable; only the gift of death can give the Impossible gift of forgiveness. Only the Impossible can give the gift of Yes!, which is before and after pardon, yes, pardon. Forgiving names the love that is absolute, without before or after, both before and after all giving, which is responsible for all giving and takes responsibility for and does justice to all giving without obligation or guilt, without price or return. Forgiveness is the secret name of the love that is responsible for all giving, all offering and accepting, for every faith, every hope. Forgiveness names the secrecy of the gift without telling who shares the secret or how the secret can be shared yet still kept. Forgiveness names the secrecy of all that has happened and must happen again in the name of Love.

## The Sin of Existing

Derrida's lecture, "To Forgive," is itself a confession and a plea for forgiveness of what he had done in *Circumfession,* a confession and request for the reader's forgiveness of the confession(s) that he had made in writing in *Circumfession.* But here, as always, the confession, even the confession of a confession, is not made in his own name; it is written from another, from another writing and from the writing of another, Vladimir Jankélévitch.[6] Derrida's confession and request for forgiveness is a gift that Jankélévitch's writings offer and Derrida accepts. It is in fact the Gift of Death that Jankélévitch gives himself in writing that offers Derrida what he accepts and offers to return in the form of a confession and plea for forgiveness of what he, Derrida, had done in writing *Circumfession.* Jankélévitch's suffering of the aporia of forgiveness is revealed in the writing of *Le Pardon* and *L'imprescriptible.* In those two works, Jankélévitch takes responsibility for contradicting himself regarding forgiveness. In his lecture, Derrida quotes Jankélévitch:

> I have written two books on forgiveness: one of them, simple, very aggressive, very polemical [*pamphletaire*] whose title is *Pardonner . . .* and the other *Le Pardon* which is a philosophy book in which I study forgiveness in itself, from the point of view of Christian and Jewish ethics. I draw out an *ethics* that could be qualified as *hyperbolical* (Derrida's emphases), for which forgiveness is the highest commandment; and, on the other hand, evil always appears beyond. Forgiveness is stronger than evil and evil is stronger than forgiveness. I cannot get out of this. It is a species of oscillation that in philosophy one would describe as dialectical and which seems infinite to me. I believe in the immensity of forgiveness, in its supernaturality; I think I have

repeated this often enough, perhaps dangerously, and on the other hand, I believe in wickedness (*mechanité*). (TF, 29)

Here is the gift of death that Jankélévitch's writing offers and Derrida accepts: "I believe in the immensity of forgiveness; and on the other hand, I believe in wickedness." Death is not an idea or a conceptual event, something that happens to concepts; persons suffer death. Death is an experience of human existence. Famously for Heidegger, death is the privileged experience of human existence, Dasein, in that it is the experience of the possible Impossibility of Dasein's existence as a whole. Death is the Impossibility of all possibilities, the hyperbolic extremity of possibility, the possibility of there being no possibility at all. The possibility of Impossibility as a kind of certainty, though not a certainty of thought or even of fact, but a certainty of anticipation, the absolute ontological horizon against which all ontic possibilities must necessarily be projected. Jankélévitch's writing confesses this death as the undergoing and suffering of the Impossible in the lived experience of the impossibility of reconciling two beliefs, which for him are not mere passing opinions or heuristic hypotheses, but beliefs which, through repeated avowal, even to the point of danger, perhaps mortal danger, have taken on the force of conviction. They have become so closely identified with him and his practice that in a figurative law court there would be "sufficient evidence" for him to be convicted and punished for being the person, the one, who is singularly responsible for these contradictory, unlivable beliefs, and therefore of his being guilty of the injustice, the unjustifiability, of those beliefs. Derrida seems to be intent on displaying the Gift of Death that Jankélévitch is giving himself and offering to Derrida, perhaps in anticipation of the need to ask pardon (of the reader) both for the gruesomeness of that death in writing, for it is gruesome enough that Derrida shies away from displaying it or allowing it to present itself "to the end," but also for what might be seen as his (Derrida's) failure at least until now to make sense of this Gift of Death offered in writing and accepted in writing in such a way that Derrida himself becomes responsible for it and needs to ask to be forgiven for failing to do justice to it in a way that implicates him, in writing, in its gruesome pathos that cries out for justice, responsibility—and forgiveness.

Jankélévitch's death in writing is indeed gruesome. In the Foreword to *L'imprescriptible: Pardonner?* ["Should We Pardon Them?"] written in 1971, Jankélévitch asks, "Is it time to forgive, or at least to forget?" Derrida notes that the response Jankélévitch makes there, "in horrified fear before the risk of a forgiveness that might end up engendering a forgetting, Jankélévitch says 'No' to forgiveness," seeming to ascribe a duty of nonforgiveness, in the name of the victims, a moral or ethical duty of which "imprescriptibility," as in the case of "crimes against humanity," would be the legal inscription. Jankélévitch concludes that the time for forgiveness cannot be now, that forgiveness is now impossible, because as he says, "Forgiveness died in the death camps." With this, Jankélévitch takes on himself responsibility for the association of the impossibility of forgiveness with death, the equation of the death camps and the deaths of the victims of the Shoah with the death of forgiveness, that is, with the unforgivable. Jankélévitch risks the mortal danger of identifying himself with the "Unforgivable."

Derrida identifies two axioms at work in Jankélévitch's arguments for the unforgivable crimes of the Shoah, axioms that Derrida says are "far from self-evident." The first axiom is that forgiveness is unimaginable unless it is asked for, explicitly or implicitly, commenting that "this difference is not nothing." At stake here for Derrida is the question of whether the breaking of the symmetry between forgiveness asked for and forgiveness granted, their dissociation, might not be a necessity of any forgiveness "worthy of this name" (TF, 27). The second axiom is that when the crime "crosses the line of radical evil" and becomes a "crime against humanity," in that way it becomes unforgivable on the grounds that forgiveness must remain a human thing, and this is impossible when the crime exceeds the scope and horizon of the human imagination, like the distance across galaxies or the speed of light, when, in other words, the crime is against the very image of the human as such. In such a case, the offense exceeds the limit of the possibility of being human. To cross this line into radical evil is to realize the possibility of the unforgivable, to make the impossibility of forgiveness a genuine possibility. Both of these axioms are inscribed in the horrible possibility of the death of forgiveness itself that Jankélévitch imagines and that might be viewed as the image of a "second death," the death of humanity that follows upon or is infernally inspired by the radical evil of the death of human beings undertaken as a "final solution":

> Forgiveness! But have they even asked us for forgiveness? It is only the distress and the dereliction of the guilty that would give forgiveness a meaning and a reason for being. When the guilty are fat, well nourished, prosperous, enriched by the "economic miracle," forgiveness is a sinister joke. No, forgiveness is not for swine and their sows. *Forgiveness died in the death camps.* Our horror before that which understanding cannot, properly speaking, conceive of would stifle pity and its birth . . . if the accused "could inspire pity in us." (TF, 28)

It is at this point that Derrida asks pardon for not going on to quote Jankélévitch's remarks that follow because they are so violent and angry. Derrida believes that they can and should be passed over in silence because they brought Jankélévitch to his death—*de mortibus nil nisi bonum*—that is, to the death he suffered in writing in the contradictory beliefs that he says he will hold to the death and of which he convicts himself: "I believe in the immensity of forgiveness . . . and on the other hand, I believe in wickedness." Death comes whenever the right hand discovers what the left hand is doing. But Derrida also catches, in the context of this self-imposed death sentence, a glimmer of hope, which is the necessary condition of realizing simultaneously both the horror of the death of the human and the pathos of suffering in a single human death— in this case, Jankélévitch's death in writing. In the above passage, the fatality and mortal danger of the aporia of forgiveness are revealed as the death that beliefs must suffer, the death which must come to all believing that is not merely credulity but rather the believing that is questioning, that believes in questioning, believes as questioning. Jankélévitch admits that the ethics of which forgiveness is the highest commandment is a "hyperbolic" ethics. He admits that it exceeds the ethical economy of the tradition of "Christian and Jewish ethics," which he studied philosophically in *Le Pardon*. That ethical economy, which views the exchange of forgiveness granted for forgiveness sought as a circulation of guilt, confession, repentance, expiation, redemption, salvation, and so on, is, according to Derrida, the strongest traditional logic of forgiveness to be found in the religious and spiritual "semantics of forgiveness" in the history of European responsibility that was his concern in *The Gift of Death*. The question of a "hyperbolical ethics" through which he identifies himself with Jankélévitch, at least insofar as it remains alive as a question in Jankélévitch's writing, is the gift of death Derrida finds historically and concretely offered and that he accepts as a leading question in writing "To Forgive." That question turns on the way in which forgiveness is both present in that history of responsibility, the way that tradition presents itself according to its own strongest logic, and at the same time is incompatible with it, the way in which the history of justice and responsibility suffers the death of its own self-destruction (*aufhebung*) through its climax in forgiveness, as in Nietzsche's writing. This instability reveals itself within the history of forgiveness itself, which leads to the self-destruction of forgiveness, the death of forgiveness and the death of humanity as the verdict rendered by the self-destructive indictment of justice and responsibility rendered in the name of the victims of that excess of human death, the unimaginable transgression of the limit of human death-dealing that "Shoah" names. This self-destruction requires of us, Derrida says, "once again the force to rethink the naming of the possibility of the impossible or the impossibility of the possible." In other words, it requires us, "once again" to rethink the unthinkable death as the aporia of forgiveness revealed through death, as death, through and as death itself:

> Where, in effect, we find the unforgivable as inexpiable, where as Jankélévitch in effect concludes, forgiveness becomes impossible, and the history of forgiveness comes to an end, we will ask ourselves whether, paradoxically, the possibility of forgiveness as such, if there is such a thing, does not find its origin: We will ask ourselves if forgiveness does not begin in the place where it appears to end, where it appears impossible, precisely at the end of the history of forgiveness, of history as the history of forgiveness. More than once we would have to put this formally empty and dry but implacably exigent aporia to the test, the aporia according to which forgiveness, if there is such a thing, must and can forgive only the unforgivable, the inexpiable, and us do the impossible. (TF, 30)

This is the challenge, trial by combat, to the death, by which Derrida takes his heading from Jankélévitch and for him as well. For Jankélévitch's death in

writing in the face of the aporia of forgiveness is a witness and testimony to
the history of forgiveness, not *in abstracto* but *in concreto*. He is a living witness in death to those who live in death, who are remembered in the death of
the tradition that has gone up in smoke and to which he testifies by believing
in both the immensity of forgiveness and of wickedness. Jankélévitch gives
his life in writing to testify that this self-destructive, self-contradictory belief
has died and must be remembered by refusing to forgive, by forgetting about
forgiveness. If there is to be any hope of passing over this death and passing
on this tradition of forgiveness, Derrida says that we will have to question it
to the end. "The axiom that we will perhaps have to call into question is that
forgiveness must still have a sense, and this sense must be determined on the
basis of [*sur fond de*] salvation, reconciliation, redemption, expiation, *I would
even say sacrifice*" (TF, 30; emphasis added).

Derrida's evocation of the deconstruction of the economy of sacrifice in
*The Gift of Death*, which in different forms had been a central theme of his
writing throughout his career, is of signal importance here in his treatment of
forgiveness. This treatment speaks to his overriding but "less well understood"
religious concern. Derrida's attention to forgiveness, particularly his identification of it and with it, as being an even more original form of secrecy than the
Gift, seems to mark an attempt to face up to the experience of conversion he
undergoes in the writing of *Circumfession*. In "To Forgive," he is attempting to
fathom, within the limits of understanding, what he had confessed there: that
the truth of forgiveness, a truth that cannot be known but can be done, is the
only truth for which human existence can take responsibility. It is the truth of
responsibility. In order to do justice to that truth, it must be done in the register of love, a love that is the extremity to which one is led along the path traced
out by faith and hope in the face of the finality of death.

In "To Forgive," this path through faith and hope to love, understood as
the final (in the face of death) truth of forgiveness, is traced out in the figure
of Jankélévitch's death in writing as he faces up to the question of forgiveness
in the face of death as the unimaginable historically realized figure of the aporia of possibility and impossibility. The extremity of suffering that this aporia
provokes and instigates in human experience appears in the way Jankélévitch
is driven to probe the raw nerve of the wound to humanity that the Shoah
opened up, cutting to the bone and to the heart. Derrida chooses to explore
the sense of the inexpiable and its possible connection to the unforgivable in
order to situate the point in experience at which the full force of the aporia of
the possible and the impossible makes itself felt, at the extremity of human
suffering. Recall that there were two axioms that Derrida identified at work
in "Shall We Pardon Them," both of which he finds questionable: first, that
forgiveness granted must be effected through forgiveness requested; second,
that forgiveness must remain on a human scale and therefore can be effaced
as a possibility by the sheer excess of radical evil. Derrida links the inexpiable
to a semantic family all the members of which he feels have their genesis in

the economy of sacrifice. Tracing this lineage back from the "imprescriptibility" of crimes against humanity, the blood-line passes over to notions of "the irreparable, the ineffaceable, the irremediable, the irreversible, the unforgettable, the irrevocable, the inexpiable" (TF, 31). In all these cases, Derrida finds that there is a shared feature from which they derive the efficacy and force of a commandment, divine or quasi-divine in its authority: [Thou shall] not . . . The force of the "not" might be taken either as that of logical necessity or of moral sanction, but in either case, the effective point situates both the crime and its consequences for perpetrator and victim within the realm of impossibility. Derrida notes that impossibility in this case stands in a direct relation to temporality: it is the "passed" quality of the deed that seems to make forgiveness impossible:

> But in all cases, one should not and/or cannot go back over a past. The past is past, the event took place, the wrong took place, and this past, the memory of this past, remains irreducible, uncompromising. This is one way in which forgiveness is different from the gift, which in principle does not concern the past." (TF, 31)

Three points are here to be noted. First, forgiveness is to be associated with temporality. Second, "being past" is to be associated with a particular form of finality. And third, forgiveness is to be associated, through distinction, with the gift, by way of the suggestion of a difference that bears specifically on the way in which both might be "impossible." Derrida goes on to draw a further consequence of the temporal dimension of the putative impossibility of forgiveness in the face of the inexpiable and all of its semantic cousins:

> One will never have treated forgiveness if one does not take account of this being past, a being-past that never lets itself be reduced, modified, modalized in a present past or a presentable or re-presentable past. It is a being past that does not pass, so to speak. It is this im-passableness, this impassivity of the past . . . which we would have to analyze relentlessly. . . . Without this stubborn privileging of the past in the constitution of temporalization, there is no original problematic of forgiveness. . . . Forgiveness, forgiveness [*la pardonéité*] is time, the being of time insofar as it involves [*comporte*] the indisputable and the unmodifiable past. (TF, 31–32)

It might be further noted here, by way of parenthesis, that this notion of the absoluteness or finality of the past with regard to the problematic of forgiveness certainly bears on the sense of the religious conception of "original sin," of a guilt which, because it will not "pass," therefore can and must be "passed on" from one human generation to another. It is a guilt that is impassible and hence impassive to any human suffering that might expiate it within some economy of sacrifice and redemption. The whole problematic nexus between the sacrifice of Isaac and the sacrifice of Jesus that was at stake in *The Gift of Death* returns here in the situation in which the tension of symmetry and asymmetry between the two is a decisive question that will have to be faced, but which now appears associated with the aporetic structure of the tension between possibility and impossibility temporally and historically instantiated.

Yet a further parenthetical observation. The temporalization of the problematic of forgiveness as it might be seen to relate to the notion of "original sin" involves the differential association of the temporality of forgiveness with the temporality of the gift that Derrida noted. The temporality of forgiveness necessarily involves the past, while that of the gift hinges on its "originality," its constitution of a future as possible in a new or original way. An important ambiguity or element of questionability, a path of further questioning arises here in that one might ask what the relation is between the aporia of possibility/impossibility as it is at work in the differentiated, but necessarily associated, temporalization of forgiveness and the gift. Both of these issues that link the aporetics of forgiveness and the aporetics of the gift together in the nexus marked by "original sin" are issues that bear immediately on both Derrida's enterprise as a whole, and particularly in *Circumfession,* as well as the possible (and impossible) discourse that might flow between his texts and those of Dante.

Returning now to the text of "To Forgive," there occurs what might be interpreted as a moment of "impasse," or arresting of the movement of the text that mimics the arrest of the movement of life in the face of death, an appearance of the face of death itself in the features of Jankélévitch's own face in writing. This moment places in suspense and sets trembling the question of the relation of the formal aporetic structures that Derrida has been delineating, both the general structure of the possible/impossible, and the central but more specific structure of the unforgivable/forgiveness, as well as the question of the possible (impossible) differentiation of the aporetic logic of forgiveness from that of the gift all along the lines of their temporalization. This moment occurs when Derrida turns to the last extremities of Jankélévitch's death-throes in writing, the way the latter traces the line where human criminality crosses over and exceeds the boundary of its possibilities and moves into the territory of impossibility, into the realm of "crimes against humanity," which are characterized by their scope, intensive rather than extensive, and which target not specific human beings or any class of human beings—the Jews for example—but effectively strike at the very possibility of being human, thereby dealing mortal danger, dealing death to humanity as such, making real the possibility of the impossibility of human existence, whatever that might mean, in a radically original yet historically determinate way. Jankélévitch writes:

> Racist crimes are an assault against men as man: not against this or that
> man. . . . No! The racist was truly aiming at the ipseity of being, that is, the
> human in all men. Anti-Semitism is a grave offense against men in general.
> The Jews were persecuted because it was they, and not at all because of their
> opinions or their faith: it is existence itself that was refused them; one was
> not reproaching them for professing this or that, one was reproaching them

for being . . . it is not obvious that a Jew must exist: a Jew must always justify himself, excuse himself for living and breathing . . . A Jew does not have the right to be, existing is his sin. (TF, 43)

Derrida underscores the notion of a "sin of existing" as Jankélévitch uses it polemically here in relation to the implied: "for the German," whatever that might mean. By identifying the racism of the Nazi as the pass by which human criminality transgresses the boundary of radical evil into the realm of "crimes against humanity," Jankélévitch succeeds in evoking the specter of a death that deals death not only to human beings but to "humanity," to the possibility of being human, thereby raising the question of the impossibility of human existence itself in the notion of "the sin of existence." But once this possibility is raised, like a deadly infectious virus or a metastasizing cancer, it cannot be contained. If there *could be* a "sin of existing," if it is possible that existing could be sinful, guilty, in itself a transgression of justice and good, if existence could be evil for some in some specific way, then, so to speak, all hell breaks loose. Once the possibility of absolute monstrosity is summoned up, then it becomes impossible to contain it, to cage or quarantine its lethal rampage; in that moment the question of the impossibility, the death, of humanity itself (whatever that might mean) has taken hold in the world, has gained dominion over existence itself. It then makes of existence itself an economy of guilt in which all are implicated. It goes without saying that this implication of "originary guilt"—the guilt of origination, the sin of beginning or coming to exist—this "original sin," could not be limited to "human" existence, no matter where the line of demarcation is drawn between the "super-human," who decides and deals death and the "sub-human," who is dealt death as a final solution. Rather, it necessarily spreads to all who are guilty of existence, including God, if God is taken to exist or to give existence. In other words, if there is an unforgivable crime or sin, if there is sense to the word "unforgivable," then that sense would extend the "not" of impossibility absolutely. Not even God could forgive—or be forgiven—the unforgivable. Jankélévitch's inexorable sense of justice makes clear, against his own intention or in the contradiction of his intentions, that the search for absolute justice severed from the possibility of absolute forgiveness, which it makes impossible, must lead to the end of existence itself in the self-destructive fires of an all-consuming sacrifice for the guilt of the inexpiable sin of existing. In "To Forgive," Derrida sits shivah at the death, in writing, of Jankélévitch, performing the work of mourning, yet looking for a way that the Gift of Death might come to pass in and through this occurrence, might pass over the death of forgiveness and the end of time, might pass on and come to begin again. "Yes!" "Come!"

Here all trembles—truly trembles, before the "No!," the power of the "not," the possibility of final impossibility. All tremble before death, the death of men and women, the death of humanity (whatever that might mean), the death of God, the end of time, the *eschaton.* A reversal of force has occurred so powerful that it has swept Nietzsche away completely and suddenly—in an instant, as if in judgment—it is as if he never existed, as if he had never traced the genealogy by which justice immolates itself in its own self-destructive coming to climax in forgiveness. Now the refusal of forgiveness, the saying of an absolute "No!" to forgiveness in the figure of the unforgivable, the self-immolation of forgiveness in sacrifice to the "implacable," to the unbending, unyielding call for absolute justice has dealt death everywhere, in the name of justice (can you believe it?), as the name of justice, for the sin of existence. Who could believe that guilt could extend so far? How would we know that guilt could be so predatory, so ravenous, as to consume existence altogether, to swallow it whole? Tremble at the power of death, at the bite of death. Tremble at the death of humanity (whatever that might mean)! Can you believe it? Can you believe that the sin of existing might be, apparently must be, unforgivable . . . unless, can you believe it? . . . there is the impossible hope of forgiveness, or the hope of an impossible forgiveness—which is it?—or again, and again, and again—an impossible hope or a hope of an impossible forgiveness *and* an impossible justice (can you believe it?). Impossible! (Can you believe it impossible?) Which is it? "I do not know" (Derrida says). All is trembling!

## REVISING THE SCENE OF FORGIVENESS

> The aporia is the experience of responsibility. (Derrida)[7]

> I would dissociate the scene of forgiveness from the scene of repentance. ("On Forgiveness," 63–64)

Let us revisit the scene of forgiveness as Dante imagined it for himself. Now we may be able to catch a glimpse of him rewriting the scene of Jankelvitch's death in writing at a price even more terrible than the one Derrida witnesses at the writing of the hope of forgiveness. That price is the price of hope. In Canto xxx of *Purgatorio*, Dante, the penitent pilgrim of the narrative now stands alone before Beatrice in the Earthly Paradise atop the mountain, bereft of Virgil, of writing, and of the promise of writing. Her first words, the beginning of her address to him, are: "Dante, because Virgil leaves you, do not weep yet, do not weep yet, for you must weep for another sword" (*Purg.*, xxx, 55–57). This is the opening scene of their reconciliation, if we can still use this word in the context of a discourse on forgiveness. Derrida thinks it is questionable. Therefore, it seems best interpreted in the context of the poem as a scene opening on the possibility of forgiveness, and equally, opening up and revealing the impossibility of forgiveness. As such, the movement toward the face to face encounter of Dante and Beatrice in the Earthly Paradise must be read as staging the revelation of a secret by way of its encryption in their flesh made word, word given and received as food. The poet sets the scene in a movement of trembling, trembling at the sight of Beatrice, trembling in the sight of Beatrice. It is also set at the site of mourning, at the work-site of mourning, where Dante is told to forget, forget the loss of Virgil, forget the loss of the figure of writing, forget the loss of the work of repentance, which is the work of mourning, the healing of wounds, the wiping away of scars. He is told to stop the work of repentance and mourning that now is finished, so as to begin a different mourning, a new mourning—mourning for the death of forgiveness, for the Gift of Death which is forgiveness, to begin to suffer again in a new way, to weep and to mourn the Gift of Death which must bring joy. Beatrice enjoins him with a new commandment, commanding new tears, commanding him to let the waters of death flow, the waters of two rivers, the rivers that flow from two different sources, flow in two different courses without confluence yet keeping together, in a form and figure that mimics the constant flow of the structure that is abstractly called "aporia," but which is felt in the flow of blood and tears as the experience of responsibility.

Before Beatrice speaks her commandment, her injunction of tears in the voice of divine command that blends the tone of both father and mother, when Dante first catches sight of her, at her site on the other side of the river, the (m)other/woman, she is inscribed in the pageant of signifiers traced by the Hebrew and Christian scriptures in the place of the Eucharist, holding the place of the "God-man" who is displaced here and appears as the griffin who is in her traces. She takes the place of the God made man (which can be hyphenated several ways) and so takes the place of the Other (God)/death, (Beatrice: (m)other/woman//god/death). She takes the place of the Word made flesh made food and so holds the place of one who feeds with one's own flesh. At this sight, Dante turns to say to Virgil, "Not a drop of blood is left in me that does not tremble (*tremi*): I know the tokens (*segni*) of the ancient flame" (*Purg.*, xxx, 46–48). Suddenly, he realizes that Virgil is gone, gone back to Limbo, that state of suspended animation that suffers nothing except the impossibility of hope. This is not because those who dwell there refuse to hope but because they are not aware that hope is possible, because they have not been shown how to hope. Virgil, his hope up to now, has gone from Dante and he stands before her, the other/Other, hoping against hope, hoping for the impossible, for a new hope, the hope of forgiveness for which he has not asked, cannot, will not ask. The other power, the power of the "not," of the impossible, is calling out in the throbbing pulse of his blood and in the burning of the immolating fire in the streaming of tears—he is crying rivers now, rivers through which he must pass. Virgil, the mother to whom he turned a moment ago "with the confidence of a little child that runs to his mother when he is frightened or in distress" (*Purg.*, xxx, 43–45), and whose loss he now mourns as "the sweetest father, to whom I gave myself for my salvation" (*Purg.*, xxx, 50–51). Dante cries tears of passion, which is suffering; he sheds tears of mourning, which is suffering. His tears fall for father and mother. He cries tears for the loss of his father and mother, in writing, a loss which for him calls no less for tears than the loss of all the fathers and mothers of all the others: "nor did all that our ancient mother lost keep my dew-washed cheeks from turning dark again with tears" (*Purg.*, xxx, 52–54). The setting of the scene is domestic and familial; it is the dream place where humanity would be at home, in the Garden, the original home, the place where human existence originally takes place and where all economies originate, the scene where all economies are set. In the drama that Beatrice is orchestrating, Dante is being scripted (is scripting himself through the Other) to suffer multiple role reversals: Virgil's role as father/mother is reversed into the role of Beatrice as father/mother; her role as mother is reversed into the role of the "ancient mother who lost all"; his role as innocent child is reversed into that of the guilty child, and will again be reversed into that of a man (Adam, the new Adam) who is neither innocent nor guilty, but suspended in forgiveness, by forgiveness, between the two. The script they are following revisits the scene of forgiveness that has already pardoned the scene of the sin of existing. Through all that follows, no word of forgiveness asked or granted passes between Dante and Beatrice. Forgiveness does not exist for them. They forgive forgiveness in the name of responsibility, in the name of humanity, in the impossible hope of the joy of humanity.

Then like one who commands with authority (*come ammiraglio*, "like an admiral") she "directs her eyes at me beyond the stream," at the one beyond the stream who is separated from her (she is beneath her veil that does not let him see her distinctly), the one who is beyond the stream and the veil, beyond the vale of tears. She continues, "royally and ever stern in her mien, 'Look at me well: indeed I am, indeed I am Beatrice! How did you deign to climb the mountain? Did you not know that here man is happy?'" (*Purg.*, xxx, 73–75). This exchange of names, this economic transaction of naming, of identification through looking, this regard of recognition, which is paradoxically occurring for the first time, takes place under erasure, under the erasure of Dante's abject request for pardon for mentioning his own name in writing, "when I turned at the sound of my name, which of necessity is registered here" (*Purg.*, xxx, 62–63). He asks pardon for improperly mentioning his proper name, which is not his property but has been given as a token of recognition by Beatrice. It will prove to betoken the Gift of Death—one of Beatrice's other, improper names that she will also give him. She has offered him this gift, but he has not yet accepted it, because he has not yet given the gift of death either to himself or to her. His death and her death exchanged an-economically, the other exchange of the gift of their other names, of their deaths. Her name is given over the erasure of another signature: "*Guardaci ben! Ben son, ben son Beatrice.* Look at us! I am, I am Beatrice." Beatrice is the other name for the signature, "I am who I am," the signature of the lawgiver, the name given to Moses to avoid speaking the proper name (if there is one), the name given as a placeholder for the name that cannot, should not be given, the name that is unforgivable to speak, because perhaps it names the unforgivable.

To be forgiven the story has to be written again from the beginning differently. The rewriting is the forgiving and the tears are the ink, the transubstantiated sacrament of the blood which the sword of her words releases with its cut. This sword, her version of the story, is keen and double-edged; she uses it to circumcise his heart:

> For a time I sustained him with my countenance: showing him my youthful eyes I led him with me turned toward the right goal. So soon as I was on the threshold of my second age, and had changed life, this one gave himself to others. When from flesh to spirit I had ascended, and beauty and virtue were increased in me, I was less dear and less pleasing to him and he turned his steps along a way not true, following false images of the good which pay no promise in full. (*Purg.,* xxx, 121–132)

"This one gave himself to others." Yahweh's message to the whole tribe through the prophets: you gave yourselves to others. Other gods, idols, other laws, other nations. The spirit of Yahweh\Jehovah lives on in Beatrice, the jealous lover. But also the Spirit of Jesus, of Resurrection—"on the threshold of my second life . . . and had changed life . . . and ascended (to) beauty and virtue increased in me." She has him collared and is tightening the noose. The sword of her words is cutting him short, cutting him to the quick, cutting him off without recourse. Now she drives home the point, "he turned his steps along a way not true, following false images of the good *which pay no promise in full.*"

You Judas! You lowest of the low; you devil's food. I spit your name out of my mouth, for only Satan could abide the taste of you on the tongue. After the so-called god of your love raped my mouth with the eating of your (false) words made (false) flesh of your false heart, you betrayed me for thirty pieces of silver, for tokens of an economy that can never pay promises in full. Pay promises—of writing, to say of me in writing what never has been said of woman before. You will write me? With what tool? With the flesh and blood of your heart? But where will you lay your hand upon it, how will you find it in you now that you made me swallow it whole in the picture show of your dream. Never been said of "woman"—of the "other," woman! What could pay *that* promise in full? Nothing! Except perhaps what I myself, will give you as gift, par-don, the gift of forgiveness. "For I am Beatrice, I am," the god-bearing image in writing of death, of life in the face of death. Behold, I am doing a new, impossible thing. I will write you! I will write your confession for you, name you as the one—guilty of what you did. I will let you see yourself through my eyes, which for a long time have been filled with tears for you. But you must sign it in you own name, which is impossible, so you may make your mark, in your own style, in tears for blood, and words for flesh.

> "Say if this is true: to such an accusation your confession must be joined!" Confusion and fear, together mingled, drove forth from my mouth a Yes such that eyes were needed to hear it . . . So did I burst under that heavy load, pouring forth tears and sighs, and my voice failed along is passage. (*Purg.,* xxxi, 5–21, *passim*)

But prayers and tears are not enough; the words are necessary. She needs what had been promised: what had never been said in writing of woman before, not since Adam; the truth—what he had done, who he was. "Weeping I said, 'the present things (*cose presenti*), with their false pleasure, turned my steps aside, as soon as your countenance was hidden'"(*Purg.,* xxxi, 34–36).

So already in this scene of face-to-face encounter, Dante's script has anticipated the questions Derrida says he has about the scene of forgiveness, about the address at which the scene of forgiveness is set and about who addresses and who is addressed in the name of forgiveness. He says,

> . . . the address of forgiveness must forever remain, if there is such a thing, undecidably equivocal, by which I do not mean ambiguous, shady, twilit, but heterogeneous to any determination in the order of knowledge, of determinate theoretical judgment, of the self-presentation of an appropriable sense . . . (TF, 36)

This heterogeneity of the address of forgiveness to every "name," every determination in the order of knowledge and representation that founds the prohibition against idolatry, raises at least two more specific issues for Derrida: first, he ponders whether the scene of forgiveness can and must be fixed at the site of the face-to-face encounter of the one who asks for and the one who grants forgiveness (TF, 34); second, he examines whether the scene of forgiveness is a human scene or a divine scene. In other words, there arises question of the "limit" of forgiveness, which, like every question of the human and divine, is at bottom a question about the cut or boundary that separates the realms of the possible and the impossible (TF, 44–45). This second question, the second form of the same question, speaks to the issue of passing over the limit that separates the human and divine. Dante inquires if indeed it does separate, or how it separates, so that one must ask whether the crossing of this boundary, which is the relation of life to death, is possible or impossible, whether the crossing of that boundary is a transgression, sin, or crime, or an intercourse and communion that is generative and nourishing. Dante forces us to ask how it could possibly be separated.

Derrida's gestures of response to both questions are similar. In the first case, he questions the nonsubstitutability of the victim and criminal in the scene of forgiveness, enacted as the stricture that their encounter take place face-to-face, at least in the sense of occurring in the name of persons whose identities are open to one another and who give their address to one another, with no substitution of a third for the singular one or other. But Derrida asks, "Is this possible? Is such a head-to-head, such a face-to-face possible?" And he wonders aloud whether "from the outset," from the very setting of the scene, forgiveness implies, "as if by hypothesis," the appearance on the scene of a third party whom it nonetheless must, should exclude. Concerning the second form of the question, he draws out the implication of this gesture toward the aporetic structure of forgiveness, because the limit between the human and the divine is "not just a limit among others," but is itself the very experience of "limitation itself," if limit has a self, the experience of passing on or through or not being allowed to pass on or through, of being stopped or not. This is the question of experience itself, of all that passes through experience or that stops experience, the experience of experience ending, the experience of the "Yes!" and the "No!"; the experience of possibility and impossibility, of life and death. Derrida puts it in two ways, the first structural and the second concrete:

> We thus dissociated on the one hand unconditional forgiveness, abso-
> lute forgiveness . . . absolutely unconditional forgiveness that allows us to
> think [*donne a penser*] the essence of forgiveness, if there is such a thing—
> and which ultimately should even be able to do without repentance and the
> request for forgiveness, and on the other hand conditional forgiveness . . .
> that is inscribed with the set of conditions of all kinds . . . yet the distinction
> between unconditionality and conditionality is shifty [*retorse*] enough not to
> let itself be determined as a simple opposition. The unconditional and the
> conditional are, certainly, absolutely heterogeneous, and this forever, on either
> side of a limit, but they are also indissociable. *There is in the movement, in
> the motion of unconditional forgiveness, an inner exigency of becoming effective,*
> manifest, determined, and in determining itself, bending to conditionality.
> (TF, 45; emphasis added)

So at the general and abstract level of the aporetic structure of forgiveness the question of the undecidability of the address of forgiveness involves the further questions: Whom does forgiveness involve? Is it limited to the absolute singularities of the criminal and the victim? Where does forgiveness occur? Is it only in the face-to-face encounter of these two? How does it become effective? Is it only effective when forgiveness is asked and granted on the basis of conditions like repentance and reconciliation? Is there a limit to what can be forgiven? Are there inexpiable and, therefore, unforgivable sins? Is forgiveness limited to the human? to the divine? Or does the limit of the unforgivable somehow extend beyond the limit of both human and divine power to forgive, so that there might be crimes that are absolutely unforgivable? Does the power of forgiveness, absolute forgiveness, if there is such a thing, somehow exceed, perhaps even *also* exceed the limit of both the human and the divine, opening up the possibility of a third modality of possibility beyond (or through) the aporia of possibility and impossibility? These are the strings of aporia that tremble across the sounding board of the discourse of forgiveness as Derrida tries to attune himself to it.

But to such questions there can only be one truthful response: "I do not know." Derrida acknowledges:

> . . . there is no theoretical statement about forgiveness. Each time I make a
> theoretical statement about the event of forgiveness I am sure that I miss it.

> [ . . . ] What then regulates my use of the word forgiveness . . . ? Well
> here I must say I do not know. I have no knowledge of this. I can know what
> is inscribed in the concept of forgiveness that I inherit, so I work on that
> heritage. . . . From within this possible knowledge, I discover this extraor-
> dinary excess. . . . [and] about this I have no knowledge and I cannot speak
> of it in a theoretical fashion. But I can nevertheless think—I can think what
> I cannot know—I can think of the desire to forgive beyond economy—or to
> be forgiven beyond economy. I have a thought of this gracious and uncon-
> ditional forgiveness. . . . It is out of this desire or thought, which exceeds
> knowledge, that I speak, that I organize this discourse; but it's a very unsafe
> discourse, as you realize. ("On Forgiveness," 53–54)

This thinking of what exceeds thought, however, thinking in the direction of excess, and thinking through the "unsafe" structure of discourse
given as aporia contains within itself as both its origin and motive force a
desire to become concrete, determinate, and singular, to become effective
in experience. As Derrida said earlier, "There is in the movement . . . of
unconditional forgiveness an inner exigency of becoming effective, manifest, determined, and in determining itself, bending to conditionality." In
the tradition that most effectively determines itself in Dante's writing this
notion of "bending to conditionality" expresses itself in the Pauline idiom of
*kenosis,* to which we shall have to return. But in the context of the lecture
"To Forgive," Derrida offers a gesture of this inner exigency of the aporetic structure of forgiveness to concretize the tension that flows between its
absolute polarities and to make itself manifest in experience, to become flesh
and blood. Derrida honors this exigency by memorializing a final episode in
the account he has given of Jankélévitch's death in writing, the death that is
suspended within the absolute polarity of his two writings, *Le Pardon* and
*L'imprescriptible.* Derrida recounts a letter sent to Jankélévitch by a young
German, Wiard Raveling, who speaks at length of his complex experience
of being German in the wake of the Holocaust, without himself having personally experienced it:

> I myself have not killed any Jews. Having been born in Germany is not
> my fault, or my doing. No one asked my permission [thus he poses from the
> outset the immense question, which will remain with us, the question of guilt
> or forgiveness according to the legacy, the genealogy, the collectivity of a *we*
> and of which *we*-Derrida]. I am completely innocent of Nazi crimes; but this
> does not console me at all. My conscience is not clear, and I feel a mixture
> of shame, pity, resignation, sadness, incredulity, revolt. I do not always sleep
> well. I often remain awake at night, and I think, and I imagine. I have night-
> mares that I cannot get rid of. I think of Anne Frank, and of Auschwitz . . .
> (quoted in TF, 38–39)

Jankélévitch responded with the following letter:

Dear Sir, I am moved by your letter. I have waited for this letter for thirty-five years. I mean a letter in which the abomination is fully assumed and by someone who has had no part in it [*n'y est pour rein*]. This is the first time I have received a letter from a German, a letter that was not a letter of a more or less disguised self-justification. Apparently, German philosophers, "my colleagues" (if I dare to use this term) have nothing to say to me, nothing to explain. Their good conscience is unperturbable. [Injustice or ignorance of Vladimir Jankélévitch as if a letter addressed to him personally were the only reparation possible—Derrida] You alone, you the first and no doubt the last, have found the necessary words outside the political commonplaces and pious clichés. It is rare for generosity, spontaneity, and a keen sensitivity to find their language in the words we use. And such is your case. There is no mistaking it. Thank you [pardon beseeched: a gift that calls for thanks—Derrida]. No, I will not come to see you in Germany. I will not go that far. I am too old to inaugurate this new era. Because for me it is a new era all the same. For which I have waited too long. But you are young, you do not have the same reasons as I. You do not have this uncrossable barrier to cross. It is my turn to say to you: When you come to Paris, as everyone does, knock on my door . . . We will sit down at the piano. (quoted in TF, 40)

Derrida's reflection on these two letters, this exchange of names under erasure, over two signatures that cross and even meet (they did meet) reveals what he takes to be the embodied experience of the aporia of forgiveness. Raveling writes in the hope, undoubtedly sincere but perhaps not thought all the way through to the very end, of the question it nonetheless clearly expresses: Who am I (for you)? Who are you (for me)? Can forgiveness have a meaning between us? And Jankélévitch's response, equally sincere, even if also unspoken: I do not know. The discourse between them stops, it dies, in the very act of its being undertaken. For Derrida, this is not the story of an episode, an instance, failed or successful, innocent or guilty, of forgiveness. Rather, it is an account of the instant in which it becomes possible for the question of forgiveness in its full aporetic character to be raised again, raised from the dead among whom Jankélévitch had consigned it, to be asked and go on being asked without the pretense of knowledge, but with an urgent sense of the exigency of the question itself, an instance of decision and therefore of responsibility, regarding forgiveness, regarding the question of the very possibility and impossibility of history as the history of forgiveness going on, and what it would mean for this history to go on responsibly. What responsibility can one—or the other—take for the question of the possibility of an impossible forgiveness? It is precisely at this point, at the point of the extremity of passion, of suffering the contradiction of the aporia that is not merely a structure of thought but always necessarily of experience as well, at the point where the hope of knowledge dies, that the question can be raised, and always raised again, not simply reiterated or repeated, but transformed into the hope of new experience, where the question can be "passed over" and passed on as hope itself (if hope has a "self").

This hope of beginning again, this hope in the secret promise of beginning, like every hope, rests on faith (can you believe it?). The belief, or faith, or trust on which this question rests is not a belief in the meaningfulness of the question of forgiveness, or in human questioning generally, or in divine answers or revelations, or even in divine questioning (whatever that might mean; however it could take place). Rather, this hope rests on belief in questioning the impossible *as impossible*. It is a belief in an impossible questioning which, although impossible, nevertheless must and therefore can be done. It is belief in the impossible: to believe such a belief is to believe in death, to believe in death as a gift, to hope for death through belief in death as a gift, to hope for death to seal and keep the impossible promise of life, to keep the promise in its very death, to keep the promise which life is in and through the perjury against that promise which death is. If forgiveness is, as Derrida has said, before the Gift, if it is the for-giving which gives giving, the forgiving that allows giving to pass on as promised, to pass on as promise, despite the necessary perjury, the perjury made with the promise, perjury as the counterpromise, then forgiving would perhaps occur when the promise, which has always already been emptied by the perjury that is its counterpromise, is allowed to pass on, when it is passed over through a belief that is absolutely impossible, a belief that credits the impossible, credits impossibility, credits death as the sign, the countersign of the counterpromise. When questioned, forgiveness becomes the pass-word, the countersign to the question of the sign, the counterpromise, the perjury that allows the promise to pass on. Belief and hope in death are the pass through which forgiveness passes over every perjury of every promise, passes over the perjury that is the "sin of existing," and allows the empty, perjured, criminal, sinful promise of existence, never fully kept, to pass on, thereby keeping its secret promise. Belief and hope in death are the pass through which forgiveness allows life to pass on as the (empty) secret (empty) promise of beginning, of always beginning again. Belief and hope pass over into love, the love that forgives the gift.

Forgiveness as the Gift of Death that gives giving, or love—what can be said of forgiveness as love or of love as forgiveness, of the gift of love or the forgiving of the gift? Of course no theoretical statement is possible. It is impossible to speak or think the Impossible. But it can be thought as a question regarding the ways in which the traditions have imagined, figured, and passed on the question of the Impossible, together with the desire and the belief and the hope in which it has been figured. For Dante this traditional figure of faith and hope in forgiveness as the Gift of Death is "resurrection," or more accurately, the Resurrection of Jesus. Resurrection names the countersign that death for-gives to the economy of sacrifice that ends, that dies once and for all, with Jesus on the cross (so the story goes). The cross is the sign of contradiction, the self-contradiction of the economy of sacrifice, which, like every economy, pays no promise in full. The sign of the cross is the sign of the original perjury that is the sinful secret of the original promise, the secret, perjured promise of Genesis. The Cross is the sign of the Covenant that begins its promise anew by raising the question in the form of sacrifice and leaving the question suspended in the aporetic structure of contradiction, the other sign of the cross in thought. This suspended question of the Gift of Death, how the promise can pass over through death, gives a new sign, a new structure of the question in the sign of the cross, and the Resurrection gives the countersign in the revelation of forgiveness as the secret of the giving of the Gift of Death.

When Beatrice speaks to Dante she speaks only of Resurrection and of his failure to believe in her death as the offer of the Gift of Death. She accuses him of perjury of his promise to her to write of her what had never been written in verse of woman before. She accuses him of perjuring his promise to write her secret, the secret that cannot be known, cannot be spoken because it is no secret; it is the impossibility of the existence of a secret, the secret of the impossibility of existence, the secret of forgiving the transgression of the possibility of the impossibility of existence, forgiving the sin of existence, forgiving existence by giving death, not as a penalty or as a price, not as sacrifice or as redemption, but as the countergift, the countersign, the counterpromise that for-gives the gift.

Beatrice speaks only of Resurrection. She speaks of it as the secret that has been given over into her keeping, into the keeping of woman, like the women who went to Jesus' tomb, bearing gifts to give the dead while all the others, all the men who had betrayed him, kept themselves hidden in the false secrecy of fear and guilt. The women went and trembled; the men did not. They had to be told by the women, the women who had been entrusted with the new secret, the new beginning of the secret, the secret of the Gift of Death. The women had been told to keep it secret by sharing it, making it open, making it an open secret so as to make visible the empty tomb, to reveal the empty secret or the secret of the perjured promise. "He is not here." He is not present, he is absent, he is Other. You will recognize him only in the sign of the breaking of the bread and the passing of the cup. He is the secret of the gift, which nurtures life, the secret Gift of Death, the secret that cannot be known but must be kept in the passionate suffering of the Impossible, the suffering of believing and hoping the Impossible, which passes over into love: Love, which is the third, the Other of life and death.

Beatrice does not forgive Dante. She only commands Dante to say "Yes!" to her accusation. She writes his confession for him in her own words over her own signature under the erasure of an Other's signature and requires only that he countersign it. He makes no confession of his own, and does not ask for forgiveness. His only statement, his only confession is the confession of Everyman to the sin of existing, "The *present things* (*le presenti cose*), with their false pleasure, turned my steps aside, as soon as your countenance was hidden" (*Purg.*, xxxi, 34–36). His sin is the sin of existence, of all existence, of all "the present things," as if he were saying 'the things you have presented, the things that are presentable, and re-presentable, without you when you were hidden in death, encrypted in death, when I could no longer read you among the present and represented things because you saw and spoke in secret, spoke of the empty secret, of the secret of what is not present, what is not given, spoke of what is forgiven, these let me lose sight of you in death, lose sight of your resurrection which is the secret that I had thought to write of you, but which now you write in me, with which you cross me and which I countersign with my tears, with rivers of tears through which I must pass, through which I must be carried by the other women who keep your secret. Yes, I broke faith with you when I substituted the present things for the hope of your death which is the gift of your love, the gift of your death.'

It is done. He passes through the waters of his tears, passes through the waters of baptism into death, the death that wipes away every tear in which the ruins of memory are written, the death that heals the memories that must not, cannot be forgotten, preserving the ruins of memory that are passed over and passed on by remembering differently. He passes through the Gift of Death, through the Resurrection that for-gives the gift of the empty perjured promise and begins a new life that remembers the suffering as joy.

## DOING THE TRUTH IN (FAITH, HOPE AND) LOVE—THE FINAL TRUTH OF FORGIVENESS

> Derrida's secret is the secret without (*sans*) truth, the secret of the *sans*, the secret confessed in a confession without truth. So this confession does not bring into the light of day the unconcealed truth of his secret self, because such a secret he does not know, and this because there is none. There is no truth beyond the truth one "does," the truth one "makes" of oneself, *facere veritatem,* in one's heart by confessing it. (*PTJD,* 290)

There is no truth except the truth one confesses, the truth of what has been done in the name of "my God," a truth which must be written as confession in "my" heart by the Other/"God."

Dante believes that forgiveness has happened, that forgiveness has been done in him, in his experience, that it has been written in his heart by Beatrice as the confession that he transcribes in his *Commedia.* He can believe that the impossible truth of forgiveness has happened in his experience and in his heart and in his writing, because he believes that this impossible truth of forgiveness has already been done in the Resurrection of Jesus, which has been inscribed in the heart of humanity as its history and in the heart of Beatrice, which she in turn has written in his heart, and which he in turn has written in his poem as his confession of the history of what has been done in him, the history he has become, the history of his responsibility and freedom, the responsibility and freedom of his promise that has been forgiven him and that he now keeps in secret written on his heart and in the poem.

Derrida too believes that forgiveness has happened, that forgiveness has been done, done to him in his experience. He believes that it has been written in his heart by Georgette, his (m)other, as the confession that he writes in his *Circumfession.* He believes that the impossible truth of forgiveness has happened in his experience and in his heart and in his writing, because he believes in writing, believes that this impossible truth has already been done in writing and must always be done anew. He believes that writing is the trace-mark of the history of forgiveness, of forgiveness as the final, absolute truth of the Secret Promise of the Gift, which never appears, never leaves a mark, but happens in writing as the history of responsibility. "One always writes in order to confess [the truth]; one always writes in order to ask forgiveness" (*Circum.,* 49). Responsibility decides the history of forgiveness by confessing in writing the truth one has done, the truth that one has made, the truth that has been done, made, and written in one by an Other, and for which one has accepted responsibility, the only truth for which one could possibly claim responsibility, claim to "know," or be held responsible for.

Derrida believes in writing as the history of forgiveness because he has found that history written in him, written in his flesh and blood, the flesh of his circumcision and the blood of his heart. In the flesh of his circumcision, he finds written the mark of the Promise, of the covenant between God and Abraham, the mark of responsibility for the decision regarding the cut of sacrifice, the decision that Abraham makes in the instant of responsibility, but that is deferred and dispensed by God. Derrida finds written in the flesh of his circumcision the mark of responsibility for the decision that keeps the secret of that Promise by deferring the final decision, the decision that finally gives the Gift of Death, and by substituting the cut of decision in the instant for the cut of sacrifice that never ends. This deferral through dispensation and substitution traces the figure in history of the Jew, of the Jewish blood that flows in Derrida's heart. The figure of Jewish responsibility, the Jewish history of responsibility, is marked by the experience of deferral as the way in which the secret Promise of the Gift is kept as dispensation from the economy of sacrifice through the substitution of the decision of faith. But this figure of Jewish responsibility is also a figure of responsibility written in a Jewish style. The history of Jewish responsibility for the secret promise is itself a particular shibboleth, a style of secret password, for the secrecy of the promise of the gift, the promise of giving, in all the possible historical styles that its impossibility might effect. The secrecy of the promise and the impossibility of the gift leave their mark on the history of responsibility inscribing *différance* into every writing of every history of responsibility. This *différance* becomes apparent according to the style by which the promise cuts off the one who is chosen to receive it, and cuts off his children and his children's children, from those who are excluded, the way the chosen one and the chosen people are set apart in a promised land, which is carved out for them from all the others. To be chosen as the child of the Promise is to be cut off, separated, kept in secret from all the others and from the Other. This too Derrida finds written in his flesh and blood.

This history of responsibility that Derrida finds written as a difference in the writing of history, he rewrites according to the figures of prophetic judgment and messianic justice in the history that he writes, which, like all writing, is a history of confessing and asking forgiveness. It is the history of responsibility that he writes according to the confession that has been written in his flesh and in the blood of his heart by all the others of his writing, especially by his (m)other in *Circumfession,* and the Other, especially in *The Gift of Death* and in "To Forgive." It is the history of his belief in writing, of his hope in writing, and of his love of the others/Other that is revealed in the testament of his writing. It is his testament, his testimony given as confession, a confession of his love that he finds written in the trace of *différance,* which he believes is the signature, always under erasure, of forgiveness, the erasure, which is the mark of forgiveness, the mark of the style in which the history of responsibility is written. This love of *différance,* the mark of forgiveness written as the history of responsibility, which must always be decided again and written again, is the writing of his experience of the love that gives the gift by for-giving, the love that is given as the forgiveness of the Gift of Death.

Death is the Impossible; death is the unforgivable. Death is the possible impossibility of the Gift and of the for-giving that gives the Gift. Death is the possible impossibility of forgiving and the impossible possibility of forgiveness. Love is the Gift of Death for-given. Love is the for-giving of the Gift of Death. Before the Gift is forgiveness. Before the Gift, love as for-giving the Gift, as giving the Gift of Death. Death keeps the empty secret which is the perjured promise of the Gift. Forgiving death keeps the secret promise by giving the Gift, by giving death as its gift. Love names the forgiveness that gives the Gift of Death. For Dante, resurrection names the love that for-gives death and gives the Gift of Death, which keeps the promise of writing as confession. "Every confession is written in the register of love." Every confession asks for the Gift of Death, every confession asks forgiveness of death, for-gives death, forgives the refusal of death, the refusal of forgiveness, the refusal of the promise of the gift, the refusal of the Gift of Death.

## CHAPTER FOUR

# Paradiso: Turning Tears into Smiles

Chapter 4 examines the difference that emerges when Derrida's *Memoirs of the Blind* is read alongside Dante's *Paradiso* in an attempt to respond to the question, "What is the difference between Dante and Derrida, and what difference does it make for the concerns that they share and the style of writing that marks their relationship?" Both texts are configured as "Pictures at an Exhibition," that is, as studies of the ways in which faith, hope, and love can be portrayed as structures of personal identity through studies of human figures and faces. Derrida examines a series of self-portraits, studies of blindness, and "sacred allegories," which he selected for an exhibition he was asked to curate at the Louvre shortly after *Circumfession* was written. Step-by-step, he leads the viewer through a deconstructive tour guided by the "hypothesis of sight" to the final revelation that the truth of the eyes is expressed neither by vision nor by knowledge, but by tears. Quoting Andrew Marvel, "Only human eyes can weep." The course of the exhibition reveals that the aporia of faith can be seen differently as the aporia of the eye: how to read the ambiguity of the text written by the eyes, written in the eyes in the water of tears—tears of sorrow, tears of joy.

Dante's *Paradiso* can be read as a Book of Joy: the Joy of Resurrection received as the Gift of Death forgiven. Dante spreads out his Book of Joy across the sweep of the whole universe as a kind of (self-portrait) gallery of human religious identity, which exhibits how tears of sorrow come to be converted into smiles of love, revealing the smile as the essence of the mouth, before and beyond either speaking or eating. The smile of the mouth is the scripture of forgiveness, the trace of love given and accepted as the Gift of Death, the love which is final because it does not end, but as Resurrection, always begins again. Dante and Derrida are as different as mouth and eyes that play across the human face, writing, each time differently, the singular identity of the One who is always Other.

## ENJOYING FORGIVENESS: THE FREEDOM OF LOVE

"Let me raise only one point concerning blindness, which is symptomatic of the general question I have about the relationship [Ambrosio] is unfolding for us. In general, whenever Derrida's texts are entered into association, *mutatis mutandi*, with classical religious texts one must remain alert to a general and massive mutation. By this I mean that Derrida is a pilgrim who in a very serious sense is lost, errant, who does not know where he is going, for whom there is no unique name—God, for example—that cannot be translated into or reduced to some other name. If he were to be found among the pilgrims on the way to Canterbury he would be like a pilgrim who never heard of Canterbury and is not convinced that Canterbury is the place he needs to go. Thus, while Plato talks about the Good beyond being, Derrida likes to say that he is interested in the Khora beneath being. If Derrida is a pilgrim, he is a blind pilgrim who needs a walking stick. Now the question I have is whether the blindness [one] finds in Dante is the blindness of the "beyond being," of a river of light, a celestial blindness that comes of being blinded by the sun of unbearable brightness, as in Marion's "saturated phenomenon," and hence a certain beatific vision of Beatrice, and whether this is not different from Derrida, who is speaking of a khoral blindness where there is no light or sun, where one is blinded not by the splendor of the secret [but] by its darkness, by the secret that there is no secret. If, as I suspect, that is so, and if that is symptomatic of what divides Derrida and Dante, then I would want to know what difference this difference makes for [Ambrosio's] analysis, how this difference affects the other correspondences he has unearthed." (John Caputo, "Response to Ambrosio")[1]

Derrida is not Dante. This much has been clear from the beginning and must remain so. Caputo is quite right to ask, in the face of the study of the significance of the deep resonances of language, images, and concerns that one discovers moving back and forth across Dante's texts and Derrida's, what are the differences between them and what difference these differences make. In fact, from the beginning, the concern of this study has not been to compare and contrast Dante and Derrida, so much as to engage the questions they engage, which are primarily questions about faith, hope, and love, about responsibility, and about writing. The overriding merit and lasting contribution of Caputo's work in *The Prayers and Tears of Jacques Derrida* has been to reveal those concerns on the part of Derrida as the impetus and motivating passion, if not the direction, for the journey which his texts have taken over the years. Caputo has attempted to argue, convincingly in my view, that it is precisely Derrida's "passion for the Impossible" that constitutes his "religion without religion." While radically departing from any of the "concrete messianisms" of the religions of the sacred scriptural heritage of Judaism, Christianity, and Islam, it is nonetheless both genuinely religious in its passion and itself a historical "messianism" precisely in that it *departs from* that specific religious tradition.

The difference that Caputo's question inquires after in the above citation does not express a skepticism about the authenticity of Dante and Derrida's shared religious concerns, but candidly endeavors to understand what the difference is that allows them actually to share and participate in those concerns precisely as human concerns, that is, as historical concerns that always occur in the singular instant of decision. It is the occurrence of the singular instant of decision that constitutes both history and religion, which constitutes religion as the history of responsibility. It is precisely the difference between them that qualifies both Dante and Derrida to make confession, to bear witness, and to offer testimony regarding the human experience of the singular instant of decision that constitutes religion as the history of responsibility. For it is responsibility, the question of responsibility, that frees history to begin, just as it is history that evokes responsibility.

The point of Caputo's question, then, would seem to be how the specific historical and personal difference regarding religion between Dante and Derrida opens up a communication and a communion between them. Rather than being disabling or distancing, this difference would be, to speak like Derrida for a moment, the quasi-transcendental condition of possibility for there being a relationship between the two, and for the significance, whatever it might be, of that relation. Of course, if we are to look for this effective difference between them, we must look for it in their writing. But because that difference and its significance must necessarily be ascribed to the style of their writing, we must attempt to resist the temptation to conceptualize that difference reflectively. Because such a difference would be between singularities, or at least between singular styles of writing, which must elude conceptualization, our approach will be to trace the figure of their difference in the texts that express their own experiences of conversion. By taking a turn into religion at a certain moment of forgiveness each turned more consciously into a place of secret joy. So it is the singular style of joy written on the face of each that is the destination of our journey here.

Two texts: Dante's *Paradiso* and Derrida's *Memoirs of the Blind;* an accidental, though not an arbitrary pairing. *Memoirs of the Blind* is continuous and consanguineous with *Circumfession* in ways that are startlingly similar to the continuity and the consanguinity of *Paradiso* to *Purgatorio*. This "startling" experience is precisely the one that occurs when one recognizes in the photograph of a child, perhaps even one's own, a resemblance of eyes, or mouth or line of the jaw, to the parent, perhaps even oneself, which the "direct" view of sight in passing, in person, the present view of presence, fails to reveal; yet the substitute, the intermediary medium, the photograph, immediately makes this resemblance unmistakable—the "trick" of the lens, the "transposition" from "in front of your face" to "in your hand." It is this "startling" recognition of similarity, of resemblance, of continuity, consanguinity, kinship and spectral, ancestral memorialization—it is the "start" it gives that demands attention. It provides the link between Derrida and Dante, that is between their texts, because it is their texts, like the photographs in the example above, that reveal the as-yet-unseen, or until now differently seen, similarity (or is it a difference seen differently?). It shows itself by displacement, by transposition, by intermediation and dislocation from "in front of one's face" to "in the palm of your hand." Look at how many "starts" we get here: it is startling to see the trace of the weepy Jackie of *Circumfession* now revealed in the master hand of "curator," the deployer of the Louvre exhibition on blindness and seeing—how not to see in the open, *l'ouvre*. It is equally startling to see the trace of the weepy Dante of the Earthly Paradise at the helm of his vessel, a sort of Starship Enterprise, warning off those who might scuttle along in his wake attempting to brook the deep sea voyage from which he has just returned like some Ishmael:

> O you that are in your little bark, eager to hear, following behind my ship that singing makes her way, turn back to see again your shores. Do not commit yourselves to the open sea, for perchance, if you lost me, you would remain astray. The water which I take was never coursed before. Minerva breathes and Apollo guides me, and nine Muses point out to me the Bears. (*Par., ii, 1–9*)

But most of all, it is startling to see again how these two texts, a book of blindness and a book of vision, accomplish the same trick of "disposition," displacement, substitution, from in front of your face to in the hand; how they accomplish in the writing, in the medium of intermediation, the "turn" of recognition, the turn into conversation and communion, the turn into communication and intercourse. Dante and Derrida resemble one another not so much in what they write, but in that they write, in that they enjoy writing, or better, much better, in that they are "en-joyed," by writing. They are en-joyed by the Impossibility of faith, of hope, of love, of responsibility, of religion, of life—and write about the religious life (without religion) as the history of responsibility for the Gift of Death. They are en-joyed by and in the writing of human religious life. By seeing Dante and Derrida portrayed in the ways that they write, seeing them portrayed in the trace of their traces, and in the trace of their traits, we see a relationship that is startling, not despite the differences, but because the similarity lies precisely in their way of differing, the way of differing that is im-proper to both of them. We recognize their kinship and consanguinity in that they both *differ in writing,* they both differ in that they write the difference of the singular instant of decision that constitutes responsibility, constitutes religion, constitutes history, and constitutes religion as the history of Western responsibility. In and through all differences of image and metaphor, style, and historical situation, differences of a depth and profundity too vast to do more than "sketch," the claim we have been tracing here is that Dante and Derrida are startlingly recognizable as blood-kin, because tests have been made, analyses done, types taken and matched, of the blood in which they write, of the blood and water (of tears) that is the ink of their writing, of the blood by which and for which they differ in writing.

Blindness and vision—these are matters of the blood, of the family, of men and women, of faces and portraits, of memory and representation, of paradox and substitution, all of which belong together in an impossible intimacy of infinite extension, and in a vast distention of a concentrated secrecy impossible to penetrate. To everyone's wonder and the dismay of all, Dante and Derrida forestall every academic discourse of comparison and contrast by having always already begun their communication and communion, their intercourse of absolute rivalry and absolute singularity, the wildest and most impassioned dance of seduction, inciting a tremor of intimacy that solicits its mate with the sheer self-containment of its own identity. Their texts dance a dance of ecstatic joy that possesses itself wholly in its fascination for the wholly other, the other that can for it never be whole and therefore is wholly needed. The *Paradiso* and the *Memoirs of the Blind* are not finally then books of vision and blindness; they are books of joy, the joy that arises only within the blind spot that faith alone introduces into the field of vision, the religious ecstasy of the Impossibility of the whole, which wholly impassions us as human beings and wholly identifies the joy that makes us whole in our need.

All this makes the present study a work of nearly impossible presumption: the vast presumption of faith. It presumes familiarity with the works of Derrida discussed here, *Circumfession, The Gift of Death, Memoirs of the Blind,* and "To Forgive," and with Dante's *Vita nuova* and *Commedia.* But it also impossibly presumes faith, faith in the religious concerns of those writings, and faith in writing as the work of faith, faith in the prayers and tears of writing, for Derrida and Dante startle us precisely in their faith in writing, their faith in writing as the work of praying and weeping, their faith in the hope of writing, which is the hope of the Impossible, their hope of the joy of love, which is written in the faces of persons human and divine, faces that are Impossible to read but are always doing the truth of freedom—the truth of beginning and ending history.

*Memoirs of the Blind* proceeds in the play of several presumptions, which are confessions and therefore enactments of blindness: first, on the hypothesis of sight, that is on the hypothesis that all seeing and all knowing, all *voir* and *savoir,* are themselves hypotheses; second, on the presumptive substitution of drawing for writing; and third, on the dissolution of the eye into the organ of weeping and tears. This dissolution presumes and portrays the necessary return of organic life to water in the degeneration of the culture of life into its genetic elementarity, which is therefore the return, in the end, to the beginning, to beginning again. The eye envisions death in weeping and tears; it sees life through tears, sees it through death, and so sees it as the gift of death, which is to say, sees life as always necessarily beginning again. This leads to the recognition of a fourth presumption at work in *Memoirs of the Blind:* that the vision of the eye originates in the blindness of faith. The hypothesis of sight means that seeing presumes faith universally. All seeing is a work of faith that entrusts itself to the work of the hands that grope toward what they see in another way, or better, grope toward seeing in the way of the Other. Drawing, like writing, is the work of the hands, hands as substitutes for eyes, hands that do not grasp, but feel in the manner of groping, as with the blind man's staff or the stylus of the one who gropes, the draftsman or the writer, the one who entrusts him- or herself to ways traced out, to the traits that are put down, hypothesized, put *in place of* what one hopes to find out but cannot see. "Hypo-thesis" means that which is put down as the starting place from which the "argument"—the venture ship, the Argosy—sets out in the hope of returning laden with treasure; the "aesthetic" level of the "given" from which phenomenological reduction proceeds and on the presupposition of which it operates, reducing it, dissolving it into the flow of time, which is the abstract image in reflection of the flow of water—the ancient image of marking time is to count tears. The substitution of drawing for writing, Derrida's personal concern, is marked with an ambiguity on which Derrida remarks that it seems to mark a tie to his older brother, whose draftsmanship was a constant source of obvious family pride. This, however, engendered in Jacques a constant sense of inadequacy and the failure to please, to gain notice, to satisfy, so that his family repeated the unspoken substitution of Jacob for Esau. The ruse of disguise to beguile the blindness of paternal blessing, the necessary sacrifice of one son to preserve another in the inexorable economy of patriarchy, patrimony, and patri-parricide once again emerges here as the necessary legacy of the archetype of "brotherhood," the mark Cain bears for the murder of Abel, the token of the dual/duel of victimization that is at the root of the binocularity of sacrifice.[2] It betokens a necessary conflict of perspective and mutual destruction that the "unity of vision" (and knowledge) requires, and further, requires to be concealed. Derrida's curatorial responsibility for the exhibition in the Louvre, which he instantaneously decided, at the beginning, to characterize as "how not to see in the open (l'ouvre/Louvre) or how to read between the lines, seeing through the blinds"—seeing through the blind spots—which are all the slits and cuts with which the inevitable jealousy and murder instigated by the competitive demand for sacrifice lacerate the field of vision.[3]

This sibling rivalry is the first confession Derrida makes in and through the writing of *Memoirs of the Blind*, which is of course a companion and guide to the exhibit that he has arranged, a script to trace his scripting of the drawings. This is a work of mourning for the brother whom he has killed for the sake of the "paternal blessing." (Derrida's relative silence regarding his father, at least in these texts and in contrast to all the traces of his mother in passing, unexcused by any accident of "autobiographical" fact, is another of the many signatures under erasure with which the exhibition and its script are signed). He must mourn the brother who is killed with and buried under writing, in a sepulcher whitened by the myth that the discourse that traces the course of the exhibit is about drawing. It is, of course, about drawing; but in writing about drawing Derrida can write about writing without naming it properly, write about it under erasure, under an improper name. Jacques writes and his brother draws—quite different, but they are after all brothers, and the story among brothers is always the same: jealousy, violence, murder in the economy of blood that circulates through the veins of sacrifice, one of the oldest of family values.

The point here, of course, is that it is their blood relation and blood-guilt that Derrida is confessing in the exhibition and in its scripture. He is confessing it now in the light of the faith of the conversion described in *Circumfession*. He is seeing himself in the only way that one ever sees oneself, through the making of a self-portrait, which means through the eyes of the other. The mirror that the narrow act of artistic self-portraiture provides is always only a "mechanical" though tantalizing and provocative exercise of the sin of narcissism, which too is required by the economy of sacrifice and its state of debt. The economy of sacrifice and its state of debt requires such narcissism. The exhibit and its scripture is a Derridean self-portrait in the act of confessing and testifying and witnessing to the scene of forgiveness that has occurred in the rewriting of his story from his mother. The love that is dis-covered in/on/at the scene of forgiveness, seen in faith through the tears in which that scene is written, written in water, in blood and in ink, this love begins the world again. The exhibition traces a course marked out by the groping stick/stylus of a blind man who sees the world through the veil of tears as a place of joy. This place of joy, however, is not one from which darkness and death are simply banished, any more than blindness is simply the absence of sight—the absence of a present presence. Such an anemic paradise, as a place of joy, would be a double overdraft—the absence of an absence—the privation of a privation. Rather, this paradise that Derrida is enjoying, having (almost) died and gone to heaven in the Louvre, is the vast ocean onto which Dante's river Eunoe flows, the waters of "good memory," of healed memory, of the preservation of the ruins of memory and the memory in ruins. There were other waters through which Dante had first to pass, the waters of Lethe, the waters of memory of a life that is always "ruining," always already "ruined" by death, always already starting to be ruined. But these are the waters of memory as the work of conserving ruins, burying the dead, memory as the work of mourning, keeping faith with the dead in the hope of the Gift of Death. The place of joy is the place of keeping faith with the ruins of life in the hope of the Gift of Death. It is the place of love, of the free intercourse, the free flowing together, running together all the wellsprings of life into the falling waters of death, falling like tears of joy and tears of sorrow. Derrida is rewriting his life, writing a new life, still seen through the veil of tears of sorrow, but now turning into a stream in which tears of joy flow freely from the scene of the Gift of Death, of death forgiven, of a gift for-given.

So *Memoirs* is a book of the dead as well as the blind; it is written for joy at the Gift of Death that he has been given from his mother. It traces a certain tendency in Derrida toward "exhibitionism." He makes an exhibition "in the open" to demonstrate the conversion and transformation of his exhibition "in secret" (*Circumfession*) of his circumcision. All his writing, perhaps all writing, shows the trait of exhibitionism in *retrait*. The exhibition is the confession of the forgiveness of his writing, the writing from which the name of God was absent and which the mother feared had been forgotten by her son. She wept over that writing and bathed it in her tears, so that through her tears for him, through tears that were for him, through this veil of tears he could see and enjoy his writing, could come to love the writing that had killed his father, killed his brother, and had all but killed his mother, until, *in extremis*, in his last-minute race with death to find his way back to her, he discovered that love was still his most difficult ally.

In this place of joy, he is also rewriting his dreams. He remembers the very bad dream—like Dante's dream of "heart-eating"—of a "duel" between two old blind men who are fighting and who turn on him and threatened to harm his sons, the uncircumcised sons over whom he grieves in *Circumfession*, just as his mother grieves over him. No appeal to authority, for example Freud's authority, need be made here for the meaning of the dream: Derrida interprets it for himself and for us in the exhibition, there confessing the joy of his resurrection in the transformed vision of faith that he now displays for all to see, just as he had displayed, at the "start" of his conversion in *Circumfession*, the mark of faith in his flesh. He exhibits it in the painting in which the exhibition culminates, the painting by Daniele da Volterra, *Woman at the Foot of the Cross*, weeping for the death of her son. The woman, his mother, who has now written herself into the heart of his story, weeps in him for the death of the son, for the death of all sons, and he weeps for the death of his sons in the demand for sacrifice that took Abraham's son, took the son of YHWH, took Georgette's son, and has taken his sons, the demand for the cut that cuts off every mother's son, the cut that remembers death, remembers the death that is not yet forgiven, the ruin of life remembered without the Gift of Death that is for-given.

In *Memoirs of the Blind* Derrida is writing his vision of life, his life, the course of his life in writing, confessing his life as he now sees it through eyes bathed, circumcised in tears, confessing it to be a vision of paradise, the place of a secret joy, the joy of the Secret of life, of the Secret of always beginning again, life as the Gift of Death. Like Dostoevsky's Father Zossima, he confesses that now he sees life through the eyes of faith, eyes blinded by tears and weeping, the tears of the other that are for him, tears that express the love of the other for him, which is now written in his heart. The "hypothesis of sight" spreads out and opens up the course of his exhibition of the traits of faith; it rewrites his vision of his life in writing with the difference that it is traced in the traits of the drawings that he scripts here to tell the course of his journey and to illustrate through what he writes: the joy of all that he has written and now begins to write again

The "hypothesis of sight" tells the story of the conversion of seeing through the blindness of drawing into the hope that incarnates itself as writing: the substitution of hands for eyes. All "seeing" is always "seeing as," and the "as" signifies the process of conversion that occurs in language as what Derrida calls "archi-writing." The hypothesis of sight seems to be a gesture toward a theory of kinesthesia, an an-economic free play of interchange among the senses, which does not simply allow or tolerate substitution, but blesses it by enacting and memorializing the passing over. It commemorates a certain "allowance," a passing on and passing over amid the ruins of memory, the acceptance of the shibboleth or deceptive password that forgives the original sin of substitution. Adam and Eve were not to taste of the fruit of the tree of the knowledge of good and evil that guarded the way to the tree of life at the center of the garden. Presumably, they were to enjoy it by looking at it. Theirs was to be a joy of the eyes, not of the hand or the tongue; they were not to touch it with their hands or their tongues, not to taste of it or even talk of it as they did with the serpent, not to smell the aroma that wafts only when the skin is pierced. The substitution of tongue and hands and ears and nose for eyes was their sin, and with them substitution became the pattern of all sin, the "original sin" that makes substitution a guilty act, a debt of deception that must always be paid off, redeemed, and saved at the price of incurring a new debt. This pattern continues on and on without end, setting up the deadly economy of sacrifice without forgiveness, always withholding and deferring the Gift of Death, in which there can be no substitution, which can and must always only be forgiven.

That the hypothesis of sight directs the course of Derrida's exhibition of the joy of conversion that opens up the scene of forgiveness to be seen only by eyes that are bathed in tears would seem to account for all of the major lines of development by which that hypothesis is articulated in and through the drawings it deploys. Based on the original hypothesis of blindness as the necessary "other" of seeing, the exhibition traces the "history of salvation" in the Jewish and Christian testamentary scripture as it reveals itself through various episodes of the intercourse between blindness and seeing. This is always a business between fathers and sons within the history of the lineage that both traces the economy of sacrifice that descends from Abraham and inscribes in the flesh of every mother's son the mark of the covenant. This mark is certainly different than the mark of Cain, but a cut nonetheless. It also traces the dispensation and the healing of blindness, which is the work either of the angel of the Lord or of Jesus. Such a reading of the hypothesis of sight accounts in the first place for Derrida's focus in the exhibition on the "transcendental blindness." Such blindness, he implies, is the necessary structure of the self-portrait that is the work of "everyone who says mine." This gesture toward blindness as quasi-transcendental structure of every attempt at self-representation puts Derrida's signature at the end of the script of the exhibition under erasure. In the same way it deflects responsibility for this script as a scripture of responsibility for rendering the history of his faith in the promise of the writing in which he has always been profiling himself. It accounts too for the inclusion of the drawings that portray "sacrificial blindness" in the story of those on whom blindness is visited as the price that must be paid for some gift of strength or talent that blinds them to the blindness of faith on which the gift depends, and so requires the demonstration of forgiveness that is before the gift, and through which alone the gift must pass and be passed on. Finally, the hypothesis of sight accounts for the drawings that show the decisive instant of conversion that must necessarily pass through the blindness of faith to enter into the transformed vision which, specifically in the case of St. Paul, reveals the "Way." This way is located at a certain juncture along the street called "Straight"—the *via diritta* from which Dante had strayed. It is a path that had not been seen prior to the blindness of conversion, in the "open," but which now opens up and is seen in a new light.

All this leads to the final vision of blindness, Daniele da Volterra's *Woman Weeping at the Foot of the Cross,* the only woman—other than the interviewer/interlocutor with whom the scripting of the exhibition unfolds—to play a significant role in the story of this exhibition. All of Derrida's other confessors are men. Significantly, she appears only after the pilgrim who follows the way of the exhibition to its end, has passed through the "ruins of memory," which above all else signify the condition of the one who confesses and so self-portrays himself:

> In Christian culture there is no self-portrait without confession. The author of the self-portrait does not *show* himself; he does not teach anything to God, who knows everything in advance (as Augustine never ceases to recall). This self-portraitist *does not lead one to knowledge,* he admits a fault and asks for forgiveness. He "makes" truth, to use Augustine's word, he makes [*fait*] the light of this narrative, *throws light* on it, in order to make the love of God grow within him, "for love of your love."(*MB,* 117)

Derrida goes on to quote Augustine's lament over "the concupiscence of the eyes" by which one is drawn away from the inner truth by outward appearance of the "simulacrum."

> And all these things are additional temptations to the eye that men follow outwardly (*foras*), inwardly (*intus*) forsaking the one by whom they were made, ruining (*exterminantes*) what he made of them. But, oh my God, my Glory, for these things too I offer you a hymn of thanksgiving. I make a sacrifice of praise to the One who sanctifies me (*Confessions,* 10. 34).

Derrida goes on to ask rhetorically whether Augustine means to condemn all Christian painting, condemn art as un-Christian. His response: "not at all, just so long as conversion saves it" (*MB,* 119). What does this mean, and specifically, what does it mean for Derrida's art show, for the exhibition of drawings that he has arranged to stand in for, as a kind of allegory, to substitute for the course of his writing? Derrida turns to a discussion of Jan Provost's *Sacred Allegory*—a painting that depicts the Resurrected Christ and Mary as Queen of Heaven sitting on either side of the globe of the earth. The two are gazing

upward in rapt contemplation at the monocular "Eye of God" appearing as the
Sun at the center of the burning fire of the Empyrean, flanked by the Lamb
of the Apocalypse. Derrida's interest in the painting is focused exclusively on
one aspect: the way in which it shows the "quasi-transcendental" condition of
possibility, not solely of Christian art, but of the Christian vision of faith. Of
the painting he says:

> . . . [it] must always be able to be contemplated as the representation or
> reflection of its own possibility. He puts on the scene, in stages, the opening
> scene of sacred painting, an allegorical self-representation of this "order of
> the gaze" to which any Christian painting must submit. This putting to work
> of the self-presentation does not suspend—no more than it ever does—ref-
> erence to the outside, as is so often and so naively believed. The desire for
> self-presentation is never met, it never meets up with itself, and that is why
> the simulacrum takes place. Never does the eye of the Other recall this desire
> more sovereignly to the outside and to difference, to the law of dispropor-
> tion, dissymmetry, and expropriation. *And this is memory itself.* To "contem-
> plate" this picture this way, the gaze must become Christian; it is not that
> it must be already converted, but learning to see the divine condition of the
> picture itself, learning to see on this condition, *which is possible only in a hymn
> or prayer.* (*MB*, 121; emphasis added)

The condition of art, insofar as it can be religious (which here Derrida
refers to as becoming Christian), is the same as the condition of seeing insofar
as either can be true: each must be in the process of becoming (converted to)
the vision of faith. For the vision of faith is the vision that sees itself beheld,
held in the gaze of the One, the monocularity that always already forgives the
im-possibility of seeing and forgives all that substitutes, all the simulacra that
the eye sees without seeing the eye that beholds it, forgives it, and makes it able
to see in the light in which it is seen. "And this is memory itself." Memory is
confession of the ruin of experience that is not the result of a fault of attention,
a lapse of care, or any failure of the work of preservation, but is a witness to the
law of disproportion, dissymmetry, and expropriation by which desire always
exceeds itself and so always necessitates the forgiveness that must freely pre-
cede it. Before the gift, before the mutuality of the gaze, before the exchange
of desires that always exceed themselves, is forgiveness, which passes on judgment and passes on desire to begin again in the gift of desire's death:

> A Christian drawing should be a hymn, a work of praise, a prayer, an implor-
> ing eye, an eye with joined hands, an imploring that is lifted up, an imploring
> of surrection and resurrection . . . like the eyes of the Son and his mother [in
> the painting] who look in the same direction. Imploration, revelation, sac-
> rifice: . . . this allegory shows the eye of the Other only by unveiling the
> allegory of showing itself, the allegory of drawing as apocalypse . . . [which
> means] nothing other than a revelation or a laying bare, an unveiling that

renders visible the truth of truth: light that shows itself, as and by itself. This is an apocalypse of painting—as Christian painting. Everything here is at once overturned and put back in place, from on high to down below, from top to bottom and all the way through. (*MB*, 121–22)

But "apocalypse" has another meaning that is by no means secondary, but necessary to the first: the event of a catastrophe or a cataclysm. At the same time that order and proportion are inscribed and incised by the cut of the stylus, in the instant of decision when the eye passes from seeing to overseeing, in the moment when eye passes over into hand and forgets what it was seeing in favor of the work that the hand is making, in that moment of sacrifice, the cutting off of sight, in that moment of apocalyptic judgment, which is also the hymn of praise, the eyes are not alone, they are seconded by another, they "mean" something else, they mean differently. For a moment they hold back, hold in reserve, the tears that necessarily mourn the victim of the sacrifice, mourn both the necessity of the structure and the demand for the sacrifice. At that moment of blind sacrifice, the eyes hold back, hold onto the tears that would implore, in vain, for mercy, for dispensation of the demand, for what will come from what will not, cannot come, and so the tears come in the wake of the work. "Order and ruin are no longer dissociated at the origin of drawing—and neither are the transcendental structure and sacrifice—even less so when drawing shows its origin, the condition of its possibility, and the coming of its event: a work" (*MB*, 122).

Every work is, in its origin, a sacrifice of praise; every hymn that lifts its eye to heaven in gratitude or joy has bloody hands. Every work that flows like blood from the instantaneous cut of decision falls into the abyss of blindness, leaving sight behind, cut off from the gaze that holds it, forgets that it is beheld. It can be redeemed from its khoral exile, its being cut off and alone in the instance of calling, which is "mine" and mine alone, by that other eye, the other in the eye that holds back tears, holds tears in reserve to mourn the death that is necessarily mine alone, imploring in tears that the sacrificial blindness not be final/fatal, but that it call forth a new vision, the vision that sees through tears:

> A work is at once order and ruin. And these two weep for one another. Deploring and imploring veil a gaze at the very moment they unveil it. By praying on the verge of tears, the sacred allegory *does* [*fait*] something. It makes something happen or come, makes something come to the eyes, makes something well up in them, by producing an event. It is performative, something vision alone would be incapable of if it gave rise only to representational reporting, to perspicacity, to theory or theater, if it were not already potentially apocalypse, already potent with apocalypse. By blinding oneself to vision, by veiling one's own sight—through imploring, for example—one *does* something with one's eyes, *makes* something of them. One does something to one's own eyes. (*MB*, 122)

This double-dealing of the eyes *deplores* the sacrificial blindness into which they are drawn by the "concupiscence of the eyes" at the demand of desire. In the same instant, however, in the face of the desire of the Other that can never be met, the eyes *implore* forgiveness for the death of sight, cut off by the hand, with tears that well up and are held in reserve in the eyes, the other "doing" that reveals a "second sight" that sees through tears. Every work of praise undoes itself by imploring the gift of death, imploring that death give its gift, the gift of beginning again. The necessity of death to which the sacrifice of the hand witnesses by its blindness invokes and reveals a second function of the eyes. They are converted to a second sight, the necessary, needed other of sight:

> Now if the tears *come to the eyes*, if they *well up in them* and if they can also veil sight, perhaps they reveal, in the very course of this experience, in this coursing of water, an essence of the eye, of man's eye, in any case, the eye understood in the anthropo-theological space of allegory. Deep down, deep down inside, the eye would be destined not to see, but to weep. For at the very moment they veil sight, tears would unveil what is proper to the eye. And what they cause to surge up out of forgetfulness, there where the gaze or look looks after it, keeps it in reserve, would be nothing less than *aletheia*, the truth of the eyes, whose ultimate destination they would thereby reveal: to have imploration rather than vision in sight, to address prayer, love, joy or sadness rather than vision in sight. Even before it illuminates, revelation is the moment of "the tears of joy." (*MB*, 126)

This "difference" of the eyes is the apocalyptic revelation of the destination other than sight. That destination arrives as the imploring of the gift of death in the moment of sacrificial blindness that is the necessary pain/penalty demanded by the desire of the other, which cannot be seen even while it beholds, by the gaze that cannot be met. Derrida sees this difference revealed in Jan Provost's painting *Sacred Allegory* in the figure of the sexual difference of mother and son. It is this difference that constitutes the specific difference that reveals the truth about human sight. Quoting the poet Andrew Marvel in reference to John Milton, the blind poet, author of *Sampson Agonistes,* "but only human eyes can weep," Derrida recalls the forgetfulness of death, and therefore of the gift of death, which is characteristic of animal sight, even of the seeing of the *animal rationalis*. He says that "only man knows how to go beyond seeing in knowing [*savoir*], because only he knows how to weep . . . Only man knows how to see this [voir ça]—that tears and not sight are the essence of the eye" (*MB*, 126). This is the allegory of sexual difference, of all sexual differences across their entire spectrum and in all their spectral apparitions. It is the allegory of deploring and imploring, this "other story" or "story of (the) Other," or "Other of the story," which plays out beyond the normal course of intercourse in the transformation of constant conversion, in the process of becoming other, which means beginning again. This "sacred allegory" of sexual difference that is revealed in the final moment of Derrida's scripting of the exhibition, this last play of his deployment of the exhibition about the truth of the eyes revealed as the constant conversion of sight into tears, about the constant conversion of drawing into writing, about the constant conversion of the faith that the son calls "mine" into the love of the mother that constantly calls him, has in the end the effect of a question: "From where and from whom this mourning or these tears of joy? This essence of the eye, this eye water?" (*MB,* 127). And when the spectral voice of the interlocutor, the voice of the (other) woman, asks "isn't that exactly what happened to you, as you explained earlier [referring to the recent facial paralysis that fixed one eye in an unblinking and so unwashed stare]," he responds, "Exactly." This, all of this, is what happened to him: in the exhibition he exhibits his conversion, the blindness of his conversion, just as in *Circumfession* he exhibited his circumcision, the mark of the call to conversion written in his flesh and which he confessed in that work that he had not forgotten. Here in *Memoirs of the Blind,* he writes the script that guides the exposition of his constant conversion, the conversion that he said had been going on constantly in his writing "for a longtime now." The exhibition is a revelation of this conversion amid the ruins of memory, ruins in the form of faces, faces in ruins in the form of names, names written and names held in reserve, faces and names welling up in memory. Together, they are the source of tears in remembrance of seeing without seeing, of seeing without seeing the gaze that beholds us, the gaze that holds in memory the source of all that one calls "mine."

Derrida places as Epilogue to this course of tears, the text of Marvel's poem on Milton:

> How wisely natured did decree,
> With the same eyes to weep and see!
> That having viewed the object vain,
> We might be ready to complain.
>
> Open then, mine eyes, your double sluice,
> And practice your noblest use;
> For others too can see, or sleep,
> But only human eyes can weep.
>
> Thus let your streams o'erflow your springs,
> Till eyes and tears be the same things;
> And each the other's difference bears;
> These weeping eyes, these seeing tears.
>              (Andrew Marvel, "Eyes and Tears")

And the final word that frames the vision of the Epilogue, the last interplay of his lady who makes trial of him:

> "Tears that see . . . Do you believe?"
> "I don't know . . . one has to believe. . . ."

The exhibition is Derrida's self-portrait blinded by the faith that he has just finished confessing in the text of *Circumfession*. The writer of that text had exhibited there his circumcision, in the "hellish" memory of the covenant written in his flesh to remember the Promise and its demand of sacrifice. But the writer of *Memoirs of the Blind* now portrays himself welling up in tears, tears of joy that flow from the springs of memory, the common source of weeping and seeing, the common source of two streams of memory, forgetting and recollection, Lethe and Eunoe. That common source is death, the event of all memory in its difference; death which holds in reserve, which holds within itself its gift, the gift that flows through the waters of forgiveness. Shakespeare's 64th Sonnet poses the question of tears in this way:

> Ruin hath taught me thus to ruminate:
> That Time will common and take my love away.
> This thought is as a death, which cannot choose but weep,
> To have, that which it fears to lose.

And Derrida:

"From where and from whom this mourning or these tears of joy? This essence of eye, this eye water?"

"I do not know . . . one has to believe . . ."

## DANTE'S PORTRAIT GALLERY

### Imagining Joy

The Glory of the All-Mover penetrates through the universe and reglows in one part more, and in another less. I have been in the heaven that most receives of His light, and have seen things which whoso descends from up there has neither the knowledge nor the power to relate, because, as it draws near to its desire, our intellect enters so deep that memory cannot go back upon the track. Nevertheless, so much of the holy kingdom as I could treasure up in my mind shall now be the matter of my song. (*Par.,* i, 1–12)

Dante's *Paradiso,* his song of vision, does not beg the question of difference. In fact, it begins precisely there. In it, Dante endeavors to trace the course that difference runs back along the tracks that it has inscribed in memory, back to the horizon from beyond which it is always and everywhere coming, back to edges of the universe, back to where light and memory, indeed everything, are cut off, like the thread of life itself in death, back to where light and memory, poetry and life begin and end, and then beyond to where they are always beginning again. The *Paradiso* "locates" itself in difference, by passing through the question of difference and passing over into the reality of its occurrence, its truth (which is always the same). This "pass-over" happens, it takes place, in writing—in the writing of the poem. In its writing, Dante does the truth of difference by identifying himself with and in and through its occurrence. He identifies himself with and through and in the faith, the hope and the love that trace the way in which the truth of difference is done, tracing that way as the fulfillment of a movement of "constant conversion," a movement that is always passing over into responsibility for one's personal identity: Who have I been? Who am I? Who will I become?—the three "ek-stacies" of personal existence of which Heidegger speaks. Dante's vision of the *Paradiso* is his continuing testimony and witness, his Gospel, telling the truth of what he has seen: the truth of difference, the occurrence of the absolutely Impossible that has been, is being, will be done in him, from Another. It is his testimony to the way difference happens in the singular instant of decision that passes over into the responsibility of personal identity through which the truth of the absolutely impossible Secret is done and takes flesh and blood. It is his testimony to "freedom," the freedom that allows the Impossible to be true and to be done, the freedom that allows the Impossibility of difference, that lets the Impossible be: for-given, before and after every question, be for-given as the Gift of Death—death, the Impossibility of any possibility at all. Dante testifies in the *Paradiso* to the way difference happens as the freedom of personal identity.

In the poem's own language and imagination, the *Paradiso* is Dante's met-aphor for the experience of Joy, which is revealed for the blind eyes, washed in tears, of faith in the resurrection of Jesus. It has already been suggested here that what Derrida writes of as the "Gift of Death" might be connected to Res-urrection as the central and primary metaphor of Christian faith. In Christian belief, Resurrection reveals the impossible Secret of the history of freedom, the Secret that there is no secret, through the image of the empty tomb. The resurrected Jesus is a "new creation," the "first-born of the dead," and the "new Adam." What does this mean? First, it implies that the resurrected Jesus is nei-ther a "resuscitated corpse" nor the spectral apparition of an "immortal soul." Rather, in death the history of the person of Jesus, his identity, truly ended; he died, "body and soul." Furthermore, it implies that, in the decisive instant of Resurrection, the whole truth of that personal history began again anew, "body and soul." The resurrected Jesus is both truly the same person, the same identity that was written in the history of his life and death, and at the same time truly different. But again, what does this mean: How does the same happen differ-ently? How does history begin anew "in the middle" of history? What happens to history when it happens differently? Resurrection is the central metaphor of Christian faith because only here, at the site of the empty tomb, can the question Who is Jesus? be truly asked, and it is this question, as a question, which encrypts the impossible Secret of both the identity of Jesus as a person and the history of all personal freedom, both human and divine. For the blind eyes of faith, which can see only through tears, the truth of Jesus' identity can be revealed only in and through his death; only death can reveal his identity as a whole, that is, in its genuine singularity. The way he dies changes the way his life happens to those and for those whom he dies forgiving. "Father, forgive them for they know not what they do." Forgive whom? Forgive what? How does forgiveness happen in this singular, decisive moment which, for Christian faith, reveals not simply a change in the identity or history of Jesus, or even a change in the way history happens, but reveals the secret of difference, which is itself impossible. It is the revelation of the way that history happens as difference, thereby revealing all history to be the history of "freedom," the freedom that allows difference to happen, the freedom which, from the beginning to the end, in the middle, at the center of all beginning and ending, lets the singular occur decisively, lets the cut occur that decides the figure of the instant, the singular instant, the decisive stroke that makes all the difference. Freedom lets difference be, allows all that begins and ends to begin again, begin anew, begin differently. Freedom allows all that is the same, must necessarily always be the same, must necessarily happen finitely in time and space, to happen differently, which is to say, to happen as history. The history of freedom is the history of the Impossible Secret, the history of difference. Freedom names the for-giving of the Gift of all that happens as history, of all that happens differently, of all that happens in the same way, beginning, ending, and beginning again anew. Freedom names the Gift of Death, names the way the Gift of Death happens: as forgiving. And Christian faith reveals the naming of the Gift of Death happening as forgiving, the Resurrected Jesus, writing the name of this forgiving as the personal identity of Jesus. It reveals the name that had been encrypted, the name that is signed under erasure, signed by the empty tomb, written in the broken cryptography of the empty crypt, the name of the Open Secret, the empty secret of the Impossibility of death, the empty Secret of the Impossible gift that death gives, the impossibility that is death.

Freedom, happening as forgiveness, lets difference be. Forgiveness passes on and passes over judgment—not its own judgment, but the decisive stroke of the Other that cuts the wound of death into the flesh of life, cuts off life from death, cuts "Yes" from "No," beginning from end. Difference is death; forgiveness lets difference be and so lets death happen differently. Those nearest to Jesus, those who had witnessed the events of his life constantly posing the question of faith, Who do you say that I am? eventually decided, *in extremis*, to betray him, decided not to witness his death, not to suffer with him the question his death posed, Who do you say, finally, in truth, I am? When they decided to flee in the face of the Other's death, decided not to let his death happened to them, decided not to let his death be for them, decided to let him be alone in death and hide themselves from death in fear, they cut themselves off from him, cut themselves off from his truth. Only the women remained to witness the question through to the end, to witness the truth that was encrypted in the question of the end, the encrypted truth of its beginning again. So the women weeping at the foot of the Cross had to bear witness to the message they received at the site of the empty tomb: He is not here. He is not here in death. His death is happening differently. How the memory

of the words the women had reported from the Cross, "Father, forgive them
. . ." must have burned then in their hearts, been inscribed in fire and blood
into the flesh of their hearts now that they had heard the *news:* his death is
happening differently. The Secret of the Resurrection is neither in the empty
tomb nor in the apparition stories that stem from it. Rather it is in the way
that the question Who is Jesus? is resurrected in their hearts and begins to
happen anew, differently, at the testimony of faith, at the testimony of those
(women) who had witnessed the end. They witnessed the truth that can only
be done in the end, in death, the whole truth of the beginning in the end, the
truth of forgiveness as the final word that lets difference, the cut of death, be,
allows it to happen, allows forgiveness to make all the difference.

Consequently, Resurrection does not mean simply either the beginning of
a "new" history, in the sense of a separate chapter, or an alternate history, in the
sense of rewriting history by giving it a new beginning and a new ending. It
does not mean a new narrative so much as a new way of narrating that begins
and ends in the middle. It does not mean a new history, but a new, entirely
different way of writing history, which traces the figure of history as the history of freedom. But tracing the figure of freedom means a new way of writing
personal identity, a new way of naming, a new way of writing personal names,
a new way that the Word becomes flesh and the flesh becomes word. The Resurrection names a new creation, a new "Adam," a new "firstborn," a new way of
beginning again, a new way of forgiving the Gift of Death, a new way of writing the history of forgiving and a new way of forgiving history in writing.

In summary then, in the poem's own language and imagination, the *Paradiso* is Dante's metaphor for the fulfillment of freedom's journey to relational
identity, his way of taking responsibility for the question, Who am I? which is
inseparable from the questions, Who are we? and Who is Jesus? His response is
that the responsibility of freedom fulfills itself by tracing its identity in the figure of Joy. The challenge of the *Paradiso*, for Dante the poet and for the reader,
is to imagine the reality of joy—a reality that Dante insists is "transhuman";
it exceeds our natural capacity as human beings. In other words, it is a gift
that can only be experienced once we have become "innocent" again by having
accepted the Gift of Death, which, in Christian terms, is Resurrection, the forgiving of death, the forgiven and forgiving death, the necessary death of the
desire of the Other, death forgiven as Gift, the gift of a "new" life, the constant
conversion of death into new life, the transformation, the "transhumanizing" of
life through tears into the blindness of faith, through the prayer of the hands
and heart into the work of hope, and through the doing of truth into the joy
of love. The Gift of Joy and the Gift of Death: these are not two separate gifts,
but one single, continuous movement of becoming, through forgiveness, who
we are in relation to the whole of reality, including divine mystery.

For Dante, tracing the figure of personal identity in Christian imagination, this movement unfolds as a journey into ever-increasing *light*, to which
Dante's eyes must gradually adjust, as he continues what began in his reunion

with Beatrice: he is learning to see himself through her eyes. As they begin their journey into Paradise, she looks directly into the sun, and he looks at and follows her. His relationship to her becomes one of discipleship, just as those who fixed their eyes on Jesus and followed him gradually were lead to discover their true identity in the role they were given to play in the cosmic drama of salvation history.

The problem of imagining a joy that exceeds the scope of human individuality and liberty of choice is precisely the problem of imagining that we are actually welcome to have a place of our own and to be at home in the divine creation of a cosmic community of love. This is why Dante sets the stage on which the journey will unfold across the full sweep of the physical universe as he understood it—the nine spheres of the heavens, and beyond the Empyrean, which, far from being infinitely remote, is the true center of all relationship, and as such, is always immediately here and now. The cosmic dynamics of light, space, and time become in Dante's poetic imagination metaphoric representations of the *"physics of freedom."* This mystery reveals itself concretely and particularly through each detail of Beatrice and Dante's journey. By following her and learning to see himself at home on the stage of all human history, Dante's consciousness gradually matures into that "passionate understanding"[4] of who he is in relation to the whole, which is both the body and the soul of Joy. This unity and integrity of human existence is represented metaphorically in Christianity by the resurrected Christ, whom Dante will briefly glimpse just prior to the final vision. In the *Paradiso,* Dante is imagining the joy of experiencing his participation in the resurrection of Christ, into which he was baptized in the Earthly Paradise; Dante's resurrected body is incarnated in the words of the poem and his soul in their meaning. Together they express and embody, they "incarnate" the passionate understanding of Joy.

From another perspective, we can approach the problem of imagination that the *Paradiso* poses by reflecting on the distinction between *happiness* and *joy.* "Happiness" means the fulfillment of our natural human capacities. Its origin is in Greek philosophical thought and is most fully articulated by Aristotle in the *Ethics.* There he defines happiness as the activity of life in accordance with "perfect virtue," that is, in accordance with reason, which is the general form or structure of all virtuous activity. To give Aristotle and Greek thought generally its due, he does not mean "reason" as abstract, conceptual thought alone, but rather the human capacity to understand and participate in the reality of Nature's activity as a whole. This is the origin of the idea of Natural Law as the norm of morality. To be happy is thus to act deliberately in conformity with the law of nature insofar as it can be understood and applied to human living.

So far, so good; but from the perspective of the Christian imagination, the concept of happiness does not go far enough. It expresses only a philosophical version of the promise of the "old law," which must be and has been surpassed by the "new law" of Love, revealed in and by Christ. The Joy promised by this new law is the joy of love. It is this Joy toward which Dante and Beatrice are journeying, and it follows that this promised joy must be understood as exceeding the happiness that is the natural result of human moral living. E. M. Forster expresses the incommensurability between the two when he says in the final pages of *Howard's End:*

> Actual life is full of false clues and sign-posts that lead nowhere. With infinite effort we nerve ourselves for a crisis that never comes. The most successful career must show a waste of strength that might have moved mountains, and the most unsuccessful is not that of the man who is taken unprepared, but of him who has prepared but is never taken. On a tragedy of that kind our national morality is duly silent. It assumes that preparation against danger is in itself a good, and that men, like nations, are the better for staggering through life fully armed. The tragedy of preparedness has scarcely been handled except by the Greeks [in the tragedies]. Life is indeed dangerous, but not in the way morality would have us believe. It is indeed unmanageable, but the essence of it is not a battle. It is unmanageable because it is a romance, and its essence is romantic beauty.

Will we do violence to Dante's poem to read it, especially the *Paradiso,* as a romantic comedy? Certainly not; the violence would lie in reading it in any other way. If joy is a gift of Love, then we may well have to prepare ourselves to receive it; this is the argument of the *Purgatorio.* But once prepared, we must be willing to follow the lead of another into that territory where we could not lead ourselves or make our way alone. Having taken responsibility for that part of our identity that is formed by our own choices, we must be prepared to discover the meaning of those choices and the identity they have given us in the eyes of an Other who has also made choices in relation to us, choices that have always preceded ours and always have responded to them in the full measure of Love.

This leads to a final consideration that is central to the interpretation of the *Paradiso.* The "physics of freedom" and relational identity is *differential.* Freedom makes a difference within the identity of relationship, and at this level of meaning, it is true to say that only freedom makes any difference. Dante introduces this central theme in the first lines of Canto i of the *Paradiso,* and it echoes throughout all that follows: "The glory of the All-mover penetrates through the universe and reglows in one part more, and in another less" (*Par.,* i, 1–3). Each sphere of the heavens that Dante and Beatrice visit and each of the souls they encounter in them is differentiated in a hierarchy of more or less, higher and lower. Yet we are told explicitly that this hierarchic differentiation obtains only from the perspective of Dante's human experience. From the perspective of the "center," which is the truth of divine Love, all are arrayed in their proper place in relation to that one mystery, forming the petals of the White Rose, in an arrangement that is differentiated in such a way that all are equidistant from the center without being near or far.

Initially, in Canto iii when he meets Piccarda, Dante is confused by this situation and asks why she does not desire to be "higher up." What is Dante trying to understand for himself and express to the reader through this problem? By now we should recognize it as another form of the basic "tension of opposites," the problem of the One and the Many, that characterizes all language and understanding of human existence in language. It is the basic structure of metaphor and of personal identity: relation, the necessary belonging together of sameness and difference. All are the same in that they are "enjoyed" fully and absolutely, yet that joy is differentiated. Each is identified by a unique relation between themselves and God *and* God itself is identified by a unique relation to each and all as the "center." The image is that of a circle. The circle is precisely the relation among each of the points of its circumference with its center, and the center is defined by its relation of differentiated equality with every other point. Well and good for the geometric figure, but what does its metaphoric application to personal identity mean? Perhaps that the "physics of freedom" pertains to qualitative relationships where meaning arises from a process of mutual codetermination, rather than to quantitative relationships where meaning is determined "metaphysically," that is, hierarchically and unilaterally by reference to a fixed absolute standard that can measure all relations, quantify them, because it does not itself participate in any of them. The pilgrim's view of the souls and their spheres leads to the confusions of hierarchy because it has not yet mastered the "differential equations" through which the meanings of joy are expressed. This "mastery," however, is not acquired as an individual achievement, but through discipleship—that higher form of apprenticeship through which is learned not a skill, but love, the joy of being centered and at home in the mystery of the whole.

In the following excerpt from Dostoyevsky's *The Brothers Karamazov,* from the section titled "The Russian Monk," Fr. Zossima, the venerable old holy man who guides (therefore, a type of Virgil) the young monk Aloysha Karamazov, speaks of the conversion of his older brother, Markel, during an illness. As we shall see, the idea of the "blessed life" he articulates here closely parallels Dante's vision of the life of the blessed in the *Paradiso,* particularly in the metaphor of the White Rose, and for that reason is quoted at length:

> It was the beginning of Lent, and Markel would not fast; he was rude and laughed at it. "That's all silly twaddle and there is no God," he said, horrifying my mother, the servants, and me too. For though I was only nine, I too was aghast at hearing such words. We had four servants, all serfs. I remember my mother selling one of the four, the cook Afimya, who was lame and elderly, for sixty paper roubles, and hiring a free servant to take her place.
>
> In the sixth week in Lent, my brother, who was never strong and had a tendency to consumption, was taken ill. He was tall but thin and delicate-looking, and of very pleasing countenance. I suppose he caught cold; anyway, the doctor who came soon whispered to my mother that it was galloping

consumption, that he would not live through the spring. My mother began
weeping, and careful not to alarm my brother she entreated him to go to
church, to confess, and to take the sacrament, as he was still able to move
about. This made him angry, and he said something profane about the
church. He grew thoughtful, however; he guessed at once that he was seriously ill, and that that was why his mother was begging him to confess and
take the sacrament. He had been aware, indeed, for a long time past that he
was far from well, and had a year before coolly observed at dinner to our
mother and me, "My life won't be long among you; I may not live another
year," which seemed now like a prophecy.

Three days passed and Holy Week had come. And on Tuesday morning
my brother began going to church. "I am doing this simply for your sake,
mother, to please and comfort you," he said. My mother wept with joy and
grief; "his end must be near," she thought, "if there's such a change in him."
But he was not able to go to church long; he took to his bed, so he had to
confess and take the sacrament at home.

It was a late Easter, and the days were bright, fine, and full of fragrance.
I remember he used to cough all night and sleep badly, but in the morning
he dressed and tried to sit up in an armchair. That's how I remember him
sitting, sweet and gentle, smiling, his face bright and joyous, in spite of his
illness. A marvelous change passed over him; his spirit seemed transformed.
The old nurse would come in and say, "Let me light the lamp before the holy
image, my dear." And once he would not have allowed it and would have
blown it out.

"Light it, light it, dear, I was a wretch to have prevented you doing it. You
are praying when you light the lamp, and I am praying when I rejoice seeing
you. So we are praying to the same God."

Those words seemed strange to us, and mother would go to her room and
weep, but when she went in to him she wiped her eyes and looked cheerful.
"Mother, don't weep, darling," he would say, "I've long to live yet, long to
rejoice with you, and life is glad and joyful."

"Ah, dear boy, how can you talk of joy when you lie feverish at night,
coughing as though you would tear yourself to pieces."

"Don't cry, mother," he would answer, "life is paradise, and we are all in
paradise, but we don't see it; if we did, we should have heaven on Earth the
next day."

Everyone wondered at his words; he spoke so strangely and positively, we
were all touched and wept. Friends came to see us. "Dear ones," he would say
to them, "what have I done that you should love me so; how can you love anyone like me, and how was it I did not know, I did not appreciate it before?"

When the servants came in to him, he would say continually, "Dear, kind
people, why are you doing so much for me; do I deserve to be waited on? If
it were God's will for me to live, I would wait on you, for all men should wait
on one another."

Mother shook her head as she listened. "My darling, it's your illness makes you talk like that."

"Mother darling," he would say, "there must be servants and masters, but if so I will be the servant of my servants, the same as they are to me. And another thing, mother, every one of us has sinned against all men, and I more than any."

Mother positively smiled at that and smiled through her tears. "Why, how could you have sinned against all men, more than all? Robbers and murderers have done that, but what sin have you committed yet that you hold yourself more guilty than all?"

"Mother, little heart of mine," he said (he had begun using such strange caressing words at that time), "little heart of mine, my joy, believe me, everyone is really responsible to all men for all men and for everything. I don't know how to explain it to you, but I feel it is so, painfully even. And how is it we went on then living, getting angry and not knowing?

Dante and Dostoyevsky seem to share a similar style of writing joy. They both write it as a smile through tears at the recognition of the singular responsibility that is "mine" in the face of the all the others.

## Only Human Mouths Can Smile

And as a pilgrim who is refreshed within the temple of his vow as he looks around, and already hopes to tell again how it was, so, taking my way upwards through the living light, I led my eyes along the ranks, now up, now down, and now circling about. I saw faces all given to love, adorned by the light of Another, and by their own smile, and movements graced with every dignity. (*Par.*, xxxi, 43–51)

From where, from whom, this mourning, or these tears of joy—I do not know; one must believe. (*MB*, 127)

As tears are to the eye, so a smile is to the mouth: both express the meaning of what comes to pass and so takes place organically as life, specifically human life. Tears and smiles reveal the truth of the face, the organic identity of the person, as the free interplay of the part with the whole, the mysterious relation of the many to the one, the different to the same, the present to the absent. In the book of the face is written the historical narrative of a freedom and a responsibility that exist nowhere but there. In the integrity of the face, specifically in the byplay of eyes and mouth, the whole story is told—the identity of everyone who says "mine." Only human eyes may weep; only human mouths can smile.

The key to understanding the difference between Dante and Derrida is to understand the difference between the tears of the eyes and the smile of the mouth, the by play through which together they give expression to the face. Eyes and mouth animate the face: they give it a soul, a meaning-ful identity capable of judgment, of responsibility for truth and deception, for love and hate. The face is the original organic metaphor, the first writ-ten text—the word made flesh. Both Dante and Derrida are masters of face-writing, of portraiture and self-portraiture. The difference between them is the difference in their way of writing faces, the difference between Derrida's dialect of prayers and tears and Dante's dialect of hymns of praise and smiles. These are differences of tone, inflection, cadence, and colloquialism. The dif-ference in their writing is a difference of religious dialect: not the difference of dialect between a Jew who rightly passes for an atheist and a philosopher and a Roman Catholic who rightly passes for mystic and a poet—this would be to miss the point altogether, to hideously misread and disfigure their self-portraits. Rather, the difference in their writing is one of religious dialect in a sense that precedes any historical determination according to a religion. They both write the face of religion as "messianic," but the style of their messian-ism differs; the stylus of each is guided by a different hand, they write in and with different hands—and hands are the agents and ambassadors of the face. Dante and Derrida write messianic religion differently, but both write it as the text of human faces, as the sacred scripture of personal identity, of freedom and responsibility, as the Book of Revelation of the holy face, as the revelation of the face as holy.

How do eyes and mouth differ within their interplay across the organic integrity of the face? The beginning, but only a beginning, of a response might be to recognize that the eyes are binocular and stereoscopic; the mouth is monoral and monotonic. Their byplay transpires across the bridge of the nose, the central stroke that articulates the open space of their distance, sep-arating the eyes and leading toward the flair of the nostrils, which repeat the binarity of the eyes in proximity to the singular horizon of the mouth, where linear tensility masks latent circularity. As framed by the ears, the face lies open as playing field, arena, game board, articulated by the potential matrices of ones, twos, threes, and fours; circles, lines, triangles and squares, ovals and rectangles whose combinatorial possibilities are unlimited, but mouth and eyes alone are mobile, and in this way they are the foci of expression. Mouth and eyes do the same thing: they write the history of freedom, of definitely articulated events of meaning, in the texts of human faces. But they do so differently. Only human eyes can weep, only human mouths can smile. The tears of the eyes are ambiguous, in accord with their essential binocularity: there are tears of mourning and tears of joy. But the smile is singular in its significance: it recognizes and records the singularity of the Impossible and the impossibility of the singular. It is the primary and original comedic ges-ture; it marks the freedom of responsibility in the face of what cannot be, what properly should not be, but constantly occurs and occurs improperly, yet decisively. Heidegger, quoting Leibniz, asks, "Why is there anything at all, and not much rather nothing?" Existence is absolutely impossible—*ex nihilo nihil fit*—yet existence occurs, literally all the time and all over the place; it occurs as absolute singularity, decisively, historically, always only in one time and one place; existence is, strictly speaking, ridiculous. The smile recognizes and accepts responsibility for the absolute singularity of reality's ambiguity as a whole, the unbreakable bond of unyielding necessity by which the Impossible, the "No!" is in constant ambivalent intercourse with the open field of the possible, the "Yes!" the force of affirmation from which the singular event, the historical occurrence of the singular, emerges. The smile takes responsibility for itself and signs itself with the mark of the singular, signaling acceptance of the impossibility that is the necessary other, the generative partner of every possibility. The essential structure of reality is impropriety, beyond the reach in its historical occurrence of the tyranny of the principles of noncontradiction and sufficient reason. The smile is the original comedic gesture because it signs the acceptance of the other as such, the other as ambiguous, as necessary, the Other as death. The smile is the gesture of freedom and responsibility because it expresses forgiveness. Freedom is always first forgiveness. Freedom always first for-gives the impropriety of existence, the Impossibility of the Gift. Freedom for-gives the impossible love that gives the gift, for-gives the Impossible desire of the Other. The Other is, strictly speaking, impossible. The desire of the other is madness: the gift of the other necessitates death—yet it happens all the time. It is written in the Holy Book of the Face under the name of Love. Octavio Paz puts it this way:

> We live with phantoms, and we are ourselves phantoms. There are only two ways out of this imaginary prison. The first is the path of eroticism, and we have already seen that it ends in a blind wall. The question of the jealous lover—What are you thinking about/What are you feeling?—has no answer except sado-masochism: tormenting the Other or tormenting himself. In either case the Other is inaccessible and invulnerable. But we are not transparent, either, for others or for ourselves. This constitutes humanity's original sin, the brand that marks us from birth. The other way out is that of love: surrender of self, acceptance of the freedom of the beloved. Madness, an illusion? Perhaps, but it is the only door that leads out of the prison of jealousy. Many years ago I wrote: Love is a sacrifice without virtue. Today I would say: Love is a bet, a wild one, placed on freedom. Not my own; the freedom of the other.[5]

Only human mouths can smile, because to be human is to recognize the necessity, the freedom, the responsibility to forgive existence and to forgive, to wholly forgive, the whole of existence, from before the beginning until after the end, to smile on the Other in the name of love. The smile traces that figure of recognition on the face, and so, from the womb of the mouth, through the pass of the smile, the laughter of life is born in the name of a love, which is forgiven as the Gift of Death.

## "Singing the Holy Smile"

"Open your eyes and look on what I am; you have seen things such that
you are become able to sustain my smile." I was as one that wakes from a forgotten dream and who strives in vain to bring it back to mind, when I heard
this proffer, worthy of such gratitude that it can never be effaced from the
book which records the past.

Though all those tongues which Polyhymnia and her sisters made most
rich with their sweetest milk should sound now to aid me, it would not come
to a thousandth part of the truth, in singing the holy smile, and how it lit up
the holy aspect; and so depicting Paradise, the sacred poem must needs make a
leap, even as one who finds his way cut off. But whoso thinks of the ponderous
theme and of the mortal shoulder which is laden therewith, will not blame it if
it tremble beneath the load. It is no voyage for a little bark, this which my daring prow cleaves as it goes, nor for a pilot who would spare himself.

"Why does my face so enamor you that you turn not to the fair garden
which blossoms beneath the rays of Christ? Here is the Rose wherein the
Divine Word became flesh; here are the lilies by whose odor the good way
was taken."

Thus Beatrice; and I who to her councils was all eager, again gave myself
up to the battle of the feeble brows. (*Par.*, xxiii, 46–72)

Canto xxiii of the *Paradiso,* together with Canto xxiv, form a hinge on
which pivots the transitional passage into the third and final movement of the
third and final Cantica of the poem. Recognition, therefore, of the cardinal significance of the context in which the above citation occurs might lend at least
an initial and limited plausibility at this juncture to the use of it as a herme-
neutic point of entry into the great circulation of meaning within the *Paradiso,*
which so often prompts even its own author to despair of taking responsibility
for charting a course through its vast and deep currents. Nevertheless, the intersection in the passage cited above of a pivotal turn in the course of the narrative with the central metaphor of the Cantica's poetic structure offers a bearing
for interpretation that is well suited to the concern to understand the significance of the difference between tears and smiles, between Derrida and Dante.
Specifically, the passage serves as a point of concrete application for the three
overarching interpretive themes in the Paradise identified earlier: discipleship,
joy, and the differential physics of freedom, insofar as all three are rooted in the
identity of Beatrice, written in her face as the figure of her smile.

The transitional context of the citation is briefly as follows. Having
completed the journey through the first seven planetary stations, the Moon,
Mercury, and Venus (the first tercet), the Sun, Mars, and Jupiter (the second tercet), and Saturn, the sphere of the contemplatives, Beatrice has urged
Dante to look down and retrace the course from the place at which they have
arrived to the inhabited portions of the earth from which they departed. This

visual perspective rehearses the trace in memory of the movement from the beginning of the pilgrim's journey *"nel mezzo del cammin di nostra vita,"* that is, the journey that before the beginning and after the end is situated in the middle of human life, at its center, in the soul, that is, in the meaning of the events that are now being written in the book of his memory from the book of her face, and which subsequently have been transcribed in the book of the poem. After this summary resetting of the scene, a new vision begins to unfold, which she announces:

> And Beatrice said, "Behold the hosts of Christ's triumph and all the fruit ingathered from the circling of the spheres!" It seemed to me her face was all flame, and her eyes were so full of joy that I must needs pass it by unde-scribed. (*Par.*, xxiii, 19–24)

First, the poet insists anew on what he has more and more urgently affirmed since he entered Paradise: that the experience that is occurring is impossible, impossible to remember fully, impossible to convey in words or to comprehend in meaning; yet it is so compellingly true that the journey must be done again in writing. It must begin again and be done as truth in love, the love of Beatrice done again as the love of writing. The vision described in the citation is of the "Church Triumphant," the souls of those who have identified themselves through faith with the resurrected Christ, who appears in the vision as a Sun which, among the sweep of all the spiritual bodies visible at this unimaginable height (if "height" it be), shines and illuminates all the others as much as the sun outshines all other heavenly lights seen from the earth. So the vision constellates itself around three types and sources of light: the divine writing of the Resurrection on which Dante cannot look for more than an instant (*Par.*, xxiii, 33); the celestial light of the souls, which shine of themselves with the writing enkindled in them by the light of Christ (this is the structure of "revelation" in Dante's poetics); and finally the light of Beatrice's face and of the joy, which her eyes reveal. It is at this point that she enjoins him, "Open your eyes and look on what I am; you have seen things such that you are become able to sustain my smile" (*Par.*, xxiii, 46–48). Even at this advanced stage of the journey, Dante cannot even begin to look into the light of the Resurrection, the source of all revelation, yet in the instant during which that light strikes his eyes, he is changed decisively. Now he can sustain the full radiance of Beatrice's smile and see in it her truth—the truth by which and for which he must now see himself situated in a larger companionship and society than that of hers alone. For she is soon to leave him, of necessity. In order to complete the journey and return into the middle of his own life in the full freedom of responsibility, he must pass into his full identity amid the society of the Church as a whole, for it is only at the center of the whole Church that the Resurrection can be revealed as his own personal center.

This accounts for the extraordinary drama of the events that are to be recounted in the following three cantos, 24–26. The pilgrim is now in the sphere of the Fixed Stars, and specifically in the constellation of Gemini, his own birth sign and therefore an index of the singularity of his own vocative identity, the one to which he is personally and historically called as human, as Christian, as citizen of Florence, as lover of Beatrice, and as poet. Here he must stand scrutiny by three great Apostles, representatives of the whole Church: Peter, who examines him on faith, James who examines him on hope, and John who examines him on love. Appropriately, it is during the encounter with John that there occurs the episode of temporary blindness that contrasts sharply with the leitmotif of *Memoirs of the Blind,* yet ensures the symmetry of complementarity between the two in their face-writing, specifically with the difference between eyes and mouth. Through this examination, Dante, although still seconded and mentored by Beatrice must declare his own identity, identify the truth of who he is—a possibility now open to him because he has, in sustaining Beatrice's smile, experienced the revelation of the truth of who she is, the truth that she has done in loving him. Now he must declare the truth of who he is in terms of the understanding of the faith, hope, and love by which he must yet do that truth in the love of Beatrice, of God, and of writing, the love that will give the gift of the poem.

What does Beatrice mean in saying that he "has become able to sustain [her] smile?" What does Dante see in Beatrice's smile now for which he was not able to shoulder the responsibility in writing up to this moment? He sees revealed the truth of who she is, that is, the truth she has been doing in love for him, the truth she has been doing in love in him since the time of her first revelation to him when they were both nine (she "is a nine"). It is the truth she has been doing in the middle of his life, in his soul, his identity, since the beginning of his journey, since, sent by Lucy, sent by Mary, whom she is about to reveal to him now, she sent Virgil to guide him through hell and up Mount Purgatory. This is the truth she has been doing in love in and for him, since, through tears of repentance at their reunion in the earthly Paradise, he first glimpsed again her eyes above the veil. Even at the words of his confession, her mouth beneath the veil was still without a smile, but since then she has been gradually revealing more of her smile as he has become more capable of the light that in truth was nothing the other than the radiance of her smile. Now he looks with his own eyes at the light of truth that throughout their journey through Paradise he has been learning to see through her eyes. Now, as she compels him by the command of her mouth to sustain her smile, he becomes as "one that wakes from a forgotten dream, and who strives in vain to bring it back to mind" (*Par.,* xxiii, 49–51). Wakes indeed from a dream; he wakes ultimately from the dream of heart-eating that revealed the untruth, the dark light, at the center of his life, at the center of his love for her. The dark light, which is at the center of his life, is the untruth, unlight, at the center of all light and all revelation, in the Other as such, in the freedom of the Other, in the responsibility of the Other for the desire of the Other, which is Impossible, the desire and love that freedom must necessarily forgive, so as to let the gift of Love, which is the Gift of Death, be given. This is what he sees in her smile as he wakes from his lifelong dark dream into the light of consciousness and identity that he must now, in the examination, begin to call "mine." This revelation, proffered him as gift by her words, the offer of a gift of love by the forgiveness that smiles the truth of what had been refused because it is Impossible, he now finds "worthy of such gratitude that it never can be effaced from the book which records the past" (*Par.*, xxiii, 52–54). That revelation is now written in the book of his memory, the ruin of memory, the memory that is written in ruined lines, the memory of ruin of all that is past because it has been passed over, has been for-given and so is always already past, but in gratitude is recognized as forgiven. All memory is memory of forgiveness. Paradise is the memory in gratitude of all things ruined and past, of all things forgiven. Paradise is written in gratitude in the book of memory, the book written in the holy face.

At this point in the unfolding vision, the face-writing takes a turn that must be recognized as "deconstructive" in the strict sense, that is, as a style that is as characteristic of Dante, especially in the *Paradiso*, as it is of Derrida. The trace of the vision-writing, the eye-writing, the smile-writing, the memory- and face-writing is abruptly cut off by Dante to acknowledge again as he has from the beginning that each and every stroke of the writing is itself a cut, a cutting off, a ruining; each stroke of the writing is stricken by death, is the Gift of Death that must be forgiven if it is to go on beginning again:

> Though all the tongues which Polyhymnia and her sisters made most rich with their sweetest milk should sound now to aid me, it would not come to a thousandth part of the truth, in singing the holy smile, and how it lit up the holy face; and so, depicting Paradise, *the sacred poem must needs make a leap, even as one who finds his way cut off.* But who so thinks of the ponderous theme and of the mortal shoulder which is laden therewith, will not blame it *if it tremble beneath the load.* (*Par.*, xxiii, 55–66; emphasis added)

The poet's vocation is to sing praise; ultimately, praise to whatever is divine. But this vocation is impossible. No amount of divine inspiration, not even the sucking tongues of every poet who ever lived, nursing at the breasts of all the sister-tribe of Muses, could avail now to tell one thousandth part of the truth that has been told, as the death knell had always already told for Dante's love and for his writing, for his love of writing, in the face of Beatrice, signed with her holy smile. His writing of her, of her love, of the truth of her that had been done in her love, had always, from before the beginning and after the end, been cut off by the stroke of death, had always already been the Gift of Death, the death figured in the dream of heart-eating, the lifelong dream from which he is now awakening to find his writing, his love of writing, cut off by the cut of his love's smile, the smile that traces the cut of her mouth that he had raped with the enforced eating of his false heart by the false divinity of false love of false writing—a writing that had always already been doomed to fail, as it still

is doomed to fail now. So it causes him to tremble, to tremble under the ponderous (*ponderoso*) theme (*tema*), the crushing weight of the responsibility that
was first put on him when he first met her, met his freedom and was called
to write; no, not to write, that was the bad dream, called to be written by that
face, to have the book of the holy face transcribed in ruins in the book of his
memory, the memory of forgiveness, copied in the book of his face, mirrored
in the book of his poem. It causes him to tremble, and who can blame him. It
must be, has been, forgiven—though not by any mechanical or merely fateful
destiny. "It is no voyage for a little bark, this which my daring prow cleaves as
it goes, nor for a pilot who would spare himself" (*Par.*, xxiii, 67–69).

The image here retraces the course he has been taking throughout the
*Paradiso* directly back to its embarkation, to the image evoked in the invocation of an inspiration that comes from beyond the range of the mortal gods,
beyond the Muses, beyond Apollo to its source in the divinity beyond the
gods, beyond God, to a gift, to a vocation to writing, that is impossible to give,
which can only be forgiven:

> Oh you who in your little bark, eager to hear following behind my ship
> that singing makes her way, turn back to see again your shores. Do not com-
> mit yourselves to the open sea, for perchance, if you lost me, you would
> remain astray. The water which I take was never coursed before. Minerva
> breathes and Apollo guides me, and nine Muses point out to me the Bears.
>
> You other few who lifted up your necks betimes for bread of Angels, on
> which men here subsist but never becomes sated of it, you may indeed com-
> mit your vessel to the deep brine, holding to my furrow ahead of the water
> that turns smooth again. (*Par.*, ii, 1–15)

Here Dante acknowledges the figure of the divine source of this vocation to the love of writing in terms that, as shall emerge, closely parallel those
evoked by Derrida in describing the apocalyptic origin of all sacred art in *The
Memoirs of the Blind*. The image of the vessel, the ship that furrows the unceas-
ing, rhythmic undulation of the waves, is uncertain in its seaworthiness. The
power of writing, of all art, of all cutting and marking, every decisive stroke,
every choice, depends on a divine condition that sustains the enabling daimonic inspiration of Minerva, Apollo, and the Muses. Only those who have
"lifted up their necks betimes for the bread of Angels," may follow beyond this
point into the *Paradiso*. This condition is absolute: the journey can be taken
and sustained only on the condition of "Eucharistic" faith, a faith that realizes
itself as "Thanksgiving," as a hymn of praise born of gratitude.[6] This is the
faith of face-writing, faith in the Word become flesh and flesh become word,
faith in resurrection of the body, faith in the eating of the resurrected body
and the drinking of the resurrected blood, faith not just in the Resurrection of
Jesus, but faith in resurrection as the Gift of Death, the "general resurrection,"
as universal in its promise as death is itself. It is faith in the universality of revelation as the promise of every scriptural history of personal identity written

by freedom in the Book of the Holy Face. It is faith in the Gospel of Beatrice because that Gospel is transcribed in her face from the Gospel of Jesus written in his holy face, which is now being written again, transcribed from her face into the book of his memory, written in his heart and traced in his face, and retraced in his poem. Her face is his Holy Writ, and his poem is his testimony in faith to the bread of her word, which is from the flesh of her body in the hope of Resurrection, articulated by her face and her smile, which is not yet done speaking to him. The vision of her smile now directs him beyond her face to that of another, the Other (woman), whose name is prefigured and transcribed in the name of the Rose: "Why does my face so enamor you that you turn not to the fair garden which blooms beneath the rays of Christ? Here is the Rose wherein the Divine Word became flesh" (*Par.*, xxiii, 70–73).

Beatrice here directs Dante beyond her own testament and its authority to the singular source of all Christian testamentary witness, the Gospel of Jesus, the "Good News" of the Divine Word made flesh, written in the flesh and face of Jesus by having first been written in Mary's flesh and face. She is first among all the Other-women, the one by whom Beatrice was sent to Dante, as was testified to Dante in the revelatory Annunciation brought by the angel Virgil at the outset of the journey. The original scene of Annunciation is enacted now again, not reenacted, here in Dante's experience. In the vision, the truth of the angel happens again, the same truth that happened to Mary is happening again now to Dante differently. He sees a light descend from the Source, Jesus, to crown the beauteous sapphire [Mary] by which the brightest heaven is "ensapphired." The medium finds its voice in the vision to say:

> "I am angelic love, who circle the supreme joy that breathes from out the womb which was the hostelry of our Desire; and I shall circle, Lady of Heaven, until thou shalt follow thy Son, *and make the supreme sphere more divine by entering it.*" (*Par.*, xxiii, 103–108; emphasis added)

Here finally the full impact of the vision's truth claim, revealed from Beatrice's smile, strikes home upon his eyes, the last stroke in the "battle of the feeble brows," to which he has surrendered himself at her command. It falls to Mary, not simply to lead the way for them both, as for all, into the highest sphere, but to do the Impossible, to do the (impossible) truth of love in love. Here is revealed the truth of the "leap" that Dante's poem must take and of the burden of responsibility for the "ponderous theme" under which both poem and poet "tremble": she, Lady of Heaven, in following her Son must "make the supreme sphere *more divine* by entering it (*farai dia \ più la spera supprema perché li entre*)." Rightly do both poem and poet stagger under the force of the blow, the mortal stroke, the stroke of the mortal, which writes the divine in words of flesh. For once this dissemination of the Word has seeded itself and germinated in the flesh, then gestation of the divine in history grows rampant and never ceases to come to birth, it never ceases to become *more divine*! There can be no Sufficient Reason for this violation of the Law of

Non-Contradiction. The Rose is without why, the "hostelry of our Desire," of all desire of the Other, which is impossible and therefore can never be given, never be taken as given, but remains always the focus of all wonder, revealing in its name and face what is more than divine, what alone can make the divine reveal its truth and so become more divine, revealing the love that cannot be given, but must always be forgiven and so can always begin again.

Now it is possible to recognize that in this canto Dante has anticipated the penultimate scene of Derrida's *Memoirs of the Blind* and has painted in the poem his own version of Jan Provost's *Sacred Allegory*. A brief reminder of Derrida's interest in that painting will serve to underscore the significance of the occurrence of the image here in Dante's *Paradiso,* itself a "sacred allegory." Derrida says of the painting that it "must always be able to be contemplated as the representation or reflection of its own possibility" (*MB,* 121), because it shows the exchange of glances between human and divine vision that makes painting possible. He goes on to say that the painting "puts on the scene, it stages, the opening scene of sacred painting, an allegorical self-presentation of this 'order of the gaze' to which any Christian drawing must submit" (*MB,* 121), precisely because it portrays the impossibility of the desire of the Other, that is, the divinity, strictly speaking, of the Other insofar as it is impossible. This is the "order of the gaze," hierarchized and dissymmetrical, and this, he concludes,

> . . . is memory itself. To contemplate this picture in this way, the gaze must become Christian; it is not that it must already be converted, but it must be in the process of conversion, learning to see the divine condition of the picture itself. Learning to see on this condition, which is possible only in hymn or prayer.
>
> A Christian drawing should be a hymn, a work of praise, a prayer, an imploring eye, an eye with joined hands, an *imploring* that is lifted up, an imploring of surrection and resurrection . . . like the eyes of the son and his mother who look in the same direction. (*MB,* 121)

Memory itself is the origin of all mimesis, of all art insofar as it could be understood as mimetic. This is not to say that an aesthetic of mimesis can account exhaustively for the phenomena of art, but rather that all art, however else it might be interpreted, must also be interpreted mimetically, that is, as born from the memory of the Other, from the exchange of the gaze that envisions and remembers that Other even as it turns its gaze to another. Memory remembers the Other as such, as the One that is impossible, and therefore divine, therefore as the One that cannot be given or taken as given, but must be remembered as fore-given, and therefore must be forgiven. But the order of the gaze structured in this way, Derrida says, is not simply religious; it must *become Christian;* it must be in the process of learning to see the "divine condition" of the painting, that is, learning to see on the condition of the divine—in other words, on the condition of the Impossible, the impossible desire of the Other. This conversion or learning to see the divine condition of sacred art—perhaps the divine condition of all art—is possible only in a "hymn of praise," which, at least here in Derrida's text, turns immediately into a "prayer, an imploring eye, an eye with folded hands. . . ." But is a hymn of praise, sung by the mouth, the same as "an imploring eye, an eye with folded hands"? Surely both are rightly called prayers. But one is sent upward and the other beckons downward, begs a downward movement, a condescension. Nevertheless, the condescension is invited by a surrection, a lifting up of the hands. Then too, the raising up of the hymn of praise is predicated by a resurrection, a rising up again of what has been buried, gone under after being struck down, undergoing the mortal stroke of death. So the movement of prayer is necessarily a double gesture, a double movement, a circulation that is prevented from circling back on itself, from closing its circuit, by the Impossibility of its desire of the Other, allowing and necessitating that is always beginning again, to resurrect, to be born again, born anew, a new creation, not merely a repetition, that, in other words, it happened historically.

There is a further dimension, however, to the intertextuality that moves between Canto xxiii of *Paradiso* and the role of Provost's *Sacred Allegory* in *Memoirs of the Blind*. "Like the eyes of the Son and his mother who look in the same direction . . ." Jesus and Mary, Dante and Beatrice, Jacques and Georgette, Monica and Augustine—all configure the "order of the gaze" of which Derrida is speaking here: not specifically in that they figure as son to mother (although Dante's use of the mother/child metaphor in regard to his relationship to Beatrice is sustained and dominant enough to easily accommodate this usage), or yet simply as male and female, but insofar as both the parent-child relation and the male-female relation gesture ambiguously toward the singularity of the Other as such, toward the singularity of all "those who say mine," and further toward the singularity of the relation of difference between the two. In the first instance, no one asks Who is the Self? but rather, Who am I? No one, in the first instance asks Who is the Other as such? but rather, Who is Jesus? or Who is Beatrice? or Who is Georgette? so that finally one must ask, "From where, from whom, this mourning or these tears of joy?

The images of Mary and Jesus in Provost's painting and in Canto xxiii of the *Paradiso* help to locate more precisely the question prosecuted here, What is the difference between prayers and tears in Derrida's writing and the hymns and smiles in Dante's poem. But they do not yet in themselves answer that question; that is to say, they do not respond to it in a fully responsible way. To proceed in that direction requires fleshing out what is implied in the "sacred allegory" of Beatrice's smile as it plays out in the vision considered above. In what sense can Beatrice's smile become the source of revelation for Dante of the truth and full reality in experience of the final configuration of the divine in the person of the resurrected Jesus in relation to the human, and in the first instance to Dante's own personal identity? And in what sense can the vision of Beatrice's smile require the recognition by Dante of the historical necessity that, impossibly, the divine can be augmented, become more divine, by Mary's entrance into it? Provisionally, we might attempt to focus the matter in the following way in anticipation of further development. The *Commedia* offers three distinct testimonies that are nevertheless inseparable from one another: testimony to the love of Beatrice, to the love of God, to the love of writing. These are not, however, testimonies of Dante's love of Beatrice, of God, of writing. Rather they testify to the love that comes from Beatrice done in him, the love that comes from God done in him, the love that comes from writing done in him—which three, perhaps, all are One. They are the one love that comes through death, which is done in all as the Gift of Death, done in him and in all as forgiveness, done therefore differently in him and in all, done not so much in him and in all, but *as* him and *as* all, done as identity; done, not so much as finished, but as final.

The image of Provost's *Sacred Allegory* carries yet one more implication in this context. Not only does the representation of Jesus and Mary, mother and son, configure the relation of Dante and Beatrice as the opening whence this celestial vision issues, it also configures the relation of Jacques and Georgette, it enthrones them suspended in the space between the divine and the human eyes that determine the "order of the gaze" in which they are fixed. So now there are three questions that issue from the vision of the painting, or rather three sets of questions, each set comprising the same three questions that had to be addressed above to the relation of Dante and Beatrice, three sets of three questions regarding the love that is envisioned between the two lovers as determined by the order of the gaze in which they are fixed; the love that in each case—Jesus and Mary, Dante and Beatrice, Jacques and Georgette—is from the Other (woman) and is done as the identity, the final truth, of the one who bears responsibility for his own (style of) face-writing. The three questions about love bearing on each of the three pairs of lovers ask after the love of/from the Other (woman), the love of God, and in the love of writing. These questions configure the relation of the faces, the style of the face-writing, in each relation as it is fixed by the order of the gaze that constantly converts from the binary polarity of the divine, both the possible and the impossible, to the singularity of the human, which is the decisive event of the historical.

Of Jesus, the face-writer, the Word made Flesh, the Holy Face of the Resurrection, it must be asked Who is this Jesus whose divinity becomes more divine when it is written in the flesh of Mary from her face and from her mouth at her word of praise and petition, "Yes, come"? Of Dante, the poet of comedic praise, it must be asked in the reading of the poem, Who is this Dante who is here taking responsibility for the face he gives himself in the final vision of the poem, the final word on the visage of the divine, the face that is written from the smile of Beatrice? Of Derrida, the continual confessor of the empty Secret, it must be asked in following the course of his writings that trace the ruins in memory of his conversion, Who is this Jacques who in this way is taking responsibility for the ruined alliance that is traced in his flesh in the face of the eye of his mother who weeps at the foot of the Cross by which the name of God has been crossed out and rewritten under it, as if in shame, over and over again in what he writes and continues shamelessly to go on writing? Finally it must be asked of all, of every mother's son, of all three, if these three are not one; if all do not face the same question, Who are you? How are you taking responsibility in your face-writing for the love that has been done in you as a truth that comes from the Other (woman), the love which is the Gift of the Death of the Other (woman), so that you can go on writing only in the faith and hope of the Resurrection of that love which, as the Gift of Death, must be and can only be forgiven? How can you take responsibility for what can neither be given nor received, neither prayed for in petition nor praised in thanksgiving; for what can be, must be always already for-given, and so forgiven? How can forgiveness happen? How does it come to pass so as to be passed-over? How does forgiveness come to be written in the face as the Joy of Resurrection?

## "FACES ALL GIVEN TO LOVE . . ."

> And as a pilgrim who is refreshed within the temple of his vow as he looks around, and already hopes to tell again how it was, so, taking my way upwards through the living light, I led my eyes along the ranks, now up, now down, and now circling about.
>     *I saw faces all given to love, adorned by the light of Another, and by their own smile,* and movements graced with every dignity. (*Par.,* xxxi, 43–51; emphasis added)

According to this text of Dante, joy animates the face through the interplay of a light that is from Another, focused through the binocularity of the eyes, and inscribed in the singularity of the smile that is one's own, the trait that passes, normally under erasure, for the signature of whoever says "mine." The final four Cantos of the *Paradiso,* xxx through xxxiii, have to do with finality, the enigma of finality, which is different than an ending, a conclusion, or an arrival at a destination or goal. It might perhaps later be said that they have to do precisely with the Gift of Death. In the poem, Dante makes this difference between "finality" and "finish" clear in the opening image of the above citation, "And as a pilgrim who is refreshed within the temple of his vow as he looks around, and already hopes to tell again how it was. . . ." The destination, the point of the vow in the goal of the journey, is always already inscribed in the ruins of memory; it is itself "monumental," taking the form of a "sacred allegory" that configures in its figural line the trace of the Other(s), whose essential binocularity ordered the gaze that is, even in the instant of fulfillment, already passing over into beginning again. All that is most telling, every decisive stroke, is ordered, commanded of necessity, toward retelling, not in the

form of original to simulacrum, or of presence to representation, but in the triadic logic of life, death, Resurrection, beginning again, a logic not of concept,
or even of praxis, but of personal identity. This is a logic of truth done in love,
written in faces, a logic that is governed by the Principle of Relational Identity,
for which the principle of Noncontradiction is the substitute, and by the Principle of (in)Sufficient Reason, which substitutes for the Law of Love, which
is a law of excess. The telling "again" is the supplement to every narrative and
metaphor, to every "sacred allegory" of art and every prayer of the heart, the
responsorial psalm to every hymn of praise and petition, "Yes! Again!" The
vision Dante has at the end of the Paradiso, the "final vision," is a vision of
the truth of finality, the joy, written in faces, of the Resurrection, that is, the
"apocalyptic" vision of the "second coming." This apocalypse comes not as the
end point of history, but as the freedom that is history and that gives itself the
finality of having its own law, of having itself as law, the law of historical finality, the law of always beginning again, always having to sign itself in the light
of Another, with its own identifying mark of its sovereign "Yes! Again!"

   It is the finality of this sovereignty of free relational identity written in
the face of joy animating the interplay of eyes and mouth that Dante traces so
closely and artfully in the narrative and metaphoric progression of these concluding cantos, which can only be sketched in outline here. The discipline of
constant conversion governs that progression through a series of substitutions
that finally lead, not to a "prime mover" or first and final cause, but to the dis-
covery of the empty tomb, the empty Secret of the Promise, the secret promise
of always beginning again, of passing over, the Gift of Death, which can only
be for-given and therefore must be forgiven for never finally arriving, for never
arriving finally, but must be accepted in faith, hope, and love in the Eucharistic
response, "Yes! Again!

   The progression of metaphors that Dante's "sacred allegory" of the "final
vision," of the vision of the finality of freedom as the truth and law of history,
comprises the following elements, each of which will be considered individu-
ally: (1) the limit of the eyes and the death of writing; (2) the "river of light," the
conversion of the eye; (3) the White Rose, the apocalyptic vision of the general
Resurrection; (4) the departure of Beatrice, experienced as the Gift of Death in
writing and the arrival of Bernard as Beatrice's substitute; (5) the quasi-divine
sovereignty of Mary; (6) the final vision of the divinity of the Other as Trinity,
together with the figure of Resurrection as the truth of Incarnation.

1. *The death of writing and limit of the eyes*—Canto xxx opens with the drama
of the second episode of Dante's blindness, temporary but decisive in the
process of constant conversion which he is undergoing. Like the first episode
at the end of the examination on love conducted by the "Beloved Apostle,"
St. John the evangelist in Canto xxvi, the episode signals that the blindness
of faith, which sees through tears, is in fact a necessary element in the process
of "constant conversion," neither transitory nor simply instrumental, but a

necessary moment of the recurring rhythm of historical identity. The singularity of the Point of Light (Christ), which Dante had been unable to endure yet and which prefigures the final vision, recedes now from the field of vision of the ninth sphere, the *Primum Mobile*. Opening out from Beatrice's smile unto the utmost horizon of vision, the pattern of recurrence begins again, reconfiguring itself differently:

> . . . not otherwise the triumph that plays forever round the Point which overcame me, seeming enclosed by that which it encloses, was gradually extinguished to my sight, *wherefore seeing nothing and love constrained me to return with my eyes to Beatrice.* (*Par.*, xxx, 10–15; emphasis added)

At the literal level of the story, Dante, guided by Beatrice, has now seen all there is to be seen, surveyed the entire created universe, both physical and spiritual. Nothing remains to be seen. The allegorical possibilities for interpretation here are of course multiple and compelling: the Nothing as the "other face" of God, who is absolutely other to creation; the Nothing as not simply the metaphysical Other of Being and Truth, but as Freedom, as Sartre and even perhaps Heidegger would have it. But more compelling than traces of interpretation is the stroke by which Dante points the line of the writing back to its proper focal point, the face of Beatrice "wherefore seeing nothing (*nulla vedere*) and love (*amor*—the word echoes back across every trace that marks the journey from the first vision of Beatrice and the false dream of the false face of divinity under the name Amor in the *Vita nuova*) constrained me to return with my eyes to Beatrice." Love and the "nothing to see"—not blindness as the limit of sight but the limit of the Other of the eye, the nothing written in the Other as its empty Secret—*together* constrained his eyes to repeat the pattern of returning again to her face. But here the finality inscribed in this text, every text, of face-writing begins to be revealed:

> If what has been said of her so far as here were all included in a single praise, it would be too slight to serve this present turn. The beauty I beheld transcends measure not only beyond our reach, but I truly believe that He alone who made it can enjoy it all. At this pass I concede myself defeated more than ever comic or tragic poet was defeated by a point in his theme; for, as the sun does to the sight which trembles (*trema*) most, even so remembrance of the sweet smile shears my memory of its very self. From the first day when in this life I saw her face, until this sight, the continuing of my song has not been cut off, but now my pursuit must desist from following her beauty further in my verses, as at his utmost reach must every artist. (*Par.*, xxx, 16–33)

Love and the limit of the Other of the eyes come together to reveal the truth of death, of a death in writing, a death of writing, the necessity of Death which alone can give Death's Gift, can give death as a gift, the gift of love, which can be given only as the for-given and for-giving death. Now his life in writing, what was once his "new life," is able to tell the truth of his love of her beauty by writing the truth of his love of writing, which is that it had always first been written in him by her, the death which he had so long refused to face: it is the face of her death, the face which is the Gift of her death, the Gift given to him now as the death of his writing, which now must begin again in love differently. She, in the flesh of his writing, writes her death as the defeat of the writing he had falsely called "mine"; she now is the point (*punto*) which defeats his writing, as a moment earlier his eyes were defeated by the singularity of the Point (*punto*) of Light. Christ who had withdrawn in favor of Beatrice as the giver of death to the substitution of Dante's hands for his eyes, his substitution of all the love of writing for the love of Beatrice for the love of Christ, his substitution of one for all the others. Now he writes the truth of his writing, faithfully writes the death of his writing in the hope that has been written in his heart by the love that is written in her face. And in that instance of surrender to the necessity of death, surrender to the need of death, the "sweet ally," he becomes finally obedient to the authority of her face-writing in him:

> . . . with the act and voice of a leader whose task is accomplished she began again, "We have issued forth from the greatest body to the heaven which is pure light: light intellectual full of love, love of true goodness full of joy, joy that transcends every sweetness." (*Par.*, xxx, 38–42)

A new light, a new seeing, a new writing with a new "sweetness" (*dolzore*) of style, the resurrection of the old *"dolce stil' nuovo,"* in which he had tried to write the false love of her life, occurring now as the Gift of her Death in writing. In a flash of vivid light, his eye is quenched, the salvation (*salute*) recalling her salutation (*salute*) which he had so eagerly sought and so thoroughly mistaken for salvation in the *Vita nuova*. She now tells him that this salvation is the embrace into which love receives those whom it "quiets (*queta*), in order to prepare the candle for its flame" (*Par.*, xxx, 52–53).

2. *The River of Light*—As these words of hers come within him, Dante immediately experiences himself "surmounting beyond my own power, and such a new vision was enkindled in me that there is no light so bright that my eyes could not have withstood it" (*Par.*, xxx, 57–60). Then he sees "a light in the form of the River," between two banks festooned "with marvelous spring," and "living sparks" arising from the water like "rubies set (*circumscrive*) in gold," and dropping amid the flowered grass, then rising again "as if inebriated by the odors," to plunge again into the stream. All the elements of the vision, she lets him know, are "shadowy prefaces of their truth," a kind of allegorical pageant like the one that preceded the arrival of Beatrice herself on the shores of the double rivers, Lethe and Eunoe, of the Earthly Paradise. Here the vision prefigures the vision of the White Rose that is to follow, the blossoms signifying humanity, which he will see "in those aspects which you shall see at the last judgment," that is, in bodily form, unlike the "souls" that he had met all along his journey. The vision of the White Rose signifies the general resurrection

at the last judgment and expresses the final meaning of history; history is life embodied as the single blossom comprising every singularity passed over from the history of freedom done in love.

But first she says to him, "you must needs drink of this water before so great a thirst in you be slaked" (*Par.*, xxx, 73–74). There now occurs the decisive instance of conversion, marked by an equally telling image:

> No infant, on waking far after its hour, so suddenly rushes with face toward the milk, as then did I, to make better mirrors of my eyes, stooping to the wave which flows there that we may be bettered in it. And even as the eaves of my eyelids (*palpebre*) drank of it, so it seemed to me out of its length to have become round. (*Par.*, xxx, 82–90)

Drinking with one's eyes! It is natural enough to speak of drinking in the vision of something delightful, but in this context the image reveals the true source of the kinesthetic image: the infantile memory of seeing with the mouth, of seeing the beloved face beyond the stream, as the source of the stream that feeds life. An image drawn from the out of the ruins of memory, drawing back to the scene of forgiveness enacted "beyond the stream" of forgetfulness in the earthly Paradise where Dante first beheld again "the lovely eyes" above the veil that hid the desired smile. Eyes and mouth, seeing and eating/drinking here are revealed in their unitary source: the face of love, glimpsed amid the ruins of memory, from which one may learn to smile at the satisfaction that quiets desire. In this image another garden scene is recalled, the flowering and fruiting of Paradise in *Genesis,* the scene of the original substitution, the scene which is figuratively reversed here, as if to forgive the original "sin" by reversing its polarity and allowing it to become the *"felix culpa,"* the happy fault that becomes not only the occasion but the means of salvation. Just as in Hell, sin, first glimpsed in the lust of the eyes and the romance of writing in the story of Paolo and Francesca, finally revealed its truth through images of eating, devouring the other as the means of the final betrayal of the Other, so here the love that begins with the desire of the eyes that "swell" (*torge*) more and more is finally to be quieted through the slit of the mouth. All history revealed as the interplay of eyes and mouth, imagined in the conversion of the linearity of history into the singularity of an identity and the circulation of an economy of excess that is without addition or subtraction, near or far, because now in the play of eyes and mouth across the face the triadic inclusiveness of its circulation comprises not simply self and Other, but also the other(s), all the other others, face to face.[7] This is the image of the White Rose that Dante now beholds.

The conversion of the eyes into the passage for food immediately reveals the authority for its truth claim as Dante now sees the circle fulfilled within itself with the human fruiting of the history of love:

> Then, as folk who have been under masks (*larve*) seem other than before, if they doff the semblances not their own wherein they were hid, so into

greater festival the flowers and the sparks did change before me that I saw
both courts of Heaven made manifest. O Splendor of God whereby I saw the
high triumph of the true kingdom, give to me power to tell how I beheld it!
(*Par.*, xxx, 91–99)

3. *The White Rose*—It seems reasonable to speculate that the great penultimate image of the final vision, the White Rose that comprises "both courts" of
Heaven, angels, and humans, is also drawn, like the River of Light, from the
ruins of personal memory; Dante's individual experience to be sure, but also
the memory of persons as the most basic structural configuration of history, as
that memory would have been familiarly displayed in another form of "sacred
allegory," the Rose Windows of the greater churches of Dante's culture, those
splendid specimens of a different style of face-writing, a different configuration of the interplay between the light of divinity and the fractive singularity
of human faces. Row upon row of petal-faces forming the flowering of love
in the script of salvation history, the history salvaged out of the ruins of the
memory of persons, each of whose identity witnessed and testified to a singular, decisive event of revelation of the truth done in love.

As if to underscore the essential figural structure of this image of the history of personal freedom, the interplay of human and divine personal freedom,
Beatrice introduces Dante to the vision of the Rose in explicitly civic, and even
poetically overdetermined political terms: "Behold the great assembly of the
white robes! See our city, how wide is its circuit! See our seats so filled that few
souls are now wanted here!" (*Par.*, xxx, 130–132) The image of the Rose is first
expressed in terms at once apocalyptic and vernacular, the heavenly Jerusalem
and the Tuscan *commune*, indeed his native Florence, exile from which had
lingered in his life like gall, as bitter as mother's milk is sweet. That this lofty
vision of Paradise as the community of Justice is indeed the image in conversion of enduring hope amid the ruin of memory in exile is attested shortly
after in the text in an image so poignant yet palpably comedic, offset by this
scene of high solemnity, that it calls attention to itself with an art far beyond its
standard simile form, and in that sense is indicative of Dante's poetic genius,
which holds the sublime and the mundane in constant and controlled tension:

> If the barbarians, coming from such region as is covered every day by Helice
> . . . when they beheld Rome and her mighty work, when Lateran rose above
> all mortal things, were wonder-struck, I, who to the divine from the human,
> to the eternal from time had come, and from Florence to a people just and
> sane, with what amazement must I have been full! Truly, what with it and
> with the joy, I was content to hear naught and to stand mute. (*Par.*, xxxi,
> 31–42)

It is in fact quite right to say that what seems to impress Dante most
forcefully, at least initially, in the vision of the Rose is its integrity, a wholeness
that exceeds both mechanical unity and even the organic homeostasis of

physical life. It bodies forth a form of community that could arise only through a divine Providence capable of disseminating its own freedom without limit, and this according to a differential function so absolute in both its originality and its finality that, in comparison, our own contemporary physical theories of General and Special Relativity, of quantum mechanics and the Uncertainty Principle, would be to our own culture as the physics, optics and astronomy of his own age were to his poetic imagination, "shadowy prefaces," pregnant with truth, although ordered in relations of inverse polarity. Whereas the physics and cosmology of Dante's age modeled themselves on the symmetry of order, proportion and clarity, and so dictated the structure of his portrayal of the physical world from the pit of Hell to the pinnacle of the earth on Mount Purgatory and beyond to the summit of the celestial spheres, his account of the integrity of the Rose, which is detailed later in the text, can be described as a physics of the resurrected body, the physics of the "body-politic" in a state of Justice that can only be realized in a "second coming," in a Judgment Day that is always yet to come. It is a differential physics of freedom that shares with classical physics and metaphysics of Being the metaphor of Light as its absolute standard and model of order and proportion, but which unlike it, and like contemporary physics and astronomy takes light to be the "improper" standard of total relationalism ("relativity" does not mean "relativism," not the totalitarianism of every individual, but a totality of relation, of the total interrelation of all events such that the singularity of each is absolutely constituted by that of all the others). This is the differential physics of freedom, rooted in the totality of interrelation and finality of interdetermination that takes the law of identity as its standard, the absence of any fixed standard that nonetheless happens as the absolute limit of all possibility against which the singularity of every historical event becomes determinate, the Impossible: Light, the absolute limit of the possibility of all occurrence; Light, the original impossibility that capacitates every real possibility of history. In the beginning, as the condition of beginning, before all beginning, God said, "Let there be Light," and in the end, in a final Word that is the end of all beginning, God will say "Let there be Light."

This differential physics of freedom and its law of identity is the precise point of the citation quoted above, "I saw faces all given to love, adorned by the light of Another and their own smile, and movements graced with every dignity." In the vision of the White Rose, through eyes converted by drinking in the River of Light, Dante now sees the revelation of the truth that Beatrice's smile has been doing in him all along his journey, and particularly the truth that was done from her face through his eyes and out of his mouth in his confession of faith, hope, and love made under the sign of Gemini, his birth sign, in the sphere of the Fixed Stars. That revelation is the Rose: the flowering of truth as beauty in the radiant Light of Joy. The connection between the confession and the vision is both immediate and direct, and therefore also essential to understanding the significance of the vision. Here in sum is the whole of his matured theology, his poetics and indeed his identity as a person: the face can reveal the true identity of the person, because it reveals the truth about personal identity, about what it means to be a person and to have an identity. Personal identities are the fundamental and ultimate realities of all history, because all history is the history of personal relationships of freedom. When those relationships are "given over to love," they are suffused with the radiance and beauty, the light of Joy, the Joy of the Resurrection, the Joy of the "Yes! Come! Again!" that is totally and finally written in the text of the face from the Other that is always at the center of all the others, the center through which the desire of the Other, every desire of every other, passes and is focused at its absolute limit in the radiant intensity of undiffused Light on the face through the eyes. This Light animates the face with a soul of its own, a soul capable of feeding on the desire of the Other and transforming it in a process of constant conversion into its own identity.[8]

In his confession to Peter, James, and John, Dante figuratively takes as witness the whole Church, the whole apostolic community that is born of and nurtured by the witness of confession, which is always witness to and confession of forgiveness, the for-giving that lets the Gift be given. In his confession in the presence of Beatrice, his original witness, Dante the pilgrim must say, and Dante the poet must write, his identity, confess who he is in the faith that sees through eyes blinded by tears; who he is in the hope of what will be done in him by the desire of the Other that leads him on; who he is in the love that is the Gift of the Other, and therefore the Gift of Death (figuratively, the "second blindness" that is about to occur), the gift that can only be forgiven, and therefore can and must always begin again, the Gift that gives the Whole, the gift that can be wholly given because it must first be wholly forgiven, the gift that fulfills desire and brings peace by wholly identifying itself with the desire of the Other, by wholly identifying the relation, the persons in relation, the persons who are the relation, by giving the relation of giving and forgiving, by giving the giving and the forgiving faces. "I saw faces *all given* (*süadi*) to love (*carità*)."[9] Dante must write his confession, confess his identity in writing, by taking responsibility for the question "Who am I?" as a person, that is, as a freedom, as one who can and must say "mine," as one responsible for both a "Yes!" and a "No!" and therefore finally capable of joy or despair, as one responsible for the mark of judgment, the signature of freedom, what is written across the line of the mouth, what is most its own, what is written in the face through the eyes on the mouth from the face of the Other, as one who is responsible for one's own smile, the signature that says "Yes! Come! Again!" as if to say, "I am wholly satisfied, I am whole and at peace in your coming and therefore wholly desire that you come again and again, world without end—because the Gift of Death is the forgiving of every end."

What Dante sees in the Rose is the community of confessors in whom justice is wholly done to the responsibility of freedom for the text that is written on its face, as its face, the responsibility to take oneself and others at face value, the beauty of the face that is adorned with the light of Another, for what is written in the face is what is first from the Other, from the impossible light of the Other, from the light and in the light of the impossible desire of the Other. But each faced is also adorned with its own smile, the mark of the freedom that chooses to say "Yes! Come! Again!" and in so saying signs itself with the mark of peace. With this smile that each calls "mine" playing across the mouth, each and every one wholly identifies with the desire of the Other that does not eat in order to devour the Other, so as to finish the hunger of desire, but eats eucharistically, eats to celebrate the hunger of desire and finalize it, make it wholly without end by forgiving the end.

### 4. *The Departure of Beatrice and the Arrival of Bernard:*

> My look had now taken in the general form of Paradise as a whole, and on no part had my sight paused; *and I turned with rekindled will (e volgeami con voglia rïaccesa)* to ask my lady things as to which my mind was in suspense. One thing I purposed, and another answered me: I thought to see Beatrice, and I saw an elder clad like the folk in glory. His eyes and cheeks were suffused with benign gladness, his mien kindly such as befits a tender father. And, "Where is she?" I said at once; whereon he, "To terminate [finalize] your desire Beatrice has urged me from my place, and if you look up to the circle that is third from the highest tier, you will see her again, in the throne her merits have allotted to her. (*Par.*, xxxi, 52–69; emphasis added)

The departure of Beatrice configures the vision, reveals the order of the gaze, according to which the vision of the Rose, the vision of the Joy of Resurrection, reveals its truth. Specifically, it reveals the truth of the vision in its finality, the sense in which it envisions a finality of Joy that is without end because it always begins again. According to the differential "physics of freedom" which Dante is poetically theorizing in the Empyrean, the finality of Joy arises from the resurrectional structure of love, the structure of the Gift of Death, forgiven and forgiven. When he has taken in the general form of Paradise, but without pausing on any specific part, the process of continual conversion still governing his movements, he turns again with rekindled will ("*volgeami con voglia rïaccesi*" notice the poetically genial, semantically fortuitous mirroring in the words for "turn" and "will," *volgeami* and *voglia*, reflecting their interrelation in the structure of experience from which they arise) to say "Yes! Come! Again! Come to continue this intercourse ours." But now the same running together of love begins, again, to happen differently: in language intentionally reminiscent of Beatrice's commission to Virgil, and in keeping with the differential function of parental gender, Beatrice, his lady-mother, must undergo conversion into another "kindly father," as Virgil had been kindly to him in conducting him to the place where he could see Beatrice again, so Bernard will give him safe conduct to the Other of Beatrice, the other woman, the one who was before Beatrice in the order of love and forgiveness, the Other/

woman of Dante's destiny, the Other woman of all destinies, the woman who
is Other to the Divine, who is divinely Other, the woman who as Other to the
divine allows the divine to become different, "more divine," in her face. Dante
must have another lady-mother, and in order to do so, he must be guided by
another father, equally courtly in his own way to the chivalric Virgil of Canto
ii of the *Inferno*, for whom Beatrice's slightest wish was his command. But for
the moment, at this instant in the text, Bernard's larger functional role is secondary to his role in assisting Dante immediately and peacefully to reenvision
Beatrice and resituate himself within the limitless field of difference that now
is the free space of their relationship:

> Without answering I lifted up my eyes and saw her where she made for her-
> self a crown as she reflected the eternal rays. From the region which thunders
> most high no mortal eye is so far distant, were it plunged most deep within
> the sea, as there from Beatrice was my sight. *But to me it made no difference,*
> *for her image came down to me unblurred by aught between.* (*Par.*, xxxi, 70--78;
> emphasis added)

Another rendering of the last sentence of this citation would have it,
" . . . but distance was no hindrance, for her semblance reached me undimmed
by anything between."[10] However one chooses to translate the poetically com-
pressed image, its affirmation is poignant and powerful: difference is not primarily a function of time and space, and the cut of difference, if it is clean, does
not necessarily produce the disease of infection or rupture. This turn into difference within their relationship is necessary to "finalize" (*terminar*) his desire;
it is born of the difference that is the first and, therefore, the final condition of
desire, and of the love that wholly identifies itself with that desire. And so it
puts into Dante's mouth, through his eyes, from her face, a farewell as beautiful in its integrity as perhaps has ever been written, because of, not despite, its
poetic economy:

> "O lady in whom my hope is strong, and who for my salvation did endure to
> leave in Hell your footprints, of all those things which I have seen I acknowl-
> edge the grace and the virtue to be from your power and your excellence. It is
> you who have drawn me from bondage into liberty by all those paths, by all
> those means by which you had the power so to do. Preserve in me your [mag-
> nanimity] so that my soul, which you have made whole (*sana*) may be loosed
> from the body, pleasing unto you." So did I pray; and she, so distance as she
> seemed, smiled and looked on me, then turned again to the eternal fountain.
> (*Par.*, xxxi, 79–90; my translation)

Clearly this speech is Dante's rewriting of the last section of the *Vita
nuova*, and as such, is his way of allowing her, in writing, to give him the Gift
of Death, of her death, the death she gives him here, the gift of her difference,
the gift of herself as Other, of her death without limit or measure, her death
as the river of light from which she turns to him and to which she re-turns

in continual conversion. Dante had refused the Gift of her Death in the *Vita nuova,* especially in its finale without finality, in the promise to write of her what had not been written in rhyme of woman before. This was a promise he could not keep, the promise of writing that was not his own to make, the promise whose secret had first to be written in him, through his eyes and on his heart, from another, an/other woman, from another Beatrice, a Beatrice who had become other, through death and the Gift of Death, who through resurrection had become another Beatrice. Now here he acknowledges that all that is written in him and all that he has written is from her . . . and at this she smiles, and then turns again.

"So did I pray . . ." A prayer of thanksgiving in gratitude that does not promise writing because it realizes that the promise of writing has been kept in him, in the cryptography of her death, the face-writing that he now confesses has been written as the secret truth of his identity, as an empty secret and an empty tomb, because he is not there alone, is not in secret: he is from her and with her, and she is with him from an Other, across the free play of difference without limit, in the constant conversion of love without end. And so she smiles . . . and turns again.

5. *The "quasi-divine" Sovereignty of Mary*—The vision of Mary as Queen to which Bernard directs Dante after the departure of Beatrice is the penultimate movement of the poem, on which the climax of the whole depends. In this the poetic and dramatic structure of the *Paradiso* follows the pattern established in the structure of both the *Inferno* and the *Purgatorio.* In those Cantiche, the focus of dramatic attention is centered on the encounter which precedes the concluding scenes which are, in the *Inferno* the figure of Satan, and in the *Purgatorio* the pageant of the Church and the Empire. These concluding scenes, though of great symbolic importance, are highly allegorical, to the point of being figural schemata of meaning, standing in sharp contrast to the highly realized humanity of the scenes immediately preceding each of them: the encounter with Ugolino in the *Inferno,* the reunion of Dante and Beatrice in *Purgatorio,* and the vision of Mary culminating in the prayer of St. Bernard to her on behalf of Dante in the *Paradiso.* This emphasis on the human person, indeed on the high drama played out in distinct registers on the faces of the protagonists of the each scene, is emblematic of what is most distinctive, in fact decisively singular, in the poetics of the *Commedia:* its Incarnationalism, that is to say, its absolutely singular insistence on locating the full revelation of the truth of all history, human and divine, in the identities, the faces, of persons; that is, in the history of the freedom of persons, human and divine, in the flesh and blood features and events of that history. The fullness of divine mystery is revealed always, only and altogether in the process of constant conversion whereby the Word becomes flesh, and flesh becomes again word. Nowhere in the poem is Dante's Incarnationalism more apparent than in the dramatic, as opposed to the structural, climax of the

Paradiso, where Mary's Queenship is affirmed as the absolute condition of the allegorical vision of the divine into which Dante may pass only through her. In it, Mary is acknowledged as the singular, decisive Other on which all the others depend: on whom Beatrice depends for the original motive force of her mission to Dante, on whom Dante depends for the "finalization" of his desire, on whom God depends to enter decisively into history.

Bernard thus directs Dante to Mary:

> "Son of Grace, this joyous being," he began, "will not be known to you if you hold your eyes only down here at the base; but look upon the circles, even to the most remote, until you see upon her seat the Queen to whom this realm is subject and devoted." (*Par.*, xxxi, 112–117)

Just as the Rose itself is the image in Dante's converted sight of the confession of faith, hope, and love by which he identified himself, so too, the whole Rose, with its myriad face-written identities, is only the unfolding of the dyadic vision of Christ as the singular Point of Light and Mary as the Rose across which that light plays, the two eyes of the face of Joy which Dante experienced immediately before his confession of identity in *Par.*, xxiv–xxvi, "Here is the Rose wherein the Divine Word became flesh" (*Par.*, xxiii, 73–74). Mary is the Rose and the Rose is the whole of Paradise, which in Dante's earlier vision had been enclosed in Mary the Rose just as Jesus had been enclosed in her womb so as to become flesh. As Beatrice is to Dante, so Mary is revealed as being to the divine mystery, the necessary Other through which the divine can become "more divine" through its incarnation in history. It is in this way that the earlier vision, *Par.* xxiii, 106–108, prefigured the necessity that Mary enter into the supreme sphere so as to make it "more divine." No doubt this would constitute heresy to a theologian of Absolute Being in the Middle Ages, or in any age for that matter. Perhaps it might be condoned as the flight of fancy of poetic imagination. But to take either of these views would be to miss the faith, hope, and love, singular to Dante, which animate the face of the poem with the light of Joy, by which Dante named it properly, the *Commedia*. His faith, his hope, and his love are en-joyed by Mary. Through her, from her, in her, he will see the divine—but not the *face* of God, or if he does, he will not be able to resurrect in writing that face from out of the ruins of memory. The final face, the final smile he sees is Mary's, and from her face and smile he passes over into God—and then back into the human. Her face, her smile, the one she calls her own, is the one across which the "light of Another" must play in order to reveal itself.

Doubtless powerful cross-currents in Dante's individual experience and his culture are revealed in this final structural choice that Dante makes for his poem. Turbulent forces have shaped the voyage, forces of which Dante forewarned the reader at the start of the voyage of the *Paradiso*, "O you that in your little bark . . . turn back to see again your shores" (*Par.*, ii, 1–4). The entire religious, political and social history of patriarchy and the schizophrenic repression and simultaneous exaltation of the Other as woman, are surging and ripping beneath the surface of Dante's text; all of this tumult had been present since he began to write of Beatrice. In fact, in his writing the massive tides of the repression of the Other as Western history, as the history of the West, and the history of religion, that is, the history of responsibility and freedom of the West, have taken on face and flesh and name and for one glorious moment, in the prayer of St. Bernard, Dante, the master of his own ship of poetry, holds together all the power and tumult of those forces, the same forces Nietzsche would later describe as "this monster of energy," in the peace of total and final tension:

> "Virgin Mother, daughter of thy Son, humble and exalted more than any creature, fixed goal of the eternal counsel, thou art she who didst so ennoble human nature that its Maker did not disdain to become its creature. In thy womb was rekindled the love under whose warmth this flower in the eternal peace has thus unfolded. Here thou art for us the noonday torch of charity, and below among mortals thou art the living fount of hope. Lady, thou art so great and so availest, that whoso would have grace and has not recourse to thee, his desire seeks to fly without wings. Thy loving-kindness not only succors him who asks, but oftentimes freely foreruns the asking.
>
> "In thee is mercy, in thee pity, in thee munificence, in thee is found what ever of goodness is in any creature. Now this man, who from the lowest pit of the universe even to here has seen one by one the spiritual lives, implores thee of thy grace for power such that he may be able with his eyes to rise still higher toward the last salvation. And I, who never for my own vision burned more than I do for his, proffer to thee all my prayers, and pray that they may not be scant, that with thy prayers thou wouldst dispel for him every cloud of his mortality, so that the Supreme Pleasure may be disclosed to him. Further I pray thee, Queen, who *canst do whatsoever thou wilt*, that thou preserve sound for him his affections, after so great a vision. Let thy protection vanguish human impulses. Behold Beatrice, with how many saints, for my prayers clasping their hands to thee."
>
> The eyes beloved and reverenced by God, fixed upon him who prayed, showed us how greatly devout prayers do please her; then they were turned to the Eternal Light, wherein we may not believe that any creature's eye finds its way so clear. (*Par.*, xxxiii, 1–45; emphasis added)

Nothing could be clearer: for Dante everything depends on his lady-mother, the Other (one), the Other as woman. Here we have arrived back at precisely the penultimate scene of Derrida's journey through the open space, the space of revelation through the blinds, where Provost's *Sacred Allegory* is displayed. But the two curators at this point arrange their display of portraits somewhat differently. Derrida comes finally to Daniele da Volterra's *Woman Weeping at the Foot of the Cross*. Dante instead reverses the order of display: Mary's portrayal by St. Bernard of Clairevaux as the human mother of her son and human creature of her creator, the (m)other-woman who, like Dante's other-woman, would one day weep, this trauma of human flesh and eyes and faces comes first and the allegory follows, the allegory depends on the truth of the human face. This is the allegory of God: the allegorical schema of the Trinity as the Light of the Joy that plays on human faces, the allegory of the incarnation by which the Word of God plays across the history of faces.

6. *The Final Vision:*

> O Light Eternal, who alone abidest in Thyself, alone knowest Thyself, and, known to thyself and knowing, lovest and smilest on Thyself!
>
> That circling which, thus begotten, appeared in Thee as reflected light, when my eyes had dwelt on it for a time, *seemed to me depicted with our own image within itself and in its own color* wherefore my sight was entirely set upon it. (*Par.*, xxxiii, 124–132; emphasis added)

What does Dante see in the "final vision," revealed to him through the eyes and from the face of Mary? In response to Bernard's prayer, Mary turns her eyes into the Divine Light. Mary's eyes are converted into the light. Dante chooses his words carefully even as he avers the final inadequacy of writing, the cutting off, cutting out of words: *"indi a l'etterno lume s'addirizaro"* (*Par.*, xxxiii, 43), her eyes "address themselves," they turned into the address of the eternal light, the secret proper place of the divine reveals itself first as encrypted, ciphered and signed in, as the turn of her eyes, the conversion of her eyes into "eternal light," and, through the conversion of her eyes, Dante's eyes to are converted into that same light. "Bernard was signing to me with a smile to look upward, but I was already of myself such as he wished; for my sight, becoming pure, was entering more and more through the beam of the lofty Light which in itself is true" (*Par.*, xxxiii, 49–54).

In the vision of Mary's face, with the vision that is from her face, Dante begins now to see "for himself," for his self, now identified with her, by her, at the prayer of all the others, is in her face and she is in him, as together they are both in the light. This turn is punctuated by the memory of writing, and by the ruins of memory in writing. The choreography of continuous conversion in its final "instant" is drawn by Dante with a sovereign sense of the irony of writing as the memory of the Gift of Death, the ironic structure of writing as the ruin of memory and the memory of ruin:

> Thenceforward my vision was greater than speech can show, which fails at such a sight, and at such excess memory fails. As is he who dreaming sees, and after the dream the passion remains imprinted and the rest returns not to mind; such am I, for my vision almost wholly fades away, yet does the sweetness that was born of it still drop within my heart. (*Par.*, xxxiii, 55–63)

Everything that is written "thenceforward" in the vision, like everything that has progressively been written in the poem, is written in conscious imitation of the style of writing itself, in the style that is "proper" to writing, in the style of the irony of writing as the Gift of Death, of writing as the improper memory of ruin and the ruin of memory, as the memory of a Secret which is absolutely empty, the memory of "pure" Light, light that reveals nothing, light that plays only within and across itself, "O Light Eternal, who alone abidest in Thyself, alone knowest Thyself, and known to Thyself and knowing, lovest and smilest on thyself." (*Par.,* xxxiii, 124–126)

The irony of writing is the memorial structure through which the Gift of Death takes place, the "style" by which it reveals the empty Secret that resides amid the ruins of memory as the memory of ruin, the light that reveals nothing of its face or its smile, the gift that from the beginning could not be given but only forgiven in and as Death, as the forgiven and forgiving Death, the Gift of "pure Light," which measures without measure, the Light that forgives every vision and forgives the original sin of substitution: the substitution of mouth for eyes, of eating for vision, the for-giving of the smile, the smile that smiles on and so forgives itself its empty, guilty Secret of Impossibility, the impossibility of the Gift, the impossibility of the desire of the Other, the impossibility whose name is Love.

The writing of the final vision proceeds according to the ironic structure of writing itself as the memorial marker of the Gift of Death, forgiving the impossibility of Love by tracing in writing the ruined memory of the Light's own smile. And it does so for the sake of the Other, in memory of all the others who are to come:

> O Light Supreme that art so far uplifted above mortal conceiving, relend to my mind a little of what Thou didst appear, and give my tongue such power that it may leave only a single spark of Thy glory for the folk to come; for, by returning somewhat to my memory and by sounding a little in these lines, more of Thy victory shall be conceived. (*Par.,* xxxiii, 67–75)

The writing of the final vision is to be a poor but reverential commemorative of the Joy of the Resurrection, "Thy victory," for all those who are yet to come. The writing is the gift of the glory of the Light to all the others. Here Dante locates the proper address of the writing, which he calls his own: its destiny and destination is in all those who are "yet to come," who are still coming, who are still astray, who are wandering in disarray, who still have not been given their own place in the Rose as the Gift of Death. At the end of the *Vita nuova,* he promised to address his writing to Beatrice but in so doing he went astray; he misaddressed the promise of his writing by substituting the "to" for the "from," and so misaddressed those for whom and to whom it could be written.

Now able to look fixedly into the Light, to properly address his eyes to its empty, secret site/sight the Light undergoes another conversion, or rather accommodates and shows itself hospitable to his continual conversion:

> In its depth I saw ingathered, bound by love in one single volume, that which is dispersed in leaves (*si squaderna*) throughout the universe: substances and

accidents and their relations, as though fused together in such a way that
what I tell is but a simple light. The universal form of this knot I believe that
I saw, because in telling this I feel my joy increase. (*Par.,* xxxiii, 85–93)

The first image which the Light reveals enfolded within itself, as it was
enfolded within the center of the Rose, as Jesus was enfolded in the womb
of Mary, is the book, the book of the scripture of the face-writing that was
enfolded in the integrity of the Rose. In the universe this book is dispersed and
disseminated through all the cuts, all the inscriptions of every scripture that
appears in the semblance of books that are bound in flesh, those books that
are not bound into the organic integrity of faces, books that can be dispersed
in leaves (*si squaderna*), which can deconstruct themselves into "signatures"
superimposed over the erasure of prior identities. One might even discern in
this image the necessary deconstruction of every "metaphysics," every system
of knowledge that expresses itself in terms of "substances and accidents and
their relations." For the physics of freedom can have no "metaphysics," and
its scripture can find its coherence only in the integrity of identity that binds
according to the necessities of love, that is, according to the absolute impossibility that each and every cut of difference, which might always have been
different, should ever be otherwise than it has been done in the history of
freedom which is written in faces "all given to love." This is the "love-knot"
that Dante now believes he sees, binding all to all, in the total responsibility of
forgiveness, the "truth" which is now attested, not by vision or by any evidence,
but by the Joy he feels growing in his heart at the ruined memory of this
absent vision. The Joy of the heart as testimony substitutes for the evidence of
vision, testimony to the impossibility of all substitution, the impossibility of
substitution for the singularity of identity within the totalized and finalized
integrity of the Light of Joy that plays according to the differential physics of
freedom across the scripture of face-writing:

> Thus my mind, all rapt, was gazing, fixed, motionless and intent, ever enkin-
> dled by its gazing. In that Light one becomes such that it is impossible he
> should ever consent to turn himself from it for other sight; for the Good,
> which is the object of the will, is all gathered in it, and outside of it that is
> defective which is perfect there. (*Par.,* xxxiii, 97–105)

The Light reveals itself finally as impossibility, as the impossibility of difference, the impossibility of the Other, the impossibility of any "other sight,"
or site of any other at all. It reveals itself as the Impossibility which is the
only possible satisfaction, the only possible "Good," of that desire of the Other.
Such desire is strictly impossible, but, in the instant of decision, it can be done,
as truth, in love.

On this impossible point of Light, the vision now turns again, marking
the turning point with the trace of the irony of its being done, of its truth
being done, in love, in writing, in the love of writing, marking too the memory

in ruins of the lady-mother, the Other-woman in whose womb the vision that is now being birthed, had been enfolded: "now will my speech fall more short, even in respect to that which I remember, than that of an infant who still bathes his tongue at the breast" (*Par.*, xxxiii, 106–108). The Impossible continues to forgive the need of constant conversion, "altering itself to me," as a second image appears within the light:

> Within the profound and shining subsistence of the lofty Light appeared to me three circles of three colors and one magnitude, and one seemed reflected by the other, as rainbow by rainbow, and the third seemed fire breathed forth equally from the one and the other. Oh, how scant is speech, and how feeble to my conception! and this, to say what I saw, is such that it is not enough to call it little. (*Par.*, xxiii, 115–123)

Despite the now-familiar irony of the confession, the poet's apology for the approaching death of writing in writing, the death-watch over the dwindling stream of breath to be cut into words, still bears credible testimony to the Gift of the final vision as the Gift of Death that can only be for-given. The image of the Trinity as it is written here, in the image of the composition of Light according to its refraction into the three "primary" colors, the first form of its revelation and the image of the first articulate Word of history, can, in the primitive simplicity of its figural representation, only be forgiven. It is only a cipher of the Word that gives all other words but is itself impossibly inarticulate. Rather than as a theological insight or revelation, the ironic "little" that the figure more significantly reveals is the original structure of three, the original community of integrity, of which the doctrine of the economic Trinity, its procession within itself as it smiles in love on itself, is the simulacrum. The original image on which Dante's poetic vision has all along been centered is the face, the human face as it is configured by the eyes and the smile, the binocularity of the eyes and the singularity of the smile. These are three that unfold now in the abstract structural schema of the Light. The Light of revelation, for Dante at least, always originates as the light that plays across the text of the human face. Now in his vision he retains only the figural schema of that revelation that all along has guided him, encrypted as the empty Secret that cannot be told but must be shared. It is the manner of sharing that constitutes the final turn of the vision, culminating in the instant of the final revelation. First, he gives the formula of that secrecy, the seal of absolute secrecy that must be confessed as absolute and final truth before the empty Secret can be shared: "Oh Light Eternal, who alone abidest in Thyself, alone knowest Thyself, and, known to Thyself and knowing, lovest and smilest on Thyself" (*Par.*, xxxiii, 24–26).

How is this to be done, sharing, in writing, the empty Secret that there is no secret, that the truth of the Secret cannot be revealed, but only "done" in love? How is the Impossible to be done? What shape or figure will the event of the Impossible take? How could it enter into history, the history of religion, of responsibility, of freedom? What name would mark the proper place of its occurrence? Dante cannot say, because he cannot remember; he can only recall this much:

> That circling which, thus begotten, appeared in Thee as reflected light, when my eyes had dwelt upon it for a time, seemed to me depicted (*pinta*) *with our image* (*de la nostra effige*) within itself and in its own color, wherefore my sight was entirely set upon it. (*Par.*, xxxiii, 126–132; emphasis added)

Finally, in the end, as it was in the beginning, the Light resolves itself only into "our image"; that is all that can be said amid the ruin of memory. "Our image" is all that can be shared of the empty Secret of the Impossible in Dante's vision; "our image" is the only depiction he can remember seeing at the height of his vision in the purity of Light. But he goes on to assure us that this image does reveal the truth, the whole truth: in our image lies encrypted the Secret of every secret, the Secret knowledge of knowledge itself, the forbidden fruit that remains forbidden but can still be shared, even as Adam and Eve shared it by eating it, becoming guilty of the substitution that had been expressly forbidden. But our image is their image, and their image is the image and likeness of God. As God made Adam and Eve in God's own likeness, as he smiled on them and in them, Dante here writes God in effigy, in the lines of our image; God's smile-upon-himself in the image of our smile. In this way he shares the secret that cannot be revealed, because it is Impossible, but must be shared, the guilty, empty Secret of the Impossible desire of the Other, in which all share the same image, which must be shared because it cannot be given, must be shared as always already given, as for-given, forgiven and forgiving, must be shared as the Gift of Death, death in whose image all persons, divine and human, share. Death is our image. In Dante's final vision, the Light of God, in the form of the second Circle, in the middle, the center of the community that figures the face of God, resolves itself in our image, reveals itself as the Resurrection, the Gift of Death.

Dante seals and finalizes his vision with an image of secrecy as canonical to the classical Greco-Roman humanist tradition as the image of the economic Trinity is to the Christian tradition: the image of the "Vetruvian figure." He anticipates the image that in the hands and in the drawing of Leonardo da Vinci would become emblematic of the Christian Renaissance revival of classical humanism. The Roman architect Vetruvius' image was a way of keeping the secret of the "golden proportion" that is encrypted in the mortal flesh of the human body, the secret knowledge of "Man the measure," the unspeakable "measure without measure," of the invisible Light that sheds light on every figure, of the unspeakable Word that could only be figured in the number that cannot be written or spoken or thought, the irrational, disordered, dis-array of number that contains the secret of the relation of the circle to the square, the relation from which all spacing could be proportionately measured:

As is the geometer who wholly applies himself to measure the Circle, and finds not, in pondering, the principle of which he is in need, such was I at that new sight. I wished to see how the image conformed to the circle and how it has its place therein; but my own wings were not sufficient for that, save that my mind was smitten by a flash wherein its wish came to it. Here power failed the lofty phantasy; but already my desire and my will were revolved, like a wheel that is evenly moved, by the Love which moves the Son and the other stars. (*Par.*, xxxiii, 133–145)

The problem of "squaring the circle," of moving discreetly through every degree of difference, the "four" of the square, which measures all time and space, the four points of the compass, the four seasons, the four elements, reconciling the "power principle" of dyad to the impossible, decisive instant of the singular, of this Dante confesses his own wings insufficient. Yet, in an instant the impossible is done in him and he becomes in himself, he is identified by the Impossibility of his desire. In the death of his lofty fantasy, he becomes what it could only image as "too little," and in the hunger of desire and the choice of the will he is moved by the Love that cannot be known but which all history has done, the love that moves the Sun and all the other stars, which moves as the Other and all the others.

# In *Memoriam:* A Smile in Passing . . .

Less a conclusion than a reconfiguration of the question, a re-figuring performed as an exchange of roles, personae, masks, the study ends with an unmasking of Dante as no more "Christian" than Derrida; Derrida as no less religious than Dante. Yet this does not settle the question of who each of them is, their identities as religious writers, writers of religion as responsibility for one's own face, for one's own responsibility to face up to death, writers of the scripture that death writes in, on, as one's own face.

By returning to the second essay of *The Gift of Death,* omitted from discussion until this point, and taking up again the precise sense in which Patočka's Essays are "heretical," one last aspect of the relationship between Dante and Derrida as religious writers is revealed: the way in which both of them, like Patočka, are religious "heretics," claiming to take responsibility for their own faith and their own way of going on in writing by choosing a way that they call their own—the faith of tears, the faith of smiles, the faith of a face that I call mine.

Conclusions, like so much else, are impossible. Yet, memory must be served: the dead who have passed on must be buried, and the living must pass on, continue passing on until they too have passed on. The living must give death a pass and themselves take a pass on death, must pass over death because death has passed over them, even as it has passed over the others, the dead, differently, so that they, the living, might do what all the living can and must do, memorialize the dead and memorize death, bury the dead in memory, in remembrance of the Gift of Death. All praise is gratitude; all worship, all that is held sacred, comes from remembering the Gift of Death, from remembering to pass on, from remembering to pass over death in memory of death's passing over those who have yet to pass on. The Gift of Death reveals the Secret of passing on, the Secret of both living and dying, the secret which both the living and the dead keep buried in memory and encrypted in their memorials. Death passes on the Secret of passing on, keeps its Secret by passing it on to be kept, buried in memory, by the living and the dead. Death is the Secret which is impossible to keep, which can be kept only in passing on. Death is the Impossibility of the Secret and the Secret of impossibility: the secret impossibility of the Gift, of all giving and taking, of Love, of Justice, and of course of Forgiveness, which is before the Gift, the Secret of the Gift. Forgiveness names the trace in memory of the Impossible Secret which Death keeps by giving it as a Gift, a gift which is not any present, a gift which is given as an empty promise, a gift which is passed on and passed over as promised and promising, a gift which is given and taken, as the promise of always beginning again, a promise which is kept buried in memory and is memorialized in the living as the constancy of conversion, the living who must keep (by) passing on, must always begin again; it is the promise of the Messiah, to always come (yet) (again).

For Christianity, forgiveness is signified by encrypting it in the promise and hope of Resurrection, the revelation that keeps the secret by showing it. Forgiveness is the style of tracing the trace buried in memory of the Impossible Secret that death keeps by passing on, passing over, by giving it as its Gift. The Resurrection of Jesus, the impossible desire of the Other that promises always to begin again, reveals in Christianity the secret name of God, reveals the secret of God in the name of Jesus, the Messiah who has died, risen, and will come again. The whole of the Christian "gospel" lies in bearing witness to the name of Jesus, as resurrected Lord, who reveals forgiveness as the Secret Impossibility of the Love that forgets itself, to be kept and passed on in memory, witnessed and worshiped as Way, Truth, and Life. But how is it possible to keep the promise of the Impossible Secret precisely by revealing it as the Gift of Death, that is, by revealing it through what Patočka might think of as the most advanced technology of cryptography for which Europe can and must take responsibility, can and must claim as its own:

> The narrative is genealogical but it is not simply an act of memory. It *bears witness*, in the manner of an ethical or political act for today and tomorrow. It means first of all thinking about what takes place today. The organization of the narrative follows a genealogical detour in order to describe the current European return of mystery and orgiastic mystification; in order to describe it but more particularly *to denounce, deplore, and combat it*. (GD, 35; emphasis added)

These sentences begin the second of Derrida's four essays in *The Gift of Death*, which is entitled, "Beyond: Giving for the Taking, Teaching and Learning to Give, Death."[1] The narrative referred to, at least proximately, is Patočka's delineation of the history of religion in "Is Technological Civilization Decadent, and Why?" as the history of responsibility and specifically, insofar as its civilization is inextricably bound up with Christianity, as the history of European responsibility.

For the immediate purposes of the present consideration, we can summarize the import of Derrida's treatment of Patočka's essay in "Beyond" as follows. It will be recalled that in the first essay of *The Gift of Death*, "Secrets of European Responsibility," Derrida has already traced the basic outline of Patočka's treatment of the genealogy of responsibility, which is also the history of religion, beginning with what Patočka refers to as "orgiastic or demonic mystery," the fundamental erotic impulse toward fusion and nondifferentiation, which in a sense might be viewed as the driving force at work in the practice of "magic." Magic practices the transgression of boundaries of the "orders of nature," those clear-cut lines of differentiation that mark the domains of the vegetative and animal, the human, and the super- or preternatural. Patočka sees the first major development of religion in the West in the transformation of the demonic by its *incorporation* into the Platonic conception of the soul, which takes possession of itself precisely by the enforcement of a discipline on the erotic drives of the body and so masters and subjugates them, exercising dominion over those forces so as to be able to direct them toward its own proper purpose, the Good.[2] Patočka emphasizes that this incorporation in no way annihilates or eliminates the orgiastic and demonic drive, but rather preserves it by incorporation through the disciplinary force of the way of living known as the "care of the soul" as its first principle, and which Plato identifies in the *Phaedo* as the "practice" of death. So in this Platonic conception of responsibility, the soul exists and excels precisely insofar as it succeeds in learning to practice death, to make death its own, to gain dominion over it by making it a practice. Specifically, responsibility is achieved through the soul's practice of separation, liberation, and withdrawal from the body, which it nonetheless continues to subjugate and use to fuel its drive toward the Good and its attainment of immortality prefigured by the experience of contemplation—itself a return in shadow of the subjugated demonic drive. Ultimately, this conception resolves itself into one of consumption, and if Dante is correct, finally predation: the soul feeds itself on the dominated and subjected body, in an unending, futile attempt to make itself proof against death, a vampire that "lives" the borrowed life of refusal of the Gift of Death.

The second transformation Patočka describes is the inclusion of the Platonic soul into the Christian experience of the *mysterium tremendum* through what he refers to as a movement of reversal or *repression*, whereby the Platonic soul, which still retains the force of orgiastic mystery incorporated within itself, is itself "held in check" by the transformation of the objective Platonic Good into Goodness, the personal gaze that beholds without being beheld, and holds the Christian soul within the grasp of the love that forgets itself and renounces itself in favor of its Gift, which is given without reserve. "God is love, and he who abides in love abides in God and God in him" (1 John 4:16). Again, the return of the orgiastic impulse toward fusion, incorporated in Platonism and repressed and held in check in Christianity by the gaze of self-forgetful love, returns as the disguised memory of its repressed principle of transformation—sacrifice. This genealogy of incorporation and repression of demonic mystery, first by the Platonic soul and then by the Christian *mysterium tremendum*, contains within itself what Derrida would recognize as a history of secrecy, the secret history of religion as mystery-dealing, and what Patočka recognizes as the "heretical" implication that Christianity has yet to think through fully how it has come to be responsible for itself and what it has yet to do and be in order to be responsible to and for itself.

In the final gesture of "Secrets of European Responsibility," in which Derrida has deployed Patočka's genealogy of European responsibility as this history of religion, which itself is a history of mystery-dealing, Derrida underscores his concern to examine both responsibility and religion especially in their relation to politics and, even more pointedly, with regard to the possibility or impossibility of finding a place for a history of Secrecy within, even at the heart of, politics, a secret history of politics, which would be also a history of Secrecy, and perhaps even the Secret of all histories, finding it, locating it, revealing it precisely so as to keep it, take responsibility for it precisely as—Secret. The essay concludes:

> Like the *polis* and the Grecian politics that corresponds to it, the Platonic moment incorporates demonic mystery in vain; it introduces or presents itself as a moment without mystery. What distinguishes the moment of the Platonic *polis* both from the orgiastic mystery that it incorporates and from the Christian *mysterium tremendum* that represses it, is the fact that in the first case one openly declares that secrecy will not be allowed. There is a place for secrecy, for the *mysterium* or for the mystical in what proceeds or follows Platonism (demonic, orgiastic mystery or the *mysterium tremendum*); but according to Patočka there is none such in the philosophy and politics of the Platonic tradition [including here Aristotle's politics]. Politics excludes the mystical. Therefore whatever there is in Europe and even in modern Europe that inherits this politics of the Graeco-Platonic provenance, either neglects, represses, or excludes from itself every essential possibility of secrecy and every link between responsibility and the keeping of the secret: everything that allows responsibility to be dedicated to secrecy. From there it takes very little to envisage an inevitable passage from the *democratic* to the *totalitarian*; it is the simple process that takes place by opening up such a passage. The consequences will be most serious; they deserve a second look. (*GD*, 33–34)

Derrida here sounds an ominous note of danger contained, thinly veiled if at all, in this consideration of mystery and secrecy and the attempt at their exclusion from politics. Perhaps he even has in mind a sort of prophetic tone to be discerned in Patočka's analysis, anticipating, foreseeing, forewarning, perhaps even for-giving his own death. Just a short time after writing this, he was killed at the hands of the Czech "secret–police," the ones who work in stealth—in a sort of dissimulation of secrecy that everyone knows about because they fear it—so as to "police" secrecy, to make sure that no one really has any secrets, to make sure that the very possibility of secrecy remains an impossibility by attempting to wrest secrecy's sword—death—its secret weapon, from its hand

and to wield it themselves, against secrecy itself: Death in a duel with itself to keep its secret.

This perhaps accounts for the turn that the second essay of *The Gift of Death*, "Beyond: Giving for the Taking, Teaching and Learning to Give, Death," takes in order to try to get a "second look" at the "serious consequence" that Derrida (and certainly Patočka) prophesy will follow from this opening up of a passage from democracy to totalitarianism, which "inevitably" must follow from the violence done in order to exclude secrecy, responsibility, and in a certain sense religion from the realm of the political. Perhaps the passage that Derrida envisages is the passage opened across Patočka's own visage, the wound to his head that killed him, sustained perhaps—nobody knows—at the hands of the Secret Police. Perhaps the turn which the second essay takes is Derrida's work of mourning, his memorial to Patočka's death, the turn by which Derrida remarks the turning off of two different passages, two different ways of passing on, two different ways of giving and taking death. Perhaps all this, the turn that the second essay takes, makes Derrida's essay itself a sort of "purloined letter," as Patočka mentions openly in his essay to mark and memorialize, Derrida observes, the presence of Heidegger in the essay, even though his name is markedly unmentioned. "This vision of being reduced by the entity has been presented in the work of a great contemporary thinker without credence having been given or attention paid to it" (cited in *GD*, 39).

Heidegger, "the great thinker" who is everywhere present in Patočka's essay and in his thought as a whole, goes unnamed, and unnamed in the most open and remarkable way, perhaps as a memorial gesture on Patočka's part to the fact that "this vision of being reduced by the entity" has gone without credence or attention, is in danger of becoming a dead letter, of its message being lost, the message about the relation of force to death, cloaked and hidden so artfully, encrypted for safekeeping by Heidegger in his discourse on Being, so as to keep it out in the open by virtue of its not being understood, most importantly as we have come to learn, by Heidegger himself. (Perhaps it is not a good idea to demythologize Heidegger altogether.) Perhaps here in this essay Derrida is doing to Patočka what Patočka did to Heidegger—burying him, for safekeeping, burying his death, burying Patočka's face-writing of death, the death written on his face, burying it out in the open of his writing on the relation of force and death, so as to keep its secret, the secret of substitution, the way in which the writer is present as a purloined letter by being hidden out in the open, by being kept as an open secret in this discourse on passing on, on death, on secrets.

In Derrida's essay "Beyond," this encryption of Patočka takes the form for Derrida of a reading with Patočka of technology and the culture of technology as "decadent," as a decaying of responsibility which opens up a passage for the return of the incorporated and repressed, the dead and buried force of demonic and orgiastic mystery in the specter of a cult of death. For Patočka, who in this is following Heidegger, such decadence is masked and dissimulated under the guise of a metaphysics of force, a simulacrum of Being as force, that holds sway by dissimulating force in its specifically technological effect: boredom, anesthesia. This is the symptom which Heidegger had diagnosed as the effect of the narcotic or *pharmakon* which technological society administers to self-medicate and inoculate itself against the anxiety which announces the apprehension of death, its own inevitable anticipation of death's inevitability. Heidegger, however, identifies this anxiety as the authentic call to conscience and the possibility of Dasein's taking possession of its own authentic existence as a whole, its own proper responsibility, in its self-identification as being-toward (or "in the face of") death.

Yet Derrida makes a point of noting that Patočka's relation to Heidegger in the essay is conspicuously not straightforward: "Heidegger is *alluded to* as though, for one reason or another he is not to be named, whereas others like Hannah Arendt are named, in the same context and to make a similar point" (*GD*, 38). Derrida further notes that Patočka employs formulations like "mythology" in referring to the metaphysics of force that Heidegger would never have used:

> Heidegger would never have said that metaphysical determinations of being or the history of the dissimulation of being in the figures or modes of the entity developed as *myths* or *fictions*. Such terms would be more Nietzschean than Heideggerean. And Heidegger would never have said that metaphysics as such was of itself "untrue" or "inauthentic." (*GD*, 38)

Yet Patočka does say this, Derrida notes, and the mention of Nietzsche in this context will prove significant later in the essay. And, in saying this, Patočka crosses Heidegger's discourse on the authentic dissimulation of being as a metaphysics of force with his own doubling of this image as an inauthentic dissimulation of genuine secrecy. On the one hand, Heidegger is everywhere present in Patočka's essay, memorialized as the one whose thought brings out into the open the necessity of dissimulation, "without credence having been given or attention paid to it" (*GD*, 39). Yet, on the other hand, Derrida interprets Patočka's gesture of leaving Heidegger unnamed by stating:

> However, if one holds to a logic of (inauthentic) dissimulation that dissimulates (authentic) dissimulation by means of the simple gesture of exposing it or exhibiting it, of seeing in order to see or having it seen in order to see (which is Heidegger's definition of "curiosity"), *then one has here an example of a logic of secrecy*. It is never better kept than in being exposed. Dissimulation is never better dissimulated than by means of this particular kind of dissimulation that consists in making a show of exposing it, unveiling it, laying it bare. *The mystery of being is dissimulated by this inauthentic dissimulation that consists of exposing being as a force, showing it behind its mask, behind its fiction or simulacrum.* (*GD*, 38–39; emphasis added)

For Patočka, Derrida implies, Heidegger himself, as well as his work, is hiding something, holding something back, trying to keep something secret precisely by revealing it, as if (authentic) dissimulation could be revealed as such by revealing it as "necessary," as if a revelation of the *necessity* for being to conceal itself, and by so doing excluding the question of responsibility from the *"Seinsfrage,"* the question of Being in its difference from beings *and* its difference from Dasein, trying to use difference to mask and dissimulate the separation of the question of responsibility from the question of Being. In this, Heidegger would seem to be what he so openly proclaimed himself *not* to be, to be a Greek, and at least in Patočka's sense, a Platonic Greek. Heidegger is following in the footsteps of the Plato from whom he so famously gestures his separation, the Plato whom Heidegger made a show of understanding better than he understood himself—the "he" is intentionally ambiguous here—making a show of understanding Plato better than he (Plato) understood himself, but in Patočka's implication better than he (Heidegger) understood himself, precisely in keeping from himself, keeping secret from himself the open Secret of Secrecy, that *there is* no secret.[3] Secrecy, then, is not a matter either of beings *or* of Being, but of Dasein, or more accurately, of Dasein or the soul, what Plato called the "soul," not in its separation or difference from the body or the name and face of personal identity and responsibility for personal identity, but precisely in the identity of responsibility. By substituting Being for the person and substituting necessity for responsibility, Heidegger remains a Greek despite his protestations of having taken a step back behind the history of metaphysics or even behind Nietzsche, for in identifying Nietzsche as the last metaphysician, here too he dissimulates dissimulation by revealing it as necessary rather than as a matter of personal responsibility—whatever that might mean.[4]

But this ambivalent and equivocal presence of Heidegger without a name is not itself the focus of either Patočka or Derrida's primary concern in their respective essays; rather it is symptomatic of that concern. Patočka's treatment of Heidegger passes over the dissimulation of dissimulation toward which it gestures, forgives it, we might say. Having memorialized it as a kind of death, it passes on to Heidegger's treatment of authenticity as the call to conscience that arises for Dasein's way of being-toward-death. Derrida emphasizes the importance for Patočka, as one element of his project of thinking the history of European responsibility, of a point of contact which Patočka sees between Christianity and Heidegger's thought. For Patočka, the Christian notion of the mysterium tremendum thought of precisely as gift, and a gift of self-forgetting love that has the trait of a mystery which has the last word, a mystery that is precisely a *law of love*, drawing into the closest proximity with Heidegger's concept of *Jemeinigkeit*, the absolute self-identity of Dasein, which it has in virtue of death as its "ownmost" possibility, the one possibility of which it can most authentically say "mine." Derrida comments:

In order to understand in what way this gift of the law means not only the emergence of a new figure of responsibility but also of another kind of death, one has to take into account the uniqueness and irreplaceable singularity of the self as the means by which—and it is here that it comes close to death— *existence excludes every possible substitution.* Now to have the experience of responsibility on the basis of the law that is given, that is to have the experience of one's absolute singularity and to apprehend one's own death, amounts to the same thing. Death is very much that which nobody else can undergo or confront in my place. My irreplaceability is therefore conferred, delivered, "given," one can say by death. It is the same gift, the same source one could say the same goodness and the same law. It is from the site of death as the place of my irreplaceability, that is of my singularity that I feel the call to responsibility. *In this sense only a mortal can be responsible.* (GD, 41; emphasis added)

*"Existence excludes every possible substitution."* This statement reverberates as initial impulse and lingering echo throughout the present discourse, as it does throughout *The Gift of Death,* particularly in its concern with the question of sacrifice, and the relation of the notion of sacrifice to that of the Gift of Death, and still for Derrida, beyond or rather before the Gift, to the question of Forgiveness, where, in this last stage of the present inquiry, the figure of Dante can already begin to be discerned as they make their way toward one another.

More immediately, however, Derrida turns to clarifying the sense in which, for Heidegger, the absolute singularity and irreplaceability that is Dasein's most original and fundamental responsibility is conferred by death. This amounts to clarifying what it means to give and take death. Heidegger proceeds from the assertion that, "No one can take the Other's dying away from him" (*Keiner kann dem Anderen sein Sterben abnehmen.* S.Z. 47, 240). This amounts to a clarification of both the possibility and impossibility of "dying for another," or, in other words, of sacrifice. One can never die for another absolutely in the sense of taking away the necessity for the other to die; one can never substitute one's own death for the death of the other except in some particular circumstance and only for a time. In other words, sacrifice is always derivative and partial in regard to the singularity and irreplaceability that death confers. In a similar sense, Heidegger says, "dying is something that every Dasein itself must take upon itself at the time" (*Das Sterben muss jedes Dasein jeweilig selbst auf sich nehmen,* ibid.). In other words, it is the interplay of this possibility and impossibility, the impossibility of this *abnehmen,* the taking away of the Other's death, and the possibility of this *aufnehmen,* the taking on oneself of one's own death, that simultaneously determines the ways in which death can and cannot be given. Derrida comments:

Because I cannot take death away from the other who can no more take it from me in return, it remains for everyone to take his own death *upon himself.* Everyone must assume his own death, that is to say, the one thing in the world that no one else can *either give or take:* therein resides freedom and responsibility. (*GD*, 44)

And he goes on to observe:

Thus dying can never be taken, borrowed, transferred, delivered, promised, or transmitted. And just as it can't be given to me, so it can't be taken away. Death would be this possibility of giving and taking [*donner-prendre*] that actually exempts itself from the same realm of possibility that it institutes, namely from *giving and taking*. But to say that is far from contradicting the fact that it is only on the basis of death, and in its name, that *giving* and *taking* become possible. (Ibid.)

It is important to note something that Derrida does not say, or at least not explicitly, not here: because Death is before the Gift, because the gift, like all giving and taking, comes from Death, death appears on the same site as forgiveness, which Derrida also says is "before the Gift." We shall have to return to this later.

Of course, for Derrida even if not so immediately as for Patočka, to raise this Heideggerian point is impossible without simultaneously recalling Levinas's objection to it: that it privileges my own death over that of the other, instead of recognizing that one comes to oneself as "responsible" and mortal from the position of my responsibility before the other, for the other's death and in the face of it. In the first place it is because the other is mortal that my responsibility is singular and unalienable (*GD*, 46).

But according to Derrida, Levinas reproaches Heidegger not only for reversing the logic of death and responsibility, but also for annihilating responsibility in death by his neglect of the *"adieu,"* the sense in which every *"adieu"* contains within itself an *"adieu"* that is "for God and before God and before anything else or any relation to the other. Every relation to the other would be, before and after anything else, an *adieu*" (*GD*, 47). This neglect of the *"adieu,"* Levinas would object, is ultimately a dereliction of responsibility on Heidegger's part because it portrays the death that Dasein takes on itself as a "passage into nonbeing," and as such inscribes the giving of death to oneself, this giving without gift, into the horizon of the *Seinsfrage*, from which Heidegger wishes to, or at least effectively does exclude the question of responsibility. Levinas concludes, "the relation to death, more ancient than any other experience, is neither vision of being nor of nothingness" (*La Mort et le temps*, 25).

But at this point Derrida observes that Patočka is close to both Heidegger and Levinas regarding the nexus between death and responsibility, yet differs from each of them (*GD*, 48). This leads to the decisive point of the essay, that is, Derrida's assertion that in Patočka, "we find all the same elements of agreement and disagreement [between Heidegger and Levinas concerning death and responsibility] but in an overdetermined form, and thus

radically transformed by his reference to a network of themes in Christianity"
(*GD*, 48). This network of themes comprises "the gift as Gift of Death, the
fathomless gift of a type of death: infinite love (the Good as goodness that
infinitely forgets itself), sin and salvation, repentance and sacrifice" (*GD*, 49).
In the transformative matrix of Patočka's discourse these themes emerge as
what Derrida refers to as the proposal of "a nondogmatic doublet of dogma,
a philosophical and metaphysical doublet, in any case a *thinking* that 'repeats'
*the possibility of religion without religion*" (*GD*, 49). As a thinking, this "doubling" of dogma proceeds by a logic which engenders and organically inter-
relates the themes of Christianity "internally and necessarily," independent of
the "need of *the event of a revelation or the revelation of an event.*" Such a logic,
Derrida contends:

> . . . needs to think the possibility of such an event but not the event itself.
> This is a major point of difference, permitting such a discourse to be devel-
> oped without reference to religion as institutional dogma, and proposing a
> genealogy of thinking concerning the possibility and essence of the religious
> that doesn't amount to an article of faith. (*GD*, 49)

Applying this figure of thinking to Patočka's essay and its relation to
Christianity ("Christian text or not, Patočka as Christian thinker or not")
Derrida asserts that such issues are beside the point for at least two important
reasons. First, if Patočka is taken as Christian, then his Christianity, by his own
admission and urgent assertion, is in an important sense "heretical" because it
occupies itself with the ways in which Christianity has not yet become fully
responsible for itself, has not yet thought through what it should have been or
should be. Second, if Patočka and his essay are taken to be something other
than Christian in a strictly traditional or orthodox sense (because the thinking
there does not take faith in revelation as its enabling condition), nevertheless
that thinking proceeds from a history, the history of European responsibility
and of responsibility as Europe, which is inseparable in its occurrence from its
passage through "a certain history of Christianity (and who could say otherwise?)" (*GD*, 49). Derrida concludes:

> There is no choice to be made here between a logical production, or one
> that is not related to the event, and the reference to a revelatory event. One
> implies the other. And it is not simply as a believer or as a Christian affirm-
> ing dogma, the revelation and the event, that Patočka makes the declaration
> already he referred to, as would a genealogist historian stating what point
> history has arrived at:
>     Because of its foundation within the abysmal profundity of the soul,
> Christianity represents to this day the most powerful means—never yet
> superseded but not yet thought right through either—by which man is able
> to struggle against his own decline. (117) (*GD*, 50)

Derrida thus situates Patočka's thought in a type of genealogical history that he says includes others like Levinas and Marion, perhaps Ricoeur also, and which might well be thought of as extending back without any clear limit, allowance being made for certain differences, to include "a certain Kant and a certain Hegel, Kierkegaard of course and I might even dare to say for provocative effect, Heidegger also" (*GD,* 49).

Two "conclusions" follow here as memorials. First, although he fails to mention it, is not Derrida's own name, perhaps preeminently, to be included in this tradition of thinkers "of a philosophical type" who propose a "non-dogmatic doublet of dogma, a philosophical and metaphysical [or at least quasi-transcendental] doublet, in any case a thinking that 'repeats' the possibility of religion without religion"? Was this not the entire burden of Caputo's *The Prayers and Tears of Jacques Derrida?* Second, this identification of a certain type of thinking, a certain type of philosophical thinking, which concerns itself with displaying the inner logical necessity of a possibility, in this case the possibility of a history of responsibility together with a history of European responsibility, of a history of "Europe-responsibility," a history that is genuinely both political and religious: Is this not a possibility which, as we have seen here, has in fact already occurred? This history that is revealed in and through and as its occurrence is a history which, because it is history, has neither finished occurring nor will ever finish occurring, despite the finality of its every occurrence. Has not this identification of a type of philosophical thinking and the preeminent inclusion of Derrida's name among its historical proponents been the basis for the suggestion that has guided this study throughout, the suggestion made initially in the rhetorical form of the question, Might not Derrida serve as a contemporary Virgil to guide our own reading today of Dante's *Commedia?* Derrida's style of thinking as practiced in works like *Circumfession, The Gift of Death, Memoirs of the Blind,* "To Forgive," and others *reveals* the possibility of a religion of messianic faith, hope, and love without the dogmatic fixity of any of the historical messianisms, where that fixity of dogma follows from the impulse to "teach," the impulse to evangelize, to universalize, to "go out and preach the good news to all nations," to announce with the authority of history itself what is believed to have occurred and so to have been revealed?

But of course this suggestion could be coherent only if one reads Dante's *Commedia,* in this time and place, as being itself a type of writing, a poem if not a poetics, which yields a nondogmatic poetic doublet of Christian dogma; reads it as a poem concerning which, as Derrida asserts concerning Patočka and his text, the question of whether both text and author are or are not genuinely Christian, in the end, astoundingly, must be acknowledged to be not really pertinent. For on the one hand, how can the poem be considered Christian when it blatantly and resolutely refuses to mention the name of God except by way of the circumlocutions of power and love? When it everywhere withholds as much as it can both the name and the figure of Jesus, concealing the name of the Son in the name of the mother, and encrypting the figure of

the Messiah in the figure of Beatrice or in a point of pure light? When it withholds the vision of identity even in the end when the symbol of the Trinity, the
sign of every possibility of all difference in all relation, of all revelation and all
dogma, itself dissolves into "our effigy," the human figure, the figure which forgets itself so absolutely that it remains absolutely before every name, including
that of God, of Jesus, of Mary, of Beatrice and even of Dante, who remembers
of the vision he glimpsed only "that love which moves the sun and all the
other stars?" When at its conclusion he finds himself again *nel mezzo,* at the
center of his life, at the center of history, which is absolutely final in its mortal
responsibility while at the same time is always beginning again in response to
the call of constant conversion which is inscribed in the heart by the impossible need and desire of the Other, the need and desire toward which the name
of God directs and points, always passing on and always passing over itself,
always deferring to Death, so that the very name of God becomes the way, the
*via diritta,* the path that does not stray, but passes directly on to Death, which
alone for-gives all the gifts of God and even for-gives the name of God? If
anything is apparent in the *Commedia*, it is that *it is not a Christian poem* in
that it holds back and keeps secret the name which saves, or it saves the name
from which creation and salvation arrive. It postpones and defers in every possible way the arrival of the name of the Messiah, the Messiah in whose name
faith and hope and love have occurred and whose name constantly calls all the
living to begin again to take responsibility upon themselves, take it from/in
the face of the Other, the Other who for Dante bears the name and the face of
Beatrice, and perhaps of another, whose name and face is forgotten. So that, in
the end, must we not conclude that Dante is no more Christian than Derrida;
Derrida no less Christian than Dante?

Yet, on the other hand, how could such a poem and its author be anything other than Christian when the exigency of its own poetic identity, from
beginning to end and beginning again, everywhere follows the unique pattern
of events that is revealed in and as the history of Christianity, in its dogma, in
its spirituality, in its personalities and in their witness and in its tradition of
reception and transmission of that witness, and above all in its absolute adher-
ence to forgiveness as the Gift of Death revealed in the event of the Resurrection of Jesus, an event which is not historical, but which, just as does Death for
Derrida, institutes absolutely every possibility of giving and taking while yet
itself remaining exempt from any exchange? In this way, the Resurrection constitutes for Christian faith a new creation, a new kind of history which remains
continuous with the original creation and its history of sin, yet differs from it,
begins again and always begins again a new history, a new way of giving and
taking Death as a Gift, the history of an infinite love which gives and takes
Death as the Gift of Forgiveness. The *Commedia* as a poem and in its poetics
is absolutely Christian insofar as it faithfully "doubles" the Christian teaching
of the Resurrection of Jesus as the revelation of the forgiveness of sins and
the beginning of a new history of responsibility, the history of responsibility

as forgiveness, as the impossible gift of an Impossible Love which has actually occurred in and as the historical death of Jesus, at whose name "every knee
must bend in heaven or on the earth."

So with Derrida as our Virgil, it must be said here and now that the question that would seem to separate Derrida's philosophical thinking of religion
without religion from Dante's medieval Christian allegorical poem in the
form of a romantic comedy of sin and salvation, the question of whether the
former's thinking is or is not its own peculiar messianism, heretical from the
perspective of any traditional messianism, or whether the latter's poem is or is
not Christian, more or less heretical depending on the reading, of this question
and of all others that take the same structural form, it must be said finally that
they are not genuinely pertinent. Yet this in no way contradicts the affirmation that these texts are different, that in their "doubling" of a certain history
of responsibility and a certain history of religion, the discourses they sustain
are uniquely and singularly their own. While the "doubling" that each does
faithfully replicates in its own style of writing a pattern of events as personal
history and a pattern of choices as personal responsibility, because those discourses are of different times, and because they are uniquely and singularly
timely, because they give themselves responsively and responsibly to their own
time and place, their occurrence is genuinely singular. Each is an event that
occurs "in an instant," such that the responsibility for it is unique and absolute,
impossible to share, necessary to keep in secret by testifying and bearing witness to it as an event of personal responsibility that both promises and calls
for *constant conversion to forgiveness* as the impossible truth of all existence, all
history, all faith, all responsibility, all religion, all hope, and all love. Each, in
the singular instant of existence and history, testifies to the possibility of conversion to forgiveness, which is before every Gift, before every history, every
name and every identity. Both testify to the necessity to save the name of God
from every fixed determination that dissimulates the finality of history as the
completion of history, and dissimulates mortal responsibility as a sacrificial
death which, in dispensing justice, dispenses with justice and substitutes for
it an incredible dissimulation of forgiveness as mercy. This would seem to be
the import of Derrida's concluding gambit in *The Gift of Death*, where, in the
end, finally, he invokes the voice of Nietzsche to keep the question of a genuinely impossible faith and a genuinely impossible forgiveness alive by calling
for a conversion of religious responsibility from the risk of becoming fixed
in a partialized and partializing economy of justice dispensed as mercy that
institutionalizes and enshrines itself through the finality of violence exercised
as sacrifice. Derrida says:

> In questioning a certain concept of repression *(Zurückschreibung)* that mor-
> alizes the mechanism of debt in moral duty and in bad conscience, in con-
> science as guilt, one might develop further the hyperbolization of such a
> repression (by bringing it to bear upon what Patočka says about Christian

repression). This sacrificial *hubris* is what Nietzsche calls the "stroke of genius called Christianity." It is what takes this economy to its excess in the sacrifice of Christ for love of the debtor; it involves the same economy of sacrifice; the same sacrifice of sacrifice. (*GD*, 114)

The repression that Patočka identifies with Christianity and that Derrida wishes to "hyperbolize" further, presumably in the hope of lifting that repression at least to the point where it can be responsibly thought, so opening up the possibility of beginning again to answer the call and respond to the religious promise of constant conversion, is the repression Derrida has shown to be operative in the violence of substituting the "wages" (*merces*) that the Father "who sees in secret," in this case in the darkness of the encrypted secret buried in the tomb of the dissimulation of the Gift of Death figured as sacrifice. The violence of this repression, which itself reveals the continued presence of the demonic and orgiastic impulse toward fusion in Christianity, could here be characterized as the mystagogical impulse to substitute an absolutized forgetfulness (the Good as goodness which forgets itself, "infinite love") for the Impossibility of authentic forgiveness—whatever that might mean. For Derrida, Nietzsche's unfailing nose, like a dog sniffing about in the graveyard, has caught the sense of this decadent dissimulation of death that lies buried within the whitened sepulcher of Christianity's guilty secret. According to Nietzsche's reading, Christianity cannot acquit itself of the violence that is historically inscribed in the economy of a mercy that is predicated on sacrifice. Mercy offered on the condition of a redemption purchased at the price of a sacrifice death must mask its secret guilty truth. What Christianity calls "Grace," the Gift of an infinite love, Nietzsche calls "this self-destruction of Justice." Derrida quotes Nietzsche to characterize this "properly Christian moment":

> The justice which began with the maxim, "Everything can be paid off, everything must be paid off," ends with connivance (*durch die Finger zu sehn*) at the escape of those who cannot pay to escape—it ends, like every good thing on earth, by *destroying itself* [what is translated as "destroying itself" is literally *sich selbst aufhebend*—and Nietzsche adds the emphasis: by "raising itself or by substituting for itself," Christian justice denies itself and so conserves itself in what seems to exceed it; it remains what it ceases to be, a cruel economy, a commerce, a contract involving debt and credit, sacrifice, and vengeance]. The self-destruction of Justice (*Diese Selbstaufhebung der Gerichtigkeit*)! We know the pretty name it calls itself—Grace *(Gnade)*! It remains, as is obvious, the privilege (*Vorrecht*) of the strongest, better still, their super-law (*seins Jenseits des Rechts*). (*GD*, 114)

Here, without saying so, Derrida follows Nietzsche to the scene of forgiveness, to the question of forgiveness as the question of the Impossible:

> . . . that paradoxical and awful expedient, through which a tortured humanity has found a temporary alleviation, that stroke of genius called *Christianity*:—

God personally immolating himself for the debt of man, God paying himself personally out of the pound of his own flesh, God as the one being who can deliver man from what for man had become unacquitable (*unablosbar*)—the creditor (*der Glaubiger*) plays scapegoat for his debtor (*seiner Schulderer*), from love (can you believe it? [*sollte man's glauben?*]) from love of his debtor! . . . (*GD*, 114)

Can you believe it? Echoing Nietzsche, Derrida concludes *The Gift of Death* by asking, "how can one believe this history of credence or credit?" This apparently rhetorical question, the "specter of his discourse," disturbs Nietzsche's posing of it by haunting him as well as Christianity:

As often happens, the call of or for the question, and the request that echoes through it, takes us further than the response. The question, the request and the appeal *must*, indeed, have begun, since the eve of their awakening, by receiving accreditation from the other: by being believed. Nietzsche must indeed believe he knows what believing means, unless he means it is all make-believe [*à moins qu'il n'intendele faire accroire*]. (*GD*, 115)

Derrida doubles Nietzsche's crossing of the question of Christian belief with the question Derrida hears preserved in Nietzsche's "can you believe it?" However great the distance Nietzsche wishes to put between himself and the morality of sacrifice as the history of Christendom, Derrida implies that Nietzsche's discourse cannot altogether escape becoming implicated in the event of the question of belief coming to life again, being raised up again by the power of responsibility by which questioning itself always already belongs to the Other, gives credit and credence to the Other, unless one believes that it is all "make-believe"—which, of course, Nietzsche clearly and vehemently does not—or so it would seem. Derrida here places Nietzsche, in all justice, in exactly the place where he will find himself shortly enough, perhaps already finds himself or at least will refind himself at the conclusion of *Memoirs of the Blind*, when he is asked by the feminine specter of his discourse there, regarding the testimony of Andrew Marvell's poem, "Eyes and Tears":

—Tears that see . . . do you believe?
—I don't know, one has to believe. . . .

Here the discourses on faith, on responsibility, on death, and on forgiveness all cross back on themselves and on one another, figuring forth the open secret in which all share, all persons human and divine, all who are free, all who lay claim to saying "mine" and to saying "our," all who share the open secret of the necessity, the responsibility, the guilt, and the promise of belief.

Here at this crossing Derrida rejoins Dante, *nel mezzo*, at the center, at the beginning which is the end, just that end that must begin again anew, and again and again, that end that is final because it is without end in beginning again. Derrida rejoins Dante at the scene of forgiveness that Dante calls

Resurrection and Derrida calls the Gift of Death. For both it is a scene set in writing. For both, writing appears as the trace of Forgiveness, for what must always have already begun and what must always begin again differently: forgiveness as the promise of writing, the promise destined always to be broken and which therefore must always be kept, must be kept by being written in the flesh and in the blood, written in the heart, where the flesh and the blood keep the secret of their intercourse. There flesh and blood keep the empty secret in the empty tomb of hearts that have been broken, broken by Death, broken open and broken apart by Death, flesh and blood broken and opened, disseminated and distributed, given in writing as Gift, given as food, food for the eyes, eaten with the eyes, eyes blind with tears, tears of joy and tears of sorrow, eyes of faith in which the Gift reveals itself, tears tracing the course of the revelation, tracing the history of the Gift revealed in the scripture of the face, the face-writing that is from the Other, fed through the eyes, written in the face, on the face, as the face; the Gift that is from the Other, the Gift of Death given as food eaten through the eyes, written on the face, written in light of the Other, written on the face that I call mine, written over the signature, the only signature that is mine: the text of the eyes written on the face, the text that is from the Other, written above the signature that I call mine. "I saw faces all given to love, adorned by the Light of Another, and by their own smile" (*Par.*, xxxi, 49–50).

# Notes

## INTRODUCTION

1. Of course, it still remains to be asked, "Who then is the mother of faith?" This question points in the direction of what shall prove to be a central element in the relationship of Dante and Derrida.

2. The full context of the citation is: "Such is the secret truth of faith as absolute responsibility and absolute passion, the 'highest passion' as Kierkegaard will say; it is a passion that, sworn to secrecy, cannot be transmitted from generation to generation. In this sense it has no history. This untransmissibility of the highest passion, the normal condition of a faith which is thus bound to secrecy, nevertheless dictates to us the following: we must always start over."

3. John Caputo, *The Prayers and Tears of Jacques Derrida* (Bloomington: Indiana University Press, 1997).

4. Although the literature on Dante and Derrida is regrettably limited, the significance of their relationship has been recognized and explored. I wish to acknowledge here my important debt and warm gratitude to Jeremy Tambling, who has already explored this relationship with great insight and imagination, though from a perspective and with a focus quite different from the present study. In his book, *Dante and Difference* (Cambridge: Cambridge University Press, 1988), Tambling has carefully traced the variety of ways in which the style of writing in Dante's texts, and in particular, in the *Commedia*, resist closure on any single unifying and integrating principle of identity. Tambling says, "Why Difference? A straightforward answer would be that my arguments in this book are focused on those elements of Dante's *Commedia* that break down the formal schema of the poem, and that by their capacity to differ both from themselves and from other parts of the poem effectively deconstruct the author's enterprise" (p. 1).

Tambling's convincing deployment of the evidence for a "differential" style of writing as a central element of Dante's poetics constitutes a necessary supplement to the focus of the present study. For one thing, Tambling's book, published in 1988, draws on Derrida's work prior to the writing of *Circumfession*, with which this study's engagement with Derrida begins, at least in a formal sense. More important, however, I am concerned here to ask specifically about the possible relation in the texts of Dante and Derrida between such a differential style of writing and the possibility of identifying a fundamentally religious level of human existence within which those texts are inscribed.

In addition to Tambling's, other works that make noteworthy contributions are Phillipe Sollers, *Le Divine Comedie: Entretiens avec Benoit Chantre* (Paris: DDB, 2000), and John Leavey, "Derrida and Dante: Difference and the Eagle in the sphere of Jupiter," MLN 91/1 (1976): 60–68.

Finally, I wish to draw attention to and express my appreciation for the work of William Franke, whose excellent study, *Dante's Interpretive Journey* (University of Chicago Press, 1996), I admire and from which I have greatly benefited. See also his essay, "Dante's Address to the Reader *en face* Derrida's Critique of Ontology," *Annalecta Husserlianna,* LXIX (2000): 119–131.

## CHAPTER ONE

1. At play in the juxtaposition of Neruda's experience of "being taken" by poetry with Dante's account of a similar experience in *Vita nuova* is Neruda's explicit portrayal of receiving a "vocation" without the medium of a voice. Although Dante would probably not have formulated the issue in these terms, there is in *Vita nuova* an inescapable critique of that valorization of presence and of the priority of speech to writing that Derrida identifies as the essence of logocentrism.

2. *La Vita nuova,* Dante Alighieri; Translated by Barbara Reynolds (London: Penguin Books, 1969), p. 29.

3. Robert Hollander, in his exceptionally helpful synoptic study of the relation of Dante's life to his art, *Dante: A Life in Works* (New Haven and London: Yale University Press, 2001), pp. 13–14, observes, "*Vita nuova* is, in anybody's estimation, a difficult and puzzling work. One of its students has well described it in the title of an essay, "Dante's *Vita nuova* as Riddle." It is also the first reliable evidence we have of Dante's genius. First and foremost, it has no precise or certain model in Western literature. . . . The *Vita nuova* is, as one can rarely say with such certainty, unique. Nothing in the tradition of Dante's Romance predecessors, or indeed of any precursors, serves as a sufficient model. One can only imagine the concern, even trepidation, with which the young poet assumed the office of *lector* of his own literary production. The practice was literally unheard of."

4. I am happy to acknowledge my debt to Hollander for making clear the three stages of structural development in *Vita nuova,* and the relation of the various visions of Beatrice to that development. The particular reading of this development as a process of religious conversion offered here is, however, my own.

5. The *donna gentile,* who appears for the first time in xxxv, is unidentified except for Dante's description of her: "Becoming aware of my condition, I raised my eyes to see if anyone noticed it; and then I saw a gracious lady, young and very beautiful, who was looking at me from a window so compassionately, as it seemed from her appearance, that all pity seemed to be gathered there in her." It has been argued, based on certain comments by Dante himself in *Convivio,* that this figure is a purely allegorical representation of "Lady Philosophy" to whom Dante says, perhaps with Boethius in mind, he turned for consolation in his sorrow and confusion over the loss of Beatrice. It is difficult, however, on the grounds of a variety of textual evidence to view the "window lady" as anything other a person of quite solid flesh and blood. Dante never suggests of her anything other than "noble" intentions or behavior, but describes his own reaction to her as "vile." This episode and its multiple significances are discussed by Hollander, pp. 23–24; I am following his view.

6. See Hollander, pp. 14–15.

7. He had lost her to "death" three times already: to the death of her marriage to another, the death of physical demise shortly thereafter, and, finally, the death of

his connection to her through the promise of writing when he seeks the consolations offered by the "window lady," and whoever or whatever others, substitutes all, of which she accuses him in their confrontation in the Earthly Paradise.

8. Robert Pogue Harrison has written an insightful and original interpretation of *Vita nuova*, entitled, *The Body of Beatrice* (Baltimore and London: Johns Hopkins University Press, 1988), which follows a line of interpretation, especially regarding the first dream, close to the one I offer here. In the end, he finds a different, explicitly Heideggerian, way of developing the significance of his identification of the physical body of Beatrice as the central reality of *Vita nuova* than the direction taken in this study. I believe the two are fully complementary and am grateful to Harrison for the stimulus I found in his work.

9. There is inscribed here the confluence and confusion of two images, two traditions: on the one hand, "incarnation," the emptying that keeps the secret of divine power, and on the other, the impregnation of a human by a god, divine rape, which buries the seed of immortality in the empty tomb of the womb.

10. The notion of the "an-economical," is a thematic which Derrida relies on, along with others like "excess" and "impossibility" to suggest a type of meaning structure that cannot be confined within the limits of a closed system. Literally, it evokes that which does not conform to the "rule" or "law" of the household, and therefore is "unfamiliar," that with which one does find oneself "at home."

11. As Hollander makes clear (pp. 19–20), the use of *salute* as Beatrice's first word spoken to Dante, must be given the full theological weight that the poet clearly intends. The word by which she announces her advent in face to face encounter with him is not simply a greeting or a good wish; like the word of God—which for Dante it is—it effects what it says; it is "salvation." She is here, as she will be again in *Purgatorio*, xxx, God's saving Word in the flesh.

12. See Ricardo J. Quinones, *Foundation Sacrifice in Dante's* Commedia (University Park: The Pennsylvania State University Press, 1994), for an enlightening and suggestive discussion of the intricate and intimate intertwining of sacrifice with every form of human beginning.

13. See, for example, Octavio Paz, *The Double Flame,* trans. Helen Lane (New York: Harcourt Brace and Co., 1995).

14. According to a very longstanding tradition, Dante is supposed to have spent a short period of time in the Franciscan Order as a novice. More certain, especially on the basis of both direct and indirect textual evidence in the *Commedia,* is that Dante's spirituality closely follows the pattern of St. Francis's spiritual journey, not least in the primacy given to a beloved "heavenly Lady," in each conversion story.

15. It is important to note here the direct parallel with *Inferno*, ii, where Dante explicitly recognizes the full context and significance of what he fails to see here as the true reason Beatrice deserves the praise he wishes to give even without fully understanding her worth.

16. Again, the parallels with the *Commedia* are striking, making clearer how directly the two works are linked in the process of Dante's conversion. What is imagined here of Beatrice is reimagined almost twenty years later revealed in its fullest significance as relating even more truthfully to the Virgin Mary: that she is desired in highest heaven

to complete what is lacking in the realm of the divine. This image of conversion will be examined in chapter 4, "Dante's Portrait Gallery."

17. Another significant parallel with the *Commedia* is noticeable in the words, "Whoever speaks of her and sheds no tears, His heart is stone, so evil and so base." These words carry us directly to the Ugolino episode in *Inferno*, xxxiii, where, as shall be seen, Dante's conversion reaches its turning point precisely when he recognizes himself in Ugolino.

18. In "Secrets of European Responsibility," Derrida discusses the way in which the Latin "secretum" (from *secernere*), separate, distinct, discerned is related to the Platonic conception of soul as arising through a process of separation from the body, and thus how the soul necessarily is related to secrecy (*GD*, 13); this sense of *"secretum"* derives from the Greek *krinein*, to separate, divide, to judge, all suggesting the sense of the act by which one reality is cut off from another, for example as in sacrifice.

19. See Plato, *Phaedrus*, 245a–257c, for the famous allegory of the tripartite soul as a chariot whose charioteer must control the reins of two very different steeds and so guide the chariot through its proper realm of the divine from which it has been cut off. The image makes vivid the sense of restraint moving toward repression that Patočka is describing.

## CHAPTER TWO

1. In the Introduction to his important study of Dante's sense of history, *Dante, Poet of the Desert: History and Allegory in the* Divine Comedy (Princeton: Princeton University Press, 1979), Giuseppe Mazzotta argues that the desert is a metaphor for both history and text. The desert is the place of exile both as wandering in political exile and journeying in spiritual exile toward the promised land and the new Jerusalem.

2. Derrida frequently uses the locution "God-or death," especially in *Circumfession* and *The Gift of Death*, to recall the necessary ambiguity in our use of both these words to locate the one field of meaning which first and finally identifies both the possibility and impossibility of human responsiveness and responsibility, that is, faith.

3. The irrational number represented by the Greek letter "pi." The significance of the undecidable but decisive relationship that this number represents figures centrally in the "final vision" with which the poem concludes.

4. In the remarkable commentary that accompanies her translation of the *Commedia*, Dorothy Sayers consistently refers to Beatrice as Dante's "god-bearing image"; Georgette seems to play that role for Derrida, as St. Monica did for St. Augustine.

5. A parallel is being suggested in what follows between two "places," Dante's Inferno and Derrida's "Khora." The basic Derridean text on this topic is Khora (Paris: Galilee, 1993); English translation by Ian McLeod in *On the Name*, ed. Thomas Dutoit (Stanford: Stanford University Press, 1995). For discussion of Khora in the present context of its potential significance for understanding Derrida's "religion without religion," cf. Caputo, *PTJD*, pp. 35–40, and also "Khora: Being Serious with Plato," chapter 4 in Caputo, *Deconstuction in a Nutshell* (New York: Fordham University Press, 1997).

6. There is yet another wolf story virtually present in this text, drawing on the intimate proximity in Dante's imagination of Saint Francis of Assisi, who famously played a role quite similar to Virgil's here in converting a ravenous and murderous

wolf into "Brother Wolf," thereby uniting in one figure the two dynamics of the lupine energy discussed here. The perdurance of this opposition in tension in the gothic figure of the werewolf, alternatively human and bestial is further testimony to the elemental importance of this turning point in Dante's conversion story.

7. For a succinct treatment of the "problem of Virgil" for readers of the *Commedia*, and an intelligent way of responding to it, see M. M. Chiarenza, *The Divine Comedy: Tracing God's Art* (Boston: Twayne, 1989), 24–26.

8. We shall return to consider the second essay in the final chapter of this study.

9. In *PTJD*, Caputo characterizes Derrida's notion of quasi-transcendentals as follows:

> In order to see how deconstruction is deeply affirmative, how it loves the name of God, we must first clarify that there is thus something importantly, if provisionally, "neutral" about *différance*. The quasi-transcendental work of *différance* is to establish the conditions which make possible our beliefs and our practices, our traditions and our institutions, *and* no less to make them impossible, which means to see to it that they do not effect closure, to keep them open so that something new or different may happen.
>
> A transcendental condition is a sufficient and enabling condition; a quasi-transcendental condition is insufficient and equi-disabling, seeing that the effect that it makes possible is also made unstable. . . .
>
> Transcendental conditions nail things down, pin them in place, inscribe them firmly within rigorously demarcated horizons; quasi-transcendental conditions allow them to slip loose, to twist free form their surrounding horizons, to leak and run off to exceed or overflow their margins. The problem in a transcendental philosophy is how to establish communication across the borders; the problem in a quasi-transcendental philosophy is how to keep things from running into each other and contaminating everything. But a quasi-transcendental condition is a condition of or for entities, not an entity itself; a condition under which things appear, but too poor and impoverished, too unkingly, to dictate what there is or what there is not, lacking the power to bring what is not into being, lacking the authority to prohibit something from being. (*PTJD*, 12–13)

10. This conversion, though an emphatic change of inflection in Derrida's writing, is nevertheless prepared for and implied in his earlier writing. The difference is that here it becomes his immediate and focal concern. It should be noted that this "turning" is in one sense simply a consequence, though perhaps a surprising one on first inspection, of the quasi-transcendental character of *différance*, turning on itself as it were, as it must, deconstructing itself in the text and context of Derrida's writing. A certain kinship is to be noted here with Heidegger's notion of finite transcendence in *Sein und Zeit*, and an even more important affinity for the current study, a genetic relation to Dante's use of *"nel mezzo"* to situate the time-space of the pilgrim's journey.

11. In a note to this text, Derrida refers his reader to *Glas*, p. 190, where he writes, "The 'eternal irony' of the woman will never let itself be reached behind the absolute entrenchment of this already, which is further back than the origin, older than birth, and attends death."

12. Although some scholars have disputed its authenticity, the basic starting point for any discussion of the "allegorical" style of the *Commedia* is the explanation by its author to his greatest patron and protector, Can Grande della Scala:

> To elucidate, then, what we have to say, be it known that the sense of this work is not simple, but on the contrary it may be called polysemous, that is to say, "of more senses than one"; for it is one sense that we get through the letter, and another which we get through the thing the letter signifies; and the first is called literal, but the second allegorical or mystic. And this mode of treatment, for its better manifestation, may be considered in this verse: "When Israel came out of Egypt, and the house of Jacob from a people of strange speech, Judaea became his sanctification, Israel his power." For if we inspect the letter alone, the departure of the children of Israel from Egypt in the time of Moses is presented to us; if the allegory, our redemption wrought by Christ; if the moral sense, the conversion of the soul from the grief and misery of sin to the state of grace is presented to us; if the anagogical, the departure of the holy soul from the slavery of this corruption to the liberty of eternal glory is presented to us. And although these mystic senses have each their special denominations, they may all in general be called allegorical, since they differ from the literal and historical. Now allegory is so called from "alleon" in Greek, which means in Latin "alienum" or "diversum."
>
> When we understand this we see clearly that the subject round which the alternative senses play must be twofold. And we must therefore consider the subject of this work as literally understood, and then its subject as allegorically intended. The subject of the whole work, then, taken in the literal sense only is "the state of souls after death" without qualification, for the whole progress of the work hinges on it and about it. Whereas if the work be taken allegorically, the subject is "man as by good or ill deserts, in the exercise of the freedom of his choice, he becomes liable to rewarding or punishing justice." (Letter to Can Grande della Scala, translated by Singleton in his essay, "Two Kinds of Allegory," published as Appendix in Charles Singleton, *Commedia: Elements of Structure* [Cambridge: Harvard University Press, 1954].)

13. The irony of Virgil's situation in the poem poses a crucial question to which any interpretive approach must face up. The stakes are doubled here by having proposed to take Derrida as "our Virgil." Although it must await further development, it can be said at this point that Virgil's situation, together with that of all his companions, the "virtuous pagans" of Limbo in Canto iv, who are "in suspension," is one of the strongest bonds of affinity he shares with Derrida, for whom to be "in suspense" is the necessary condition of the "sign" as such, and therefore of all writing, as well as of all who entrust themselves to writing, and especially to other writers, as Dante does here. What the implication of all this is for another aspect of Dante's relation to Virgil and its possible relation to Derrida, Virgil's exclusion from the Earthly Paradise and his return to Limbo in favor of Beatrice as Dante's "necessary other" shall prove to be one of the major burdens of present argument.

14. It is worth noting that in Francesca's recounting of the text they read, it is the man, Lancelot, who is the actor. Her assumption of the active role as narrator mirrors Dante's recognition of his initiative in scripting Beatrice's role in the *Vita nuova*.

15. For a discussion of this idea, see chapter 4, "Dante's Portrait Gallery."

16. The reading of the Ugolino episode here closely follows that proposed by the John Freccero in his important essay on the topic, "Bestial Sign and the Bread of Angels: *Inferno* xxxii and xxxiii," contained in *Dante: The Poetics of Conversion* (Cambridge: Havard University Press, 1988), pp. 152–166.

17. Here I am again following Freccero, this time in "The Sign of Satan," and "Infernal Inversion and Christian Conversion," both in *Dante: The Poetics of Conversion.*

18. I take this to be close to what Derrida means by *différance*, the necessity of difference, the necessity of the Other and all the others.

## CHAPTER THREE

1. See *PTJD,* pp. 212–215.

2. Charles Baudelaire, "The Pagan School," in *Baudelaire as Literary Critic,* Lois Boe Hyslop and Francis E. Hyslop, Jr., eds. and trans. (University Park: Pennsylvania State University Press, 1964).

3. It should noted that similar dynamic is at work in Kierkegaard with the notion of the "teleological suspension of the ethical," and even more significantly for this study, in the *Inferno.* For Dante, "damnation" is not a moral concept. It is "hyper-moral" because it moves solely within the an-economy of forgiveness.

4. For an informative and suggestive history of the evolution of the notion of Purgatory as both a theological and cultural category, see Jacques LeGoff, *The Birth of Purgatory* (Chicago: University of Chicago Press, 1984).

5. Jacques Derrida, "To Forgive: The Unforgivable and the Imprescriptible," in *Questioning God,* eds. John D. Caputo, Mark Dooley, and Michael J. Scanlon (Bloomington: Indiana University Press, 2001); pp. 21–51.

6. Derrida cites the following bibliographic information on Jankélévitch's writings in a note (#2) for *"TF,"* p. 50: Vladimir Jankélévitch, *Le Pardon* (Paris: Aubier-Montaigne, 1967). See also the little book that was published shortly after Jankélévitch's death under the title *L'imprescriptible: Pardonner? Dans l'honneur et la dignite* (Paris: Seuil, 1986), which brings together essays and talks from 1948, 1956, and 1971. The following information is appended in the note by the editors of *Questioning God: Le Pardon* is also available in Valdimir Jankélévitch, *Philosophie Morale,* ed. Francoise Schwab (Paris: Flammarion, 1998), pp. 991–1149. The articles "Should We Pardon Them?" and "Do Not Listen to What They Say, Look At What They Do" are translated by Ann Hobart in *Critical Inquiry* 22 (Spring 1996): 549–572, which also contains brief "Introductory Remarks" by Arnold Davidson (545–548). There is also a translation "Irony: A French Approach" in *The Sewanee Review Quarterly* 47 (1939). See also Emmanuel Levinas, *Outside the Subject,* trans. Michael B. Smith (Stanford: Stanford University Press, 1993), especially "Vladimir Jankélévitch," pp. 84–89. All of these articles use the spelling of his name with a *J* rather than a *Y.*

7. "On Forgiveness: A Roundtable Discussion with Jacques Derrida," in *Questioning God,* op. cit., pp. 52–72. This quotation is from p. 62.

## CHAPTER FOUR

1. John Caputo, "Response to Ambrosio," in *Styles of Piety,* eds. S. Clark Buckner and Matthew Statler (New York: Fordham University Press, 2006). I undertook

an initial exploration of the present subject matter in an essay included in that volume under the title, "Dante and Derrida: The Promise of Writing and the Piety of Broken Promises." I benefited from Caputo's responses to that essay and have tried to address them in this chapter.

2. Again, it is the merit of Quinones' book, *Foundation Sacrifice*, to have explored the interrelations of the economy of sacrifice, fratricide, and the establishment of "culture," that stand at the origins of both the cultural traditions in which Dante's poem is situated.

3. For an enlightening discussion of the importance of jealousy in Derrida's work, see Peggy Kamuf's, "Introduction," to *A Derrida Reader: Between the Blinds* (New York: Columbia University Press, 1991), especially pp. xx ff. In addition to the pun on the French, *jalousie*, meaning "jealousy" as well as "blinds," there is also the connection here to blindness and the "hypothesis of sight" which Derrida discusses later in *MB*.

4. The phrase "the passionate intellect," although not unique to her, is developed by Dorothy Sayers in her writings on Dante as being characteristic of his poetic style. In it she captures something important, not only about Dante but also about the relationship between him and Derrida. The "passionate intellect" could well be understood as a trace in Dante's poetry of *Différance*. In addition to Sayer's own work, see also Barbara Reynolds, *The Passionate Intellect: Dorothy Sayers' Encounter with Dante* (Kent, Ohio and London: The Kent State University Press, 1989). Another commentator who follows the Sayers/Reynolds line of interpretation is Helen Luke in her extraordinary book, *Dark Wood to White Rose* (New York: Parabola Books, 1989). I know of no other single book that I would recommend more enthusiastically to a reader encountering the *Comedy* for the first time.

5. Octavio Paz, The *Double Flame,* pp. 66–67.

6. It must be acknowledged that Singleton in his Commentary on this passage, following the traditional reading, rightly associates the term "bread of Angels" with divine wisdom on which the celestial intelligences, and some few privileged humans, feed. I take the "bread of Angels" to also refer here specifically to the sacrament of the Eucharist that in Catholic faith does not simply memorialize the last supper of Jesus, but through the power of the resurrection event allows the events of the Paschal mystery, the passion, death, and resurrection of Jesus, to begin again in genuinely new events of occurrence throughout history. This connection seems to be explicitly formed in the poem by Beatrice's allegorical role in pageant of *Purgatorio,* xxix, in the place of the Eucharist, and in the *Paradiso* as revealed Wisdom. What is significant in this context is that the poet links the two roles through the metaphor of eating.

7. *See Par.,* xxx, 109–123. The paradox of excess and inclusion, community, and identity, closed and open circulation, all point to the responsibility of forgiveness of all to all, which is impossible but which Dante envisions here as done where all are face to face.

8. In his Notes to *Paradiso,* xxxi, Singleton quotes Grandgent on the metaphor of the Rose: "The figure of the Rose seems to be Dante's own, although Paradise is sometimes represented in roselike form in early Italian art. . . . The Old French *Roman de la Rose,* the great literary success of the thirteenth century, made all Western Europe familiar with the rose as a symbol of earthly love; Dante's white flower is the symbol of Heavenly love. It may be that a sight of the Roman Coliseum influenced

his conception of the great amphitheater of Paradise. The figure of the rose is also a homage to Mary, who presides in the assembly. See Albertus Magnus, *De laud. B. Mariae Virginis*, XII, iv, 33: ['And note that Christ is a rose, Mary is a rose, the church is a rose, the faithful soul is a rose']."

9. In his note to *Par.*, xxxi, 49, Singleton explains his translation of *suadi*, on which a certain weight of evidence is being placed here, as follows: "From the Latin *suadus*, meaning "conducive to" or "persuasive" in its commonest usage. In the present context, however, it seems best to take the meaning to be passive rather than active, thus "persuaded" to charity, that is, "centered on" love, "all given to" love."

10. Alan Mandelbaum, *The Divine Comedy of Dante Alighieri: Paradiso* (New York: Bantam, 1982).

## IN MEMORIAM

1. The title of the essay in French is *'Au-delà: donner à prendre, apprendre à donner—la mort.*

2. There is here in this Platonic conception of the self-subsistence of the soul the encryption, buried in memory, of Sparta, the Other of Athens.

3. There might be a sense here in which it is important to recognize a way that Plato is, *mirablile dictu,* more genuinely Greek than either Nietzsche or Heidegger, in that there is to be discerned in Plato both the metaphysical and the premetaphysical dynamism of Greek culture *as well as* the necessity of their unity.

# Index